STUDIES IN THE NĀṬYAŚĀSTRA

Studies in The Nāṭyaśāstra

With Special Reference to the Sanskrit Drama in Performance

G.H. Tarlekar

MOTILAL BANARSIDASS PUBLISHERS
PRIVATE LIMITED • DELHI

First Edition: Delhi, 1975
Second Revised Editon: Delhi, 1991
Reprint: Delhi, 1999

ISBN: 81-208-0660-3

Also available at:

MOTILAL BANARSIDASS

41 U.A. Bungalow Road, Jawahar Nagar, Delhi 110 007
8 Mahalaxmi Chamber, Warden Road, Mumbai 400 026
120 Royapettah High Road, Mylapore, Chennai 600 004
Sanas Plaza, 1302, Baji Rao Road, Pune 411 002
16 St. Mark's Road, Bangalore 560 001
8 Camac Street, Calcutta 700 017
Ashok Rajpath, Patna 800 004
Chowk, Varanasi 221 001

PRINTED IN INDIA
BY JAINENDRA PRAKASH JAIN AT SHRI JAINENDRA PRESS,
A-45 NARAINA, PHASE I, NEW DELHI 110 028
AND PUBLISHED BY NARENDRA PRAKASH JAIN FOR
MOTILAL BANARSIDASS PUBLISHERS PRIVATE LIMITED,
BUNGALOW ROAD, DELHI 110 007

TO
NALINI
MY
WIFE

PREFACE

My thesis, "Studies in the Nāṭyaśāstra with special reference to the Sanskrit Drama in Performance", submitted to the Poona University for the degree of Ph. D., is now being published after due revision.

I have made an attempt in this book to present all the aspects of the performance of Sanskrit Drama, with the help of the material available in the NŚ. and other works on Dramaturgy, and also sculptural evidence, the tradition of the staging of Sanskrit plays, and other existing dance-drama styles. The efforts of scholars like Prof. Lévi, Dr. Keith, Miss Ketkar, Dr. Raghavan, Dr. Ghosh, Dr. C.B. Gupta and others, to give the idea of the practice of the Sanskrit Drama have helped me much in this attempt of mine.

I toured in many parts of India visiting archaeological site and important museums in search of panels of dance, music ands dramatic scenes. I have not been fortunate enough to get representations of dramatic scenes which would help to give an idea of the classical stage, in Indian sculpture or painting. I went to Kerala twice to study Kūṭiyāṭṭam—the Cākyār tradition of enacting Sanskrit plays and collected as much first hand information as possible.

In the Introduction I have discussed the origin and evolution of the Nāṭya—the Indian dramatic art. While discussing the various theories regarding the origin of Indian drama, propounded by western scholars, I have made use of "The Sanskrit Drama" by Dr. Keith and "The Dramas and the Dramatic Dances of Non-European Races" by Sir W. Ridgeway. After stating the purpose of Nāṭya in the first chapter, I have given the Abhinaya in detail in the second chapter. In the third chapter Music and Dance are treated and in the fourth, the theatre, the troupe etc. are dealt with. The fifth is devoted to the Preliminaries and the staging of some scenes from the Sanskrit plays of the great Classical period. Kūṭiyāṭṭam is described in detail in the sixth chapter. In the seventh, I have offered some suggestions in connection with the presentation of

Sanskrit plays at present. There are five Appendices. Appendix A discusses sculptures suggested to be the representations of scenes from Sanskrit plays; Appendix B gives the Karaṇas of the class dance; Appendix C describes in brief, the theatre in the East and South-East Asia; and Appendix D deals with ancient Indian costumes, Appendix E is connected with Kūṭiyāṭṭam. The Bibliography and the Index are given at the end.

My efforts are mainly meant to give some concrete idea of the presentation of Sanskrit plays during the classical period, using the details of Abhinaya and music as treated in the NŚ. To understand the use of music in the Sanskrit plays, I have taken the help of Bṛhaddeśī, Abhinava's commentary, the Ms. of Bharatabhāṣya, and Saṁgītaratnākara, together with some other important works on music in published and manuscript form. Some musical instruments found in ancient and medieval Indian sculpture and painting are also given.

I am greatly obliged to Dr. M. Ghosh, whose Nāṭyaśāstra Vols. I & II are used by me in connection with the translation of the text wherever necessary. I am grateful to the late Prin. R.D. Karmarkar who took keen interest in my work throughout. Dr. V. Raghavan and Dr. Ruben were kind enough to offer their valuable suggestions and to send their own articles dealing with the present problem, to me. My thanks are due to them. But for the help of Prof. K.P.N. Pisharoti, Shri Ram Cākyār and Shri Madhav Cākyār, I would not have been able to appreciate the Cākyār performance. I am, therefore, very much obliged to them. Many other friends also helped me in various ways by providing translations in English of the relevant portions from French, German and Kannad works and sending me information or their articles connected with the problem of my research. I must thank them also. I owe my gratitude to Prof. R.N. Chapekar for his kind help in giving me English renderings of two articles of Dr. Ruben.

The Curator of B.O.R. Institute Poona, the Curators of Archaeological museums I visited and other officers of that department had been extremely co-operative. I thank all of them. I am obliged to the Editor, Matribhumi, Kerala, for allowing me to use some photographs from Nāgānanda.

I am indebted to the publishers Dennis Dobson, London,

for giving me permission to use the book 'The Chinese Theatre' by Jack Chen; I have also to acknowledge my gratitude to the publishers Faber and Faber, Ltd. London for allowing me the use of the book, 'Dance and Drama in Bali' by Beryl de Zoete and Walter Spies. The brief accounts from these books are made use of in Appendix C. I am thankful to the Popular Book Depot, Bombay, for permitting me the use of the book 'Indian Costume' by Dr. G.S. Ghurye.

I thank the authorities of the Poona University for granting me permission to publish my thesis. My thanks are due to artist Shri Kelkar from Jalgaon and artist Shri Tanksale from Dhulia for providing the sketches. Lastly, I must thank M/s Motilal Banarsidass of Delhi, who accepted and carried out the publication of this book so willingly.

Makara saṁkramaṇa G.H. Tarlekar
14-1-1975
Professor Colony, Devpur,
Dhulia.

CONTENTS

LIST OF ILLUSTRATIONS

(Numerical figures against captions relate to their pages of reference)

ABBREVIATIONS

Abh.	Abhinavabhāratī.
A.B.O.R.I.	Annals of the Bhandarkar Oriental Research Institute.
A.I.O.C.	All India Oriental Conference.
BD.	Bṛhaddeśī.
Bhā.	Bhāsanāṭakacakra.
BK.	Bharatakośa.
DR.	Daśarūpaka.
G.O.S.	Gaekwad's Oriental Series.
I.A.	Indian Antiquary.
I.H.Q.	Indian Historical Quarterly.
J.A.R.S.	Journal of the Assam Research Society.
J.M.M.A.	Journal of the Madras Music Academy.
J.O.I.	Journal of the Oriental Institute.
J.O.R.M.	Journal of Oriental Research, Madras.
J.R.A.S., G.B..& I.	Journal of the Royal Asiatic Society, Great Britain & Ireland.
K.S.S.	Kashi Sanskrit Series.
Māl.	Mālavikāgnimitra.
MBh.	Mahābhārata.
Mṛcch.	Mṛcchakaṭika.
MM.	Mālatīmādhava.
ND.	Nāṭyadarpaṇa.
NŚ.	Nāṭyaśāstra.
O.H.R.J.	Orissa Historical Research Journal.
Rat.	Ratnāvalī.
ṚV.	Ṛgveda.
Śāk.	Abhijñānaśākuntala.
SD.	Sāhityadarpaṇa.
SR.	Saṁgītaratnākara.
T.S.S.	Trivandrum Sanskrit Series.
V.S.	Vājasaneyi Saṁhitā.
Vik.	Vikramorvaśīya.

References made to the Nāṭyaśāstra are from Baroda edition of the NŚ. Vol. I (II Edition), Vols II, III & IV, unless stated otherwise.

(NŚ. I. 112 means Nāṭyaśāstra, Chapter I, verse 112 etc.)

INTRODUCTION

THE NĀṬYA : THE INDIAN DRAMATIC ART

Its Origin and Evolution

I

The Indian dramatic art is called Nāṭya in the NŚ. and is defined as, "The Nāṭya[1] is the representation of the states of the three worlds." It is not mere imitation but something more than that. It is again explained in the words of Brahman thus,—"I have[2] devised this Nāṭya as the mimicry of the ways of the world, endowed with various emotions and consisting of various situations." "When[3] the nature of the world, possessing pleasure and pain both is depicted by means of representation through gestures and the like (i.e., speech, dress and make-up and temperament), it is called Nāṭya." The meaning of the word Naṭa can be taken as an actor. "The meaning[4] of the root Naṭ is 'to act' and hence, as he acts again and again the stories of men with sentiments, states and temperaments, he becomes a Naṭa." The Nāṭya is the art of the Naṭa i.e. the dramatic art.

The various situations of life are re-lived through the dramatic art. The actor takes the rôle of the character and adopting the gestures, the speech and the mental states as well, of that character, creates before the spectators, the life that character lives, making them one with that life. Music helps this representation by intensifying the particular mood. The grace of physical movements is supplied by dance. Thus, the Nāṭya becomes the art of representation in which, speech, music and appropriate graceful gestures are all harmoniously blended.

Mainly six views are available in connection with the origin of Nāṭya. They are as follows:

(1) The traditional account given in the NŚ. and other works.

1. NŚ. I. 107.
2. Ibid. I. 112.
3. Ibid. I. 119.
4. NŚ. (Edition : Dr. M. Ghosh) Vol. II. XXXV. 95.

(2) The theories about Vedic origin.
(3) The theories based on the evidence of the Epics, Pāṇini, Patañjali and Pāli Literature etc.
(4) The Secular origin—mime, puppet-play and shadow-play.
(5) The Greek influence.
(6) Origin from dance.

I shall discuss these views briefly.

1. *The traditional account*:

The NŚ. describes the origin of Nāṭya in the first chapter. God Brahman created the Nāṭyaveda for the benefit of all the Varṇas, (Sārvavarṇika) as the Śūdras could not be instructed in the Veda. The four constituents of this Veda were adopted from the four earlier Vedas, namely, the Recitation from the Ṛgveda, the Song from the Sāmaveda, the Abhinayas (the histrionics) from the Yajurveda and the Rasas (sentiments) from the Atharvaveda. The Upavedas also were connected with it.

About the recitation and the song being adopted from the Ṛgveda and the Sāmaveda respectively, explanation is not needed. About the adoption of the histrionics and the sentiments from the Yajurveda and the Atharvaveda respectively, we can explain in the manner of Abhinava[1] by saying that in the sacrificial ritual of the Yajurveda, the priests had to go through various actions and the mental state was produced in the priest performing the various rituals of the Atharvaveda[2] having the dress such as the red turban and the like. As regards the Upavedas, we find that the Āyurveda[3] found place in the NŚ., primarily in the treatment of the Vyabhicāribhāvas. Certain diseases and their symptoms were taken and applied as characteristic symptoms of certain mental moods on the lines of Caraka and Suśruta. The Dhanurveda was made use of in the representation of fights. The Gāndharvaveda was used in the preliminaries and in the actual perfor-

1. See NŚ. Vol. I., pp. 15-16.

2. A view is propounded by Prof. Jaitly to prove that the constituents of sentiment i.e. Bhāva and Vibhāva and through them, the manifestation of Rasa is seen clearly, first in the Atharvaveda. 'रसानाथर्वणादपि'—a paper read in the A.I.O. Conference 1959.

3. See 'Suśruta, Caraka and Bharata': R. K. Sen. I.H.Q. March 1954, pp. 68-80.

mance in the form of Dhruvā songs and as an accompaniment to various movements. The Sthāpatyaveda was necessary for the construction of the theatres.

Bharata, as the NŚ. tells us, arranged a performance with his hundred sons, in which the three styles of dramatic action, Bhāratī (verbal), Sāttvatī (grand), and Ārabhaṭī (energetic), were employed. Brahman asked him to employ Kaiśikī (graceful) also. The material for this, that is, the dance with fitting dress was obtained from Śaṅkara. This graceful style gave rise to the sentiment of love. Hence, women were also needed. The Apsarases were handed over to Bharata for this purpose. These divine nymphs were expert in the embellishments of dramatics. The dramatic art then became full-fledged.

The preparation for the first performance to be presented by Bharatas lacked grace. The vigour of action necessary for the sentiment like the Heroic was there but the delicacy necessary for the sentiment like the Erotic was lacking. This performance presented the story of the defeat of demons by gods. The occasion was the festival in honour of Lord Indra. The demons disliked it and created trouble. These trouble-makers were beaten to death by Indra with the banner-staff (Jarjara). Still the remaining evil spirits began to create terror. Hence, the open-air performance was shifted to the closed theatre. The nature of the Nāṭyaveda was then explained by Brahman to pacify the demons. "The Nāṭyaveda treats both the good and the evil, showing that the good is rewarded and the evil punished. It takes into account acts and ideas of the demons as well as of the gods, as there is no exclusive representation in it, of either of them. The Nāṭya represents the life of gods, demons, kings, householders and the great sages alike."

The Abhinayadarpaṇa[1] also records the traditional view of Brahman giving the Nāṭyaveda to Bharata. The Bhāvaprakāśana gives two accounts. According to the one,[2] Nandikeśvara came to Brahman and taught the Nāṭyaveda and its application to him. The Tripuradāharūpaka was performed by Bharatas who were given the instruction in the dramatic art by Brahman. According to the other account,[3] Śiva asked

1. Abhinayadarpaṇa, p. 2.
2. Bhāvaprakāśana, p. 56.
3. Ibid., pp. 285-286.

his pupil Nandikeśvara, whom he had taught the Nāṭyaveda, to instruct it to Brahman.

We do not arrive at anything concrete, historically, with these traditional accounts. The origin of the dramatic art goes to Brahman according to one tradition and to Śiva according to the other. The origin of Vṛttis necessary for the drama is attributed to Viṣṇu in the NŚ. If we are to rely on the NŚ. tradition, we find that Brahman is responsible for the origin of Nāṭya, Viṣṇu for Vṛtti and Śiva for class dance.

2. *Vedic origin*:

Prof. Max Müller made a suggestion in connection with the hymn to the Maruts (ṚV. I. 165) that the 'dialogue was repeated at sacrifices in honour of the Maruts or that possibly it was acted by two parties, one representing Indra, the other the Maruts and their followers'. Prof. Lévi developed this suggestion in detail. As the arts of music and dance are found developed in the Vedic age, it may be assumed that the Ṛgveda knew dramatic spectacles. Hence according to Prof. Lévi the dialogues were reproduced by the priests, assuming the roles of Gods and sages, to bring vividly before the people, the majesty of the Gods and their laws. Prof. Schroeder held that the dialogue hymns and also certain monologues in the Ṛgveda are relics of Vedic mysteries. He says that the close relation of music, dance and drama is seen among many people; Gods as dancers are known to Vedic religion. This can be explained only on the assumption that the priests were used to see the performance of ritual dances. Dr. Hertel supported this theory of the dialogues as mystery plays. The dialogue[1] hymns are regarded as precursors of the later classical drama by M. M. P. V. Kane.

As regards the dialogue hymns, we find that the dialogues in some cases clearly possess dramatic quality, e.g. the dialogue between Purūravas and Urvaśī (Ṛv. X. 95), or between Saramā and Paṇis (Ṛv. X. 108), or between Yama and Yamī (Ṛv. X. 10) etc. The monologue of drunken Indra presents a peculiar feature. In one Ṛc[2] the gesticulation is essential

1. The History of Sanskrit Poetics (1951), p. 315.
2. Sāyaṇa on Ṛgveda X.119.9.
'इह वा अन्तरिक्षे नि दधानि इह वा द्युलोके इति हस्तेन निर्दिशति'।

to understand the meaning. Indra says, "Ha ! May I place this earth here or there? (इह वा, इह वा)". These words need gesticulation. Sāyaṇa, the commentator, adds the remark, 'points by hand'. This indicates that the recitation was accompanied by movements of hand and the like. Dr. I. Shekhar[1] points out in this connection that the NŚ. mentions the recitation alone as adopted from the Ṛgveda and the histrionics from the Yajurveda.

In connection with the dialogues and monologues in the Ṛgveda, it can be reasonably said that the recitation would have been accompanied by necessary physical gesticulation. But their dramatic representation cannot be understood definitely in the absence of positive evidence.[2]

Dr. Keith holds that the Vedic ritual contained within itself, germs of drama. Yet they are nothing but the elements. According to Miss[3] Ketkar, the earliest stage of the drama was the art of one man assuming the roles of many. The word Viśvarūpa in the Yajurveda may connote this idea. She holds that the word Śailūṣa in the Taittirīya Brāhmaṇa refers to Naṭa i.e. an actor, skilled in the four-fold Abhinaya.

As regards Miss Ketkar's view, it is not certain whether the word Śailūṣa in the Brāhmaṇas means an actor. Śailūṣa is connected with song in the Vājasaneyi-Saṁhitā (गीताय शैलूषम्), and with dance in the Taittirīya Brāhmaṇa (नृत्ताय शैलूषम्), the song and the dance being allied arts.

3. *The evidence of the Epics, Pāṇini, Patañjali, Pāli Literature etc.*

The Harivaṁśa[4] clearly refers to Nāṭaka. But its date is not earlier than the second century A.C. The passages in the Rāmāyaṇa[5] which have references to naṭas and nāṭakas have

1. Sanskrit Drama : Its Origin and Decline, pp. 5, 14.

2. Shri D.R. Mankad thinks that perhaps the Ṛgvedic dialogues and monologues represent our elementary nṛtya-types, the monologue being sung by one expert actor who may have been a bhāṇika and the dialogue being carried on by two opposite parties—'The Types of Sanskrit Drama', p. 167.

3. Bhāratīya Nāṭyaśāstra, pp. 2-4.

4. Harivaṁśa, II. 91.26; 93.28.

5. Rāmāyaṇa.II-69, 4.

no claim to an early date according to Dr.[1] Keith. Thus, the epics in his opinion cannot be said to have known the drama. He admits, of course, the strong influence of the recitation of the Epics on the development of drama. The recitation of the Epics was in vogue. Bhāratas (modern Bhāṭs) were the rhapsodes of Bharata tribe. Mahābhārata is the great Epic of the family. With the passage of time, the rhapsodes took upon them the newer art of drama. Dr. Keith then says that, hence the term Bhārata meant a comedian in later texts. The term Kuśīlava which sometimes denotes an actor is derived from Kuśa and Lava of the Rāmāyaṇa, who sang Rāma's deeds before Rāma. In a bas-relief from Sanchi, there is a representation of a group of Kathakas. With their recitations accompanied by music in some degree, the Kathakas danced and indicated by gestures the sentiments of the characters they represented. Dr. Keith understands the word naṭa occurring first in Pāṇini[2] to mean a pantomime. Mentioning the view of Mr. Weber tnat there is a reference to a pantomimic killing and binding in Kaṁsavadha and Balibandha respectively referred to in the Mahābhāṣya, he admits that at the time of the Mahābhāṣya, a primitive form of drama existed. There was acting in dumb show if not with words too. The naṭas not only recited but also sang. The special term Bhrūkuṁsa[3] was used for the actor playing feminine roles.

The influence of Kṛṣṇa cult on the Sanskrit drama is evident. The normal prose language of the drama is Śaurasenī Prakrit. It was so because it was the ordinary speech of the people among whom the drama first developed into a definite shape. Śiva occupied an important place as the inventor of dance. The part of Rāma was equally significant in connection with drama. Stating these points, Dr. Keith says that it was from religion that the decisive impulse to dramatic creation was given. He opines that probably the Sanskrit drama came into being shortly after, if not before, the middle of the second century B.C.

1. Cf. The Sanskrit Drama, pp. 28-49.
2. Pāṇini. IV. 3. 110 & 111.
3. Mahābhāṣya. IV. 1-3.

Regarding the Mahābhāṣya[1] passage, Dr. Raghavan[2] takes the show of the Śaubhikas (Śobhanikas) as the presentation of the story through action unaided by words. Dr. Dasgupta,[3] accepting the authority of Kaiyyaṭa explains Śaubhikas as teachers who trained the actors in the matter of actual acting or demonstrated how Kaṁsa is killed by Kṛṣṇa or Bali is fettered and says further that this demonstration is a visible demonstration given by the instructors while superintending over the acting of their disciples.

Prof. Hillebrandt accepts the view that the granthikas took parts. With regard to the change of colour, he says that the supporters of Kaṁsa on the stage showed the dominant sentiment of fury while those of Kṛṣṇa were reduced to manifest fear as their sentiment.

In this view, the followers of Kṛṣṇa, the invincible, exhibit fear as the dominant sentiment. This does not look credible. Dr. Ridgeway[4] also thinks that the granthikas divided themselves into two parties. Those representing the followers of Kaṁsa had their faces blackened and those of Kṛṣṇa had their faces red. Kṛṣṇa, the black, was different in colour from the rest of his race. Hence, it is but natural that the Yādavas should be represented with red faces. The change of colour is understood by these scholars in the case of the performers.

Three modes of the representation of these episodes are described in the passage concerned. In the first, there is the actual representation by the performers of drama; in the second, through pictures; and in the third, through the words alone by the granthikas. When the granthikas describe effectively

1. Mahābhāṣya.III. 1.26.

ये तावदेते शोभनिका नामैते प्रत्यक्षं कंसं घातयन्ति प्रत्यक्षं च बलिं बन्धयन्तीति । चित्रेषु कथम् । चित्रेष्वप्युद्गूर्णा निपतिताश्च प्रहारा दृश्यन्ते कंसकर्षण्यश्च । ग्रन्थिकेषु कथं यत्र शब्दगडुमात्रं लक्ष्यते । तेऽपि हि तेषामुत्पत्तिप्रभृत्या विनाशादृद्धीर्व्याचक्षाणाः सतो बुद्धिविषयान् प्रकाशयन्ति । आतश्च सतो व्यामिश्रा हि दृश्यन्ते । केचित् कंसभक्ता भवन्ति केचिद् वासुदेवभक्ताः । वर्णान्यत्वं खलु पुष्यन्ति । केचिद्रक्तमुखा भवन्ति केचित् कालमुखाः ।

2. The Sanskrit Drama and Performance, p. 14.

3. A History of Ṣanskrit Literature, Classical Period, p. 637.

4. The Dramas and Dramatic Dances of Non-European Races, pp. 141-142.

in words these incidents, the audience becomes one with the episodes. Those partial to Kaṁsa would have their faces darkened when he is killed, and those that are devotees of Kṛṣṇa would have their faces reddened in anger. In this explanation the change of colour is understood to be in the case of the audience, which seems to be more reasonable.

From Saṁyutta[1] Nikāya, the naṭa appears to be a comedian who by his speech with truth and fiction combined, made people laugh and enjoy. Dīgha Nikāya mentions Sobhanagarakam. In Burmese it is Sobhanakam. Buddhaghoṣa explains Sobhanagarakam (V.L. Sobhaṇagam) as Naṭānam abbhokiraṇam (i.e. a troupe of actors). According to Dr. Wijesekera, these naṭas were either the same persons referred to in the Mahābhāṣya as Śobhanikas or at least their precursors in the art.

The naṭa[2] and nartaka are mentioned in the Arthaśāstra. The Naṭasūtras of Śilālin and Kṛśāśva are referred to by Pāṇini. From Naṭa the word Nāṭya is derived in the sense of the practice of the Naṭas (naṭasya dharmaḥ) or the sacred traditional work of the Naṭas (āmnāyo vā). This means that the traditional works of the Naṭas existed at least in the times of Pāṇini and the Naṭa as a class did exist. We know from the Mahābhāṣya that the Naṭas used to sing and perform and from Saṁyutta Nikāya that their art was connected with speech also. If Śaubhikas were the instructors of the Naṭas then the Nāṭya[3] in the times of Pāṇini was nothing but the full-fledged dramatic art.

4. *The Secular Origin*:

Mime: Prof. Hillebrandt and Prof. Konow think that it is an error to look to religious ceremonies in explaining the origin of drama. According to them, a popular mime existed, which with the epic, lies at the bottom of the Sanskrit Drama. The use of Sanskrit and dialects in classical drama is claimed as

1. ...'नटानं भासमानान यो सो नटो रङ्गमज्झे समज्जमज्झे सच्चालिकेन जनं हासेति रमेति ॥' Gāmaṇi-Saṁyuttam; Saṁyutta Nikāya IV, p. 306.

Cf. Buddhist Evidence for the Early Existence of Drama: Dr. Wijesekera; I.H.Q. XVII, pp. 196-206.

2. Arthaśāstra. II. 27.25.

3. Pāṇini. IV. 3-129.

a proof of popular origin. The mixture of prose and song and the union of both with music and dance, the simplicity of the Indian stage, the Vidūṣaka and the preliminaries are all given as pointing to popular origin. Prof. Konow finds in Yātrās, the evidence of the secular origin.

It may be accepted that the mimetic character is natural to man. But "Prof.[1] Hillebrandt himself adduces proof that the western parallel of the Vidūṣaka is connected with religious ceremonies rathei than a secular creation." And we know, the Yātrās are essentially connected with religion.

Puppet-play : Dr. Pischel holds that the puppet-play is the source of Sanskrit drama. This play was in vogue in ancient India. The word Sūtradhāra would point to the leader of the puppet-play who holds the puppets by threads.

In regard to this view, we may say that the instinct of imitation is so strong in man that it is more reasonable to understand the existence of drama first and the use of puppets introduced later on. The Vidūṣaka came from drama and not from the puppet-play. The word Sūtradhāra denotes holding the thread of Nāṭya or his connection with the Naṭasūtras. It[2] is possible to think that Indian puppetry exercised some influence on practices of the live stage (e.g. the convention of swoon).

Shadow-play: According to Prof. Lüders the Śaubhikas in the Mahābhāṣya were the persons who explained matters to the audience to supplement either dumb actors or shadow figures. The recitation of the Epics was illustrated through the use of shadow figures. This, united with the art of the Naṭas, gave birth to drama.

We know that[3] the word Śaubhika has no relation to shadow and it is not explained in that sense by any authority. The term Chāyānāṭaka which is interpreted as shadow play may denote a drama in the state of a shadow. The oldest of these species is the Dūtāṅgada of Subhaṭa (13th century A.C.).

The word Leṇaśobhikā in one of the Mathurā inscriptions

1. The Sanskrit Drama : Keith, pp. 50, 51.
2. Cf. The Classical Drama of India, H.W. Wells, p. 96.
3. The Sanskrit Drama : Keith, pp. 55-56.

is taken by Mr. Jacob[1] to mean a woman who operates a shadow play. The Sītābengā cave is thought to have served as a shadow theatre.

I think it is better to understand the word 'Leṇaśobhikā' as 'cave-actress' as is done by Prof. Luders.[2]

5. *The Greek influence*:

About the Greek influence in the creation of Sanskrit drama we can see that there are marked differences between the Greek drama and the Sanskrit drama. Scholars like Dr. Raghavan,[3] Dr. Keith and Mr. G. Banerjee, have shown that the Sanskrit drama is indigenous. The Indian drama is distinguished from the Greek drama, on account of its rich variety of dramatic form and the absence of anything like Greek tragedy and the chorus. In comparison to Bharata's theatre, the Greek theatre was very large. The theory of Rasa is a great achievement of Bharata. The word Yavanikā for curtain need not be taken as indicating the Greek influence. At the most the word may point to the idea that the Indian curtain had its material from Ionian cloth. The highest influence of Hellenism in India was in the First century B.C. But we know that the Sanskrit drama was already well-established by that time.

6. *Origin from dance*:

After knowing all these views in connection with the origin of the Sanskrit drama, we finally come to the part played by the dance in regard to the origin of the dramatic art in India. The classical Sanskrit plays available to us from Bhāsa onwards are the finished products of the Indian drama. Hence it is obvious that the beginning of this art must be much earlier than the earliest available classical plays.

The dance tradition in India is very old. Dr. Ghosh[4] holds that a ritual dance connected with Śiva, in course of time,

1. Cf. 'The Shadow Theatre in Greater India and in Greece' : Jean Przyluski.
Journal of the Greater India Society. Vol. VIII. No. 2, pp. 83-91.
2. 'Indian Caves as Pleasure Resorts' : Prof. Luders; I.A. Vol. XXXIV, pp. 199-200.
3. See The Sanskrit Drama and Performance, pp. 15-16.
4. Contributions to the History of Hindu Drama, pp. 5-7.

gave rise to drama. Dr. Oldenberg[1] maintains that the origin of drama is to be found in the sacred dance accompanied by gestures of pantomimic character. This would give rise to drama, after being combined with song and later enriched by dialogue.

It is true that dance existed first and then drama came into being. Hence their relation should be clearly known. In the Ṛgveda, the word nṛtu[2] occurs in the sense of dancer. Uṣas is described as revealing her beauty like a dancer removing the garment in the form of darkness (ṚV. I. 92.4). In the Vājasaneyi-Saṁhitā[3] we get reference to 'nṛtta' and 'gīta'. In the Atharvaveda[4] the root 'nṛt' is found. In the Śāṅkhāyana[5] Brāhmaṇa and in the Kauṣītaki Brāhmaṇa, 'Śilpa' is described as dance, vocal and instrumental music. In the Taittirīya[6] Brāhmaṇa we get reference to vaṁśanartinam which Sāyaṇa explains as vaṁśāgranṛtta-jīvinam (one who has his livelihood by the dance on the pole-end—a pole dancer or an acrobat). In the Jaiminīya[7] Brāhmaṇa we have 'nṛtta gīta'. In the Kātyāyana[8] Śrauta Sūtra nṛtta, gīta and vāditra are mentioned. From Pāraskara[9] Gṛhya Sūtra we know that a student should not engage himself in this triple art nor should he visit it. Thus we find in the Vedas, Brāhmaṇas and the Sūtras the word nṛtta or nṛtya for dance. In dance, acrobatics too had a place. In the Pāli Jātakas also nṛtta, gīta and vāditra are referred to often. As the art of dance was very old, going back to the Indus Valley Civilization, it is but natural that the development of dance through hundreds of years would give rise to different beautiful dance movements which find a scientific treatment in the NŚ., in the classification and the

1. The Sanskrit Drama : Dr. Keith—p. 26.
2. ṚV. 1.92.4.; 1.130.7; II. 22.4; VI. 63.5; VIII. 20.22 etc.
3. VS. XXXV. 6 नृत्ताय् सूतं गीताय शैलूषम् ।
4. Atharvaveda. 4.9.8.
5. Śāṅkhāyana Brāhmaṇa, 29.5; Kauṣītaki Brāhmaṇa XXIX. 5. 'त्रिवृद्वै शिल्पं नृत्यं गीतं वादित्रमिति'
6. Taittirīya Brāhmaṇa, III. 4.2.1.
7. Jaiminīya Brāhmaṇa, I. 42.
8. Kātyāyana Śrauta Sūtra, XXI, p. 867.
9. Pāraskara Gṛhya Sūtra, II. 7.

description of Karaṇas (dance units) and Aṅgahāras (various combinations of dance units). This was the class dance used mostly to satisfy the gods. Dance, song and instrumental music are prescribed in connection with the Pitṛmedha rites and dance alone in Atirātra and Satrāyaṇa sacrifices. The Mahābhārata[1] tells us that the Gandharvas and the Apsarases delighted the priests in the intervals of sacrificial rites by the arts of dance and music.

In the Ṛgveda, Indra, the destroyer of enemies is addressed as 'nṛtu' and the charming goddess of dawn also is addressed by the same word, indicating thereby, the vigorous, and the gentle aspects respectively. God Śaṅkara dances vigorously at the time of the destruction of Dakṣa's sacrifice. In the twilight we have his Sandhyānṛtya.

Thus the dance with its vigorous and gentle styles is very ancient and is denoted by the term nṛtta or nṛtya. Nāṭya,[2] the dramatic art, is first referred to by Pāṇini. We find the words Bharata, Śailūṣa and Kuśīlava used to denote an actor in classical Sanskrit literature. In the list of the victims of Puruṣamedha, Śailūṣa is mentioned in connection with song and dance. Dr. Ruben[3] has mentioned a class of naṭas existing in India, who are rope-dancers. This rope-dance belongs to the religion of God Śiva. The word sūtradhāra, the rope-holder, is suggested by him to be associated with the rope-dance. The naṭa is to walk on the rope stretched from the summit of the cliff. The word Śailūṣa is interpreted by Dr. Ruben as one who camps on the rock. The word Śilālin is also connected with the naṭas as the teacher. The oldest teacher of the naṭas and his pupil might have been called in this way. This can be associated with the rope between the cliffs and Śiva, the lord of the mountains. In his account[4] of pre-Āryan tribes in India, he has mentioned the primitive

1. MBh. Aśvamedha Parva, 88.40.

2. Dr. Trigunayat is wrong when he says that the root 'naṭ' is found in The Ṛgveda, VII. 104.23. (The root is 'Naś' & not 'naṭ'. Seth Govinddas Abhinandan Granth, p. 423.)

3. 'Über Die Ursprunge Des Indischen Dramas, Ankara 1940, pp. 213-233.

4. Über Die Literatur Der Vorarischen Stämme Indiens—1952, pp. 117-121.

drama of the Santals, in which the role of the goddess of the village, the god of the village and the mountain-god are played by men in their flower festival. In the case of Uraon, at the Sarhul festival, the marriage of the Sun god with the Mother Earth is celebrated wherein the roles of these gods are played by the priest and his wife. Thus Dr. Ruben thinks that a source of Hindu drama can be traced in such dances where a rope-dancer dances as the god Śiva in his form as the Lord of the dances and the giver of fertility.

A statue of a female dancer is found in the Indus Valley Civilization. A broken male statue is identified as giving us the famous posture of Naṭarāja. Shri. I. Shekhar[1] favours the non-Āryan origin of the Sanskrit drama. According to him, Bharata was a scion of the non-Āryan family of the artistes who did his best to secure recognition for the members of his troupe. When Bharata felt helpless and depressed due to the curse on the Naṭas, he found a non-Āryan patron in the person of Nahuṣa. The Naṭarāja Śiva is the non-Āryan God. Shri I. Shekhar further states that the use of gestures recommended by Bharata in portraying various situations in a drama, presuppose the existence of certain traditions in the field of choreographic dramaturgy.

In ancient India there was a fusion of Āryan and Non-Āryan cultures. But as regards Bharata, we find that Bharatas were an Āryan tribe mentioned in the Ṛgveda. The word Kuśīlava denoting the twin brothers Kuśa and Lava, who sang the Rāmāyaṇa were, of course, the Āryan princes. The Sūtas who were the reciters of the Purāṇas were connected with dancing also in the Vedic period. The Śailūṣas too were connected with dance and music in the Vedic period. According to the account of the Cākyārs, the dramatic art was taken to Kerala by a Sūta family. The Naṭas were concerned with singing, speaking and acting. In the dramatic troupe the NŚ. mentions Bharata, Naṭa and Kuśīlava. Bharata is described as an expert in adopting various roles, Naṭa as an expert in acting and Kuśīlava in playing various musical instruments. Later, the word Kuśīlava and Śailūṣa also are used to denote actors. When the actor in general lost his status in society due

1. **Sanskrit Drama : Its Origin and Decline, pp. 35-40 & pp. 45-47.**

to loose morals, the word Kuśīlava got the interpretation of 'one having bad character'.

Bharatas stage the first dramatic performance. One method of warfare i.e., Nyāya is connected with Bharata. The verbal style is also specially related to Bharatas. In the dance and music practised by the Sūtas and Śailūṣas as professional classes, the speech and dress and make-up were perhaps lacking in the beginning. The performance of the Bharatas might have been with speech and the necessary natural gesticulation in confoımity with the recitation of the dialogue-hymns of the Ṛgveda and later on, the narration of the ancient legends. The class of artistes called Naṭas, combined the different features of mimicry and used to present the ancient stories of heroism in the form of dialogue and song, adopting roles of different characters with befitting dress and makeup. Thus their art became the full-fledged dramatic art, which had a very delightful effect on the spectators. The play became really a Krīḍanīyaka. The art of the Naṭas primarily had the perfection of histrionics. It seems that the Bharatas adopted it and hence the treatise was named by Bharata as the Nāṭyaśāstra. In course of time, all these i.e., Bharata, Kuśīlava, Naṭa and Śailūṣa became synonyms as the original distinction of their professions was merged in the single profession of the actors.

The dance was at first only an expression of joy consisting of various simple rhythmical movements of the body. Many a time it was accompanied by song. This was pure dance void of any gesticulation. The various simple and graceful movements gradually became complicated to heighten the element of grace in dance. The different movements of the different parts of the body were classified and the classical dance was established. In the dance pattern the song that was sung was sometimes interpreted. The words could be expressed by the gestures of the hand or hands and the facial expression. But all this was in keeping with the rhythm. Hence though the classical dance could also have the gesticulation, all this gesticulation was governed by tempo and beats. Śiva's dance interpreting the song is referred to by Abhinava[1] quoting Kohala. The theme of the song was the destruction of Tripura by Śiva.

1. NŚ. Vol. I. p. 180.

It was sung by Nārada and rendered into Abhinaya by Śiva. Thus the dance was developing in combination with Abhinaya. On the other hand, the natural instinct of imitation which is all the while powerful in man was responsible for the art of imitation of the striking incidents from life. In the imitation of various characters involved in these incidents, with their language, action, dress etc. the art of representation i.e., the actor's art was born. The earliest dramatic performances recorded in the NŚ. were concerned with fights. The victories of the gods over the demons were celebrated by representing them on festive occasions. This was Anukṛti, imitation. The dress and make-up, the angry challenges, the deceit and excitement and the actual fight, augmented by appropriate music constituted the success of the performance. The adoption of dance supplied the grace of action. Only the male actors participated in the beginning but soon the actresses were introduced to enrich the art. Now the themes of love as well could be handled effectively.

The Nyāyas connected with warfare are described in detail in the NŚ. In the worship of the stage, we find fights as an item. The same word 'raṅga' was used for the arena as well as the theatre. This helps us to understand the beginning of the dramatic art as connected with the imitation of the fights.

The monologue and the dialogue as forms of speech were already there in the time of the Ṛgveda. Speech was used more and more in the representation. The development of the plot according to the necessity of the theme in one act or more acts and the styles of action necessary for the particular type of the performance gave rise to varieties of plays. The variety of languages such as Sanskrit and Prakrits to suit the types of characters became also a necessity.

When the first two plays were performed before Śaṅkara he asked to add classical dance to the preliminaries to make them more striking. This dance provided more and more conventional gesticulation. Due to this manner of gesticulation the root 'nṛt' is used in the NŚ. and elsewhere also in the sense of gesticulating in the play.

The effort to call the Nāṭyaśāstra, the fifth Veda, the pūjā in connection with the stage, the relation with gods, Brahman,

Viṣṇu and Maheśa, the occasions of the performances which were the festivals in honour of the deities, the preliminaries to satisfy the deities, all these point to the religious connection of the drama.

The well-settled practice of the earliest available classical dramas presuppose the existence of Sanskrit drama at least a few centuries earlier. The NŚ. (200 B.C. to 200 A.C.) gives such minute details of the dramatic art that it must have had a long tradition of centuries to possess such perfection. Hence, it is reasonable to conclude that in the times of Pāṇini, the Sanskrit drama was definitely in vogue.

II

The NŚ. describes the ten Rūpakas (types of plays). It is obvious that the author of the Nāṭyaśāstra had a large body of plays available to him for such a classification. If we study these types we can trace the course of the evolution of the Indian drama up to the period of the NŚ. The term Rūpa or Rūpaka is used for play, as primarily it is visual representation. These ten types are—Nāṭaka, Prakaraṇa, Samavakāra, Īhāmṛga, Ḍima, Vyāyoga, Aṅka, Prahasana, Bhāṇa and Vīthī. It was[1] possible to have the features of one Rūpaka into that of the other.

Let us now see the salient features of these Rūpakas as given by Bharata.

Nāṭaka: It has for its subject-matter a well-known story (drawn from tradition). The hero is a celebrated king of exalted character. (If he is divine, he should appear in human form). His exploits and amorous deeds are treated. The divinities may appear as subordinate element. It has proper number of acts that is, five to ten and has Praveśakas (interludes.) It presents the life of kings which is full of varied actions representing various states and sentiments arising out of pleasure and pain. The plot is developed properly through the five stages—the beginning (prārambha), efforts (prayatna), hope of gaining the aim (prāptyāśā), certainty (niyatāpti)

1. Abh. "अन्ये त्वाहुः । एकैकस्य रूपकस्य दश दश रूपाणि संभवन्ति । तथा च वीथ्यङ्गानां सर्वत्र संभवः । परगतवचनानुरूपभाषणरूपभाणयोगश्च किंब्रवीषीत्याकाशभाषिते । एवमन्यदपि ।" NŚ. Vol. II. P. 408.

and securing of the aim (phalāgama). In the act, the part of the play is fully expressed but the germ of the plot is not wholly disposed off. The act should not be too long and at the end of it all characters leave the stage. An act should cover the action that can happen in the course of a single day. Actions of anger, favour and grief, the end of curse, flight, marriage, and commencement of miracle and its appearance should be directly presented in the act (or sometimes indirectly also).

[Aṅka (act) is so called because by means of states and sentiments it causes the meaning of the play to mount or to grow in the heart of the audience. Aṅka is also derived from aṅka, the mark, as it is characterised by various sentiments.]

When incidents that are to be finished in the course of a single day cannot be accommodated in one act, they should be presented in an interlude (Praveśaka) after closing that act. Incidents that may take place in the course of a month or a year are also to be described through Praveśaka. But the time element should not exceed a period of one year. When in an act any person goes out on business to a distant land, it should be indicated after closing the act (by Praveśaka). In Praveśaka the conversation of the attendants should be in Prakrit. The battle, loss of kingdom, death, siege of a city, should be presented through Praveśakas and not by direct representation. The death of the hero should never take place; either his escape, capture or truce should be effected. The attendants or the followers of the hero should be four or five. The exalted situations should come in the latter part of the play. The Marvellous sentiment should find place at the conclusion of all plays.

Prakaraṇa : The plot and the hero are the creations of the poet's imagination. It is similar to Nāṭaka but the life to be delineated is that of a Brahmin, a merchant, a counsellor, a minister or a family priest or a caravan leader. Thus, the hero is never a king. Characters like dāsa (servant), viṭa (parasite), and courtesans would have a place here. The heroine may be a noble woman or a courtesan. There should be Viṣkambhaka[1] (supporting scene) in brief in Sanskrit, with

1. Abhinava says, in Prakaraṇa, in regard to the hero, the middling characters would be mostly there as associates of the hero. Hence the possibility of having Viṣkambhakas. NŚ. Vol. II. p., 433.

middling characters similar to Praveśaka. It may present middling characters or both middling and inferior characters. In between the two acts, Praveśakas should also be used. It has no divine element nor kingly luxury.

[Nāṭikā: It has characteristics from both, Nāṭaka and Prakaraṇa. It has king as a hero but the plot is the outcome of the poet's fancy. A maiden attached to the harem or the one connected with the music-chamber, serves as a heroine. It should have mostly female characters and graceful gestures. It consists of four acts. It should have dance, music, recitation and love in union in ample measure. Occasions of favour, anger, hypocrisy and royal etiquette should be there. The typical characters here are, the hero, the queen, the female go-between and the attendants. The Nāṭikā,[1] having the features of both, Nāṭaka and Prakaraṇa, is included in them and as such needs no separate mention as another variety. Thus the number of Rūpakas would be kept as ten.]

Samavakāra: Well-known Gods and Demons constitute its characters. It has three acts, three kapaṭas (three kinds of deceits), three vidravas (three kinds of excitements) and three types of love. It has the duration of eighteen nāḍikās (one nāḍikā is equal to 24 minutes). The number of heroes is twelve.[2] The first act has the duration of twelve nāḍikās and contains laughter as it has love due to passion, excitement, deception and Vīthī. The second is similar in nature and has the duration of four nāḍikās. The third act that brings the play to the end, has the duration of two nāḍikās. The acts should have different incidents that are loosely related. The three kinds of excitements are—(1) due to battle and flood; (2) caused by storm, fire and big elephant; and (3) siege of the city.

The three kinds of deceptions are due to (1) devised plan, (2) luck, chance or accident, (3) enemy's strategy causing joy or sorrow.

1. NŚ. XVIII. 61.

2. Abhinava records two views regarding the number of heroes. According to one, the number of heroes in each act should be twelve while the other view states that the hero, his rival and their two associates, these four in each act make up the total of twelve in three acts.
NŚ. Vol. II., p. 437.

The three kinds of love are—(1) love in relation to duty, (2) love due to material gain, and (3) love due to passion. When one gets one's desired object while carrying out one's own duty it is love together with duty. The duties consist of observance of vows, and practising of austerities and penance. When one acts to obtain material gain or the enjoyment of pleasure for some material gain, it is love together with material gain. When there is a seduction of a maiden or the enjoyment of a woman secretly or with excitement, it is love due[1] to passion.

Īhāmṛga: It has the divine hero engaged in fight for divine lady. The plot is well-knit and convincing. It has mostly vehement males and has its construction based on feminine anger. It should have commotion, excitement and angry conflict. The plot of love is to be based on causing discord among women and carrying them off and oppressing the enemies. When the killing of persons is about to take place, the battle should be avoided by some artifice.

Ḍima: It should have a well-known story of exalted heroes. It should consist of four acts and six sentiments omitting the Erotic and the Comic. It deals with incidents like earthquake, challenge and angry conflict. It should abound in deceit and jugglery and the use of many models. It possesses sixteen heroes and is full of characters like Gods, Nāgas, Demons, Yakṣas and Goblins. The styles are Sāttvatī and Ārabhaṭī with many states.

Vyāyoga: It has the duration of one day and possesses few female characters. As in Samavakāra many males take part in it but it does not have that length as it consists of one act only. The hero[2] is well-known, but not a god, a king or a sage. According to the DR. he should be a haughty man (uddhatanara). In it there should be fight, personal combats and angry challenges and conflict. Vyāyoga has exciting sentiments.

1. Abhinava mentions here that the woman is one that is belonging to others, e.g. Ahalyā enjoyed by Śakra. NŚ. Vol. II., p. 440.

2. See—Abhinava—NŚ. Vol. II., p. 445—
दिव्यैर्देवैः नृपैः ऋषिभिश्च नायकैः न निबद्धोऽयं भवतीत्यर्थः ।

Utsṛṣṭikāṅka or Aṅka: The story here is either well-known or otherwise. The males participating in it are other than the divine ones. The sentiment of pathos is mostly found here. After the fight is over, there are many bewildered movements and lamentations by women. It has only Bhāratī style.

Prahasana: It has two varieties. The śuddha (pure) variety has comic disputations by Bhagavats, ascetics, Brahmins, and others and it also abounds in jocular remarks by low persons. The parts of the story in it are possessed of the particular states with language and behaviour natural to them, giving uniformity to the plot. The saṁkīrṇa (mixed) variety has courtesans, servants, eunuchs, parasites, rogues, and unchaste women as its characters. These appear with their immodest dress, movements and behaviour. Some popular scandalous topic or hypocritical incident should be introduced in it through the disputations of pretenders. The elements of Vīthī should be judiciously used.

Bhāṇa: It is to be acted by a single character narrating one's own experiences or describing those of others. Other characters, though they are not present on the stage, are made to speak through one only, that is present—he is Dhūrta or Viṭa. This is done by making him repeat the words that are supposed to be addressed to him, together with his replies in course of Ākāśabhāṣitas. He thus develops the story through this manner of speech and appropriate physical movements, in a gradual manner. It should have one act and should include many movements, expressive of the various conditions of Dhūrta or Viṭa.

Vīthī: It may contain all the sentiments and has one actor or also two. It has the characters of the three types—superior, middling and inferior. It has the use of thirteen constituents. These constituents are—

(1) Udghātyaka—The words with obscure meaning are connected by[1] men with the words other than those intended by the speaker, in order to explain them.

(2) Avalagita—When something occurring in relation to anything is made to accomplish something else.

1. NŚ. Vol. II., p. 453; F.N. 5—रप

(3) Avaspandita—When auspicious or inauspicious meaning of the word is grasped, it is explained otherwise skilfully.

(4) Nālikā—The sportive answers are given to deceive the other.

(5) Asatpralāpa—Even though the learned speaks what is beneficial in the company of fools, it is not accepted as such.

(6) Vākkeli—When a single or more striking replies are there.

(7) Prapañca—The untrue words of mutual praise of two are uttered in the interest of one, creating laughter.

(8) Mṛdava—With proper reasons, the merits are turned into defects and vice versa, in repartee.

(9) Adhibala—When words spoken by others or by oneself in course of a dialogue lead to their mutual modification.

(10) Chala—The words having different meanings create anger and laughter.

(11) Trigata—Due to similarity of words, many meanings are connected skilfully in it by means of modification etc. or it is the conversation[1] among the three (i.e. Sūtradhāra, Vidūṣaka and Pāripārśvaka in the preliminaries) with comic sentiment.

(12) Vyāhāra—Anything liable to occur is described vividly in the presence of the hero with a sense of little laughter.

(13) Gaṇḍa—It is the undue combination of words due to excitement, confusion, quarrel or reviling; it consists of many words of abusive type.

Vṛttis (*styles of speech and action*):

Bharata gives four Vṛttis—Bhāratī, Sāttvatī, Ārabhaṭī and Kaiśikī, the use of which is at the basis of the difference between the different varieties of plays. Vṛtti is man's activity in the direction of achieving the aim of life. This is the theme of all literature. Hence, the Vṛttis are called the mothers of Nāṭya—the constituent elements of all dramatic works (and hence poetry also). Out of the ten types of plays Nāṭaka and Prakaraṇa should have all the four styles while the others should be without the Kaiśikī.

The origin of style is connected with the fight of Viṣṇu with the demons Madhu and Kaiṭabha. The demons challeng-

1. NŚ. Vol. II., p. 458; F.N.१९.

ed the Lord for a battle. They fought with their fists and knees using various harsh words of mutual conflicts, shaking the ocean as it were, by words of censure. Lord Brahman, listening to their wordy warfare spoke, "Is this Bhāratīvṛtti proceeding from speech alone, increasing stage by stage? Please kill them." Then Lord Viṣṇu said, "I have created this Bhāratīvṛtti for the purpose of my work. This will be the style of speakers abounding in words. I shall kill them today." The two demons fought with perfect gestures and movements of the limbs as they were experts in the method of battle. The earth felt an excessive burden due to the steps of Viṣṇu planted on earth in the course of the fight. The Bhāratī style was born there. This is another derivation of the word Bhāratī from the word bhāra (the burden), which was felt by the earth.

The jumping movements of the wielder of Śārṅga bow, sharp, intensely brilliant and full of sattva (i.e. strength) and without any confusion, gave rise to Sāttvatī style.

The God moved sportively with various aṅgahāras and tied up the tuft of his hair gracefully. This gave rise to the Kaiśikī style.

Ārabhaṭī was produced by various personal combats which were full of energy and excitement and which arose out of many foot-movements.

The various acts the Lord introduced arising out of the Vṛttis, were worshipped by Brahman with words expressive of them. The destruction of the demons was effected by body movements, strange, uneven, clear and graceful too. This would be the method of personal combats among people, to be called nyāya, in the release of weapons. It is stated also that the Bhāratī style rose from Ṛgveda, Sāttvatī from Yajurveda, Kaiśikī from Sāmaveda and Ārabhaṭī from Atharvaveda. The Vedic origin, of course, forms a supplementary part of the story of the origin from the fight.

We have seen that the first dramatic performance was connected with warfare in which many heroes fought. In this story of the personal combat between Viṣṇu and Madhu and Kaiṭabha the styles of action are again connected with fight. Introduction of the element of grace came from the dance of Śiva. Some previous[1] commentators of the NŚ. who under-

1. NŚ. Vol. I., p. 23.

stood that the dance of Śiva seen by Brahman referred to the dance of Pārvatī also, maintained that Brahman saw the presentation of Kaiśikī by Pārvatī. But Abhinava says that it is wrong. For, it is possible even for men to perform graceful action. Viṣṇu produced the grace by tying up the locks.

Dr. V. Raghavan[1] has made clear the conception of Vṛtti as follows—"Nāṭya is the imitation of action and each action has its characteristic mood or atmosphere with respect to the man in action as well as the sahṛdaya who sees the Nāṭya. The mood or atmosphere is Vṛtti. Hence Bharata says that the dramatic action or drama is born of Vṛtti. Different types of drama present different kinds of action as characterised by different atmospheres. So Bharata says that Vṛtti is also that factor which differentiates one type of drama from the other." He explains Bhāratī as connected with the Bharatas, Sāttvatī with the Sāttvatas (the race of Kṛṣṇa), Ārabhaṭī with the Ārabhaṭas and Kaiśikī with Kaiśika or Krathakaiśika (the ancient capital of Vidarbha country, the home of grace and beauty). When the speech is the prominent mode of expression, it would be Bhāratī style. Hence that would come under Vācikābhinaya. The mental action—the Sāttvikābhinaya would be Sāttvatī. The bodily action would be Āṅgikābhinaya. When it is forceful it would give rise to Ārabhaṭī style and when graceful to Kaiśikī style.

According to Dr. V.S. Agrawal[2] these styles are connected with regions. Bhāratī belongs to the Bhārata region or Kurukṣetra; Sāttvatī to the region of the Sāttvatas i.e. the Yādavas of Saurāṣṭra; Kaiśikī to Krathakaiśika i.e. Vidarbha and Ārabhaṭī to the country of Ārabhaṭas i.e. the region to the west of Indus and south of Baluchistan, inhabited by people called Arabitae or Arbiti. In that region there is the river Arabius. This last region marked the end of Bhāratavarṣa which he thinks to be the ancient Ārabhaṭa region.

The styles are described in the NŚ. as follows—

Bhāratī—It is to be employed by males and not by females. In it, speech is prominent and the language used is Sanskrit.

1. See 'The Vṛttis'—by Dr. Raghavan. J.O.R.—Madras 1932, Vol. VI. pp. 346-370; 1933, Vol. VII., pp. 33-52.

2. Harṣacarita—Eka Sāṁskṛtika Adhyayana, pp. 33-34.

As it is used by Bharatas, it is called Bhāratī. Its four varieties are, Prarocanā, Āmukha, Vīthī and Prahasana. Prarocanā is used in the preliminaries to attain success, prosperity, good luck, victory and removal of all sins. Āmukha (prologue) contains conversation with interesting words relating to the topics concerned, of the actress, clown or assistant with the Sūtradhāra. The use of varieties of Vīthī or any other manner of conversation is made. Āmukha has five varieties—udghātyaka, kathodghāta, prayogātiśaya, pravṛttaka and avalagita. Udghātyaka and avalagita are the elements of Vīthī. In kathodghāta, the character enters the stage taking up a remark of the Sūtradhāra. In prayogātiśaya, the Sūtradhāra himself remarks and introduces the beginning of the play and then the character enters. In pravṛttaka, the Sūtradhāra describes something, having recourse to the particular period such as the season etc. and the character enters on the basis of that. Any of these five should be used suitably.

Bhāratī style is characterised by speech. It was used by Bharatas; hence it is the verbal style i.e. the pāṭhya. Gradually, the element of speech became more important in plays which expressed the whole range of action. In the earlier plays, actual combats were represented. But in the later plays, we find that these were also reported through speech.

In the actual play, speech together with all the mental and physical action, is present. But in Prastāvanā, there is no scope for mental and physical action; hence it appears that later[1] works connected Bhāratī with Prastāvanā only.

Having arisen in connection with fight, this style has the absence of women. Dr. Raghavan also says in connection with this Vṛtti that at first, the actors were male. They spoke Sanskrit. The definition of Bhāratī refers to that stage. In later times, Bhāratī is everywhere in perfect drama.

Sāttvatī[2]—It has exuberance of joy and absence of sorrow. It has representation by words and gestures couched in the spirited language. The Heroic and the Marvellous sentiments

1. DR. Dhanika, p. 95.
2. Abhinava explains Sāttvata from sattva i.e. mind, and सात्त्वतो गुण: as मानसो व्यापार:
Sāttvatī is endowed with sāttvata quality.

NS. Vol. III., p. 96.

are connected with it; the Erotic and the Pathetic have no scope. The characters are mostly the majestic ones defying each other. Its four varieties are as follows—(1) Utthāpaka is the challenge to fight; (2) in Parivartaka, the thing that caused the rising up is given up and some other thing is undertaken due to need—it is the change of action; (3) Sallāpaka has various words of abuse or insult, whether arising from challenge or not; (4) Saṁghātyaka is the breaking of an alliance due to mantra, artha or vākyaśakti—either owing to luck or one's own fault.

From these four elements of Sāttvatī, it becomes clear to us that it has the warfare as its province. It might have been then, the way of fighting connected with the Sāttvata race.

Ārabhaṭī—It has mostly the qualities of Ārabhaṭas, the bold persons. It has deception of the various kinds and words full of hypocrisy, falsehood and jugglery also. It has four varieties—(1) Saṁkṣiptaka—In this there is significant workmanship, presentation of abundant model works and striking dresses. It relates to some condensed matter. (2) Avapāta—There is occurrence of fear and joy, acts of panic, calamity and confusion in it. The entries and exit are quick i.e. hurriedly effected. (3) Vastūtthāpana—In it the representation manifests combination of all sentiments based either on panic or its absence. (4) Sampheṭa is full of excitement. There are many fights, personal combats, deception and abundance of striking by weapons and splitting.

Ārabhaṭī seems to be a mode of fighting, relating to Ārabhaṭas and hence their violent manner. Ārabhaṭī is connected with the sentiments of Raudra, Bhayānaka and Bībhatsa. According to Dr. Agrawal,[1] this violent style was produced by the mixture of Hallīsaka and Rāsa. Hallīsaka, in his opinion, is derived from the Ionian Elysian. The ancient Ārabhaṭa region had the Indian Rāsa and Ionian Elysian mixed. The Ārabhaṭī naṭas are described by Bāṇa as dancing with their hair wafting about due to the vigorous movements. This dance style in which the hair are left untied and the head and the whole body shaken violently is peculiar to Baluchi and Kabayali people.

1. Harṣacarita—'Eka Sāṁskṛtika Adhyayana', pp. 33-34.

Kaiśikī—It has charming costumes and it relates to women. It is full of various kinds of dancing and singing and has acts dealing with enjoyment of love. It consists of the following four elements—(1) Narma—It abounds in remarks made in jest, based on love. The Heroic sentiment is absent. It is threefold—(a) that concerned with jealousy and anger (b) words of rebuke and (c) self-reproach and deception. (2) Narmasphuñja—It has the first meeting of lovers and words and dresses exciting the passion of love. It ends in fear. (3) Narmasphoṭa—It has many states which contribute to the Erotic sentiment. (4) Narmagarbha—The hero, due to necessity, acts incognito, with his qualities like intelligence, beauty, riches etc. This style is connected with the Erotic and the Comic sentiments.

Kaiśikī which was a later addition to the dramatic art was clearly meant for the atmosphere of music, lovely dresses and scenes etc. with women conducive to the Erotic sentiment. It might have been then, the style of action connected with Kaiśika, the short form of Krathakaiśika.[1]

The styles, then, are meant to produce the particular atmosphere of the particular play which has the particular sentiment like the Heroic or the Erotic as the principal one. Accordingly, though all the four styles found place in dramatic action, their judicious use created the two main divisions of the plays corresponding to the two main sentiments, the Heroic and the Erotic. The Marvellous, the Furious, the Terrible, the Odious and the Pathetic also were natural in association with the Heroic in which the theme was warfare. Hence, the Kaiśikī style which abounded in dance, music and as such the women characters had little scope in such types of plays. But Nāṭaka and Prakaraṇa were marked by the prominent use of the graceful style in addition to the other three styles because grace of speech and action together with effective use of music and dance was necessary in them. Of course, the hero of the drama was heroic but at the same time, his love affairs too were to be delineated. Hence in Nāṭaka, Kaiśikī was essential and as such, the presence of women was a necessity. In Prakaraṇa, the sentiment of love was dominant and hence Kaiśikī was

1. Cf. 'The Vrttis' by Dr. Raghavan.

essential. We find that among other varieties, Samavakāra, Ḍima, Īhāmṛga and Vyāyoga are connected with the themes of war actually and Utsṛṣṭikāṅka with the effect of war. Hence all these have no use of the Kaiśikī proper. Bhāṇa, Prahasana and Vīthī are connected with the atmosphere which is characterised by speech more. Love in Bhāṇa is of low type. Vīthī abounds in witticism and clever speech. Prahasana is full of jokes creating laughter. That is why there is no proper scope for Kaiśikī in these. Thus we see that the four styles distinguished the plays in two broad divisions first and then according to their use in various proportions further distinguished them from one another. In the plays which are said to be devoid of Kaiśikī, Kaiśikī is not totally absent; but it is subordinate. It is possible to have a Nāṭaka like Mudrārākṣasa devoid of Kaiśikī.

Scholars have discussed the development of the plays from the point of Vṛttis or the number of Acts and actors. The Stages are given as, from one[1] Act one actor plays to the plays of one Act and more than one actor and then to plays with three or four Acts having many characters and lastly the plays with five to ten well-knit Acts. The development from the point of view of Vṛttis[2] is given as, (1) plays like Bhāṇa which had Bhāratī Vṛtti as prominent; (2) then Sāttvatī was added and it became more prominent, (3) later Sāttvatī had in addition, Ārabhaṭī also and then ; (4) the types with all the four Vṛttis like Prakaraṇa and finally the (5) perfect Nāṭaka. Dr. Raghavan[3] has traced the evolution from Vīthī to Prahasana and finally to Prakaraṇa by slow stages. This is one line of development according to him in which the presentation of ordinary men from society is found. The other line of the dramatic development is the heroic one. The first dramas staged i.e. Amṛtamanthana and Tripuradāha, celebrating the deeds of gods slowly developed into Nāṭaka. In this development some features of the Social Play & the Heroic Play were intermixed.

The first performances dealing with the themes of battle

1. 'Contributions to the History of Hindu Drama' by Dr. Ghosh, p. 8. 'The Types of Sanskrit Drama' by D.R. Mankad, p. 165.
2. Cf. Bhāratīya Nāṭyaśāstra, by Miss Ketkar, pp. 359-363.
3. 'The Vṛttis' by Dr. Raghavan.

with many divine heroes fighting against the demons required a large stage. These open-air performances would have been successful due to the exciting nature of the plays. This heroic type was connected with religious festivals. The NŚ. mentions the performance of the first play in which preliminaries with the Nāndī in particular, formed the part of the performance. This means that the form of the drama was fixed even in this first play. The Raṅga which was the open-air stage for combats, races and dances etc. included the representations of important events in the life also, by the actors. When the play developed it was bifurcated from this Raṅga and had its own Raṅga where dance and music were employed as entertainment to the audience and the propitiation of the deities for which the performances were arranged. Side by side with the heroic plays another type also would have come into existence like Vīthī, having superior, middling and low types of characters and one or two actors to represent stories to evoke various sentiments. Such a performance required minimum accessories and used witty repartees. The Bhāṇa with one actor had low type of love for its theme. The actor's skill was really praiseworthy in the success of Vīthī and Bhāṇa. Prahasana with many characters of lighter type was also popular due to the exposition of hypocrisy. As the make-up and dress etc. for the various characters were required in Prahasana, it became a farcical play which might have been very popular from the ancient time. These three types had speech as the dominant feature. Leaving aside the earlier Prahasanas like Mattavilāsa or Bhagavadajjukīya, some of the later Prahasanas (e.g. the Muṇḍita-Muṇḍa) indulge in coarse vulgarity connected with sex. The humour, sometimes amounting to vulgarity, the wit and the ridicule of the hypocrisy in these farcical plays entertained the masses. Prahasanas used Prakrits mainly, which added to their popularity. These plays of mass entertainment also have the regular form in which Prastāvanā with Nāndī is there.

When the heroic plays were begun to be enacted in closed theatres the change in the nature of these plays was but natural. Though the large theatre was necessary in the beginning to accommodate large number of characters and the properties, the medium size theatre was fixed as most suited afterwards as the adoption of class dance brought the subtleties in Abhinaya. The entries and exits through the green-room were also fixed. The songs were kept into background and the speech became more prominent. The use of entrance and exit songs became necessary. The grace in the acting became more marked. In the Īhāmṛga the hero was still divine and fight was the strong motive. In the Vyāyoga, instead of god, a haughty man became the hero, though many actors took part in it and duels were represented. The Utsṛṣṭikāṅka was connected with the pathos due to the lamentation of ladies bereaved of their husbands killed or wounded in the battle. The mortal characters participated in it and not the divine ones. Thus the way for the human hero was paved. In the Nāṭaka, the perfect heroic drama, a noble king became the hero. As his valour and love were treated, the fuller human life came to be represented on the stage. In the Prakaraṇa the hero belonged to a lower status than the king. The stage had a green-room with two doors and a place for orchestra. The curtain was gradually introduced to effect the entries of the characters. In the earlier stages of evolution there would have been a time when the songster gave the story in songs and the actors gesticulated it. In the perfect drama the songs were used to give the mood etc. of the character. Hence, the musicians were placed in the background. The Preliminaries were carried out in detail by the Sūtradhāra to pacify the deities and to tune the hearts of the spectators to the performance.

When the poets expressed the situations in their plays in beautiful effective language, the niceties of modulations of voice became necessary. So the medium size theatre became most suitable.

In the presentation of the earlier types battle scenes were prominent. The description of Ḍima points to the ample use of model works. Though Śṛṅgāra is there in Samavakāra, it is subordinate. In the perfected Nāṭaka, the subtleties of acting became more important for which, appreciative spectators were needed. Hence, we find in the Prologues of the plays, a request by the Sūtradhāra to the learned spectators. The expert judges were seated to decide the winner of the dramatic competitions. In the case of difference of opinion, the experts in various professions were consulted. Thus it would be seen that the plays suited to popular taste and those appreciated by art connoisseurs were getting differentiated. Before concluding his commentary on Samavakāra, Abhinava[1] says that by its performance on the occasion of Devayātrā, the devotees full of faith become pleased while the women, children and the ignorant get interested due to exciting themes of fighting etc.

The plays were studied from the viewpoint of the stages in the development of the plot, the main incidents and the subordinate ones, and the junctures. The effort of the hero is to be delineated in five stages—namely, the beginning, the striving, the attainment slightly suggested by the means, the visualisation of the certainty of success and the attainment of the result. The means which are conducive to the attainment of the result are also five—the Bīja i.e. the seed; the Bindu, the prominent point; the Patākā, the subordinate incident; the Prakarī, the minor episode; and Kārya, all the effort for the purpose of the main plot. In the Patākā, the characters get their purpose also served while helping the hero. The character in the Prakarī, which is introduced for helping the hero has no purpose of its own, and has no continuity. Bīja, Bindu and Kārya would be necessary in all plays while Patākā and Prakarī would be used when required. The plot is developed through five saṁdhis i.e. junctures—the Mukha (opening in which the germ is created,) the Pratimukha (progression), the Garbha (sprouting of the germ), the Vimarśa (pause over the germ that has sprouted) and the Nirvahaṇa (bringing together the objects of all the junctures). The Nāṭaka and Prakaraṇa are to have five junctures. The number of junctures used is according to the nature of the play e.g. Ḍima and Samavakāra would have no Vimarśa; Vyāyoga and Īhāmṛga would be without Garbha and Vimarśa while, Prahasana, Vīthī Aṅka and Bhāṇa would have only Mukha and Nirvahaṇa. Each juncture has its Aṅgas i.e. the sub-parts which are 64 in all. Abhinava has stated that the Mukha has twelve sub-parts, Pratimukha thirteen, Garbha has thirteen, Avamarśa (Vimarśa) has twelve and Nirvahaṇa has fourteen. But in his commentary he has

1. NŚ. Vol. II., p. 441.

explained with illustrations thirteen sub-parts of the Avamarśa juncture. Thus the total number comes to sixty-five. The Daśarūpaka drops Prārthanā in the Garbha juncture and keeps the number sixty-four. According to one view mentioned by Abhinava,[1] one of the sub-parts of Avamarśa is dropped and according to the other, Praśasti from the Nirvahaṇa is not to be counted. There is some difference[2] as regards the nomenclature of the sub-parts of the junctures.

These sub-parts of the junctures are treated in the NŚ. to show how the plot should be well-knit from the viewpoint of the language used in it. They are to be used sometimes mixing two or three of them. The sub-parts of the junctures are meant for the perfection of the play and what particular sub-parts are to be used in the particular juncture, depends upon the expert poet. It can be reasonably said that the rigidity regarding the particular sub-parts in the particular junctures cannot be enforced. Their purpose is to guide the playwright for an ideal play.

The plays are divided into acts. The events which are not needed to be represented on the stage but are necessary for the understanding and progression of the incidents in the plot are made to be known to the spectators through interludes called Praveśaka and Viṣkambhaka. The former has Prakrit speaking characters only and the latter has either Sanskrit speaking middling characters (in its pure variety) or middling characters and low characters, both (in its mixed variety). The Praveśaka having only low characters seems to be a later convention. Prof. Karmarkar[3] is right when he says that there seems to have been in the beginning only one variety of prelude i.e. Praveśaka. For, in the NŚ. the Praveśaka alone is mentioned while describing Nāṭaka, while Viṣkambhaka (supporting scene) is given in connection with Prakaraṇa. The Praveśaka in the classical plays never comes at the beginning of the first act. There are three other explanatory devices also, which are added later on. When somebody e.g. Sūta etc. introduces

1. NŚ. Vol. III., p. 56.

2. See—'The Theory of the Saṁdhis and the Saṁdhyaṅgas' by Dr. T. G. Mainkar, pp. 23-24 & 34-145.

3. 'Dramatic Terms—Praveśaka and Viṣkambhaka' A.B.O.R.I. Vol. XXXV, pp. 122-128.

some matter from behind the curtain it is called Cūlikā. In Aṅkāvatāra an Act is introduced at the end of the previous Act, without breaking its continuity; it relates to the purpose of the germ. When the opening of an Act is introduced beforehand by a male or female character, interrupting (the subject-matter of the previous Act), it is called Aṅkamukha.

The element of dramatic irony was supplied through the four Patākā-sthānas. When some matter is already taken in hand and another matter of similar nature is suggested through an accidental idea, it is known as Patākā-sthāna due to its nature of indication like that of a Patākā, i.e. banner. Ten aspects of Lāsya are described in the NŚ. in connection with plays. The Daśarūpaka explains them in connection with the Bhāṇa. Abhinava states that they too become useful in Nāṭaka. These Lāsyāṅgās having Lāsya, the gentle dance as their principal element are to be performed by one individual and as such, are outside the scope of the Nāṭaka proper. Their use would have been allowed for striking effect in the presentation of plays.

The Lāsyāṅgas are described as follows:

(1) Geyapada—The song is sung by the singer (seated) in accompaniment of instrumental music.

(2) Sthitapāṭhya—A woman separated from her lover and burning with the pangs of love recites in Prakrit, full of sentiment.

(3) Āsīna—It is sitting steady being overcome with anxiety and sorrow, without any instrumental music.

(4) Puṣpagaṇḍikā—It has songs and various dances accompanied by various movements of men, performed by women.

(5) Pracchedaka—It has a woman, who being afflicted by moon-light (thus excited with passion), clings to her lover even if he has done wrong.

(6) Trimūḍhaka—It has even metres, abounding in manly states, that are composed of delicate words.

(7) Saindhavaka—In it there is the representation of a lover who has failed to keep the appointment, using

Prakrit, accompanied by well-performed Karaṇas (of Vīṇā and the like).

(8) Dvimūḍhaka[1]—In it there is a song of caturaśrapada full of sentiment and states, used for the sake of striking effect, with Mukha and Pratimukha parts. According to Abhinava[2] there is stepping in four directions used in it, after performing caturaśra.

(9) Uttamottamaka—In it there is a composition in various metres with many sentiments, having Helā and Hāva.

(10) Uktapratyukta—It has combination of speeches and counter speeches due to anger or pleasure, having words of censure, set to music.

Citrapada—It has a woman burning with the fire of love and diverting her mind by looking at the form of her lover drawn in picture.

Bhāvika—In it there is a woman burning with the fire of love and manifesting various states, seeing her lover in dream.

Abhinava does not admit the Citrapada and the Bhāvika which are treated by some among the Lāsyāṅgas; for he says that the Lāsya is given by Bharata as daśavidha and in the chapter on Tāla also the ten Lāsyāṅgas are treated in the NŚ.

Some of these Lāsyāṅgas have other definitions also, having more stress on dance and music. The theme of Lāsya is to be a poet's creation similar to a Prakaraṇa. Hence in addition to the ten situations worked out as the ten Lāsyāṅgas, appearing in love dramas, two more are also treated by some.

The language to be used is given as twofold in the NŚ., the Sanskrit and the Prakrit. In this connection the NŚ. gives all the necessary instructions regarding the metre, the beautifications and the merits and demerits of the language to be used in the plays. The Sanskrit language is to be used by the heroes

1. S.D. VI. 220. Dvimūḍhaka is given as Dvigūḍha

2. 'चतुरश्रपदक्रमम्' is explained by Abhinava as 'चतुरश्रं कृत्वा क्रान्तदिक्चतुष्टयं: पदै: क्रमणं यत्रेति ।" NŚ. Vol. III p. 73.

of all the four types—Dhīrodātta (noble and exalted), Dhīralalita (noble and gay), Dhīroddhata (noble and haughty) and Dhīrapraśānta (noble and calm). These heroes may use Prakrit when occasion demands it. Prakrit is to be used by a Bhāgavata, Tāpasa, Unmatta, Bāla, Nīca, by those possessed of lower spirits, and females etc. Sanskrit is to be used by Parivrāj, Muni, Śākya, Cokṣa and Śrotriya. Thus, the superior and middling characters are to use Sanskrit and others, Prakrit. The queen and the courtesan may use Sanskrit to suit special occasions. The divine nymphs should use Sanskrit but they may use Prakrit when on earth. Seven regional Prakrits and some tribal languages are also given by the NŚ. which are to be used in conformity with the characters. The suggestions made by the NŚ. regarding the use of the different dialects are meant to give some latitude to writers to use them suitably so that the characters could be marked out as belonging to their respective regions. Dr. P. L. Vaidya[1] says in this connection that the principal Prakrit dialect used in the dramas was, Śaurasenī both for prose and verse. We find that later the Mahārāṣṭrī which got prominence, was used in the verses put in the mouth of female characters, side by side, with the Śaurasenī.

The characters in the plays are of three types—the superior, the middling and the inferior, according to their superior, middling and inferior qualities and status. The instrumental music prescribed for the different characters is also given accordingly i.e. the instrumentation is dealt with separately for males and females of the superior, the middling and the inferior types. The NŚ. has given the terms of address for different persons of the three types being necessary for etiquette. The names of characters are also to be significant.

III

We can now look for the line of development of the Sanskrit drama by turning to the plays of the great classical period.

1. 'Use of Prakrit Dialects in Sanskrit Dramas'—A.B.O.R.I. Vol. XXXIII, pp. 15-25.

We have to begin from the plays ascribed to Bhāsa[1] for fuller details of the earliest available classical plays. The fragments of the plays of Aśvaghoṣa indicate the developed stage of the Sanskrit drama but being fragments they cannot throw much light on all the details necessary for minute study. Some peculiar features in the Trivandrum plays are sufficient enough to indicate that they belong to an early period from the viewpoint of the evolution of Sanskrit drama. In the earliest plays, the fights were presented directly on the large stage. In the medium-sized theatre, instead of depicting wars actually with many characters involved in them, the effect was achieved by their powerful descriptions. But the spectators were used to see the fights on the stage. Hence, in the Bhāsa plays we find duels still represented. In the further development, these also began to be reported through descriptions. The plays ascribed to Bhāsa present the middle stage in this development. The fight of King Udayana and his capture by the enemy are reported in the Pratijñāyaugandharāyaṇa. The last battle between the demons and Rāma's army consisting of monkeys and that between Rāma and Rāvaṇa are described by the three Vidyādharas in the Abhiṣeka. But in the same play, the personal combat between Vālin and Sugrīva is directly presented. The fight of Uttara with the Kauravas is reported by a soldier in the Pañcarātra. The personal combat between Bhīma and Ghaṭotkaca in Madhyamavyāyoga is directly presented while the fight between Bhīma and Duryodhana with mace is described by the three soldiers in the Ūrubhaṅga. The Bālacarita presents the combats between Dāmodara and Cāṇūra and between Balarāma and Muṣṭika. These illustrations are sufficient to prove that these plays represent that stage of the evolution in which the representation of fights on the stage was being limited to the personal combats. The size of the stage also might have been responsible to some extent for such a change. The fighting with weapons is mainly reported. The NŚ.[2] says that the attack with weapons should not be shown actually but should be pre-

1. In the thirteen plays printed in the Bhāsanāṭakacakra, there are five one-act plays, one three-act play, two-four-act plays, one five-act play, three six-act plays and one seven-act play. There is variety in themes also.

2. NŚ. XXI 224, 225.

sented by gesticulation or, if the actor is so very expert that no harm would be done by such an attack, the use of weapons could be made. This gives us the idea that the effect of representation of fight was desired more and not the actual representation. The NŚ. describes in detail the four methods of warfare which indicate their use in the earliest period of the Sanskrit theatre. One more point is, the representation of death on the stage. In the Bhāsa plays we have the deaths of Vālin, Daśaratha, Duryodhana, Cāṇūra, Muṣṭika and Kaṁsa represented actually. In the later drama Nāgānanda, we have the hero as good as dead. But this death is temporary as the hero is brought to life immediately by the goddess. The NŚ. gives in detail the representation of death while describing the abhinaya. It[1] prohibits the death of the hero which is absolutely essential for the happy ending of the play. In the verse, preceding this verse prohibiting the death of the hero, the fight, the death, the siege of a city are given as not to be directly represented but to be reported through Praveśaka. Abhinava[2] records a view in connection with the presentation of death on the stage, according to which, the death which is brought about by action connected with others e.g. the cutting of the demon's head by discus should not be represented but the death due to disease etc. not brought about by the action of others should be represented. But Abhinava points out that such a discrimination is improper. He states that the dead one cannot exit and as such, the Dhruvāgāna would have no scope. The spectators too would lose their interest. Hence, death as such should never be represented on the stage. The point becomes clear when we look at the absurdity of the dead one being on the stage who must be removed from the stage. In Bālacarita, Act V, we find the words of Vasudeva to the effect that the dead bodies should be removed (from the stage). Sometimes in folk-theatre we find that the dead one gets up and leaves the stage without causing any serious flaw in the minds of the spectators. In the Chinese theatre, the protagonist who is killed does not fall down at the end of the battle but exits at a run. The beheaded character falls to the ground for a moment and then

1. NŚ. XVIII. 39.
2. NŚ. Vol. II. p. 426.

rising up runs off the stage. Thus it can be seen that the conventions of the stage deserve consideration in regard to the question of the representation of death. By holding a curtain it would have been possible for a dead character to leave the stage or, as in the above-mentioned manner of the Bālacarita, the dead ones would have been removed from the stage. After Bhāsa no classical drama has shown death on the stage except that of the temporary one of Jīmūtavāhana in Nāgānanda. Like the wars, duels and the death also were presented in effective manner in the plays that followed those of Bhāsa, through descriptions and through their effects on the character concerned.

The consideration of language also leads to the same conclusion of the Bhāsa plays being earlier. The simplicity of the language is also an important consideration in the discussion of the evolution. In Kālidāsa, we find that the expression has become more poetic but the poetic and the dramatic go hand in hand to heighten the beauty of each other. In Harṣa, the expression has become more ornate and the use of elaborate metres is also there. This tendency is on the increase in Bhavabhūti. To distinguish Bhāsa from the later writers, the comparison of Cārudatta and Mṛcchakaṭika would prove helpful. The description of Vasantasenā's house given in short in the former play by Vidūṣaka and that extremely elaborate one given in the latter would bring about the difference easily. The classical drama was handled after Kālidāsa by playwrights who were living in the age in which classical Sanskrit had attained that level of ornateness which is found in the great Sanskrit works of prose and verse. Naturally, the dramatist also, being the product of his age, took resort to the very ornate dramatic compositions that were a source of great joy to the learned critics. The presentation of these plays on the occasion of public festivities e.g. the plays of Bhavabhūti presented at the festival of Kālapriyanātha, would have been appreciated by the learned spectators due to the highly polished expression while by the ordinary ones due to the expert gesticulation of the actors which had also attained great heights of histrionics.

We find that in the Sanskrit plays, the majority of verses is in Sanskrit. Perhaps the earliest plays contained a greater number of Sanskrit verses in simple language and much of the prose-dialogue improvised. In Bhāsa we find one verse spoken by two or three characters. This trait is found in the Mṛcchakaṭika and in Uttararāmacarita etc. The verse is split up in a peculiar manner in Mālatī-Mādhava: the first half is recited from behind the curtain, most of the third line by Kāmandakī who is on the stage and the rest of the third line and the fourth line by Makaranda after entering the stage.

When the prose dialogues with the mixture of Sanskrit and Prakrit were used more and more, the verses, conducive to striking effect were retained. The dialogue in the verse form can also be dramatic. Thus originally, the form would have been wholly in Sanskrit and later on in Sanskrit and Prakrit both for the sake of indicating reality and due to the need of the time.

The Sanskrit drama was bred in such an atmosphere where, in life, Sanskrit and Prakrit were the media of the cultured and the non-cultured in the society respectively. The use of the Prakrit dialects in Sanskrit plays of the classical period points to the fact that these, together with Sanskrit were intelligible to the spectators. The hero speaks in Sanskrit and the heroine responds in Prakrit and the hero further goes on in Sanskrit. All this would not have been possible if both were not intelligible to the characters concerned and the spectators. In the popular plays like Prahasana, the people's language, i.e., Prakrit was dominant.

Bharata mentions the use of the Dhruvā songs which were sung by the musicians. The request of Sūtradhāra to the Naṭī to sing a song is seen in the Prologue of the Pratijñāyaugandharāyaṇa of Bhāsa but the song is not sung. In his Pratimā the request is to sing a song describing autumn and the Naṭī must have sung it as the stage direction 'gāyati' is there. The actual song is not given. The songs of Gandharvas behind the scene are referred to in the Abhiṣeka. Bhāsa has introduced hallīsaka (a group dance) in Bālacarita and Pañcarātra. Kālidāsa has introduced the use of dance and music in Mālavikāgnimitra where Mālavikā is made to sing a song and render it into abhinaya before the king, the queen etc. In his Vikramorvaśīya, Urvaśī, the heroine is a heavenly dancer and hence it was possible for the dramatist to have her actions full of graceful dance movements. Thus, Kālidāsa has blended the dance, music and poetry harmoniously and has offered us a very charming Sanskrit drama. Harṣa followed this predecessor and introduced dance and music through the characters in the plays. The appeal of Mṛcchakaṭika was due to the variety of low and middle characters on the background of the noble hero and the polished, high-minded heroine Vasantasenā, an expert in dance-movements.

The author of Mudrārākṣasa struck a new path inasmuch as he did not give scope for Kaiśikī style. The drama in the hands of Bhavabhūti became very highly poetic. The Veṇīsaṁhāra of Bhaṭṭanārāyaṇa is also of such very ornate style. Later on Murāri and Rājaśekhara have developed the same highly poetic tradition. Many Sanskrit plays have been written on the line of the great predecessors after Rājaśekhara and also produced. But in these later plays the artificiality of the art is quite marked. The allegorical play of the mediaeval period has its beginning in Aśvaghoṣa's art. As regards the play within the play we find that Kālidāsa introduced the Chalika nāṭya in his Mālavikāgnimitra and later on the classical playwrights like Harṣa and Bhavabhūti actually introduced a play within the play. In the earliest plays like Ḍima there was ample scope for model works. In the plays of Bhāsa we find such characters as ocean, the serpent Kāliya, the weapons of Viṣṇu and Garuḍa introducing themselves in one verse each, the curse, the royal glory (rājaśrī)`the bull-demon etc. There is the Viśvarūpa of Kṛṣṇa in Dūtavākya. Later on the use of the model work became less prominent and only suggestive model works were employed when necessary. The descriptions of scenic situations mostly in Sanskrit verses became more and more favoured by the playwrights and hence we find a very large number of descriptive verses in Murāri, Rājaśekhara and others.

The most developed types of Rūpakas like Nāṭaka and Prakaraṇa put into background the types like Samavakāra and Ḍima etc.; that is why their early specimens have not come down to us. Bhāsa's Ūrubhaṅga and Madhyamavyāyoga are taken to be solitary specimens of Aṅka and Vyāyoga respectively by some scholars. We have the four earlier Bhāṇas in the Caturbhāṇī. As regards Prahasana, we have Mattavilāsa and Bhagavadajjukīyam as early illustrations. The early specimens of Bhāṇa and Prahasana are available as they could survive due to their being popular entertainment.

IV

The Sanskrit plays gradually became limited to the select appreciative spectators and the people's entertainment naturally sought expression in the popular type[1] of plays using prominently the elements of music and dance which were current as the means of popular entertainment throughout. The sculptural representations of many dance panels from 2nd century B.C. onwards, point to their popularity. Kohala who came after Bharata treated these plays.

The name of Kohala[2] appears in the NŚ. as the author of Uttaratantra. He has first described after Bharata, the forms of drama, other than those mentioned by Bharata, which were existing in his times. These are the Uparūpakas—the minor varieties. From the definitions[3] quoted by Abhinava it seems that some of them had music and dance very prominent in them. Nāṭī or Nāṭikā,[4] having the features of both the Nāṭaka and the Prakaraṇa is described in the NŚ. Troṭaka, which is defined as a separate variety is nearer to Nāṭaka while Saṭṭaka has the dominance of Prakrit. These cannot be properly called as Uparūpakas. They are Rūpakas themselves. The other varieties like Ḍombī, Śrīgadita, Rāsaka etc. are generally speaking devoid of much speech and are full of music and gestures. Śāradātanaya[5] separates these i.e. Nāṭikā, Saṭṭaka and Troṭaka

1. Cf. 'A Note on the Popular Element in the Classical Sanskrit Drama', by Sivaprasad—A.I.O.C. 1922 Vol. I. pp. 249-264.

2. NŚ. XXXVIII—18.

'शेषमुत्तरतन्त्रेण कोहलस्तु करिष्यति' ।

3. NŚ. Vol. I. p. 181.

4. Abhinava mentions one view according to which Prakaraṇikā is also given as derived from Nāṭaka and Prakaraṇa.

"अन्ये तु...इति प्रकरणिकापि सार्थवाहादिनायकयोगेन कैशिकीप्रधाना लभ्यत इत्याहुः ।"

NŚ. Vol. II. p. 436.

5. Cf. A Note on the name 'Daśarūpaka' by V. Raghavan. J.O.R.M. Vol. VII pp. 277-290.

and gives the rest i.e. Ḍombī etc. as Rūpakas of Nṛtyātmaka varieties. Nṛtyaprabandhas are performed by only one person. They are Ekahārya as the Bhāṇa. Lāsya mentioned in the NŚ. is the dance variety. The Tāṇḍava[1] was at first mere dance, but it approached the dramatic form when the story of Śiva's burning away of Tripura was sung by Nārada and closely following it, Śiva danced and rendered the story in abhinaya. When all the characters in the Tripuronmātha, sung by Nārada are acted by different persons we go nearer drama; though the actors are still dumb, they closely render in gestures, the theme which is sung by another set of music artistes nearby. We find in the Kathakali of Kerala this type of Tāṇḍava. Bhoja describes Nāṭikā and Saṭṭaka but leaves Troṭaka. The Uparūpaka varieties[2] named Bhāṇa, Preraṇa and Bhāṇikā adopt the 'anyāpadeśa' method of describing symbolically animals to suggest the intended idea and the dancer sings these with the gait of lion, elephant or other animals figuring in those songs. The animal symbology for clever suggestion is employed in the Nāṭakas. The animal allegory is used to suggest the scenic situation also.

Troṭaka is a variant of Nāṭaka. Saṭṭaka is a variant of Nāṭikā and differs from it by being all in Prakrit and having no introductory scenes. The acts are called Javanikāntara. The name denotes a form of dance.

Abhinava[3] quotes ancient authorities giving the definitions of Ḍombikā, Bhāṇa, Prasthāna, Ṣidgaka, Bhāṇikā, Preraṇa, Rāmākrīḍa, Hallīsaka and Rāsaka and calls them as Nṛttātmaka prabhandhas.

Dhanika[4] calls Ḍombī, Śrīgadita, Bhāṇa, Bhāṇī, Prasthāna and Rāsaka as Nṛtyabhedas. According to Hemacandra these i.e. Ḍombikā and others are 'Geya-rūpakas' based on padārthābhinaya. He has distinguished between Pāṭhyarūpaka

1. See—"A Note on the name 'Daśarūpaka' " by Dr. Raghavan.
2. See Ibid. NŚ. Vol. I. p. 172.
3. NŚ. Vol. I p. 181
4. DR. I—8.

and Geyarūpaka. In the former[1] the songs and the tempo etc. with the bodily movements are subordinate, while in the latter they are prominent. In the Rāga-kāvya the story is in the form of the songs sung according to the particular Rāga. Abhinava[2] says that Rāghavavijaya was to be sung in Ṭakka Rāga and Mārīcavadha in Kakubhagrāma Rāga. A composition which would employ several Rāgas would be Citrarāga-kāvya like the Gīta-Govinda. In the Rāgakāvya, the music was predominant in the form of the songs which were gesticulated also, for Abhinava[3] mentions Tāṇḍava in the Rāghavavijaya.

Śāradātanaya has treated the story-element also for most of these Uparūpakas. According to Dr. Keith[4] these specimens show rather the character of pantomime with song, dance and music. These[5] are treated by Dr. Raghavan and Śrī Mankad in detail. I am giving them in brief.

In Bhāṇa the descriptions of Nṛsiṁha, Sūkara etc. are given by the female dancer with terrible movements of limbs. Bhāṇikā is also based on dance having mostly Haricarita for its subject-matter. In Ḍombī the mind of the king is entertained by words suggesting concealed love, by the dancer. Rāsaka is to be performed by many female dancers with a variety of rhythm. In Nāṭyarāsaka, the dance approached nearer to imperfect drama. Prasthāna is connected with the lover's going away on travel. Whatever is performed in street, assembly, squares or temples by many characters is called Prekṣaṇaka. Nartanaka is the dance gesticulating different objects with graceful and

1. 'अथ पाठ्यस्य गेयस्य च रूपकस्य को विशेषः । अयमाख्यायते—
पाठ्ये हि—अङ्गं गीतं चेत्युभयमप्रतिष्ठितम् ।...
गेये तु गीतमङ्गं च द्वयमपि स्वप्रतिष्ठितम् ।'

Cf. Kāvyānuśāsana VIII—4. Vol. I., p. 447.

Cf. NŚ. Vol. I. p. 166.

Cf. 'Nṛtyanāṭyava Geyanāṭya' by Chaitanya Desai. Chanda (Marathi) Māgha-Phālguna 1880.

2. NŚ. Vol. I. p. 182.

3. Ibid. p. 198.

'यत्तु राघवविजयादौ सीतामूर्च्छादिव्यावर्णन्तं ताण्डवम् ।'

4. Cf. 'The Sanskrit Drama', p. 351.

5. See 'The Types of Sanskrit Drama', pp. 105-128. by D.R. Mankad 1. "Bhoja's Śṛṅgāraprakāśa", by Dr. V. Raghavan, pp. 545-574.

rhythmic movements. In Hallīsaka, the women dance in a circle with one hero at the centre. Ullopyaka should have one or three acts; battles form part of its subject. Pārijātaka has the Erotic and the Heroic sentiments, the hero being a god or a noble Kṣatriya. Sallāpaka has three or four acts, with the Heroic and the Furious sentiments. The Erotic and the Comic are absent. [Sāhityadarpaṇa gives the hero as a heretic (pāṣaṇḍa).] Śilpaka also has four acts and sentiments except the Comic. Its hero is a Brahmin. Goṣṭhī has nine or ten Prākṛta heroes and five or six beautiful heroines. (Bhoja gives it as the representation of the sports of Kṛṣṇa in Gokula and the killing of the Asuras by Kṛṣṇa.) Śrigadita should have a renowned hero and high-born heroine. Bhoja explains the name by saying that in it a heroine describes her Lord's qualities (to her friend) as Goddess Śrī, her Lord Nārāyaṇa's. According to SD.[1] it should be full of the word Śrī. In Ṣidgaka, the forcible conduct of the lover or sometimes his cunning acts are spoken in the presence of the friends. Durmallikā has four acts and its heroine is grown-up and town-bred. The secret enjoyment etc. are described in private by a female messenger in vulgar manner. Rāmakrīḍa has descriptions of seasons. Preraṇa is full of laughter and enigmatic expressions. Vilāsikā should have ten Lāsyāṅgas and Vidūṣaka, Viṭa and Pīṭhamarda.

These minor varieties generally give more prominence to dance and music. They served as popular entertainment when Sanskrit plays became limited to the select cultured audience. The popular element found a vent in these Uparūpakas and Geyakāvyas. These Uparūpakas[2] appear to be a link between the ancient classical theatre and the later popular theatrical traditions.

V

This style of the Uparūpakas with the dominance of dance and music was adopted by the traditional popular theatre of

1. S.D. VI. 294.

2. Prof. N. G. Joshi of Baroda informs me that Gurjara Viṭa and Mahārāṣṭra Viṭa are described in the Mānasollāsa. He thinks that this Gurjara Viṭa, later has become the comedian of Bhavāi, the folk-play of Gujarat and the Mahārāṣṭra Viṭa, the comedian of the Marāṭhī folk-theatre.

India when the modern Indian languages became the spoken languages of India. Sanskrit and Prakrit both became literary and hence artificial languages which could be understood only by the literary few. So the Sanskrit plays using Sanskrit and Prakrit went out of the reach of the common man. Though they were presented even after the rise of modern Indian languages, their appeal remained limited. That is why the dance-drama style, being very popular, was adopted by the theatre that emerged after the rise of modern Indian languages. We find many features of the classical abhinaya in the dance-drama types of Kathakali, Yakṣagāna, Kucipuḍi, Bhāgavatamela-nāṭaka and the Aṅkīyānāṭ etc.

The Kathakali[1] is the name given to the pantomime dance-drama of Kerala. Pantomime acting has reached its full maturity in Kathakali. Certain characters of the play wear wooden masks while others have their faces painted. Many stage practices including its very distinguished technique of abhinaya have been borrowed by Kathakali from Kūṭiyāṭṭam—the traditional presentation of Sanskrit plays by the Cākyārs of Kerala. Because of the presence of Āhārya, Sāttvika and Āṅgika abhinayas and the vācika supplied to some extent by the songs of the musicians, this Kerala art form becomes a dance-drama which has incorporated many classical elements.

The themes of the plays which are sung by the musicians to the accompaniment of instrumental music are enacted elaborately by the dancers. The female roles are played by the male dancers. There are set types of characters. The dress and make-up are very fantastic and elaborate. But it has profound undertones of moods associated with it. The majestic beauty of Kathakali head-dress and ornaments is eye-filling. A terrific character like Vīrabhadra utters shrieks or some awful cries at the moment of climax. Except this, the dancers never speak. The vocal music is provided by two musicians, the main one and his partner. The instrumental music gives prominence to Tāla. There is some provision for acting without the accompaniment of singing. The stage is about sixteen feet square, a kind of pandal not demarcated from the auditorium. The

1. Cf. "Kathakali", by K. Bharatha Iyer; Ch. II.; Marg-Dec. 1957. pp. 12-35.

light is provided by the big brass oil-lamp. A curtain is used, held by two persons, before the entry of the characters. After the invocatory verse, two dancers execute a devotional dance behind the curtain and this is followed by a pure dance performed by the Sāttvika character and his partner. When this divine pair has made the auspicious beginning, the curtain is lowered half-way to the sound of a conch and the flourish of drums, revealing the dancers under the canopy with peacock feathers and flywhiskers on their sides. This pair begins to play with the eyes, eyebrows and elegant gestures. There is a song from Gīta-govinda and then a display of skilful drumming after which, the play starts. The themes are all mythological. At the stage of climax, the awe-inspiring and frightful characters enter through the audience from behind. This practice is adopted from the earlier Cākyār tradition.

The Yakṣagāna[1] of Karnatak belongs to South Canara. The themes of Yakṣagāna are fights and warfares—the stories of the Heroic and the Furious sentiments from the Purāṇic legends. The actors of Yakṣagāna roar and perform robust dances in weird costumes. These plays are poetic dramas sung always with Rāga and Tāla. The name must have come from Yakkalagāna which is available from Andhra. The theme is sung by the musician called Bhāgavata and the actors recite extempore speeches. The stage is in open-air, a roofed square of 15′×15′. Four bamboo pillars usually decorated with mango-leaves are planted at the four corners to demarcate the stage. Just nearby a small enclosure is made with a curtain to serve as a green-room. In old days two torchbearers were placed on both sides of the stage to provide light. The Bhāgavata conducts the plays and he is the most important personage. He sings songs and the dancers dance to the rhythm of his cymbals. One or two stools are used to serve purposes like a throne etc. Members of the audience sit on the three sides of the stage and on the fourth Bhāgavata and his accompanists stand. The torchbearers come forward to throw light on actors' faces. In the preliminaries in honour of the deities songs and dance are resorted to. The comic conversation is also

1. Cf. 'Yaksha Gana' by Dr. Raghavan—Triveni Vol. VII. No. 2 and 'Yakṣagāna Bayalāṭa' (Kannaḍa) by Shivram Karanth.

there through the chief comic character Hanuman nāyaka. After the preliminaries, the songs introducing the theme are sung. If the theme is from Rāmāyaṇa, Rāma and Lakṣmaṇa enter first and if from Mahābhārata, the Pāṇḍavas. A red-coloured cloth used as a curtain, is held by two persons. If the entry is that of the Pāṇḍavas, the youngest brother Sahadeva stands with his back towards the curtain (hence to the audience). The crown alone is visible. He touches the ground and salutes the Bhāgavata, dances a little and then shows his face first and gradually the whole body is revealed by removing the curtain. Then enter Nakula, Arjuna, Bhīma and Dharma, one after another in the same manner. All once again come behind the curtain and show themselves gradually together. The vigorous dance of each displays his heroism. Thus preparation of the mind of the audience to receive the play is made. Then Bhāgavata calls the chief comic character and orders him to introduce the Pāṇḍavas. First he praises them but Arjuna and Bhīma alone are praised a lot. Then he helps Pāṇḍavas as a counsellor and ambassador and some fun is also justified in his talk. The Bhāgavata introduces the minor characters through questions like, 'Who are you?' "Why are you here?" "Whence have you come?" etc. He becomes the part and the parcel of the whole show. He repeats the moods of the characters. If the song contains speech the actor also sings in accompaniment of the Bhāgavata, as he dances. The actor starts conveying the meaning of the song and the sentiment expressed therein in a sort of musical prose. Literary appeal is secondary in the Yakṣagāna. The rhythmic movement of the feet is a special beauty of Yakṣagāna. The entry of the devil is awe-inspiring. At the end there is Bharatavākya sung by the actors. Dance claims much importance in Yakṣagāna. The music brings in emotion and the dance, grace. The dress and make-up are grand. Occasional use of the mask is also seen. The use of some hand gestures also can be noticed. As in Kathakali the female roles are played by male dancers.

In the Kucipuḍi[1] of Andhra, the dance-drama named after the village of its birth, all the roles are played by men only.

1. Cf. 'Bhagavatamela and Kuchipudi', by Prof. Khokar; Marg, Sept. 1957 pp. 27-36.

Its technique reveals remarkable balance between dance movements and footwork, expressional abhinaya and the expression conveyed through song and speech. The dancers portray through gestures and mime, song and speech. The song and speech are rendered by the dancers themselves and not by the supporting musicians alone. But some items in Kucipuḍi are to be performed solo. They are presented by introducing them as additional diversions in the dance-drama or by rendering them as independent numbers in dance-concert. Apart from being a dancer and an actor, the Kucipuḍi artiste is expected to have a high proficiency in the Sanskrit and Telugu languages and also possess a good knowledge of music. Kucipuḍi artistes claim that their art is based on the Abhinayadarpaṇa and the NŚ. The themes selected are based on the epics and Purāṇas, the Bhāgavata purāṇa in particular. The dancers present through abhinaya the aṣṭapadīs of Jayadeva. The plays are acted in the open-air on an improvised stage. When the audience assembles the Konnaṅgi who is also known as the Hāsyagaḍu appears on the stage. Being a Vidūṣaka he is grotesquely attired. His main task is to create order and attract the attention by his awkward dance movements. After his exit a prayer of invocation is sung and then the conductor of the dance-drama and the supporting musicians and drummers appear on the stage. Together they give a display of rhythm on the drums and the cymbals. The conductor next sings a prayer in honour of the goddess Bālatripurasundarī of Kucipuḍi. This is followed by an elaborately rendered Śloka in which the conductor expounds the theme and the purpose of the play and exhorts the assembly to give attention and the play commences. The principal characters are introduced by presenting them first behind a piece of cloth held by two volunteers. This improvised screen does not cover the character fully—the face and the feet are left visible. Prior to the removal of this curtain, a few steps and movements in dance are performed by the character behind the curtain. Illumination is provided by oil-lamps. Another interesting feature of earlier times was the use of a kind of powder, known in Telugu as Guggilum to provide a sudden flash of illumination at the most exciting junctures of the play. One more characteristic of Kucipuḍi is that each principal character introduces himself on the stage with a daru—a small dance and song sequence designed for each character to enable him to reveal his identity and skill in the art. This is known as the Pātra praveśadaru. These darus form the part of the actual text of the drama. Another peculiarity of the art is the addition of comic pieces which are not found in the original text. They serve to provide comic relief after tense, serious sequences. The make-up and costume have nothing elaborate in them. The language of these dramas consists of verse, prose and songs all according to texts. The metres are recited in a singing manner. The songs are mainly in Darus. Every Daru is preceded by a verse, every word of which is properly gesticulated. There is no extempore matter.

In Bhāgavatamelanāṭaka[1] belonging to Tanjore district also the characters go through their parts interpreting every piece of song and speech through abhinaya. The plays are all in Telugu. As in Kucipuḍi here too, the principal characters introduce themselves through Darus. When an actor finishes his part in a particular act or scene he does not necessarily vacate the stage. Unlike Kucipuḍi there are no dance or abhinaya items in this dance-drama which can be rendered independent of their place in the play. The make-up is simple as in Kucipuḍi. Except when Rākṣasas are shown in battles, masks have no place. The whole action is in the form of songs sung from behind as well as by characters themselves and rendered into abhinaya by them. In between these, prose lines are read out by the text-reader.

The plays of Śaṅkaradeva and his followers are called Aṅkīyānāṭ. In the Aṅkīyānāṭ of Assam, there are the preliminaries in the beginning. Two drummers and two cymbal players present instrumental music and as the tempo increases they dance also. Then the comic character enters and next the Sūtradhāra enters with the use of the curtain as in the case of Kathakali etc. The Nāndī verse is sung by him to the accompaniment of dance. At the time of Nāndī, flute also is added to the orchestra. In the Nāndī Lord Kṛṣṇa is invoked in an

1. Cf. "The Bhāgavata Meḷa Nāṭaka", by Dr. Raghavan—Journal of the Indian Society of Oriental Art—Coomaraswamy Vol. 1937, pp. 167-170.

elaborate ritual. After the Nāndī the Sūtradhāra introduces the play mostly speaking in vernacular. Sūtradhāra remains on the stage throughout the play. He explains every new entrance first in Sanskrit verse and then in the vernacular. He himself dances before introducing characters. Every important speech of the character is followed by a song. Before the starting of the play proper, the Sūtradhāra implores the attention of the public. The conch is blown at the entry of the main character. In the Aṅkīyānāṭ Rukmiṇī-Haraṇa[1] witnessed by me, first Kṛṣṇa and Uddhava entered dancing, without the use of a curtain but their entry was introduced in a song. After their exit Rukmiṇī was introduced with a song. She entered dancing with her female companion and then left the stage with her. Then the rest of the characters entered in the same manner and the story proceeded. The parents liked their daughter's choice of Kṛṣṇa but the brother opposed, being in favour of his friend Śiśupāla. In the scene of Svayaṁvara some plain stools were used to seat the various rival kings gathered in the hope of winning Rukmiṇī. After this scene, came the duel between Kṛṣṇa and Śiśupāla in which the latter was defeated and the pair Kṛṣṇa and Rukmiṇī was united. All the characters in the play entered the stage dancing to the accompaniment of the drumbeats and left the stage too in the same manner. After every speech there were dance movements by the characters. Gesticulation of verses came from the actors whereas singing was done by the Sūtradhāra. In the roles of Rukmiṇī and Kṛṣṇa there was a very powerful expression of sentiments. In this traditional dance drama of Assam, music, gestures and dance play a considerable part. The method of using both, the Sanskrit and the vernacular side by side to express the same thing is adopted by the Sūtradhāra in the narration of the progress of the play. Feminine roles are played by males.

In the Yātrā[2] performances of Bengal music, song and dance are as important as the dialogue. The feminine roles are played by young boys. The Nāndī is sung in chorus by the troupe with the director as the chief who is called Adhikārin.

1. I witnessed the performance of Rukmiṇīharaṇa at Gauhati. It was presented at the A.I.O. Conference.

2. Cf. Indian Stage, by H.N. Dasgupta—Chapter on 'Jatrās'.

Formerly, the yātrās had their themes concerned with Śakti. Kṛṣṇayātrās came into existence in Caitanya period. The Adhikārin addresses a prayer to the public for soliciting their goodwill and narrates the scope of the play. There was no sort of a green-room formerly. In the 15th century the characters spoke in Sanskrit and Prakrit and used vernacular in the song. The incidents from the youthful life of Kṛṣṇa are presented. At the completion of one episode there is a chorus by the party of singers. The setting of scenes is simple and the dress and the accessories are not elaborate.

In the Rāmalīlā of Upper India the whole acting is in dumb show. Numerous characters are there. Appropriate dresses and masks are used. Richly decorated children act as Rāma, Lakṣmaṇa and Sītā . On the tenth day Rāvaṇa is killed.

In the Rāsalīlā of North India, Rāsa dance is prominent. A devotional song praising Kṛṣṇa is sung in the Nāndī. The various incidents from Kṛṣṇa's life are presented. The Rāsalīlā-plays are operas in which the Sūtradhāra, an expert in music and his friends give the links in the story in songs. The Rāsalīlā is connected with Śrīmadbhāgavata. For the change in the dress of characters, a curtain is introduced. The whole play is presented through dance and music predominantly. These plays can be connected with the Rāsaka or Nāṭyarāsaka type of the Uparūpakas.

In the Bhavāi[1] of Gujarāt no stage is required and there is no attempt at scenery. There is a curtain used occasionally held by two men. A chorus of two or three persons helped by ordinary musical instruments, provide the music. God Gaṇapati appears on the stage in the beginning. Popular tales are enacted. There is a crude effort at the dress and make-up also. Often, the speech becomes vulgar as this is mainly a mass entertainment. The monologues or dialogues supported by the chorus reciting songs referring to the incidents form the body of the performance. The actors also join the singing.

In the Konkan districts of Maharashtra, there is a tradition of dramatic performances known as the Daśāvatārī plays. They are enacted at the time of the annual festivities connected with the local deities. The Sūtradhāra selects the theme from

1. Cf. 'Indian Theatre', by R.K. Yajnik—Chapter III.

Rāmāyaṇa or Mahābhārata and acts as the chief actor, the king hero as well as the director of the play. The dialogues are not written. The actors speak extempore dialogues keeping in mind the central theme and the incidents.

Another variety of the folk-drama of Maharashtra is Lalita. Formerly it was enacted on the last day of Navarātra in which some incidents from the Daśāvatāra were presented. The performance ended with the killing of Rāvaṇa by Rāma. In the beginning Lalita had one actor and use of songs only. Afterwards other actors and prose-dialogues were added.

The most popular folk-theatre of Maharashtra at present is Tamāśa. At the beginning of the performance, there is the salutation to God Gajānana followed by a scene between Kṛṣṇa and Gopīs. Then the play commences. The comic actor plays a very prominent role in this performance. Whatever the theme, there is not much of an attempt at costumes. There is no use of screen. The change of scene is indicated by Parikrama (moving round on the stage) and dialogue. There is no fixed stage equipment. Occasionally a stool or a chair serves as the royal throne. A bow or a sword finds place when necessary. The speeches are mostly extempore. The chief actors must be also best singers. Music, dialogue and dance are blended together harmoniously. The actors show a great talent in the gesticulation. At times the jokes are crude and sometimes vulgar because the uneducated actors present the plays before the villagers who do not possess a very refined taste. The dance has grace and also very fine expression. Many times the amorous songs are rendered into abhinaya by the female dancers effectively. Such dances are of the Lāsya (gentle) type. In the pure dance sequences the beginning is in the slow tempo with graceful movements. As the tempo increases the foot-work becomes intricate and the body movements become quick and vigorous. With the fastest tempo the dance culminates in giddy whirls. As these are open-air performances meant to entertain thousands of spectators, the singers have special training in keeping as high a pitch of their voice as possible.

The simplicity of stage, the minimum use of accessories, the ample scope for dance and music and use of one curtain or its absence are found in this regional traditional theatre of

India which I have been able to describe. It is indeed the continuation of some of the features of Sanskrit theatre which had the dance-drama style of representation.

The evolution of the Indian theatre is given by me in three broad periods—its origin and pre-classical stage, the classical stage, and the dance-drama style of the Uparūpakas which found its continuation in the regional theatre when the modern Indian languages adopted that style for the popular entertainment. The classical conventional abhinaya was handed down through the traditional teacher-pupil relation. Of course, the Sanskrit plays were also performed at the courts of kings e.g. the Kerala kings or king Bhoja of Dhara or in connection with religious festivals. The use of the vernacular to explain the Sanskrit speeches has also been resorted to in the transitional period.

The influence of the dance-drama style of the Indian theatre is visible on the theatre of China,[1] Japan and South, East Asia as well, in which the close association of dance, drama and music is found. The recourse to symbolism, the stylised gesticulation, the simplicity of the stage etc. are the features generally seen in the traditional theatre of the East and the South-East Asia.

1. The theatre in the East and South-East Asia is described in brief in Appendix C.

Chapter I

THE PURPOSE OF NĀṬYA

The Naṭasūtras referred to by Pāṇini give us the idea that the works dealing with the Actor's art existed in his time. We can infer that the different aspects of the Actor's art were studied and brought together in these Sūtras. The purpose of the dramatic art must have received great attention in such works. As the Sūtras dealt with such topics in brief, explanation was provided in the course of their studies. In the NŚ.[1] we find explanatory verses quoted by Bharata, which were handed down in the teacher-pupil tradition. Thus it is clear that before the NŚ. the dramatic art was studied scientifically, and the NŚ. has used this study suitably in proper places.

The play was meant to give delight as well as to provide instruction. As H.W. Wells[2] remarks, 'The theatre was one of the disciplines of contemplation by which peace was established within the soul'. The Greek tragedy aimed at achieving violent purgation. The Indian conception of drama avoided tragedy and aimed at repose. Even in the tragic themes of the two plays of Bhāsa, namely Ūrubhaṅga and Karṇabhāra, the ideal of a warrior i.e. the obtainment of heaven if killed in the course of fighting, is aimed at. In the Ūrubhaṅga, death of Duryodhana is presented which leads him to heaven. In the Karṇabhāra, the hero Karṇa is led to his last fight, in which, we know, he is to meet his death, befitting a noble warrior. Hence such plays also do not produce that perturbation of the mind which is effected by the Greek tragedy. In the play itself, sometimes there was a sudden change of mood, which was to be heightened by a kind of song called the Ākṣepikī Dhruvā. After such sudden changes of moods, another kind of song

1. E.g. NŚ. Vol. I. 'अत्रानुवंश्यौ श्लोकौ भवतः ।' p.290. Abhinava— अनुवंशे भवौ शिष्याचार्यपरम्परासु वर्तमानौ श्लोकाख्यौ वृत्तविशेषौ सूत्रार्थसंक्षेपप्रकटीकरणेन कारिकाशब्दवाच्यौ भवतः ।'

2. The Classical Drama of India, pp.6-12.

called the Prāsādikī Dhruvā was employed to bring about pacification of mind.

The Drama was meant to evoke Rasa. Rasa is so called because it is relished.[1] Its meaning can be accepted as 'aesthetic delight'.

The latent basic mental states are roused through imagination of the situations of life presented in the dramatic spectacle. The Vibhāvas, i.e. the characters presented and the atmosphere in which they are presented create the illusion of reality. The Vibhāvas(determinants) together with the Anubhāvas (the physical effects of the particular moods of the character) and the Vyabhicāribhāvas (transitory moods) create the appearance of life i.e. the life, the poet has tried to depict. As long as they are present before him, the spectator imagines immediately to be experiencing this life. This experience at once, awakens the permanent latent moods which are the part of his mental make-up, due to past experience in real life. Thus he experiences the life in the dramatic spectacle. He loses individuality during the time of this experience. The actor imagines himself to be Rāma at the time of the presentation and tries to act that role with appropriate dress, make-up and physical movements and creates the illusion that Rāma is actually present before the spectator. In this process the actor is not to experience really the permanent moods of Rāma; he just imagines to experience them by his imitation of gestures which Rāma, a particular type of noble nature would have exhibited. The poet creates the character of Rāma and depicts his behaviour in various circumstances proper to him. The actor tries to represent this Rāma. The probable physical movements of this particular character are inferred from the behaviour of the persons of such type in actual life. Thus, what the actor tries to imitate is the behaviour of the individual character whose movements are probable as belonging to persons of that type. Hence, even though the role of Rāma is acted, the effect is that

1. NŚ. Vol.I., p. 233. 'रस इति कः पदार्थः। उच्यते आस्वाद्यत्वात्।' According to Dr. Nagendra, the word Rasa in the sense of aesthetic delight came to be used probably during the fifth century B.C. to the second century B.C. Cf. 'Rasa Śabda kā Arthavikāsa'.
Hindī Anuśīlana-Dhīrendravarmā Viśeṣāṅka, pp. 421-427.

of a type i.e. a grand noble man. This takes the spectator beyond the mere individuality. By this experience of the behaviour of noble man in general, the spectator imagines that Rāma, the noblest is presented before him. He becomes engrossed in the activities of this character. He forgets his individuality as the experience is not limited to the individual. The experience of the moods which has left subtle impressions on his mind, gets aroused by the similar experience felt more powerfully through the representation. The experience of the reality he had, becomes identical with that produced by the illusion of reality. But as the experience effected by the illusion of reality is not that of the particular individual, but common to individuals of that class, the basis of individuality is absent. But all the experience even though felt as identical is all the while, on the imaginative level. Hence, though the experience is of joy or sorrow, anger or jealousy, it does not affect the mind as it would have affected in reality. The identity is so strongly felt that actual tears would be there due to the sorrow of the chaıacter in the spectacle. As long as the illusion persists, he would feel this identity. In this experience, whatever he feels due to the identity with that life, joy or sorrow etc. is not important. The experience itself is important. It is unique. It is different from actual reality but at the same time similar to it. This unique experience, not limited by the sense of time and place, is a source of supreme bliss to him as it is never[1] non-pleasant.

Bharata gives the analogy of enjoyment of food in explaining the experience of the aesthetic delight. Just as a well-disposed person, whose mind is free from other thoughts and thus centred on the act of eating, relishes the flavours while eating food to which various spices are added, and in this relish gets satisfaction, so also the spectatoı whose mind is engrossed in the spectacle relishes the latent permanent states aroused by the presentation of the various emotions with the help of verbal, physical and mental gesticulation and gets joy

1. ND. states 'सुखदुःखात्मको रसः ।' According to ND. the five Rasas Śṛṅgāra, Hāsya, Vīra, Adbhuta and Śānta are pleasurable due to the desirable Vibhāvas etc. while Karuṇa, Raudra, Bībhatsa and Bhayānaka are non-pleasurable due to the undesirable Vibhāvas etc.
Cf. ND. P. 141.

in this experience. Hence, these Rasas are called Nāṭyarasas (the sentiments in the dramatic spectacle).

Rasa, then, is the relish of the Sthāyibhāva (the permanent mood), experienced by the spectator. The sentiments are in the nāṭya only, which means that they are not in the worldly experience. The experience of different emotions in real life is not the one that one gets from the representation. It is 'alaukika' i.e. belonging to the sphere of reality as imagined by the poet. The sentiment is not present in the actor. He simply is the means to convey the sentiments in the drama to the spectators. Hence the actor is called the 'pātra' (i.e. pot). The pot does not relish the taste of the wine but is the means to serve it to the drinker. Abhinava[1] has recorded another view according to which Nāṭya is the representation which we witness as externally effected by the means of acting etc. It is the work of the actor. From this representation the sentiments are evoked in the spectators. Bharata has described the composition of plays in Vācikābhinaya i.e. one of the four abhinayas. He explains Nāṭya mainly in relation to the performance. The performance of plays evokes sentiments. In poetry also the sentiments would be evoked by the same mental process. But that is not the main concern of Bharata as he is dealing with Nāṭyaśāstra.

The Rasas are eight[2] : Śṛṅgāra (the Erotic), Hāsya (the Comic), Karuṇa (the Pathetic), Raudra (the Furious), Vīra (the Heroic), Bhayānaka (the Terrible), Bībhatsa (the Odious) and Adbhuta (the Marvellous). Out of these, Śṛṅgāra, Raudra, Vīra and Bībhatsa are the original ones and the rest arise out of these four. Hāsya arises from Śṛṅgāra and Bhayānaka from Bībhatsa. A mimicry of the Erotic is called Comic and the result of the Furious sentiment is known as the Pathetic. Adbhuta results out of the Heroic and that which is Odious to behold results in the Bhayānaka.

1. NŚ. Vol. I p. 291.
अन्ये त्वभिनयादिसामग्रीमयं बहिर्दृश्यमानं नाट्यं नटधर्मः
कर्म रूपमित्याशयेन नाट्याद्रसा इत्याहुः ।

2. शृङ्गारहास्यकरुणा रौद्रवीरभयानकाः ।
बीभत्साद्भुतसंज्ञौ चेत्यष्टौ नाट्ये रसाः स्मृताः ॥
NŚ. VI. 15.

When Hāsya is said to be produced from Śṛṅgāra what is meant is that the improper love produces the Comic. As Abhinava says, in the impropriety of the sentiments as Pathetic and others, Comic is produced. The impropriety is the cause of laughter. The Furious has the result in the form of death and destruction which are the sources of the Pathetic. The heroic actions cause the Marvellous sentiment and the Odious, having Vibhāvas like blood, flesh etc. cause the sentiment of fear.

The Vibhāvas, Anubhāvas and the Vyabhicārībhāvas when combined give rise to the sentiments arousing the permanent mood in the heart of the art-lover. In saying that the set of four sentiments arise out of the first four, Bharata has taken into consideration, the Vibhāvas, Anubhāvas and Vyabhicāribhāvas. Daśarūpaka[1] has tried to give the basis of the above view. According to it, the relish of poetry is fourfold i.e. at the time of the relish the mental state is fourfold having vikāsa (blooming), vistāra (expansion), kṣobha (excitement) and vikṣepa (agitation). In Śṛṅgāra there is vikāsa; in Vīra, vistāra, in Bībhatsa, kṣobha and in Raudra, vikṣepa. This four-fold nature of the mental state is due also to the remaining four i.e. Hāsya, Adbhuta, Bhayānaka and Karuṇa. Hence, the two sets are related. Hāsya would be produced by the impropriety of any other sentiment but primarily it would go with Śṛṅgāra. That means, when Hāsya is produced, it does not weaken Śṛṅgāra. But when Hāsya arises out of the impropriety of sentiments like the Pathetic etc. that sentiment is at once weakened as it becomes ridiculous. Thus in Prahasana, Bhāṇa etc. the Hāsya is produced by impropriety. There the Hāsya-rasa is prominent. Karuṇa would naturally go with Raudra, Adbhuta with Vīra and Bhayānaka with Bībhatsa. In the language of music, Hāsya is saṁvādin with Śṛṅgāra and so on.

The conception of Rasa is based on experience. Why these eight only are admitted can be explained in the following manner. The different forms of Nāṭya actually existed and the variety of effect on the spectators was also carefully studied. We get a clear description of this in the items mentioned in

1. DR. IV. 43, 44.

connection with the Nāṭyasiddhi. In the themes of the plays adopted from the Rāmāyaṇa, the Mahābhārata, mythological texts and legends or even in the social ones, the main sentiments are Vīra and Śṛṅgāra. The exploits of a brave hero would be full of fury, creating wonder and due to the destruction caused, would create disgust and fear ending in the pathos caused by the inevitable killing in the fight. While in the course of love, the hero would cause mirth to excite the feeling of love. The proper lover would strengthen his love by the comic while the improper one like Rāvaṇa loving Sītā would be an object of ridicule.

Bharata has treated the colour and deities of the different Rasas as handed down by tradition. Afterwards the Vibhāvas of the eight Rasas are given. In Śṛṅgāra, the Vibhāvas of Love in union and separation are given. The Erotic is caused when men and women both are there and it belongs to the fullness of youth. In all these Vibhāvas etc. Bharata has mentioned how the Anubhāvas are to be gesticulated. The particular situation is brought forth by the Vibhāvas. Duṣyanta hears the words of girls in the penance forest. Śakuntalā with her two friends is watering the trees. Looking at the most beautiful Śakuntalā in the company of her charming companions he is fascinated and says that the ladies in the harem are put into background by these ascetic-girls. He listens concealed, to their friendly open-hearted talk. He has the desire in him for Śakuntalā. Thus the sight of Śakuntalā, the talk of the friends, the surrounding trees and creepers affectionately looked after by them—these are responsible for making clear in the mind of the spectator the meaning of the particular behaviour of the hero. The bee troubles Śakuntalā, she cries for help and Duṣyanta goes forth. They see each other—in both seed of love is planted. Thus for the Erotic sentiment the young hero and heroine must be there. But their behaviour as lover and beloved would be made known to others in the proper context. The love in union would thus be made clear by the context such as the pleasures of the season, the use of garlands, unguents, ornaments, the company of beloved persons, objects of senses such as the songs and the like, splendid mansions, going to garden and enjoying oneself there, seeing the beloved one, hearing his or her words and playing or dallying with him or her. The context determines the nature of the behaviour of the characters. That the behaviour of the hero and the heroine is based on love is made known by the consequents such as clever movements of eyes and eyebrows, soft and delicate movements of limbs and the like, and all the other transitory states excluding indolence, cruelty and disgust. For love in separation, the context of the situation would be the same; only the lovers are separated, hence the consequents would be represented such as despondency, weakness, apprehension etc. The love in separation has the status similar to that of the Pathetic. But the difference is that in love in separation, the expectancy of reunion is there while in the Pathetic, it is absent.

Thus the Vibhāvas produce the particular sentiment in the sense that in their absence nothing could be delineated by the poet. The situation is made to be understood in its clear perspective by the consequent actions i.e. Anubhāvas. The sentiment which is depicted by the poet is thus transferred to the spectator through the gesticulation of the consequent actions befitting the particular situation that gives rise to them. By gesticulating the transitory states, the sentiment becomes strongly manifest, e.g. the artificial anger for being late at the place of appointment, annoyance till the arrival, disappointment at the failure in keeping time, the pacification caused by the lover's prostration and such other transitory states cause the basic mental state of love to be evoked fully resulting in Śṛṅgāra. Thus the characters in the story in the appropriate surrounding (Vibhāvas) with fitting gestures expressive of the mental states (Anubhāvas) and the transitory states (Vyabhicāribhāvas) cause to produce in the spectator, the sentiment meant to be depicted by the poet.

Bharata has given the Vibhāvas, Anubhāvas and the Vyabhicāribhāvas for all the eight sentiments. In this context, it is to be noted that the abhinaya is given for the Anubhāvas only. The Vibhāvas are to be dealt with by the poet, which are to be represented by creating the atmosphere either through words or other means. The Anubhāvas are to be gesticulated, which would lead the spectator to infer the sentiment.

Bharata has treated eight Rasas only. The admission of Śānta[1] as a sentiment in drama is a later development. When plays dealing with the life of Buddha e.g. that of Aśvaghoṣa, came into existence or such other plays, in which the effect on the spectator was that of Śāntarasa, this sentiment also might have been included. The experience of Śānta is more natural in case of poetry where one is free to enjoy oneself. In drama, the actor who creates by his gesticulation, the appearance of a divine hero steeped in union with the highest reality would be understood by the spectator as a tranquil person. This illusion will arouse in him the inner urge for the ultimate reality. This experience would last as long as the Vibhāvas are there. The absence of Śāntarasa plays would be a possible explanation of its non-inclusion in the number of Rasas given by Bharata.

Bharata further treats forty-nine Bhāvas. Bhāva primarily means a mental state. He considers the relation between Bhāva and Rasa. Three positions are possible—Rasa produced from Bhāva, Bhāva from Rasa or their mutually causing each other. As regards the first two, he opines that the production of sentiments from moods is seen and not vice versa. Bhāvas are so known because they cause to originate (bhāvayanti-sampādayanti), the sentiments when connected with various gesticulation. But stanzas 36 and 37 of Ch. VI of the NŚ. give us the view that there is no sentiment without mood and no mood without sentiment. Their mutual production is effected due to histrionic representation. Just as the combination of spices and vegetables lead to the flavour of food so also the Bhāvas and Rasas mutually produce each other. Abhinava explains that Bhāvas (moods) produce Rasas (sentiments) and the sentiments become the cause of the designation of the moods etc. The relation is explained as from the seed from which the tree, its flower and fruit are produced. Similarly the sentiments are the root from which all the moods are decided. The Vibhāvas, Anubhāvas and Vyabhicāribhāvas represented in the spectacle manifest the sentiments in the spectator. As such, they cause the origination of the sentiments in the spectator by arousing permanent moods. From the

1. Cf. The Number of Rasas by V. Raghavan, pp. 16-26.

view point of Rasa, they are designated as Vibhāvas etc. In this sense, their mutual relation may be understood as causing each other. Abhinava[1] describes that poetry is the tree, the actor's action like the abhinaya etc. is the flower and the relish of the sentiments by the spectator is the fruit.

Out of the two explanations 'bhavanti iti bhāvāḥ' and 'bhāvayanti iti bhāvāḥ', Bharata prefers the latter. The mental states which exist in real life are denoted by the first explanation. In poetry, the mental states depicted by the poet pervade the hearts of the readers. In dramatic representation the states are so called because they infuse the meaning of the play into the spectators through words, gestures and representation of temperament. The purport of the poem is, of course, the sentiment. When the meaning of the play, brought forth through Determinants and consequents, is made to pervade i.e. enter the heart of the spectators through the enacting of the words, gestures and temperaments, it is called Bhāva. Abhinava says that this explanation is meant in relation to both the poet and the actor. The inner idea of the playwright is made to pervade the mind of the spectators by means of words, gestures, colour of the face and the representation of the temperament—hence they are called Bhāvas. As they cause to manifest the sentiments, relating to various kinds of acting, they are called Bhāvas by those who perform plays. 'The mental[2] states fit to be relished are led to the level of conscious experience of the spectators by them'. The behaviour presented through various acting is made known distinctively by the Vibhāvas. Vibhāvas are meant here in the sense of Vijñāna i.e. distinctive knowledge. Verbal, physical and temperamental gesticulation is determined by them, hence they are called Vibhāvas. Rāma's standing up in respect becomes clear when Vasiṣṭha enters. Tears would be caused by heat, smoke, disease or even joy. The Vibhāvas determine to what the tears are due as they clearly show whether the situation is of joy etc. The acting by means of words, gestures and temperament is made to be experienced by the spectators; hence it is called Anubhāva.

1. NŚ. Vol. I p. 294.
2. Cf. Abh. NŚ. Vol. 1. p. 346.

Vibhāvas and Anubhāvas are well-known amongst the people. They are connected with human nature and as such, are not defined in detail. This means that the Vibhāvas and Anubhāvas which create the particular situation and give the connected development of that aspect of life which the poet or the playwright wants to depict, have their roots in reality. Even in the illusion of reality created by the poet, the reader or the spectator feels that it is actual reality for the time, during which he is experiencing it. As the ways of the world are manifold the playwright may choose any aspect of life and depict it in his work. His inner purpose, however, must not be based on utter absence of real life. The poet has freedom to choose what life he should depict. It depends on his subtle observation and genius.

Vibhāvas and Anubhāvas are, to a certain extent, bāhya (external) but vitally essential to the creation of the poetic world. Hence, a general mention is made of these while defining the sentiments. But it is not so with the Bhāvas (states). In this poetic world also, as in real life, the mental states are definitely fixed. Hence, their clear description is necessary. The effort to mention the forty-nine bhāvas (8 Sthāyibhāvas, 33 Vyabhicāribhāvas and 8 Sāttvikabhāvas) is the result of subtle observation of life due to which the human behaviour can be properly analysed.

The mental states are the cause of the manifestation of the sentiments in poetry. The sentiments are produced from them when they are imbued with the quality of universality. The inner idea of the poet which is in harmony with the heart of the spectator becomes the source of the sentiment. It pervades body just as the drywood is pervaded by fire.

The permanent states are like masters to whom other states resort. Just as the men having similar appearance are distinguished as the king and his servants due to the inner capacities, similarly the other states even though some of them may be similar to the permanent ones are distinguished according to their capacities. The permanent moods, when evoked, are relished as sentiments ; the other states are subordinate to the permanent moods, but they are necessary to the relish. Rati, Hāsa, Śoka, Krodha, Utsāha, Bhaya, Jugupsā and

Vismaya are the 8 dominant states, the Sthāyins of Śṛṅgāra, Hāsya, Karuṇa, Raudra, Vīra, Bhayānaka, Bībhatsa and Adbhuta Rasas respectively.

Rati is of the nature of pleasure—the joy in getting the desired object. This state permanently exists in all. When this is evoked due to the behaviour of young hero in union, separation etc. it would be the Erotic Sentiment. The other permanent mood is Hāsa (Laughter). In the exact reproduction of the behaviour of others by imitation and in parody, we laugh. Whenever we find something contrary to propriety, it produces laughter. Just as there is joy in getting the desired one there is sorrow when the dear one is separated. The separation from the dear ones, loss of glory or wealth, the death, the loss of the loved ones and such other experiences cause sorrow. When somebody or something opposes, one naturally gets angry. The insolence, abusive language, quarrel, injury, opposition and the like, cause anger. Energy relates to persons of superior type. Ordinary ones may have it to some extent. But as permanent mental state it is a characteristic of the great men only. As they are always energetic, nothing baffles them in their attempt. The truly energetic will never be afraid. Hence, fear as a permanent mental state is found only in women and persons of low type. Great men also may have fear if they have committed an offence regarding the elders. But it is not their permanent state. Just as the appearance of the beautiful would cause joy, similarly the appearance or the hearing of the most unpleasant would cause disgust. This is also a permanent state of women and persons of low character. The great man will not be so perturbed, by seeing or hearing anything that is disgusting. Astonishment is a permanent state of mind when one sees or hears something extra-ordinary e.g. magic, extra-ordinary feats of men, great excellence in artistic achievement etc. These eight are called the permanent states which are ordinarily found in the human behaviour. When the causes which are responsible for the manifestation of these states are represented on the stage these states are evoked. These permanent moods which are dominant in the particular composition are developed together with the transitory ones by the poet. The same are brought to the heart of the spectators by the representation through the medium of the actors. The similarity of these is felt at once by the spectator by which his mind is pervaded. He becomes as if one with that life on the stage. The world is full of variety. The eight mental states are found in the variety of the people. They are natural in the sense that they are commonly felt by different human beings. That is why Bharata has enumerated them differently. The way of the world, which is caused by the three qualities—i.e. Sattva, Rajas and Tamas —is possessed of the variety of sentiments.

The Vyabhicāribhāvas[1] are as follows—Nirveda (despondency), Glāni (weakness), Śaṅkā (apprehension), Asūyā (envy), Mada (intoxication), Śrama (weariness), Ālasya (indolence), Dainya (depression), Cintā (anxiety), Moha (distraction), Smṛti (recollection), Dhṛti (contentment), Vrīḍā (shame), Capalatā (inconstancy), Harṣa (joy), Āvega (agitation), Jaḍatā (stupor), Garva (arrogance), Viṣāda (despair), Autsukya (yearning), Nidrā (sleeping), Apasmāra (epilepsy), Supta (dreaming), Vibodha (awakening), Amarṣa (indignation), Avahittha (dissimulation), Ugratā (cruelty), Mati (assurance), Vyādhi (sickness), Unmāda (insanity), Maraṇa (death), Trāsa (fright), Vitarka (deliberation). They are so called because they move[2] favourably in relation to the sentiments in various ways.

The attitude of disgust and then total indifference to worldly affairs is caused due to the knowledge of ultimate reality in the case of the great learned ones. But normally despondency is seen in women and persons of low type due to poverty, disease, insult etc. These thiry-three transitory states are to be produced in a play by men and women of the superior, middling, and inferior types in conformity with, place, time and occasion.

The Sāttvikabhāvas are as follows—Stambha (paralysis), Sveda (perspiration), Romāñca (horripilation), Svara-bheda (change of voice), Vepathu (trembling), Vaivarṇya (change of colour), Aśru (weeping) and Pralaya (fainting). They are so called because they are originated in mind i. e. caused by

1. Cf. 'Suśruta, Caraka and Bharata' by R.K. Sen. I.H.Q. March 1954 pp. 68-80
2. NŚ. p. 355—विविधमाभिमुख्येन रसेषु चरन्तीति व्यभिचारिण: ।

the concentrated mind. Temperament[1] is accomplished by concentration of mind. Its nature which is characterised by horripilation, tears, loss of colour, etc. belonging to the respective mental states, cannot be effected by an absent mind. Temperament is desired in the representation as in it we have the imitation of human nature. The states to be produced in the representation are, after all, artificial. The actor has to imagine that he or she is the particular character in the play and then to act. By histrionic representation, the transitory states may be imitated simply by practice of acting. But the effects of the powerful mental states that become physically apparent, cannot be produced unless the actor is one with that particular mood. The sorrow or joy to be represented on the stage has nothing to do with the sorrowful or the joyful mood of the actor. He may be suffering from sorrow at heart. But on the stage, if the situation demands expression of joy, he must be able to express joy through his physical appearance. For such acting, the actor has to train himself by getting detached from the incidents in his own life and must be imaginatively one with the role. The physical appearance will then be similar to that of the role in the play. By such representation only the inner state of the character will be understood by the spectator. This special mental effect of the actor is termed as sattva. The temperamental states cannot be effectively represented unless the actor becomes one with the role for the time being. Hence, these are mentioned over and above the permanent and the transitory states. Tears may be due to joy or sorrow. To effect these contradictory moods, the actor has to make effort with the concentrated mind by which the tears will have proper basis. Thus it can be explained with all the eight temperamental states. If the occasion demands perspiration and the actor enacts wiping of the perspiration, in the absence of sweat on the body, the effect would be quite unimpressive. In the case of tears such acting will be ineffective.

1. सत्त्वं नाम मनःप्रभवम् । तच्च समाहितमनस्त्वादुच्यते ।
NŚ. Vol. I, p. 374.

In the play one sentiment is dominant and others are subordinate. The dominant sentiment should be represented with an exuberance of the temperament and the transitory states by mere gestures and postures as they are only to support the dominant sentiment. These temperamental states will be more in connection with the main character, who is the source of the dominant sentiment in the play. No useful purpose is served by attributing one temperamental state to one sentiment.

I have discussed so far the primary purpose of Nāṭya, i.e., to give the paranirvṛti (the highest bliss). But the secondary purpose is also equally important and that is instruction. When the spectator became one with the life depicted in the play in which good was always rewarded and the wicked punished, his mind naturally shrank from the bad qualities and turned to the good ones. In the real life often, the good suffers up to the end. But the Indian view does not believe in the final victory of the bad over the good. The good may suffer a set-back but ultimately that wins. The spectator's mind feels the lack of good qualities in him which would produce an urge to possess them. Hence, the effect of Nāṭya is described by the NŚ. as educating people. The NŚ. describes this in detail as follows —

"In[1] it (Nāṭya) there is sometimes reference to duty, sometimes to games, sometimes to wealth, sometimes to peace, sometimes to laughter, sometimes to fight and love-making and killing. This teaches duty to those bent on doing their duty, love to those who are eager for its fulfilment and chastises those who are ill-bred or unruly, promotes self-restraint in those who are disciplined, gives courage to cowards, energy to heroic persons, enlightens men of poor intellect and gives wisdom to the learned. It gives diversion to kings and firmness of mind to persons afflicted with sorrow. It provides hints to acquire wealth to those who are after it and brings composure to persons who are agitated in mind."

1. NŚ. I., 108-110.

Chapter II

ABHINAYA

The purport of the play is conveyed to the spectator through Abhinaya. Abhinaya is derived from abhi + √nī meaning 'to lead towards'. It is the medium of conveying poet's meaning in fullest degree to the spectators. The histrionic representation covers all human activity which is divided into the physical, the verbal and the mental. In the performance, dress, make-up, etc., are helpful to produce the proper effect immediately. Hence, they are also included in abhinaya. Thus the abhinaya is four-fold—Sāttvika (temperamental), Āṅgika (physical), Vācika (verbal) and Āhārya (dress, make-up, etc.).

While explaining Rasa and Bhāva, Bharata has mentioned the representation of them by the Anubhāvas, as Anubhāvas are the outward expression of the mental states. In fact, as we know from the four-fold abhinaya, the surrounding which is included in Vibhāva is also a part of abhinaya. The season, the decoration, the presence of dear people, the pleasure garden etc. are either described in words or to certain extent some of these are actually shown on the stage. Thus, either they would come under Vācikābhinaya or Āhāryābhinaya. But as the Āṅgika, Vācika and Āhārya abhinayas deal with all these things in detail, Bharata has given only the representation of the Rasas and Bhāvas by mentioning their effects in a general manner.

The Erotic—(1) in union—The Anubhāvas to be represented are clever movements of eyes and eye-brows, soft and delicate movements of limbs, sweet words, etc.; whereas those to be represented (2) in separation—are despondency, weakness, apprehension, envy, weariness, anxiety, yearning, sleep, dreaming, awakening, illness, insanity, epilepsy, inactivity (temporary) death and other conditions.

The Comic—It is to be represented by throbbing of the lips, the nose, and the cheeks, opening of the eyes wide or contracting them, perspiration, colour of the face and taking hold of the sides. Hāsya is self-centred when a man laughs himself and it is centred in others when he makes others laugh. This[1] two-fold division of Hāsya relates to its infectious nature. In the verses the Anubhāvas of the six types of Hāsya are given.

1. 'smita' (gentle smile) : slightly blown cheeks, elegant glances, teeth not visible;

2. 'hasita' (smile) : blooming eyes, face and cheeks, teeth slightly visible;

3. 'vihasita' (gentle laughter)—laughter suitable to the occasion; slight sound and sweetness, face joyful, eyes and cheeks contracted;

4. 'upahasita' (laughter of ridicule) : the nose expanded, squinting eyes, shoulder and head bent;

5. 'apahasita' (vulgar laughter)—laughter on unsuitable occasions : tears in eyes, shoulders and the head violently shaking;

6. 'atihasita' (excessive laughter)—eyes expanded and tearful, loud and excessive sound, sides covered by hands.

Smita and hasita should be employed in the case of superior characters, vihasita and upahasita in the case of middling ones and apahasita and atihasita in the case of the inferior types.

The Pathetic—This is to be represented by shedding tears, lamentation, dryness of the mouth, change of colour, drooping limbs, being out of breath, loss of memory and the like.

The Furious is to be represented by red eyes, knitting of eye-brows, defiance, biting of lips, throbbing of the cheeks, pressing one hand over the other and the like.

The Heroic[2]—This is to be gesticulated by firmness, patience, heroism, charity, diplomacy and the like.

1. Abhinava points out that when the others laugh, he also laughs even when he does not see the Vibhāvas, or having seen them has suppressed his laughter due to dignity. NŚ. Vol. I., p. 314

See 'Laughter in Sanskrit Poetics' by Dr. G.S. Amur, p. 234. Journal of the Karnatak University, Vol. VII, 1963.

2. Physical gesticulation is not given by Bharata.

The Terrible is to be represented by trembling of the hands, the feet and the eyes, horripilation, change of colour and the loss of voice.

The Odious is to be gesticulated by contraction of all the limbs, narrowing down of the mouth and eyes, vomitting, spitting and (shaking the limbs in) disgust and the like.

The Marvellous—This is to be represented by wide opening eyes, looking with fixed gaze, horripilation, tears, joy, perspiration, uttering words of approbation, making gifts, crying (incessantly) 'hā, hā, hā' waving the end of dhotī or sārī and movement of fingers and the like.

The states	*Representation by the Anubhāvas*
Permanent states:	
1. Rati	smiling face, sweet words, contraction of eye-brows, sidelong glances and the like.
2. Hāsa	smile and the like, i.e., laughter, excessive laughter.
3. Śoka	shedding tears, lamentation, bewailing, change of colour, loss of voice, looseness of limbs, falling on the ground, crying, deep breathing, paralysis, insanity, death and the like.
4. Krodha	extended nostrils, upturned eyes, bitten lips, throbbing cheeks and the like.
(i) against enemies	knitting of eye-brows, fierce look, bitten lips, hands clasping each other, touching one's own shoulder and breast.
(ii) when controlled by superiors	slightly downcast eyes, wiping off slight perspiration and not expressing any violent movement.
(iii) against beloved woman	very slight movement of the body, shedding tears, knitting eye-brows, sidelong glances and throbbing lips.
(iv) against one's servants	threat, rebuke, dilating eyes and casting contemptuous looks of various kinds.
(v) artificial	betraying signs of effort.

5. Utsāha[1]	steadiness, munificence, boldness of undertaking and the like.
6. Bhaya	trembling of the hands and feet, palpitation of the heart, paralysis, dryness of the mouth, licking lips, perspiration, tremor, apprehension of danger, seeking for safety, running away, loud crying and the like.
7. Jugupsā	contracting all the limbs, spitting, narrowing down of the mouth, heartache and the like.
8. Vismaya	wide opening of the eyes, looking without winking of the eyes and movement of the eye-brows, horripilation, moving the head to and fro, the cry of 'well done' and the like.

Transitory states :

1. Nirveda	weeping, sighing, deep breathing, deliberation and the like.
2. Glāni	weak voice, lustreless eyes, pale face, slow gait, want of energy, loss of colour of the body and the limbs, change of voice and others.
3. Śaṅkā	constantly looking about, hesitating movement, dryness of the mouth, licking the lips, change of facial colour, tremor, dry lips, change of voice and the like. Concealment of appearance to be characterised by adoption of clever gestures according to some authorities.
4. Asūyā	finding fault with others, decrying their virtues, casting glances in jealousy, downcast face, knitting eyebrows, disregard and abuse in public.

5. Mada
in the case of
superior persons—sleeping,

1. Physical gesticulation is not given by Bharata.

middling ones	laughing and singing,
low ones	crying and using coarse words.
Stages of Mada—	
(i) light	smiling face, pleasant feeling, slightly faltering words, delicately unsteady gait.
(ii) medium	drunken and rolling eyes, arms drooping or restlessly thrown about, irregularly unsteady gait.
(iii) excessive	loss of memory, incapacity to walk due to vomitting, hiccup, thick protruding tongue and spitting. When there is panic, grief and increase of terror due to some cause, intoxication is to be stopped by effort.
6. Śrama	gentle rubbing of the body, deep breathing, contraction of the mouth, belching, massaging of the limbs, very slow gait, contraction of the eyes, making hissing sound.
7. Ālasya	aversion to any kind of work, lying down, sitting, drowsiness, sleep, etc.
8. Dainya	want of self command, headache, dullness of the body, absent-mindedness, giving up of cleansing (of the body), etc.
9. Cintā	deep breathing, sighing, agony, meditation, thinking with a down-cast face, thinness of the body, etc.
10. Moha	want of movement, excessive movement of a particular limb, falling down, reeling, dazed condition.
11. Smṛti	nodding of the head, looking down, raising up the eye-brows, etc.
12. Dhṛti	enjoyment of objects attained, absence of regret for the unattained, impaired or lost, etc.
13. Vrīḍā	covered face, thinking with downcast face, drawing lines on the ground, touching clothes and the ring, biting the nails, etc.

14. Capalatā	harsh words, rebuke, beating, killing, taking prisoner, goading, etc.
15. Harṣa	brightness of the face and the eyes, using sweet words, embracing, horripilation, tears, perspiration and the like.
16. Āvega	
(a) due to portends	looseness of all the limbs, distraction of the mind, loss of facial colour, sadness, surprise, etc.
(b) due to violent winds	veiling the face, rubbing the eyes, collecting the ends of the clothes worn, hurried going, etc.
(c) due to heavy rains	lumping together the limbs, running, looking for some cover or shelter, etc.
(d) due to fire	eyes troubled with smoke, contracting all the limbs or shaking them, running with wide steps, flight, etc.
(e) due to elephants	hurried retreat, unsteady gait, fear, paralysis, tremor, looking back, etc.
(f) due to having something favourable	getting up, embracing, giving away clothes and ornaments, tears, horripilation, etc.
(g) due to unfavourable news	falling down on the ground, rolling about on a rough surface, running away, bewailing, weeping and the like.
(h) due to calamity	sudden retreat, taking up weapons and armour, mounting elephants and horses and chariots, striking, etc.
17. Jaḍatā	not uttering any word, speaking indistinctly, aversion to all work, remaining absolutely silent, looking with steadfast gaze, dependence on others, etc.
18. Garva	disrespect for others, harassing, not giving reply, not greeting others, looking to oneself, roaming, contemptuous laughter, harsh words, transgressing commands of the superiors, insulting others, etc. [In the case of persons of inferior type, (boastful)

	movement of the eyes and the limbs is to be employed.]
19. Viṣāda	looking for allies, thinking about means, loss of energy, absent-mindedness, deep breathing and the like in the case of superior and the middling types; in the case of the inferior type—running away, looking down, drying up of the mouth, licking the corner of the mouth, sleep, deep breathing, meditation and the like.
20. Autsukya	sighs, thinking with downcast face, sleep, drowsiness, desire for lying down.
21. Nidrā	heaviness of the face, rolling of the body, rolling of the eyes, yawning, massaging of the body, deep breathing, relaxed body, closing the eyes etc.
22. Apasmāra	throbbing, sighing, trembling, running, falling down, perspiration, foaming in the mouth, motionlessness, licking (lips) with tongue and the like.
23. Supta	deep breathing, dullness of the body, closing the eyes, stupefaction of all senses, dreaming, talking while asleep, closing eyes softly.
24. Vibodha	yawning, rubbing the eyes, leaving the bed, etc.
25. Amarṣa	shaking the head, perspiration, thinking with downcast face, determination, looking for means and allies etc.
26. Avahitthā	speaking otherwise, looking downwards, break in speech, pretended patience.
27. Ugratā	killing, imprisoning, beating, rebuking, etc.
28. Mati	instructing pupils, ascertainment of meanings, removal of doubts etc.
29. Vyādhi	
(a) fever with a feeling of cold	shivering, tremor of the entire body, bending the body, shaking of the jaws,

		desire for heat, horripilation, movement of the chin, narrowing down the nasal passage, dryness of the mouth, lamentation etc.
(b)	fever with a feeling of heat	throwing out clothes, the hands and the feet, desire to roll on the ground, use of unguents, desire for coolness, lamentation, dryness of mouth, crying.
(c)	other types of sickness	narrowing down the mouth, dullness of the body, downcast eyes, deep breathing, making peculiar sounds, crying, tremor etc.
30.	Unmāda	laughing and weeping without any reason, crying, irrelevant talk, lying down, sitting and rising up, running, dancing, singing, reciting, smearing the body with ashes and dust, taking grass and remains of flower-offering to deity, soiled clothes, rags, potsherd, and earthen tray as decorations of the body, many other senseless acts, imitation of others who are not present etc.
31.	Maraṇa	
(a)	from sickness	looseness of the body, motionlessness of the limbs, closed eyes, hiccup, deep breathing, not looking towards surrounding people, indistinct words, etc.
(b)	due to accidental injury	
(i)	wounded by weapons	suddenly falling down on the ground, tremor, throbbing, etc.
(ii)	snake bite or poison	gradual development of the following symptoms—thinness of the body, tremor, burning sensation, hiccup, foaming mouth, breaking of the neck, paralysis and death.
32.	Trāsa	contraction of limbs, shaking, tremor of the body, paralysis, horripilation, speaking with choked voice, etc.

33. Vitarka	various discussions, non-settling[1] of the problems, concealment of the counsel, movement of the head and eye-brows etc.

Temperamental states :

1. Sveda	taking up the fan, wiping off sweat, looking for breeze.
2. Stambha	being inactive, smileless, being like an inert object, limbs drooping.
3. Kampa	quivering, throbbing and shivering.
4. Aśru	wiping the eyes full of tears, shedding tear incessantly.
5. Vaivarṇya	alteration of the colour of the face with effort by putting pressure on the artery.
6. Romāñca	repeated thrills, hair standing on end, touching the body.
7. Svarabheda	broken and choked voice.
8. Pralaya	motionlessness, breathing gently (unnoticed), falling on the ground.

In the representation of the states, that of temperamental states is mentioned primarily as Sāttvika abhinaya. In fact, all the gesticulation of mental states may be designated as the Sāttvika abhinaya. But the prominence given to the gesticulation of the temperamental states is due to the peculiar mental effort which is necessary for their presentation. Bharata[2] has thus given first the gesticulation of temperament for, without it the real purpose of the performance would be lost.

Vipradāsa does not state the Āhārya abhinaya separately. He refers to the three others as resulting from body, mind and speech. According to him, the four styles of action are connected with them. He explains Kaiśikī as derived from Keśa i.e. hair and understands it as conducive to beauty and, Sāttvikī from Sattva, i.e., mind. The Verbal gesticulation is well established in Bhāratī and all the physical gestures are well-established in the other three styles of action. The style of action connected with mental states ultimately results in physical

1. Cf. NŚ. Vol. I, p. 374; F.N. 5.

2. It is to be noted that Bharata has stated the representation of death. Death is shown on the stage by Bhāsa.

gestures. So the forms of gesticulation which remain chiefly are two—Āṅgika (physical) and Vācika (verbal). Vācika which is the means of understanding the meaning, is not (fit to be) principal. Hence Āṅgika remains only as the principal one which is adorned or perfected by Vācika. This view of Vipradāsa[1] tells us how Āṅgikābhinaya got prominence in the art of representation.

Before starting the detailed analysis of the physical gesticulation it is necessary to understand clearly the mode of acting.[2] The gesticulation is two-fold, which the NŚ. treats under dharmī—Lokadharmī, i.e., the realistic practice and Nāṭyadharmī i.e. the theatrical or conventional practice. The dramatic representation which has natural behaviour and has activities of the ways of the world, devoid of graceful artificial movements of the limbs and has natural acting based on men and women of various types, is the Lokadharmī. Nāṭyadharmī is the practice in which the speech, activity and states are extra-ordinary as they are imagined by the poet. It has graceful Aṅgahāras (dance movements), dramatic conventions, embellishments of notes, characters represented not naturally (i.e. males representing as females and vice versa), and the words represented as having corporal form (e.g. in the play Māyāpuṣpaka, the entry of the curse of the Brahmin [3]). The words spoken by a near character are not heard by others. The speech which is not uttered is heard. The mountains, vehicles and aerial cars, the shield, the armour, weapon or banner are represented bodily. Due to the skill or necessity, an actor performs two roles in the same play. A woman with whom marriage is prohibited by Śāstra is employed in the role of a woman with whom marriage is allowed or vice versa. Dancing or walking with graceful movements of limbs and with raised steps is employed. All these are the illustrations of theatrical practice. The divisions of the stage with various procedures

1. BK., pp. 23-24.
2. Miss Ketkar understands the Śārīra, Mukhaja and Ceṣṭākṛta divisions as referring respectively to Nṛtya, Nāṭya and Nṛtta.

Bhāratīya Nāṭyaśāstra, p. 185.

3. Abh. 'यथा मायापुष्पके "ततः प्रविशति ब्रह्मशाप" इति ।'

NŚ. Vol., IIp. 216.

to be followed are also theatrical practice. Abhinava[1] explains further that the realistic again is two-fold—that expressive of mental condition, e.g., as in arrogant reference to one's ownself the Patāka hand raised on a level with the forehead, and that indicative of some external object, e.g., the Padmakośa hand used to represent lotus. The conventional also is twofold—that which is wholly meant for beautifying the representations, e.g., the use of the four karaṇas of the hand and that partially indicating popular behaviour as the use of Tripatāka hand to represent words spoken aside.

The conventional acting is inseparable, says Bharata. The dramatic[2] representation should always be produced with conventional practice. Without the use of gestures and music etc. there would be no enjoyment to the audience.

Āṅgikābhinaya—The Physical Gesticulation :

The gestures of limbs are divided into three types, Śārīra—those belonging to the body ; Mukhaja—those of the face ; and Ceṣṭākṛta—those resulting from the movements (of the entire body). The gesticulation is related to Śākhā, Aṅga and Upāṅga. Śākhā is explained as the gesticulation relating to the limbs. The limbs are divided as major and minor. The major ones are six—the head the hands, the breast, the sides, the waist and the legs ; the minor limbs are the eyes, the eye-brows, the nose, the lower lip, the cheeks and the chin. It can be seen that the minor limbs with the head as the major one are connected with the facial gestures. The movements of the other five major limbs would come under the Śārīra division while the entire movements of the body as in Nyāya, Maṇḍala, etc., would come under Ceṣṭākṛta. This whole gesticulation is Śākhā. Kālidāsa refers to the acting of Mālavikā as' 'śākhā-yoniḥ'—(i.e. resulting from the gestures of the various limbs). SR.[3] defines Śākhā as 'vicitrā karavartanā' i.e. the striking (graceful) movements of hands. This limited meaning of Śākhā is not found in the NŚ. The Abhinaya (the histrionics), has three aspects—Śākhā, Aṅkura and Nṛtta. The Aṅkura is defined as Sūcanā, i.e., it is suggestive. Dr. Ghosh translates it as

1. NŚ. Vol. II, pp. 25-26.
2. NŚ. Vol. II. XIII, p. 84.
3. SR. VII, p.37.

"pantomiming through them (i.e. gestures) is the aṅkura". Nṛtta, i.e., dance is based on dance-units and consists of Aṅgahāras. Aṅkura,[1] according to the NŚ. is the suggestive gesticulation like the sprout that indicates the future tree. Here Nṛtta is mentioned as one Vastu, i.e., aspect of Abhinaya. The meaning of Śākhā limited to the graceful hand gestures can be understood in the following manner. The single and double hand gestures were used to indicate more and more things and ideas and as we find, in the Cākyār tradition the whole story is expressed by hand gestures, i.e., Mudrās alone. Hence the importance of hand gestures in the Śākhā became so great that Śākhā denoted hand gestures only.

In dealing with the physical gesticulation, Bharata first treats the facial expressions as being the basis of emotions and sentiments. In the facial expression, the movements of head the major limb, together with the minor limbs are given in detail. Thirteen movements of head are treated. They are as follows—

1. *Ākampita and* 2. *Kampita* The head is moved up and down slowly in Ākampita while quickly and often in Kampita. The first is used in giving a hint, recognition, questioning, addressing naturally, and calling by pointing out. The Kampita is used in anger, argument, understanding, asserting, threatening and speeches with excessive questioning.

3. *Dhuta and* 4. *Vidhuta* Slow sideways, movement of the head is Dhuta while the same effected quickly is Vidhuta. The first is applicable in unwillingness, dejection, astonishment, confidence, looking sideways, emptiness and forbidding while the Vidhuta, in attack of cold, terror, panic, fever and the first stage of drinking.

5. *Parivāhita*—The head is alternately turned to the two sides. It is used in demonstration, wonder, joy, remembering, intolerance, thinking and amorous sporting.

1. In the Sāmānyābhinaya, Sūcā and Aṅkura are defined separately in the NŚ.

The Cākyārs employ the Kriyās in the representation, e.g. when the stage direction is 'sagarvam', the actor expresses the pride by his movements suggestive of the speech and then the actual speech is recited in which the meaning of the speech is expressed more effectively by the help of the physical gestures.

6. *Ādhuta*—Head is turned up once, slantingly. It is used in showing arrogant will, looking up at the object sideways and in self-esteem.

7. *Avadhuta*—The head is turned down once. It is to be used in communicating a message, calling, conversation and beckoning one to come near.

8. *Añcita*—The neck is slightly bent on one side in it. It is applicable in sickness, swoon, intoxication and anxiety.

9. *Nihañcita*—In it the two shoulders are raised up with the neck bent. It is to be used by women in pride, amorousness, light-heartedness, affected indifference, hysterical mood, silent expression of affection, pretended anger, paralysis and jealous anger.

10. *Parāvṛtta*—In it the face is turned back. It is to be used in turning away the face, looking back and the like.

11. *Utkṣipta*—It results when the face is raised up and is used in lofty objects and divine things.

12. *Adhogata*—In it the face is turned down. It is used in shame, salutation and sorrow.

13. *Lolita*—In it the head is moved on all sides. It is used in fainting, sickness, power of intoxication and drowsiness due to being possessed by evil spirit.

The glances described are thirty-six in number. Through them the dramatic representation is well-effected. The glances for sentiments are eight, for permanent moods eight and for transitory moods twenty.

Glances used for sentiments are—

1. *Kāntā*—With a feeling of love a sidelong look is cast with the eye-brows contracted. It has its origin in joy and good temper—it is used in the Erotic sentiment.

2. *Bhayānakā*—The eyelids are drawn up and fixed, the pupils gleaming and turning up. It indicates a great fear and is used in the Terrible sentiment.

3. *Hāsyā*—The two eyelids are contracted by turns and the pupils are moving and slightly visible. It is to be used to represent deceipt and produce laughter (in the Comic).

4. *Karuṇā*—The upper eyelid is brought down, the pupil is steady in sorrow, the gaze fixed at the tip of the nose and with tears. It is used in the Pathetic sentiment.

5. *Adbhutā*—Eyelashes are slightly curved at the end, pupils raised in wonder and the eyes widened. It is used in the Marvellous.

6. *Raudrī*—The glance is pitiless, the eyelids still, the pupils red and raised and the eyebrows knitted. It is to be used in the Furious sentiment.

7. *Vīrā*—The glance is bright, eyes fully open, agitated and serious, the pupils are at the level and at the central part blooming fully. It is used in the Heroic.

8. *Bībhatsā*—The corners of the eyes are nearly covered by eyelids, the pupils disturbed in disgust, the eyelashes steady and close to each other. It is to be used in the Odious sentiment.

Glances to express the permanent states are—

1. *Snigdhā*—The glance has medium expansion; it is sweet, with pupil steady and full of desire ; it has the eyebrows expressive of delight. This glance is due to love.

2. *Hṛṣṭā*—The glance is moving and slightly bent down, with eyeballs slightly visible, with winking, indicating smile. It is used in laughter.

3. *Dīnā*—The upper eyelid is dropped down, the pupil slightly swollen, turbid with tears and moving slowly. It is used in sorrow.

4. *Kruddhā*—The glance is rough, eyelids drawn up and steady, pupils motionless and turned up and eyebrows knitted. It is used in anger.

5. *Dṛptā*—The glance is steady and widened in which eyeballs are motionless. It expressess prowess. It is used in energy.

6. *Bhayānvitā*—Both the eyelids are expanded fully, the pupils tremulous in fear and the central part, as it were, coming out of the eye. It is used in fear.

7. *Jugupsitā*—The glance is soiled in which the eyelashes are contracted, the pupils covered and turning away from the object coming in view. It is used in disgust.

8. *Vismitā*—The glance is level, fully widened and has pupils greatly turned up with the curve of both the eyebrows lost due to being widened. It is used in wonder.

Bharata has first described the twenty glances to express the transitory states and then given their application. But for the sake of convenience the uses are given just after the description of each of them.

The glances to express the transitory states are as follows—

1. *Śūnyā*—The glance is soiled, motionless and has pupils and eyelids in ordinary position ; the look is vacant, unattentive to external objects. It is used in anxiety and paralysis.

2. *Malinā*—The ends of eyelashes are throbbing, the eyelids slightly closed, corners of the eyes pale and the pupils rolling. It is used in dejection and loss of colour.

3. *Śrāntā*—The eyelids are languid due to fatigue, the corners are emaciated and contracted, the glance bent down and the pupils depressed. It is used in weariness and perspiration (due to the fatigue).

4. *Lajjānvitā*—The ends of eyelashes are slightly curved, the upper eyelid fallen in shyness and eyeballs lowered in bashfulness. It is to be used in shyness.

5. *Glānā*—The glance is loose, the eyebrows, eyelids and eyelashes are languid moving slowly and the pupils sinking. It indicates epilepsy, sickness and weakness.

6. *Śaṅkitā*—The glance is concealed, alternately moving and steady, slightly raised, widened obliquely and pupils apprehensive. It is to indicate apprehension.

7. *Viṣādinī*—i.e. Viṣaṇṇā—The eyelids are wide apart in dejection, the corners upset, eyes closing and pupils slightly motionless. It is used to indicate despair.

8. *Mukulā*—The eyelashes are united and throbbing, the upper eyelids bent in the budlike manner and pupils opened in happiness. It is used in sleeping, dreaming and happiness.

9. *Kuñcitā*—The ends of eyelashes are bent slightly due to eyelids being contracted and the eyeballs also are contracted. It is to indieate undesirable things, objects visible with difficulty and pain in the eye.

10. *Abhitaptā*—The pupils are slowly moving due to the movement of the eye-lids, the glance is full of distress and pain. It indicates despondency, accidental hurt and distress.

11. *Jihmā*— The glance is hanging down, having eyelids contracted with slow oblique looks and the eyeballs concealed. It is used in envy, stupor and indolence.

12. *Lalitā*— The glance is sweet with ends contracted, smiling with knitting of eyebrows and showing signs of love. It indicates contentment and joy (in sporting, amorous moods).

13. *Vitarkitā*—Eyelids are turned in guess, pupils full blown and moving downwards. It is used in recollection and deliberation.

14. *Ardhamukulā*—The eyelids are half-opened like bud in joy, the eyelashes half open and pupils slightly moving. It indicates joy due to experiencing sweet smell, touch, etc.

15. *Vibhrāntā*—The pupils are unsteady with looks confused and perturbed and eyes wide and full blown. It is used in agitation, confusion and hurry.

16. *Viplutā*—The eyelids are throbbing first and then become steady and. fall down, pupils are disturbed and turned up. It indicates restlessness, madness, affliction and death.

17. *Ākekarā*—The corners of the eyes and the eyelids are slightly contracted, half closed and united and the pupils repeatedly turned away. It is used in looking to a distant object and towards objects separated.

18. *Vikośā*—Both the eyelids are wide open, fully blown, without winking and pupils unsteady. It is used in awakening, pride, indignation, fierceness and determination.

19. *Trastā*—The eyelids are turned up in fear, the pupils throbbing, the middle of the eye full blown due to panic. It indicates fright.

20. *Madirā*—To indicate light intoxication the pupils are rolling, eyes bent and the corners widened ; to indicate medium intoxication the eyelids are slightly contracted, the pupils slightly moving, look somewhat unsteady ; the excessive intoxication is indicated by the pupils slightly visible, look turned downwards, the eyes winking and unwinking.

The movements of pupils, eye-lids and eyebrows are then treated. The pupils have nine movements—bhramaṇa, the turning round ; valana, moving the eye-balls obliquely ; pātana, relaxing ; calana, trembling ; sampraveśana, drawing in ; vivartana, turning sideways in a sidelong glance ; samud. vṛtta, raising up ; niṣkrāma, going out and prākṛta, natural-Bhramaṇa, valana, niṣkrāma and samudvṛtta are used in the Heroic and the Furious sentiments ; niṣkrāma with calana in the Terrible ; praveśana, in the Comic and the Odious ; pātana in the Pathetic, niṣkrāma in the Marvellous and vivartana in the Erotic. Prākṛta is used in the remaining states. Bharata says that these are the natural movements of the eyeballs based on popular practice. There are eight kinds of looks—

1. *Sama*—gentle, with the eyeballs in a level position ;
2. *Sācīkṛta*—side-long, with the eyeballs covered by the eyelashes ;
3. *Anuvṛtta*—engaged in closely observing any form ;
4. *Ālokita*—suddenly seeing anything ;
5. *Vilokita*—looking back ;
6. *Pralokita*—looking sideways ;
7. *Ullokita*—looking upwards ;
8. *Avalokita*—looking downwards.

There are nine movements of the eyelids—unmeṣa, opening the eyelids ; nimeṣa, closing them ; prasṛta, expanding ; kuñcita, contracting ; sama, natural ; vivartita, turned up ; sphurita, throbbing ; pihita, closed ; and vitāḍita, when struck. Vivartita, unmeṣa and nimeṣa indicate anger ; prasṛta is used in wonder, joy and heroic mood ; kuñcita in undesired sight, smell, taste or touch ; sama in love ; sphurita in jealousy ; pihita in sleep, faint, affliction due to storm, heat, smoke, rains, collyrium and eye-disease ; and vitāḍita in accidental injury when struck.

The eyebrows have seven movements—utkṣepa, raising up of eye-brows singly or together—raising up of one eyebrow used in anger, deliberation, passion, sporting and in seeing and hearing naturally and the raising up of both used in wonder, joy and anger ; pātana, lowering down of eye-brows singly or together, used in envy, disgust, smile and smelling ; bhrukuṭī, raising up of the root of eye-brows, employed in anger with excitement ; catura, the widening of the eye-brows in a pleasing manner due to slight breathing, used in love, sportiveness, gentle objects, pleasing touch and awakening ; kuñcita, slightly bending the eye-brows singly or together, used in manifestation of affection, pretended and hysterical mood ; recita, raising up one eye-brow amorously, used in dance ; sahaja, natural position of the eye-brows, used in natural conditions.

There are six gestures of nose—

1. *Natā*—nostrils clinging together again and again ; it is used in the persuasion of women, in slight weeping at intervals and in breathing and gentle throbbing.

2. *Mandā*—steady nostrils ; it is used in despondency, longing, anxiety and sorrow.

3. *Vikṛṣṭā*—nostrils blown ; it is used in powerful smell, anger, fear and in the Furious and the Heroic.

4. *Socchvāsā*—It results when air is drawn in ; it is used in desirable smell and deep breathing.

5. *Vikūṇitā*—nostrils are contracted ; it is used in laughter, disgust and envy.

6. *Svābhāvikā*—natural ; it is used in the remaining moods.

Movements of cheeks are six—(1) Kṣāma—fallen, used in sorrow ; (2) Phulla—blown, used in great joy ; (3) Ghūrṇa—expanded, used in energy and pride ; (4) Kampita—throbbing, used in anger and joy ; (5) Kuñcita—contracted, used in horripilation and in touch, cold, fear and fever ; and (6) Sama—natural, used in remaining states.

The movements of the lower lip are (1) Vivartana—narrowing down, used in envy, pain, contempt, laughter, etc. ;(2) Kampana—throbbing, used in pain, cold, fear, anger, swiftness, etc. (3) Visarga—protruding, used in women's amours, affected indifference and in painting the lip ; (4) Vinigūhana—drawing in, used in making efforts ; (5) Sandaṣṭaka—bitten by teeth, used in anger ; and (6) Samudgaka—rounded, used in pity, kissing and greeting.

There are seven movements of the chin. They are—

1. *Kuṭṭana*—It results when the teeth are rubbing against each other ; it is used in fear, cold, fever and anger.

2. *Khaṇḍana*—It results when the teeth are repeatedly coming together ; it is used in muttering prayers, studying, speaking, and eating.

3. *Chinna*—It results when the teeth closely meet each other ; it is used in sickness, fear, cold, exercise, crying and death.

4. *Cukṣita*—It takes place when the lips are separated widely apart ; it is used in yawning.

5. *Lehita*—It takes place when the lips are licked by the tongue ; it is used to indicate greediness.

6. *Sama*—It results when the lips are slightly closed ; it is used in natural position.

7. *Daṣṭa*—It results when the lower lip is bitten by teeth ; it is used in anger.

The movements[1] of chin are due to the movements of teeth, lips and tongue.

There are six movements of the face—(1) Vinivṛtta—turned away, used in women's envy, anger, contempt and bashfulness; (2) Vidhuta—expanding obliquely, used in warding off, saying 'not so' etc.; (3) Nirbhugna—lowered, used in looking into depth etc.; (4) Bhugna—slightly expanded, used to indicate bashfulness, despondency, longing, anxiety, discipline and consultation; (5) Vivṛta—open, used in laughter, sorrow and fear; (6) Udvāhita—turned up, used in sportiveness and pride of women, in saying 'go away' in disregard and in saying 'so, indeed' and angry words.

The colour of the face is svābhāvika (i.e. natural) in natural and indifferent moods; prasanna (bright) in wonder, laughter and love; rakta (reddened) in intoxication and in the Heroic, the Terrible and the Pathetic; and śyāma (dark) in the Terrible and the Odious.

There are nine movements of the neck. They are—

1. *Samā*—natural, used in meditation, natural poses and muttering of incantations;

2 *Natā*—resulting when the face is bent down, used in wearing ornaments and embrace round the neck;

3. *Unnatā*—taking place when the face is upturned, used in looking up;

4. *Tryasrā*—resulting when the face is turned sideways, used in carrying burden on the shoulders and sorrow;

5. *Recitā*—moving round, used in feeling, churning and dance;

6. *Kuñcitā*—taking place when the head is bent down, used in pressure of weight and in protecting the neck;

1. SR. has treated them as 'dantakarmāṇi'.
SR. VII 500-506.

7. *Añcitā*—taking place when the head is turned back, used in hanging to death, arranging hair and looking very hingh up;

8. *Valitā*—resulting when the face is turned sideways, used in looking with bent neck;

9. *Vivṛttā*—taking place when the face is towards the front, used in going towards one's own place.

The second division of physical gesticulation is śārīra (i.e. of the limbs). In this division the NŚ. treats the movements of hand, breast, sides, waist, and legs with their parts, i.e., shanks, thighs, and feet. In this division the hand gestures are very important. The hand is very eloquent in the physical gesticulation. The number of hand poses is sixty-four in all, which is subdivided as the hand poses to be used in dramatic representation and those in dance. The single hand poses are twenty-four and those with both the hands are thirteen. The remaining twenty-seven hand poses are to be used mainly in dance, i.e., in the karaṇas etc. The actual number of dance hand poses which are defined, comes to twenty-nine in the Baroda edition. Miss Ketkar has not given the last two (i.e. Lalita and Valita) and has thus kept to the number twenty-seven. SR. defines Alapallava and Ulbaṇa separately. Thus the number comes to thirty according to SR. Then three more are treated in the SR. i.e., Nikuñcaka, Dviśikhara and Varadābhaya. His total then comes to seventy. Abhinayadarpaṇa classifies the hand gestures into three classes like the NŚ. There are many names which are common but there is difference as regards the number in each class and in their definitions and applications. Bharatārṇava gives twenty-seven single hand gestures, sixteen double hand gestures and twenty-two nṛtta hastas. In it, the use of twenty-seven hastas according to Bṛhaspati is also described. I have described the hand gestures in the NŚ. (Baroda edition) in the light of Abhinava's commentary and tried to take the help of Bharatārṇava and SR. whenever it was felt necessary.

Single hand gestures—These hand gestures are ordinarily used singly but at times two hands showing one of these gestures are used simultaneously. But still these are called single hands. Combined hands are always to be shown by both the hands.

1. *Patāka*—The fingers extended and closed and the thumb

bent. Uses—to represent blows struck by others, excessive heat, urging, great joy, in saying 'I too', 'of me too', 'by me too', etc. To indicate pride it is to be raised upto the forehead. This same hand with the other hand in Patāka with fingers moving should be used to represent fire, rain, shower, and shower of flowers. With both the hands in Patāka separated from the Svastika position, shallow pool of water, present of flowers, green grass, the things that are arranged and situated on earth such as offering etc. are to be represented. The same pointing downwards should be used to represent anything closed and opened, protected, covered, dense and to be concealed. With the fingers of the same hand pointing downwards and moving up and down, are to be expressed the speedy movement of the winds and waves, the breaking of the waters against shore and flood. The recaka of this hand should be used to represent encouragement, many, a great crowd of men, height, beating of drums and the flight of birds upwards. By the palms of both such hands rubbing against each other, anything washed, pressed, cleansed, pounded and holding up the hill or uprooting it should be gesticulated.

2. *Tripatāka*—The third finger of the Patāka hand is bent. It is used in calling, descent, bidding good-bye, warding off, entrance, raising up, salutation, comparing, the statement, expressing variety, touching the auspicious things or placing them on the head, the wearing of turban or crown and covering the nose, mouth, and ears. With the first and second fingers pointing downwards and moving up and down, the flight of small birds, the stream, the serpent and the bee etc. should be represented. With the third finger of this hand should be represented wiping of tears, arranging the tilaka, applying red sandal to the body and touching the hair.

3. *Kartarīmukha*—The forefinger of the Tripatāka hand is bent at the back of the middle finger. Uses—By bending downwards, showing the way, decorating the feet or dyeing them, arranging the design like tilaka etc. made by saffron and the like in the quadrangle are to be represented. By pointing upwards, biting, horn and letter are to be shown. When the middle finger is bent backwards, this hand indicates falling down, death, transgression, turning round, guess and trust.

4. *Ardhacandra*—All the fingers together with the thumb are bent like a bow. Uses—To indicate young tree, the digit of the moon, conch, jar, the bracelet, driving out by force, exertion, the thinness and fatness of waist. Women should represent by this hand girdle, hips, waist, face, tālapatra (a kind of ear-ornament) and earring.

5. *Arāla*—The first finger is bent like a bow, the thumb curved and the remaining fingers separated and turned upwards. Uses—To show courage, pride, zeal, beauty, steadiness, heavenly objects, poise, blessings and the favourable states. Women should represent by this hand tying the hair or loosening them and observing the entire body. Preliminaries to the marriage and the marriage should be represented by two Arāla hands moving round each other indicating circumambulation and their fingers meeting in the form of the Svastika. With this hand the circumambulation, the circle, the great crowd and the things arranged on the ground should also be represented. It should indicate also calling, asking not to come in, creation, saying many things, removing sweat, smelling sweet and good things. The functions of Tripatāka hands which are described before should be carried by women with Arāla hand.

6. *Śukatuṇḍa*—The third finger of the Arāla hand is bent. Uses—It is to be used to represent 'not I', 'not you' 'not to be done', invocation, farewell and saying 'fie upon you' in contempt.

7. *Muṣṭi*—The fingers are bent with their ends placed on the palm and the thumb on them. Uses—To represent blows, exercise as in fights, exit, pressing (as the pressing of teets in milking a she-buffalo,) shampooing and holding sword, staff and spear.

8. *Śikhara*—The thumb of the Muṣṭi is raised. Uses—To represent (holding of) reins, whips, goad and bow; throwing a javelin or spike; dyeing the lower lip and feet and raising up hair.

9. *Kapittha*—The first finger of the Śikhara to be bent and pressed by the thumb. Uses—To represent holding weapons like sword, bow, discus, javelin, spear, club, spike, thunderbolt and arrows and true and wholesome deeds.

10. *Khaṭakāmukha* (*or Kaṭakāmukha*)—The ring finger and the little finger of the Kapittha are raised and bent. Uses—To represent sacrifice, oblation, umbrella, drawing up reins, fanning, holding a mirror, drawing decorative patterns, powdering, holding long stick, arranging a pearl necklace, taking up garlands, holding ends of the garment, churning, drawing out arrows, collecting flowers, holding a whip, drawing out a goad, and a rope, and sight of woman.

11. *Sūcīmukha*—The forefinger of Khaṭakāmukha is stretched. Uses—(i) With the first finger moving upwards, to represent a discus, lightning, banner, blossoms, earring, zigzag movement like that of a fish, cry of approbation, young serpent, sprout, smoke, lamp, various creepers, Śikhaṇḍa (tufts of hair on the sides of head), falling down, curve, and roundness ; (ii) with the forefinger raised, to indicate stars, nose, number one, club, stick (Abhinava[1] takes 'daṇḍa' in the sense of threatening) ; (iii) with the forefinger bent and meeting the mouth, indicating those having long teeth ; (iv) with the circular movement of it, to indicate taking up everything ; (v) with the forefinger alternately lowered and raised, to indicate long day ; (vi) with the curved forefinger moved up and down near the face, to indicate a sentence ; (vii) when stretched, shaken and moved up, to indicate 'no' or 'speak'; (viii) when shaking, to indicate anger, perspiration, hair, earring, armlet and decoration of the cheeks. It should be held near the forehead to represent 'I' in pride, anger, enemy, 'Who is this ? and scratching the ear. When both the forefingers of Sūcīmukha hands are united it indicates union, and when separated separation, when crosssed quarrel and when pressed each other, the bondage. When facing each other and held separately on the left side, it indicates close of the day and when held on the right side night. When they are moving in a circle, they represent the orb of the moon ; when obliquely raised up near the forehead they represent the eye of Hara and Śakra.

12. *Padmakośa*—The fingers are pointing upwards with the thumb separated and bent and with the ends not meeting one another. Uses—To represent bilva and kapittha fruits and

1. NŚ. Vol. II, p. 43.

the breasts of women. With the ends bent, it represents accepting these fruits and flesh, offering worship to deities, offering oblation, casket, offering first funeral cake and multitude of flowers. Both the hands in Padmakośa meeting at the wrist and turning backward with fingers moving, represent the full-blown lotus and water-lily.

13. *Sarpaśiras*—The fingers with the thumb are close to each other and the palm hollowed. Uses—To represent offering of water, the gait of serpent, sprinkling of water, challenging for a duel, e.g., striking an arm, thigh, etc. in wrestling, stroking elephant's temple, etc.

14. *Mṛgaśirṣa*—All the fingers are pointing downwards close to each other and the thumb and the little finger raised up. Uses—It is moved to indicate 'here', 'now', 'it is', 'today', splendour of power, throw of dice, wiping sweat, and pretended anger.

15. *Kāṅgula*—The middle[1] and first finger and the thumb are (separated and raised up), in the position of Tretāgni, the ring finger bent and the little finger raised up. Uses—To represent raw fruits and small ones, and angry words of women, it is to be employed by turning out the thumb, first and middle finger.

16. *Alapallava*—The fingers are turned towards palm, beginning with little finger, standing on its side and separated from one another. Uses—To represent warding off 'Whom do you belong to?' 'It is not', unmeaningful words and woman's allusion to herself.

17. *Catura*—The three fingers are stretched, little finger raised up and the thumb in the midst of them. Uses—(i) To represent policy, discipline, penance, clever girl, afflicted person, deceit, proper words, welfare, truth and tranquillity; (ii) by one such hand or both moved round, openness, deliberation, moving, conjecture and shame are indicated; (iii) by the combined Catura hands alone, comparison with eyes, the lotus petals and ears of deer are to be represented. It is used also to indicate sports, love, brightness, memory, intelligence, judgement, forgiveness, nourishment, conscious-

1. Cf. 'ऊर्ध्वास्त्रेताग्निसंस्थानास्तर्जन्यंगुष्ठमध्यमाः ॥'

SR. VII. 142.

ness, affection, reasoning, union, purity, cleverness, sweetness, politeness, softness, happiness, character, question, livelihood, propriety, dress, soft green grass, small quantity, wealth, defeat, merit, and demerit, youth, home, wife, and various colours (red and yellow by moving this hand, white with raising this hand and blue by pressing it with the other).

18. *Bhramara*—The middle finger and the thumb crossing each other, the first finger curved and the remaining two, are separated and pointing upwards. Uses—To represent the plucking of flowers with long stems such as lotus etc. and earring.

19. *Haṁsāsya*—The first and middle fingers and the thumb are in triangular position, and close to each other and the remaining two fingers stretched. Uses—It indicates with the ends slightly throbbing, fineness, smallness, looseness, lightness, worthlessness and softness.

20. *Haṁsapakṣa*—The three fingers are stretched, the little finger raised up and thumb bent. Uses—It indicates offering libation of water and gifts, decoration of cheek, sipping water and accepting meals by Brahmins, embrace, excessive paralysis, horripilation, touch, unguent and massage. The amorous actions of women should be represented by placing it on the region of the breast according to the sentiment. It is to be used in their sorrow and supporting the chin.

21. *Sandaṁśa*—The forefinger and the thumb of the Arāla hand are crossing and the palm little hollowed. According to sentiments and moods, it is three-fold—(i) held in front ; (ii) near the mouth ; and (iii) by the side. Uses—(i) when held in front—to represent the plucking of flowers, arranging them, holding grass, leaves, hair and thread, holding or pulling out dart or thorn ; (ii) when held near the mouth—to indicate plucking of flowers from the stem, completing (the decoration) by collyrium stick and the word 'fie upon' in anger ; (iii) with the left hand held on one side having the end turned slightly, to represent words[1] of censure, delicacy, abuse and jealousy. It is used also to indicate painting, colouring the eyes, deliberation, stem, drawing designs and squeezing of the lac dye by

1. SR. has 'saroṣabhāṣaṇa' while NŚ. has 'sadoṣavacana'. SR. VII 181-182, NŚ. IX 115.

women. Combined with other hand, it represents wearing sacred thread, piercing a hole in pearls, etc., bow-string, fineness, arrow, targets, concentration, meditation and small quantity.

22. *Mukula*—The fingers with their ends are brought together close to one another and raised up like Haṁsāsya. Uses—To represent offering of oblation and worship of deities, bud of lotus and water lily, throwing a kiss (as by a Viṭa), contempt, scattered objects, taking meals, gold, counting, narrowing of mouth, gifts, quickness and buds of flowers.

23. *Ūrṇanābha*—The fingers of Padmakośa are bent. Uses—To indicate holding hair, taking stealthily, scratching one's head, skin-disease, lion, tiger and other such animals and taking up stone.

24. *Tāmracūḍa*—The middle finger and the thumb are crossing each other, the forefinger bent and the remaining two placed on the palm. Uses—To represent falling down with a sound, beating time, inspiring confidence, quickness and signs (e.g., calling young boys and others).

Combined (Saṁyuta) hands—

1. *Añjali*—Both the hands are in Patāka with palms joined together. Uses—To represent great gods it is held on head, respectable elders near one's face and friends, on breast. No fixed rules are prescribed in the case of women.

2. *Kapota*—Both the Añjali hands meet at their side. Uses—To indicate approach with modesty, salutation and talk with venerable persons, it is held on the breast. Women should represent cold and fear with this hand placed on the bosom and shaking. This hand released after the meeting of fingers, indicates anxious words, 'this much' and 'not to be done now'.

3. *Karkaṭa*—The fingers of both the hands are interlocked. Uses—To indicate massaging of the limbs in love condition, yawning after awakening from sleep, a big body, supporting the chin and holding conch.

4. *Svastika*—The Arāla hands are upturned and held at the wrist and are placed at the left side. Uses—By separating from Svastika position, it indicates the quarters, clouds, sky, ocean, forest, seasons, earth, flood and such other extensive things. This hand is to be used by women.

5. *Khaṭakāvardhamānaka*—One Khaṭakāmukha hand is placed on the wrist of the other Khaṭakāmukha hand either in Svastika position or facing each other. Uses—It represents love-making and salutation.

6. *Utsaṅga*—The Arāla hands are placed in Svastika position facing oneself and bent (right on the left shoulder and vice versa). Uses—To indicate touch (of the object beyond sight) and things done with great effort, acts of anger and indignation. To represent acts of jealousy by women it is pressed hard.

7. *Niṣadha*—The Mukula hand is enclosed by Kapittha. Uses—To indicate correct understanding, acceptance, holding, convention, speaking the truth and the purport ; the purport should be represented by this hand pressed.[1]

8. *Dolā*—Shoulders are loose and the hands in Patāka hanging down with fingers loose. Uses—To indicate hurry, dejection, fainting, intoxication, panic, excitement, state of illness and wound by weapon.

9. *Puṣpapuṭa*—Both the hands are in Sarpaśiras with their fingers close to one another meeting on one side closely. Uses—To indicate receiving and carrying of corn, fruit, flowers and similar things and carrying and removing water.

10. *Makara*—The two Patāka hands with the thumb raised are bent down and placed one upon the other. Uses—To represent lion, tiger, elephant, crocodile, shark, fish and other carnivorous animals.

11. *Gajadanta*—The two Sarpaśirṣa hands are touching the opposite arms between shoulders and elbow. Uses—To indicate carrying the bride and the bridegroom (to the place of marriage), excessive weight, clasping a pillar, uprooting a hill or a stone.

12. *Avahittha*—The two Śukatuṇḍa hands are bent facing the breast and then slowly lowered. Uses—To indicate weakness, pointing to one's body, the thinness of one's body and longing.

1. The definition and uses according to Kīrtidhara-pāṭha are given in verses 144, 145 and 146 of Ch. IX of the NŚ.
See NŚ. Vol. II, p. 60; footnote 4.

13. *Vardhamāna*—The Haṁsapakṣa hands. inverted (in Svastika position or without Svastika also.) Uses—To indicate opening of the latticed windows etc.

The hand gestures are to be used elsewhere also according to the purpose to be served. In dramatic representation, there is no idea that cannot be conveyed by hand gestures. The gestures described here are those that are abundantly seen in indicating different ideas. There are other popular hand gestures also which should be used freely along with the movements indicating sentiments and emotions. These should be used by men and women considering properly the place, the time, the performance and the suitability of the meaning.

The general movements of hands (hasta-pracāra) are three —(1) uttāna—upwards; (2) adhomuka—downwards; and (3) pārśvaga—sideways. The movements of the hands in different directions are given as five according to the other view,'[1] which is that of Udbhaṭa, as stated by Abhinava. It reads[2] 'उत्तानोऽधस्तलस्त्र्यश्रोऽग्रगोऽधोमुख एव च । पञ्च प्रचारा हस्तस्य... ।' But Abhinava says that अधोमुख comes under अधस्तल and अग्रग comes under उत्तान; त्र्यश्र is nothing but त्रिपार्श्वग. Shri Verma[3] has also accepted the view of three hastapracāras. Abhinava explains uttāna position, as in the representation of tongue, Tripatāka is brought near the face; pārśvaga as when the Muṣṭi is used in the representation of a bow; and adhomukha as in the representation of ocean, the use of (svastika) hand near the forehead.

All the hand movements should be embellished by expressive eyes, eyebrows and facial colour etc. in performance.

1. NŚ. Vol. II, p. 70.
2. 'उत्तानो वर्तुलस्त्र्यश्रः स्थितोऽधोमुख एव च ।
पञ्च प्रचारा हस्तस्य नाट्यनृत्तसमाश्रयाः ॥

NŚ. Ch. IX. 182.

3. Cf. 'Hasta-pracāras Three or Five', by Shri K. M. Varma.
O.H.R.J. Vol. V, pp. 195-204.

Shri Varma says pracāra in hastapracāra is the movement of the hand generated by the radius which moves the hand along with itself in a similar manner. Because of this, only three states are possible—uttāna, hand in supine position; adhomukha, hand in prone position; and pārśvaga, hand in middle position. He has given this explanation from the viewpoint of anatomy.

The experts should use the hand gestures in confirmity with the popular usage, taking into consideration the karaṇa (movements), karma (object) sthāna (sphere), pracārayukti (appropriateness) and kriyā (mode). When the superior types or objects are to be indicated, the hand gestures should be near the forehead; when middling, near the breast and when inferior, below. In superior acting, the hand movements should be scanty, in middling, medium, while in the low type (i.e. in which emotional expression is subordinate), abundant. When the objects are present, hand gestures should precede the facial expression and when they are absent, the facial expression should precede the hand gestures. To indicate the ideas, the superior and the middling types should use hand gestures with grace (as per the definitions given) while the low type should use them according to popular practice and natural habit. But on different occasions wise people should use different hand gestures with discretion. They are not to be used when following are to be represented—sadness, fainting, fear, affliction due to disgust or sorrow, weakness, sleep, helplessness, motionlessness, drowsiness, inertness, sickness, attack of fever, panic and cold, intoxication, powerful intoxication, madness, contemplation, practising penance, being oppressed by snowfall, bondage, floating in water, dreaming, confusion and manifesting depression. (Abhinava[1] adds here that the hand gestures which are indicative of the inner mood are to be used because they are like the consequents. The hand gestures indicative of external things etc. are not to be used.) In such cases, there should be use of the representation of the temperament as well as the effective modulation of voice. When both the hands are engaged, as in the case of the charioteer holding the reins and whip, the verbal representation would be there with proper stops, expressive of the meaning accompanied by various glances.

Dance hands are also described in connection with the hand gestures. They are as follows—

1. *Caturaśra*—Two Khaṭakāmukha hands held forward, eight aṅgulas apart from one's breast, the shoulders and elbows are on the same level.

1. NŚ. Vol. II, p. 69

2. *Udvṛtta*—The two Haṁsapakṣa hands are waved like a fan (palm leaf). Its other name is Tālavṛnta.

3. *Talamukha*—The two hands in the Caturaśra position forming Haṁsapakṣa are to be held obliquely facing each other.

4. *Svastika*—The Talamukha hands are crossed at the wrists.

5. *Viprakīrṇa*—The Talamukha hands are released after Svastika.

6. *Arālakhaṭakāmukha*—The two Alapallava hands with palms upwards are changed into Padmakośa hands.

7. *Āviddhavaktraka*—The two (Patāka) hands are to have a graceful movement after touching successively the opposite shoulder, elbow and (the end of) arm, with palms facing downwards.

8. *Sūcīmukha*—The two Sarpaśiras hands with their thumbs touching middle fingers, are to stretch their tips obliquely.

9. *Recita*—The two Haṁsapakṣa hands move swiftly with the palms facing upwards.

10. *Ardharecita*—The left hand should be as in the Caturaśra and the right, as in the Recita.

11. *Uttānavañcita*—The two Tripatāka hands are slightly bent obliquely and the shoulders and the elbows moved.

12. *Pallava*—The two Patāka hands are joined at the wrist.

13. *Nitamba*—The two Patāka hands are moved from shoulder to the hip.

14. *Keśabandha*—The two hands are moved out from the hair knot and held on the sides.

15. *Latā*—The two hands are stretched sideways obliquely.

16. *Karihasta*—The Latā hand is held up and swung from side to side and the Tripatāka hand held on the ear.

17. *Pakṣavañcitaka*—One Tripatāka hand is placed on the waist and the other on the head.

18. *Pakṣapradyotaka*—The Pakṣavañcitaka hands change places.

19. *Garuḍapakṣaka*—The two (Patāka) hands pointing downwards placed near the region of the hips are moved up quickly, turning the palms.

20. *Daṇḍapakṣa*—The two Haṁsapakṣa hands are moved alternately and then held out like a staff.

21. *Ūrdhvamaṇḍalin*—The two hands have circling movements near the upper part of the body.

22. *Pārśvamaṇḍalin*—The same movement is made on the one side.

23. *Uromaṇḍalin*—After circling movements, one hand is to be raised up and the other to hang down and these movements are to take place near the breast.

24. *Uraḥapārśvārdhamaṇḍala*—The Alapallava and Arāla hands are moved by turns above the breast and on the sides.

25 *Muṣṭikasvastika*—The two Khaṭakāmukha hands are bent at the wrists and moved round.

26. *Nalinīpadmakośa*—The Padmakośa hands are moved by turns with Vyāvartita and Parivartita karaṇas.

27. *Ulbaṇa*—The two Alapallava hands in Udveṣṭita are to be stretched up and waved.

28. *Lalita*—Two Alapallava hands are moved near the head.

29. *Valita*—The two Latā hands are crossed at their elbows.

The dance hands are to be used in the karaṇas of dance primarily and such as Patāka are to be used in gesticulating the meaning of words. But sometimes, their uses are mixed due to necessity. The dance hands are also single and combined.

There are four karaṇas related to hand movements. SR.[1] explains the karaṇa as the particular movements of the hands resulting in hand gestures expressing various ideas. They are—1) Āveṣṭita—The fingers beginning with the first finger are gradually turned inwards. The hand moves round with its palm facing the breast. 2) Udveṣṭita—The fingers are gradually turned outwards, beginning with the first finger. The hand moves round, away from the breast. 3) Vyāvṛtta—The same movement is there as in Āveṣṭita but the fingers are gradually turned beginning with the last finger. 4) Parivartita—The fingers are turned outwards gradually beginning with the last finger.

These hand movements should be used in dance and representation accompanying the facial expression. The movements

1. SR. VII. 543.

of arms in drama and dance are ten—oblique, raised upward, turned downwards, bent, moving round, thrown off, in Svastika, turned to back, extended and in the position of Udveṣṭita karaṇa.

The gestures of breasts are five.

1. *Ābhugna*—The breast is slightly bent, back high, shoulders slightly bent and at times loose. It is used in hurry, dejection, fainting, sorrow, fear, disease, broken heart, touching cold objects, rain and being ashamed.

2. *Nirbhugna*—Breast is raised and stiff, back depressed, shoulders unbent. It indicates paralysis, accepting with respect, look of surprise, speaking truth, mentioning one-self in haughtiness and excess of pride.

3. *Prakampita*—The breast is heaving up and down incessantly. It is used in laughter, weeping, exhaustion, fear, breathing (heavily), asthma, hiccup and misery.

4. *Udvāhita*—The breast is raised up. It indicates deep breathing, looking at lofty objects, yawning etc.

5. *Sama*—All the limbs are in Caturasra and with the breast in Sauṣṭhava. It is used in natural position.

There are five movements of sides.

1. *Nata*—The waist and one side are slightly bent and one shoulder slightly drooping down. It is used in approaching some one.

2. *Unnata*—One side with the waist, the hand and the shoulders would be raised and the other side in Nata. It indicates going backwards.

3. *Prasārita*—Both the sides are stretched. It indicates great joy etc.

4. *Vivartita* The trika, i.e., hip part is to be turned round. It is used in turning about.

5. *Apasṛta*—The side is restored to its original position from the Vivartita. It is used in re-turning.

There are three movements of the belly.

1. *Kṣāma* (*thin*)—It is used in laughter, weeping, inhalation, and yawning.

2. *Khalva* (*depressed*)—It is used in sickness, penance, weariness and hunger.

3. *Pūrṇa* (*full*)—It is used in exhalation, fatness, disease and gluttony.

The movements of the waist are five.

1. *Chinnā* (*turned aside*)—It indicates exercise, hurry and looking round.

2. *Nivṛttā* (*When the waist is turned to the front from the reverse position.*)—It is used in turning round.

3. *Recitā* (*When moved round in all directions*)—It is used in moving round on all sides.

4. *Prakampitā* (*When the waist is moved forward and backward obliquely and quickly*)—It is used in the gaits of hunchback, dwarf, and persons of low type.

5. *Udvāhitā* (When the sides of the hips are raised slowly)—It is used in the movements of fat person and the graceful gait of women.

There are five movements of the thighs.

1. *Kampana*—It results when the heels are raised and lowered repeatedly. It is used in the gaits of low type characters and in fear.

2. *Valana*—It takes place when the knee is drawn inwards ; it is used in the easy gait of women.

3. *Stambhana*—It results when the movement is stopped ; it is used in nervousness, and dejection.

4. *Udvartana*—It takes place when the knee is drawn inwards and moved ; it is used in exercise and dance.

5. *Vivartana*—It results when the heels are drawn inwards ; it is used in moving about in confusion.

There are five movements of shanks—

1. *Āvartita*—It takes place when the left foot is turned to right and the right to left ; it is used in the moving about of Vidūṣaka.

2. *Nata*—It results when the knee is bent ; it is used in sitting and standing position.

3. *Kṣipta*—It takes place when the shank is thrown out ; it is used in exercise and dance.

4. *Udvāhita*—It takes place when the shank is raised up ; it is used in movements like going quickly.

5. *Parivṛtta*—It takes place when the shank is turned back ; it is used in class dance and the like.

The movements of the feet are five. They are—

1. *Sama*—The feet are naturally placed on the ground in even manner ; it is used in natural posture. They are kept unmoved in connection with various karaṇas ; but in the recita movements they should be moved.

2. *Agratalasañcara*—The heels are raised up, the big toe extended and the other toes bent. It is used in urging, pounding, standing posture, pressing, striking the ground, moving round, throwing away, various recaka movements and walking on forepart of the foot due to the wound in heel.

3. *Añcita*—The heels are on the ground, the fore-part raised and the toes bent ; it is used in movements when the fore-part of the foot is injured, turning round, striking by foot and in various Bhramarī movements.

4. *Kuñcita*—The heels are raised up, the toes bent and the middle part is also bent ; it is used in noble gait, turning round to the right and vice-versa and the Atikrānta steps.

5. *Udghaṭṭita*—It takes place while standing on the fore-part of the foot and then touching the ground with the heel ; it is used in Udghaṭṭita karaṇa, once or more in the high or medium speed.

The leg movements are constituted of the movements of thighs, shanks and feet. The thigh should follow the movements of the feet.

After treating the gestures of the individual limbs separately, the movements of the body are dealt with.

Cārī : It is the movement of the limbs below the hip. In Cārī the movement of the foot is prominent, which is accompanied naturally by the movements of shank, thigh and also waist. Such movement of one foot is called Cārī. Both the feet moved together would be a karaṇa. A combination of three karaṇas is called khaṇḍa ; three or four khaṇḍas (according to tryasra or caturasra rhythm) make up the maṇḍala. The single Cārī movements related to each other constitute vyāyāma, i.e., the system of exercise. Cārīs are to be used in Nṛtta, i.e., class dance, in the Ceṣṭita, i.e., the gaits of various persons and fights (i.e., the duels and release of missiles). The dramatic representation is well-founded in Cārīs as no major limbs like the head, the hand etc. can proceed without them. The foot movements are divided into two groups according to their manner and use in representation. Those in which the foot movements are more related to the ground, are Bhaumīcārīs and those in which the foot movements are performed more off the ground are Ākāśikīcārīs.

Bhaumīcārīs are sixteen in number. They are as follows :—

1. *Samapādā*—Standing with the two feet close together, and nails of the toes even (and then) in[1] Samapāda Sthāna.

2. *Sthitāvartā*—One Agratalasañcara foot is drawn up to cross the other foot and this movement repeated by the other, after separating the two.

3. *Śakaṭāsyā*—The body is held upright, one Agratalasañcara foot put forward and the breast in Udvāhita.

4. *Adhyardhikā*—The left foot is at the back of the right and then the right to be moved a tāla[2] and half (tāla = short span).

5. *Cāṣagati*—The right foot is put forward one tāla and then drawn back two tālas and then the left foot drawn back with a slight jump to meet the right.

6. *Vicyavā*—The feet are separated from the Samapāda position striking the ground by their fore-parts.

7. *Eḍakākrīḍitā*—Jumping up and down with the Talasañcara foot in turn, constitutes this Cārī.

8. *Baddhā*—The two shanks are crossed to form Svastika with the sideways movements of the thighs.

9. *Ūrūdvṛttā*—The heel of a Talasañcara foot is moved outward (i.e., towards the back of the other), the shank bent and raised as it is turned towards the shank of the other. The thigh is turned up.

10. *Aḍḍitā*—One Agratalasañcara foot is rubbed against the forepart or the back part of the other.

11. *Utspanditā*—The foot is moved gradually sideways in the manner of the recaka movements.

12. *Janitā*—The foot is in Talasañcara, Muṣṭi hand held on breast and the other hand moved (befittingly).

1. Cf. SR. Commentary of Kallinātha, p. 757.
2. SR.-VII.1046 :

अंगुष्ठमध्यमाङ्गुल्यौ ये हस्तस्य प्रसारिते ।
तदग्रयोरन्तरालं तालमाहुर्मनीषिणः ।।

Tāla is the distance between the tip of the thumb and that of the middle finger, when they are fully extended. It comes to about 9".

13. *Syanditā*—One foot is put forward 5 tālas away from the other.

14. *Apasyanditā*—The reverse of Syanditā (i.e., the other foot is put forward five tālas away from the first).

15. *Samotsaritamattallī*—Moving in a circular[1] manner (forward or backward) with the Talasañcara feet (forming Svastika of the shanks).

16. *Mattallī*—Moving in a circular manner (forward or backward) with the feet (closely touching[2] the ground and shanks in Svastika) and the hands in Udveṣṭita.

These Bhaumīcārīs are to be used in personal combat, and in Karaṇas. Abhinava[3] explains that these Cārīs are used since time immemorial in personal combat, Karaṇas and Aṅgahāras and then in dramatic representation.

Ākāśikī Cārīs —

1. *Atikrāntā*—Lifting up a Kuñcita foot and putting it forward, throwing it up and then causing it to fall on the ground with the forepart.

2. *Apakrāntā*—The thighs are in the Valana posture, a Kuñcita foot is raised and then thrown down on sideways.

3. *Pārśvakrāntā*—Lifting up a Kuñcita foot so that the knee would be on the level of breast and then making it fall on the ground with the Udghaṭṭita.

4. *Ūrdhvajānu*—Lifting up a Kuñcita foot so that the knee would be on the level of breast and the second foot steady in turn.

5. *Sūcī*—Throwing up a Kuñcita foot and extending it up to the knee or above the knee of the other and then letting it fall on its forepart.

6. *Nūpurapādikā*—Drawing one Añcita foot backwards and then letting it fall on the ground quickly at the back of the other foot, with its forepart.

7. *Dolāpādā*—Lifting up a Kuñcita foot and moving it from side to side and then causing it to fall on the ground in the Añcita posture.

1. Cf. SR. VII 936, 937.
2. Cf. SR. VII 938, 939.
3. NŚ. Vol. II p. 101.

8. *Ākṣiptā*—Lifting up a Kuñcita foot and then taking it on the other side, and placing it on the ground with the heel crossing the shank of the other foot.

9. *Āviddhā*—A Kuñcita foot extended when there is Svastika (the shanks crossing and not touching each other) and bending it and then letting it fall on the ground with the heel.

10. *Udvṛttā*—The Kuñcita foot of the Āviddhā cārī taken round (i.e. the heel is brought near the region of the thigh of the other foot) and then letting it fall on the ground with a jump and moving round and then (the repetition of the same movement by) the other foot.

11. *Vidyudbhrāntā*—The foot is turned to the back and extended to touch the head moving all round.

12. *Alātā*—One foot stretched backward and then put in by turning it and afterwards caused to fall on the heel.

13. *Bhujaṅgatrāsitā*—Lifting up a Kuñcita foot (up to the region of the top of the thigh of the other), turning round the waist and the knee and the thigh also turned round.

14. *Hariṇaplutā*—The foot in the Atikrāntācārī caused to fall down on the ground after a jump and the other shank having the Añcita foot, thrown at the back of the first.

15. *Daṇḍapādā*—The foot in the Nūpurapādikā to be extended forward quickly with the Āviddha (i.e., the tip of the knee facing one's own body).

16. *Bhramarī*—With the foot in Atikrāntācārī (the Kuñcita foot lifted up), the entire body is to be turned round, moving on the sole of the foot; thus the trika is turned round.

These Ākāśikīcārīs consist of the graceful movements of the limbs. They are to be used in the release of weapons like the arrow from a bow and thunderbolt etc. The hands should precede, follow or accompany simultaneously the foot movements according to the importance of the hand gestures, the gaits or both. The hand should follow the foot movement, and the waist, the hand. After taking a step, gestures of the minor limbs should be used. When in a foot movement, the foot comes to rest on the ground, the corresponding hand should rest on the waist after its movement. The Sthānas (i.e. the standing postures) are to be used in the release of all missiles. They are six.

1. *Vaiṣṇava*—The feet are 2½ tālas apart, one foot in the

natural posture, and the other obliquely placed with toes pointing sideways, the shank is bent a little and the limbs are in Sauṣṭhava. Uses—The characters of superior and middling types should carry on their ordinary conversation in connection with the various duties in this posture. It is to be used in throwing a disc, holding bow, in patient and stately movements of limbs and in anger. In the (pretended) anger of love it is to be used in the reverse position. It is to be assumed in rebuking, distress, apprehension and envy etc. It is to be used prominently in the Erotic, the Marvellous, the Heroic and the Odious sentiments. (Abhinava[1] mentions its use in the performance of Sūtradhāra.)

2. *Samapāda*—The feet are in natural position and kept a tāla apart ; the body is in natural Sauṣṭhava. Uses—It is used in accepting greetings from the Brahmins and imitating birds. It is to be assumed by the bridegroom at the marriage ceremony, persons in the sky, in chariots and in the aerial car, persons of sects with indicatory marks and observing vows.

3. *Vaiśākha*—The feet are 3½ tālas apart, obliquely placed pointing sideways and the thighs steady. Uses—In riding horses, in exercise, exit, imitating large birds, bending the bow and the Recakas.

4. *Maṇḍala*—The feet are 4 tālas apart and obliquely placed with toes facing sideways ; the waist and the knee are in natural position. It is used in the employment of weapons like bow and thunderbolt, riding the elephants and looking at large birds.

5. *Ālīḍha*—The right foot of Maṇḍala is extended 5 tālas. Uses—It is employed in acts relating to the Furious and the Heroic sentiments, the repartees in anger and intolerance, duel of wrestlers, looking at the enemies and attacking them and the release of weapons.

6. *Pratyālīḍha*—Right foot is bent and the left extended in Ālīḍha. Uses—It is used to actually release the missiles kept ready for it.

Four Nyāyas, i.e., the ways of fighting, are to be employed in the use of missiles. In Bhāratanyāya the weapon should strike the waist, in Sāttvata, the foot, in Vārṣagaṇya, the chest and in Kaiśika, the head. With these Nyāyas arising out of the various

1. NŚ. Vol. II. p. 108.

Cārīs, various movements should be performed in the release of weapons.

Bhārata—The shield is to be held in left hand and the weapon in the right. The shield should be moved round by extending the hand and then drawing back. The sword should be brandished round the head or near the cheek. Again by turning the wrist gracefully the sword and the shield should be moved round the head.

Sāttvata—It is similar to Bhārata ; but the weapon (and the shield) are to be moved at the back.

Vārṣagaṇya—It is similar to Sāttvata ; but the weapon and the shield should be moved round the head or the weapon should be moved near the chest or the shoulders.

Kaiśika—It is similar to Bhārata ; but the weapon should be flourished over the head and made to strike[1] it.

These graceful movements of the limbs should be employed in the use of bow, thunderbolt and sword. Actual piercing or cutting or the flow of blood should not be shown on the stage. The release of missiles should be represented by these postures and gestures ; or the wound should be represented according to conventions. The Cārī-vyāyāma should be performed with Aṅgahāras possessing the grace of the limbs and accompanied by tempo (of the instrumental music). In all the movements in Nāṭya and Nṛtta there must be Sauṣṭhava. When the waist and the ears as well as the elbow, the shoulders and the head are in their natural position and the breast is raised it is called Sauṣṭhava. When the hands are moving near the region of waist and the navel, the chest is raised and the Sthāna is Vaiṣṇava, it is called Caturasra of the limbs. The four acts relating to

1. Cf. Śārṅgadharapaddhati—Pariccheda 80, Verses 75-82 & 90-92.

According to the Dhanurveda, described in the Śārṅgadharapaddhati, the sthānas are eight—Ālīḍha, Pratyālīḍha, Viśākha, Samapāda, Asamapāda, Dardurakrama, Guruḍa-krama and Padmāsana, and the Vyayas (Nyāyas?) are five—Kaiśika, Sāttvika, Vatsakarṇa, Bharata and Skandhanāman.

Cf. Kumārasambhava, edited by Prin. R.D. Karmarkar p.98 and 170.

Mallinātha has quoted from Yādava, the five Sthānas (excepting Vaiṣṇava of the NŚ.) while commenting on stanza 70 of the third Canto of the Kumārasambhava.

the bow are preparing, taking out the arrow, fixing the arrow and shooting the arrow.

The Maṇḍalas arise out of the combination of Cārīs. There are ten Ākāśa-maṇḍalas and ten Bhauma-maṇḍalas. In the fights and movements of those moving in the air, the aerial Maṇḍalas are to be used. They are to be employed also in fights, personal combats and moving about on the stage with graceful and the sportive movements of the limbs and in accompaniment of instrumental music. They are described in detail in the NŚ.[1]

Aerial Maṇḍalas are—Atikrānta, Vicitra, Lalita-sañcara, Sūcīviddha, Daṇḍapāda, Vihṛta, Alāta, Vāmaviddha, Lalita, and Krānta.

Bhauma Maṇḍalas are—Bhramara, Āspandita, Āvarta, Samotsarita, Eḍakākrīḍita, Aḍḍita, Śakaṭāsya, Adhyardha, Piṣṭakuṭṭa, and Cāṣagata.

The Cārīs should be used with proper combinations. When the aerial and the earthly Cārīs are combined properly, it is Samamaṇḍala. These should be used according to the instructions of the teachers.

The gaits—

The entry—After the upavahana, i.e., the singing of the notes of the particular melody, accompanied by instrumental music, the Dhruvā song should be started in which the place and the permanent mood of the character are indicated. (Then[2] again there should be upavahana according to Abh.) When the curtain is drawn away the character should enter. The superior and the middling characters should have the Vaiṣṇava sthāna. The breast should be raised even and Caturasra (symmetrical). The shoulders should not be raised very much and should be steady & 8 aṅgulas (aṅgula=$\frac{3}{4}$″) apart from the ears. The neck should balance the head gracefully like a peacock & the chin should be 4 aṅgulas apart from the breast. The right hand should be at the navel and the left at the waist. The distance between the feet should be $2\frac{1}{2}$ tālas. The steps should be according to the measure of his own hand. The steps should be 4 tālas wide in the case of gods and kings, two in the case of middling type and one in the case of women and low characters respectively

1. NŚ. XI. Vol. II. pp. 118-128.
2. *Ibid.*, Vol. II p. 130.

with 4 kalās, 2 kalās and 1 kalā[1] time measures. The tempo should be slow in the case of superior characters, medium in the case of the middling ones and fast in the case of inferior characters according to their nature and the mood. Thus, on such occasions, as fight etc. even the superior character will have fast tempo, and in sorrow, the inferior character will have slow tempo. In the natural gait, the superior character is to raise his knee upto waist and in the case of Cārīs used in fight, upto breast. He should go five steps towards the Northeast corner of the stage with graceful Pārśvakrāntā Cārī accompanied by instrumental music. Then placing the left foot in Sūcī near the heel of the right, the right foot should be moved. After turning round, he should go 5 steps to the other corner (i.e., North-west). Then the left foot should be in Sūcī and the right foot should be moved. After this, turning round, he should go 5 steps towards bhāṇḍa (the musical instruments). Again he should have the left foot in Sūcī and move the right foot. Thus, in all he should move 21 steps. Afterwards, the left foot should be in Sūcī and the right should be moved. This pañcapadīgamana (i.e., going five steps) is to be performed as a rule. On rectangular stage the actor should have elaborate foot movements; on the square and triangular stages the actor's foot movements should be caturasra (i.e., square type) and tryasra (i.e.. triangular type). When the character is walking with his equals, the tempo would be according to his rank, i.e., 4, 2 or 1 kalā. If the superior character is walking with the middling one and the low type characters, for one step of his the middling one would have two steps and the low ones would have four. The steps of Gods,[2] Dānavas, Yakṣas, Kings, Pannagas and Rākṣasas should be four tālas wide. All the other dwellers of heaven should have steps of medium width. But those among them who are haughty should have their gait similar to that of gods. The nature of gods is divine, of the kings semi-divine and of others human. Hence there is no fault if the kings have the steps like those of the gods. In case of hurry, madness and anger, the rules about the measure would not be applicable.

1. See chapter III, for the meaning of Kalā.
2. Cf. NŚ. Vol. II. p. 136. F. N. 4इ—देव

The gaits which are prescribed according to different types are to be performed scrupulously. In case of attack of fever, hunger, fatigue due to austerities, terror, wonder, dissimulation, longing, love in separation, sorrow and in the sportive gait, there would be slow tempo of more than 4 kalās (i.e., 6 or 8 ones). But in case of anxiety it would be of 4 kalās. In case of secret love, panic, fright, excitation, joy, hurry, hearing of unwelcome news, agitation due to seeing wonderful object, urgent work, distress, search of enemies, pursuit of offender and that of ferocious animals, the gaits should be of two kalās (or the ratio regarding the kalā should not be followed).

The Gaits in Various Sentiments

The Erotic—(a) In ordinary love-making the actor is to enter the stage with the female messenger showing the way. He should indicate his intention by Sūcā. He should walk with graceful steps in the Atikrāntā Cārī and the body in Sauṣṭhava, in proper tempo and tāla. His hands should follow the feet. (b) Secret love-making—With the female messenger only as the guide and with the lamp put out he should enter, without much decoration and with garments in harmony with the time (night). He should move with slow and quiet steps, apprehensive of any sound, anxious, looking around alertly, with body trembling and stumbling often.

The Furious—The gait of Daityas, Rākṣasas, and Bhīmasena and such others; the actor should stand with feet 4 tālas apart and move with steps 4 tālas wide.

The Odious—The actor should move in steps with Eḍakākrīḍitācārī on the cremation ground or battle field, odious to look at. The steps should be in quick succession, sometimes falling near and sometimes far; the hands should follow the feet.

The Heroic—The actor should move with swift footsteps in various Cārīs. In the excitement, the gait should be in proper kalā and tāla with Pārśvakrāntā, Āviddhā and Sūcī cārīs.

The Marvellous and the Comic—The middling and inferior characters should have quick steps in different directions in wonder and joy. In the laughter also such and other similar movements should be there.

The Pathetic—The actor should move with steps in slow tempo, with eyes filled with tears, drooping limbs, arms thrown up and down and crying. This is to be the gait of women and inferior persons. The superior characters should move patiently, having tears, with deep sighs and looking upwards. The Sauṣṭhava of the body should not be resorted to. In case of middling type, the gait should be according to mental mood. In case of the death of the dear one the actor should move with steps not raised much high, with his energy lost, breast depressed and with the consciousness lost due to grief. When struck severely the steps should be raised moderately and fall strongly. The shoulders and arms should be drooping and the body unsteady. When attacked by cold and torrential rain, women and inferior type should have slow steps, with limbs contracted and shaking, placing hands on breast, the body bent, teeth and lips clattering and the chin quivering.

The Terrible—The character should move with faltering, quick and near steps, eyes moving and wide, head shaking with frightened looks cast on both sides, hands in Kapota, the body trembling and lips dry. When a person is pursued by enemy etc. threatened or frightened and when he sees any dreadful creature or hears any dreadful sound, the same gait should be resorted to. This should be used by men and women showing prowess at times with successive Eḍakākrīḍita steps, sometimes fallen near and sometimes far; and the hands are to follow the foot movements.

The gait of merchants and ministers should be natural and in Atikrāntā Cārī, with steps 2 tālas wide, the left hand in upturned Khaṭakāmukha held on the navel and the right with the upturned Arāla near the bosom. The limbs should not be drooping nor motionless nor excessively moving. Ascetics, permanent celibates, observers of vows etc. should move with steady eyes looking at a distance of 4 hands in front, with presence of memory, with body and mind steady, with the proper sectarian mark and the modest clothes dyed in red. The Sthāna should be Samapāda and hands in Catura of which one should be extended. The steps should be in Atikrāntā Cārī, the face serene and limbs not drooping. This is the gait of great ascetics and observers of great vows. The others (those having the appearance of asceticism) would have the contrary qualities like unsteady mind etc. The other ascetics according to their vows should have a gait confused and stately or confused and modest. The ascetics of the Pāśupata sect should move with Śakaṭāsyā and Atikrāntā Cārīs with haughty steps. The person acting as blind or moving in darkness should walk with the feet drawn on the ground and hands groping for the way. The person riding a chariot should move from Samapāda Sthāna with cūrṇa[1] (simple) steps to indicate that he is moving in a chariot. He should have bow in one hand and the pole in the other. The charioteer has to be busy with the whip in one hand and reins in the other. The different animals carrying the vehicle should be represented by their pictures which would be held by the charioteer in his hand. He is to move on the stage with quick and simple steps. The gait of one in a celestial car would be the same as that of the person riding a chariot. While mounting, the body should be held up and the face turned up a little; while descending the body and the face should be bent down. To represent moving in the sky one should have aerial[2] Cārīs looking downwards. The actor should move from Samapādasthāna and have cūrṇa steps. While descending from the sky the gait is similar, with steps straight and wide, raised up and fallen down, moving round in irregular manner. The person falling down from the sky should have the hand in Apaviddha, the clothes scattered and eyes set on the ground. Ascending the stairs of a palace, should be performed with steps in Atikrāntācārī, body held up and the foot placed on the stairs. In descending the stairs the body should be slightly bent with one foot in Atikrāntācārī and the other in Añcita.[3] In climbing the tree the steps should be in Atikrāntā, Sūcīviddhā, Apakrāntā and Pārśvakrāntā. The descending from the bank of a river would be similar to the descent from a palace. Crossing the river should be represented as follows—

The gait in wading through the water should be according to the depth of the water. If the waters are shallow, the gar-

1. According to Apte's Sanskrit-English Dictionary, (p. 439) cūrṇapada is a peculiar exercise, walking backwards and forwards.

2. NŚ. Vol. II p. 152.
Abh. 'Maṇḍalāvarta is explained as circular movement by some'.

3. Cf. NŚ. Vol. II p. 186, Verse 137.

ment would be held up; in deep water, the hand should be thrown with the front part of the body slightly bent. A person being carried away by the current of water should stretch out his arms one by one pushing forward the water repeatedly and should be extended obliquely by the force of the current. The whole of the body should be active and mouth shaken. To indicate going in a boat the steps should be quick and cūrṇa with one foot in Atikrānta and the other in Añcita. In climbing the hill, the gait suited to ascend the palace should be used, with the limbs thrown up.

All these, i.e., the palace, the tree, mountains etc. are to be represented by the suggestive gestures enjoined for climbing or coming down. The elephant is to be represented by holding a goad, the horse by the bit of a bridle and the other conveyance by holding a whip. In riding a horse, the Sthāna should be Vaiśākha and the various cūrṇa steps should be used successively. For the gait of a serpent, the feet should be in Svastika and steps in Pārśvakrāntā Cārī and then the feet should be turned in Svastika again. In the gait of a Viṭa, the steps are graceful with Kuñcita foot put forward within one tāla, hands in Khaṭakāvardhamāna, gracefully fitting his nature and following the feet. The gait of Kāñcukīya should be according to age. When young, the feet should be raised half a tāla high, steady and straight, carrying his body with effort and should move as if upon mud; when old, the body should be trembling, steps raised slowly supporting on the stick and taking breath at every step. The emaciated person should have slow steps. In attack of illness and fatigue due to penance, one should move supporting himself on something with hands and feet moved slowly, the limbs trembling, belly emaciated and depressed, feeble voice, depressed cheeks, lustreless eyes and physical suffering. The person who has walked a long distance should move with slow steps, limbs contracted, rubbing the knees. The bulky person's gait would have feet raised slowly, dragging the body with great effort. In the case of the persons fatigued by exertion and having perspiration, the gait should be with the cūrṇa steps with much breathing and supporting himself. In the light and the medium intoxi-

1. Cf. NŚ. Vol. II. p. 186, Verse 138.

cation, the movement should have reeling motion with left and right foot; in excessive intoxication, the feet would be staggering, body reeling and hands unsteady. A lunatic should move with irregular steps in many Cārīs imitating various persons, with hair coarse and dishevelled and the body covered with dust, talking too much without any reason, and having changes of mind. He should stand with one foot in Nūparapāda and extend the Daṇḍapāda. Then performing the Baddha and forming Svastika, should turn round in Bhramara Maṇḍala; afterwards with outward Bhramarī he should move to the corner of the stage. He should move turning the trika gracefully and with hand in Latā, having irregular movements of the hands and feet. Lame men, cripple and dwarfs should display the physical defects for the sake of comic representation. In the case of the lame, one foot should always be immobile and the other in Agratalasañcara. The body should be lifted by the stiff foot. If he is to sit after moving he should sit by moving the other foot. This gait is to be resorted to also when the sole is wounded. When crippled in both legs, the body should be seated and the shanks bent. The movement should be by the Añcita of the Agratalasañcara foot. The dwarf should not have wide and quick steps. His body should be contracted. Vidūṣaka should move with laughable cūrṇa steps raised high, gesticulating physical defects. He should walk like a crane looking up and down with wide strides. In his natural gait he should carry the kuṭila (staff) in his left hand, and the right hand should be in Catura. He should bend down by turns one of his sides, head, hand and foot following the tempo and the rhythm. When he enjoys a dish difficult to get, his movements should be haughty. The menials etc. should walk, bending one side, head, hand and foot, with the eyes contemplating on the purpose. Śakāra is to move with cūrṇa steps in pride, with unsteady body, touching the dress and ornaments often and looking at them repeatedly, the limbs unnaturally moving due to long garments and garlands. The persons of inferior caste should move looking about, avoiding the contact of other people. The Mlecchas should walk according to the manner of their lands. The gaits of lion, bear and monkey are according to that assumed by Viṣṇu in his man-lion incarnation, i.e., standing in Ālīḍha posture with limbs confirming to it, one hand on knee and the other placed on chest looking in all directions and the chin placed on the shoulder; the steps should be 5 tālas apart. At the time of entry on the stage and in the representation of vehicles etc. these gaits should be used. The gaits which are not mentioned here should be adopted from the popular usage.

The Gaits of Women etc.

The Sthānas of women in walking and in conversing with others are Āyata, Avahittha and Aśvakrānta.

1. *Āyata*—The right[1] foot is in Sama and the other placed obliquely at the side one tāla apart, the face bright, the bosom even and raised, one hand in Latā and the other reaching the hips. Uses—It is to be employed in first appearance on the stage, offering handful of flowers, anger due to jealous love, twisting the first finger, prohibiting, pride, profundity, silence, recourse to resentment, looking to horizon, calling, dismissal, observing closely, anxiety and dissimulation.

2. *Avahittha*—The left foot is in Sama, the right foot placed obliquely at its side one tāla apart, hips slightly raised, one hand in Latā and the other reaching the hips. Uses—It is employed in conversation, determination, satisfaction, cónjecture, bashfulness, amorousness, sportiveness, grace, looking towards oneself, awaiting husband's arrival and the Erotic sentiment.

3. *Aśvakrānta*—One foot is in Sama and the other bent on the forepart either ready for Sūcī or not. Uses—It is employed in faltering, reeling, taking a bunch of flowers and keeping it, fright, supporting the branch of a tree gracefully & holding the loosened garment.

The Sthāna will be maintained till the Cārī begins. The Sthāna should be Avahittha, the left hand pointing downwards and the right in Khaṭakāmukha placed at the region of the navel, then raising up the right foot one tāla gracefully it should be placed at the outer side of the left. At the same time, the left hand in Latā should be bent towards the right side and kept on the navel. Then placing the right hand on the hip and the left hand in Udveṣṭita, the left foot should be put forward; afterwards with the right hand in Latā to move 5 steps with body slightly bent

1. Cf. SR. VII 1066, 1067.

and the head gracefully held in Udvāhita. The procedure for moving about on the stage for men should be prescribed also for women, but the steps should not be of the duration of 6 or 8 kalās as that would be troublesome for women. This is the gait for young women. In the case of women of middle age and middle type, the Sthāna should be Avahittha, left hand placed on waist, right in upturned Arāla, placed between the bosom and the navel, with steady body, neither relaxed nor stiff. In the case of maid servants when excited, due to intoxication, the movement should be with slightly raised body and hands flourished after assuming the Avahittha position, with the left hand pointing downwards and the right in Khaṭakāmukha placed on the navel. The gaits of women of superior, middling and inferior types will be similar to those of the men of different types respectively. But the steps of women would be graceful. Children should move according to their will; grace and measure are not required in their case. Eunuchs should have the gait of women only. When there is a change of role, the man, woman or eunuch should move according to the new role they have assumed. For disguise, sport or deception, woman should act the role of man or vice versa. Woman should play the role of man by his dress, speech, action and movements with steadiness, liberality of spirit and intelligence. Man should play the role of woman by having her dress, speech and looks assuming delicate, languid gait. The women of inferior caste and the Pulinda and Śabara women should have gait natural to their community. The women observing vows, practising penance of religious sects and moving in the sky should move with Samapāda. The forceful Aṅgahāras, Cārīs or Maṇḍalas should not be assigned to women.

Sitting Postures—

1. *Sitting at ease*—The feet should be gracefully kept apart (rested and bent) as in Vaiśākhasthāna and the hips slightly raised, hands on the waist and thigh.

2. *Sitting in deliberation*—One foot should be stretched a little, the other resting on the seat and the head should be slightly bent to one side.

3. *Sitting in grief*—Hands should be supporting the chin and the head resting on the shoulder with the sense and mind lost.

4. *Sitting in fainting, intoxication, exertion, weariness and dejection*—The hands should be extended and the body loose, supported on bow etc.

5. *Sitting in sickness, shame, sleep and meditation*—All the limbs should be lumped together between legs and knees.

6. *Sitting in offering libation of water to dead parents, muttering incantations, making Ācamana (i.e. sipping water) etc.*—The waist should be raised up in which the hips and the heels come together.

7. *Sitting in pacifying the beloved and pouring ghee into the sacrificial fire etc.*—One of the stretched knees should be placed on the ground.

8. *Sitting in worshipping a deity, pacifying the angry ones, bitterly crying, seeing the dead, fear of persons of low spirit, begging by the low persons, and attendance during the sacrificial work*—The knees should be placed on the ground and the face should be downcast. Ascetics practising austerities should have this posture.

The seats are two-fold—bāhya, i.e., for all people in general and ābhyantara i.e. relating to the king.

Siṁhāsana, the lion seat is for gods and kings; cane seat for family priest and ministers; the muṇḍa seat for the commander and the crowned prince; wooden seat for Brahmins; carpet seat for other princes—these are the seats in the royal courts. In the case of the female characters there should be lion-seat for the chief queen, muṇḍa seat for other queens; cane seat for the wives of the family priest and ministers; cloth, skin or carpet seats for concubines; wooden seats for wives of Brahmins and the female ascetics and the pillow for the courtesans. All other women should sit on the ground. This is the procedure in the royal court. In society and in one's home one should have seats according to his will. The seats for ascetics and sectarians should be according to their order of vows. While pouring ghee into the sacrificial fire or performing the sacrificial duty or offering libation of water to the dear departed, one should sit on a seat made of kuśa grass, muṇḍa seat or cane seat. The local persons of noble birth and possessed of learning should be greeted by offering a seat by the kings. The equals should be offered equal seat, middling medium and the superiors more elevated seat and the inferiors the ground. Wise persons should sit on the ground or on wooden seat before the preceptor, the king and the elderly persons. They should sit together with him when going in a boat, riding an elephant or a chariot.

Postures for lying down—

1. *Ākuñcita*—Limbs should be narrowed down and knees stuck to bed; it is to be used by persons afflicted with cold.

2. *Sama*—The face should be turned up and hands free, dropping downwards; it is to be used in deep sleep.

3. *Prasārita*—One arm is used as pillow and the knees stretched; it is used in sleeping happily.

4. *Vivartita*—It is lying down with face downwards; it is used when wounded, dead, thrown, intoxicated and mad.

5. *Udvāhita*[1]—Head should be resting on the hand (or shoulder ?) and the elbow pressing (the ground); it is used in the graceful reclining of the master.

6. *Nata*—The shanks should be slightly stretched and both hands loose ; it is used in laziness, fatigue and distress.

Whatever is not mentioned here in connection with gaits and movements should be accomplished according to the need of the occasion.

Kakṣyā—

The various regions which are described by poets cannot be represented on the stage in reality. That is why, the Kakṣyās[2], i.e., the divisions of the stage are described. Making use of gaits etc. the various places are to be indicated. By moving round on the stage, the locality is to be indicated and the change of locality is also shown in the same manner. All the places in the three worlds which are described in the plot would be indicated in the particular divisions. In one of the three divisions, i.e., outside, inside or intermediate, the locality should be understood and the nearness or remoteness by the few or many rounds of movements respectively.

The same place would be a palace or a mountain by the peculiar gait described for ascending them etc. Those who have entered first are inside, those afterwards outside; those who are to unite with the ones entered first, should move with the gaits

1. Cf. SR. VII. 1120.
2. See Ch. IV., dealing with the theatre etc.

etc. towards them. This region is the middle zone. The person intending to visit those who have entered first should report himself turning to the right. The Eastern direction for the purpose of representation is that which faces the drummers and the doors of the green room. If any person has to make his exit on any business, the door for exit would be the same by which he has entered. If due to some purpose he is to go along with the other character and is to re-enter along with him, or by himself, another zone would be indicated, by moving round on the stage. One is to walk side by side with equals, and with the inferior ones, surrounded by them. Maid servants should be known by their walk before the master. According to the needs of the plot gods and demigods are to move to cities, forests, seas or mountains through the sky, by aerial car or through their divine power. They are to move on the ground when they are in disguise so that they are visible like human beings. The winkless eyes of gods should not be imitated as the states and sentiments in a play depend upon glances.

From the dress, language, manners and profession you can distinguish the individual as belonging to the particular region. This is called Pravṛtti (i.e., local usage). The dramatic action of the character is in harmony with the impression we gather about him. Hence, corresponding to the four styles of action, the Pravṛttis related to the people of different regions are described as four. The regions are divided broadly into four divisions taking into consideration the common characteristics possessed by them and overlooking the minor differences. They are Eastern, Western, Southern and Northern.

1. *Oḍhramāgadhī*—People in the Eastern India like Aṅga, Vaṅga, Kaliṅga, etc. have this Pravṛtti.

2. *Āvantī*—The people in the regions of Western India like Avantī, Vidiśā, Saurāṣṭra, etc. have this Pravṛtti which is characterised by Sāttvatī and Kaiśikī styles.

3. *Dākṣiṇātyā*—The southerners have abundance of Kaiśikī. They prefer music and dance and their gestures are clever and graceful. The people in the region that lies between southern ocean and the Vindhya mountain are to have this Pravṛtti.

4. *Pāñcālī*—The people in the Northern India like Pāñcāla, Śauraśena, Kāśmīra, those residing on Himālayas and countries

to the northern side of Ganges, have this Pravṛtti. They have Sāttvatī and Ārabhaṭī styles.

Moving round on the stage would be in two ways according to the local usages; entering by the right door and the left. Āvantī and Dākṣiṇātyā Pravṛtti characters should enter by the Northern door and Pāñcālī and Oḍhramāgadhī by the Southern, [e.g. the[1] Dākṣiṇātya character entering by the Northern door, should move round in the Western direction and then in the Southern, Eastern and Northern direction successively. He should report regarding the work etc. in the same direction and then moving round on the stage in the North, East, South and West successively he should exit by the Northern door; Pāñcālī Pravṛtti character, by the reverse of this; his entry and exit would be by the Southern door. The entry in this case would be near the character who is in the inner zone.] Local uses may be combined according to the need or the occasion. The regions which have the particular local usage should be related to the dramatic representation having their respective forms of action; (e.g., if[2] the hero is from Kāśmīra, Nāṭikā would be improper, for Kaiśikī is prominent in Nāṭikā which is specially related to Dākṣiṇātyas). In plays, they are combined also. In relation to their production, the plays are of two types—sukumāra (delicate) and āviddha (forceful). Āviddha performance has forceful Aṅgahāras[3] consisting of cutting, piercing, fight, magic, occult powers, artificial objects and dress and has many men and few women. Ḍima, Samavakāra, Vyāyoga and Īhāmṛga are to be produced in this manner. In these plays Gods, Dānavas and Rākṣasas would be the characters which are majestic, haughty, possessed of valour, energy and strength. Sukumāra has roles of human beings. Nāṭaka, Prakaraṇa, Bhāṇa, Vīthī and Aṅka are of the Sukumāra type.

Vācikābhinaya

The Recitation—

Even though the language of the play may be perfect, without its impressive utterance the effect would not be fully commu-

1. Cf. Abhinava—NŚ. Vol. II. pp. 210, 211.
2. *Ibid.* p. 211.
3. Aṅgahāra is a combination of 6 or 8 Karaṇas (i.e. dance-units).

nicated. Not only this, but the difference in utterance would cause a change of meaning, which would be out of place in that situation. It is possible to have the contrary feelings like respect and contempt to be produced by the help of modulation of voice. In this connection, the recitation is described to possess six qualities essential for the effective performance. They are Svaras (notes), Sthānas (voice registers), four Varṇas (the manner of uttering notes), Kāku (intonation), six Alaṁkāras and six Aṅgas. In the utterance of dramatic language the voice modulation is the main thing. All the other qualities help the effective modulation.

The notes are seven i.e. ṣaḍja, ṛṣabha, gāndhāra, madhyama, pañcama, dhaivata and niṣāda. These notes are to be used in different sentiments as follows—madhyama and pañcama in the Erotic and the Comic; ṣaḍja and ṛṣabha in the Heroic, the Furious and the Marvellous; gāndhāra and niṣāda in the Pathetic; and dhaivata in the Odious and the Terrible. Abhinava[1] makes clear the use of the seven notes in the recitation. These notes are musical when they are possessed of rakti (produced by the specific musical intervals between these notes). These specific distances are not expected in the recitation. Only the change of voice to suit the expression is essential. That is why, the manner of utterance as high and low etc. is clearly defined. What is meant by stating the use of the seven notes in the respective sentiments is to be understood as resorting to the aṁśa, i.e., the dominant note of the particular jāti in which the dhruvā is sung. If the use of seven notes is not understood in this manner there would be no difference in recitation and singing.

Sthāna—The voice with the modulations is produced from the chest, throat, and head which is mandra (low), madhya (medium) and tāra (high) respectively. In the lute all the small intervals are used for the musical effect. In the recitation these are not necessary. Only the difference in the voice as grave, medium or high is used for effect. When conversing with a distant person, the voice would be loud; when not far away, the medium; and when near, low. Now as regards the intonation, the speech should be begun in mandra, then reaching tāra, gradually, should end in madhya.

1. NŚ. Vol. II, pp. 385, 386.

Varṇas (accents)—

Abhinava explains that they are svaradharmas, i.e., qualities of sound. They are so called because they make clear the special meaning.[1] They are udātta (acute), anudātta (grave), svarita (circumflex), and kampita (quivering). Svarita and udātta are to be used in the Comic and the Erotic; udātta and kampita in the Heroic, the Furious and the Marvellous; and anudātta, svarita, and kampita in the Pathetic, the Odious and the Terrible.

Kāku (intonation)—

There are two ways of intonation—sākāṅkṣa (with expectancy) as the sense of the sentence is not completely expressed and nirākāṅkṣa (without expectancy) as the sentence is completely expressed. The former has notes from the throat and the breast and begins with a high pitch and ends in a low pitch and its Varṇa and Alaṁkāra are not complete; the latter has notes from the head beginning with a low pitch and ending in high pitch and its Varṇa and Alaṁkāra are complete.

The Alaṁkāras—

Ucca (high) proceeds from head and is of high pitch. It is used in speaking to anyone at a distance, in wonder, in rejoinder, in calling anyone from distance, in frightening anyone and in affliction etc.

Dīpta (excited) proceeds from head and is of higher pitch. It is used in reproach, quarrel, debate, indignation, yelling (abusive speech), defiance, anger, valour, pride, sharp and harsh words, lamentation, etc.

Mandra (grave) proceeds from the breast register and is used in despondency, weakness, anxiety, longing, low-spiritedness, sickness, deep wound from weapon, fainting, intoxication and communicating secret words etc.

Nīca (low) proceeds from the breast and is lower than mandra. It is used in natural speech, sickness, weariness due to austerity, falling down in panic, fainting, etc.

1. Cf. Abhinava

'वर्णा गुणा यदि वा पाठक्रियाविस्तारका विवृण्वते प्रकटयन्ति स्वार्थविशेषमिति वा ।'

NŚ. Vol. II, p. 390.

Druta (fast) proceeds from the throat and is fast. It is used by women soothing children and in fear, cold, fever, panicky condition and communicating urgent business.

Vilambita (slow) proceeds from the throat in slightly low pitch and is slow. It is used in love, pathos, deliberation, discrimination, jealous, anger, envy, speaking something indistinctly, bashfulness, anxiety, threatening, surprise, telling faults, prolonged sickness and harassment etc.

Mandra and Vilambita intonations should be used in words containing pleasant sense and expressing state of happiness; Dīpta and Ucca in words expressing sharpness and roughness. The Vilambita should be used in the Erotic, the Comic and the Pathetic and Dīpta or Ucca in the Heroic, the Furious and the Marvellous; Druta and Nīca in the Terrible and the Odious. Thus the intonation should be used to express the sentiments.

The Aṅgas—

1) Viccheda is separating due to pause; 2) Arpaṇa is recitation which as it were fills the auditorium with graceful modulation of voice; 3) Visarga is finishing a sentence; 4) Anubandha is the absence of separation between words or not taking breath while uttering them; 5) Dīpana is gradual augmentation of notes, charming in the three voice registers; and 6) Praśamana is the lowering of the notes of high pitch without making them discordant. Arpaṇa, Viccheda, Dīpana, and Praśamana are to be used in the Comic and the Erotic; Dīpana and Praśamana in the Pathetic; Viccheda, Praśamana, Dīpana and Anubandha in the Heroic, the Furious and the Marvellous and Viccheda and Visarga in the Odious and the Terrible. Mandra, madhya and tāra notes are to be employed in all these. One should not proceed from mandra to tāra or from tāra to mandra directly. The tempos resorted to in connection with the sentiments are three—druta (fast), madhya (medium) and vilambita (slow). The medium should be used in the Erotic and the Comic; slow in the Pathetic and fast in the Furious, the Marvellous, the Odious and the Terrible.

Virāma (pause)—

The pause should be after completion of meaning and not according to the metre as the meaning depends on the pause. It is found in practice that there occurs pause even after one, two, three or four syllables. In a play, words occur containing small number of syllables in cases of Sūcā and Aṅkura. That is why, care should be taken about pause. When the two hands are busy, the recitation should be with proper eye movements and with pause expressive of meaning. In the Heroic and the Furious, the hands are mostly busy with weapons; in the Odious they are contracted; in the Pathetic, hanging ; in the Comic, pointing to something ; in the Marvellous, motionless due to wonder and in the Terrible, motionless due to fear. When the hands are thus employed in these and other movements the meaning of the words is made definite by Alaṁkāras and pauses. Pauses prescribed in verses require Alaṁkāras. They should be used when the word meaning is complete or breath is exhausted, or when there is a long compound, quick utterance or confusion of many meanings. Pause should be observed at the end of the foot of a verse or according to breath. Otherwise, the pause should be observed according to meaning alone. The long syllables with ā e ai and au are to be used in sadness, argumentation, questioning, or indignation with one Kalā time. In the Vilambita pause, the syllables would be long, but the duration should not be of more than six Kalās. Or taking into consideration the particular incident etc. the pause should be observed in a verse to suit the sentiments and the state.

In the recitation of verse, the pauses arising out of foot division are to be used; but the learned should adjust them according to the meaning.

Ungrammatical word should never be recited and metre never spoiled. One should not pause where it is not prescribed and should not have excited utterance when sorrow is to be expressed.

The Alaṁkāras and the pauses which are prescribed in the recitation of Sanskrit should be resorted to by women in the recitation of Prakrit.

Sāmānyābhinaya (*Basic Representation*)

The Sāmānyābhinaya is defined as that which is presented by the head, the hand, the waist, the chest, the shanks and the thighs simultaneously. It is produced by the representation of speech, gestures and temperament. The superior histrionic representation has the exuberance of temperament ; in the medium, the temperament is adequate and in the inferior, it is lacking. Temperament is something invisible but it is the basis of states and endowed with proper sentiments by means of qualities like horripilation, tears and the like.

The mental mood, which pervades even the body, is called sattva. The sāttvika, as the attribute of the body, is seen in the superior characters only. The excellence of women results in the Erotic and that of men in the Heroic.

The feminine graces in youth are the support of sentiments in drama and they consist of changes in respect of their faces and other limbs. The natural change is of ten kinds and the involuntary, of seven kinds. Abhinava[1] mentions that these graces of women are pertaining to the body only and they are not of the nature of mental mood. They only convey the Rati. They are exuberent in youth, unmanifested in childhood and lost in old age. The physical graces are Bhāva, Hāva, and Helā, which arise from one another being different aspects of Sattva. Sattva (Temperament) partakes of the nature of the body, and Bhāva (Feeling) arises from Temperament, Hāva (Emotion) from Feeling and Helā (Passion) from Emotion. The explanation of Bhāva[2] is the same as is given in connection with the Rasa theory. Hāva manifests itself in the changes of eyes and eye-brows and the Recaka of neck, indicative of the Erotic sentiment. Helā is the Emotion arising out of the Erotic sentiment, expressing itself in graceful movements. The natural graces of women are as follows—

1. *Līlā*—It is imitating the behaviour of the beloved persons by means of speech, gestures, and ornaments, which are delightful and inspired by affection. It is the sportive mimicry.

2. *Vilāsa*—(amorous gestures)—These are the relevant changes of the special kind relating to the standing and sitting postures as well as to gait and movements of hands, eyes and eye-brows which occur at the sight of the beloved person.

1. NŚ. Vol. III. p. 154.
2. NŚ. VII. 2.

cf. DR. II. 33 p. 51. निर्विकारात्मकात्सत्त्वाद्भावस्तत्राद्यविक्रिया ॥

According to DR. Bhāva is the first (manifestation of) change in the nature that was unaffected previously.

3. *Vicchitti* (*a careless toilet*)—The great charm which arises out of the slightly careless placing of garlands, dress, ornament and unguents.

4. *Vibhrama* (*confusion*)—It is the inversion of various things such as speech, gestures, costume and temperament due to intoxication, passion and joy.

5. *Kilakiñcita* (*hysterical mood*)—It consists of frequent combinations of smiling, weeping, laughter, fear, sickness, fainting, sorrow and fatigue due to joy.

6. *Moṭṭāyita* (*manifestation of affection*)—It occurs through the sportive imitation, amorous gestures and the like when at the mention of the lover one gets absorbed in his thoughts.

7. *Kuṭṭamita* (*pretended anger*)—It is pretended distress even though actual joy is experienced. It is produced through joy and confusion when the hair, bosom or lower lip etc. are touched by the lover.

8. *Bibboka* (*affected coldness*)—It is the indifference which women show on account of vanity and pride after they have realised their cherished desire (i.e., winning the lover's heart).

9. *Lalita* (*lolling*)—It consists of the graceful movements of hands, feet, eye-brows, eyes, lips, etc. by women.

10. *Vihṛta* (*want of response*)—It occurs when women do not make any reply to the lover even though they have heard his words, due to bashfulness or pretence.

The involuntary graces—

1. *Śobhā* (*beauty*)—It is the decoration of limbs due to beautiful form, youth and loveliness heightened after the enjoyment (of love).

2. *Kānti* (*charm*)—Śobhā which is full of the passion of love is Kānti.

3. *Dīpti* (*radiance*)—It is high degree of charm.

4. *Mādhurya* (*delicacy*)—It results when the movement of limbs is moderate in conditions, which are dīpta and lalita.

5. *Dhairya* (*self-control*)—It is the natural mental condition which is not affected by rashness and is free from boasting in all matters.

6. *Prāgalbhya* (*boldness*)—It is the absence of agitation or nervousness, in practice (as in embrace etc.) of love.

7. *Audārya* (*courtesy*)—It is the courteous behaviour in all

situations. (Abhinava[1] explains it as not speaking harsh words even in intolerance, jealousy, anger, etc.)

These graces take place in the performance which is delicate on account of the theme of love. In the sentiment of love when there are exciting states like jealousy, anger, etc., excepting Vilāsa and Lalita others may be present.

The temperamental aspects in the case of males are eight—

1. *Śobhā (brilliant character)*—Expertness, heroism, energy, aversion to mean acts, ambition to acquire great merits constitute Śobhā.

2. *Vilāsa (grace)*—When the eyes move steadily, gait is like a bull, and there is a smile on the lips while speaking, it is Vilāsa.

3. *Mādhurya (self-possession)*—When even in the great changes the natural harmony of sense organs remains unchanged due to practice (of warfare, exercise etc.), it is called Mādhurya.

4. *Sthairya (tenacity)*—Not moving from one's undertaking relating to the duty, wealth or love, irrespective of its being produced from good or evil, is called Sthairya.

5. *Gāmbhīrya (gravity)*—When the outward changes in cases of anger, joy and fear are not noticed, it is Gāmbhīrya.

6. *Lalita (sportiveness)*—The amorous movements which are not deliberate and are of tender nature, constitute Lalita.

7. *Audārya (generosity)*—Making gifts, bestowing favours and speaking sweet words to enemies as well as to one's own people constitute Audārya.

8. *Tejas (spiritedness)*—Not tolerating the insult or reproach at the hands of the enemies, even at the cost of life, is Tejas.

The physical gesticulation is described as six-fold.

1. *Vākyābhinaya (gesticulation of words)*—It is the recitation of Prakrit and Sanskrit speech composed in verse and prose, possessing meaning full of various sentiments.

2. *Sūcā*—When the meaning of a sentence is first indicated by temperament and gestures and then there is Vākyābhinaya, it is called Sūcā.

1. NŚ. Vol. III, p. 163.

3. *Aṅkura*[1]—When one skilfully represents by gestures like Sūcā the words which one has in his mind, it is called Aṅkura.

4. *Śākhā*—It is the gesticulation relating to limbs as already explained in the beginning of Āṅgikābhinaya.

5. *Nāṭyāyita*—It is the indicative histrionic representation which is employed in a drama with different practices for the sake of enlivening time, lasting till the coming together of the characters on the stage. The histrionic representation of the 'dhruvās' relating to the states and sentiments effected by means of delineating joy, anger, grief, and the like is also to be known as Nāṭyāyita. Abhinava[2] explains it in the first case as when there is a play within a play also. As regards the dhruvās he says that there is no gesticulation of each and every word but there is gesticulation of the major and minor limbs and temperament indicating joy etc.

6. *Nivṛttyaṅkura*—It occurs when one represents words spoken by other person by Sūcā.

Sense objects should be represented in the following manner—

1. *Sound*—It should be represented by side-long glance, bending the head side-ways and putting the first finger near the ear;

2. *Touch*—It should be indicated by the eyes slightly narrowed, eyebrows raised and touching the shoulder and the cheek;

3. *Form*—It should be represented by holding the Patāka hands on the head and moving the face slightly, looking intently with the eyes;

4. *Taste and* 5. *Smell*—They should be indicated by eyes slightly contracted, nostrils expanded with exhalation when they are favourable.

The favourable attitude of the mind should be represented

1. Cf. NŚ. Vol. III, pp. 170-171. Abh. explains Aṅkura by illustrating the gesticulation by Sāgarikā in Act I of Ratnāvalī, when she enacts collecting flowers after saying "I shall also collect flowers and worship Madana." This gesticulation of collecting flowers peculiar to Sāgarikā would be different from that of an ascetic. Cf. SR. VII—38. According to SR. in Sūcī the gesticulation (by hand) would precede the speech, while in Aṅkura, follow the speech.

2. NŚ. Vol. III, pp. 172-173.

by happy movements of limbs, horripilation and blooming of the face. When the unfavourable attitude is to be represented the head should be turned back, eyes and nostrils contracted and one should not look (toward the sense objects). The indifference should be shown by middle state, i.e., not expressing either too much delight or too much abhorrence.

Various types of women are described next as they are indeed the source of happiness. The types possess the nature of gods, demons, gandharvas, etc. and also birds, goblins, tigers, monkeys and such animals. After knowing a woman's nature one should approach her accordingly. According to dramatic convention, the enjoyment of love is two-fold:—ābhyantara—relating to kings in Nāṭaka and bāhya, relating to courtesans in Prakaraṇa. The women are of three classes—bāhyā (courtesan), ābhyantarā (noble, high-born) and bāhyābhyantarā (purified courtesan). The king should be united with ābhyantarā and divine courtesan, others with courtesans. The signs of courtesan's love are, casting sidelong glances, touching ornaments, itching the ears, scratching the ground with toes, showing the breast and the navel, cleansing the nails and binding the hair. Those of a highborn lady are, smiling eyes, steady gaze, concealed smile and speaking slowly with downcast eyes, replying with a smile, concealing her sweat, lower lip throbbing and nervousness.

Various stages of love to be represented are, longing, anxiety, recollection, enumeration of the lover's merits, distress, lamentation, madness, sickness, stupor and death.

Eight kinds of heroines are described according to the science of the Erotics.

1) *Vāsakasajjikā (dressed up for union)*—When the conjugal union is due, the heroine in the eager expectation of love's pleasure decorates herself joyfully.

2) *Virahotkaṇṭhitā (distressed by separation)*—She is a heroine whose lover does not turn up due to his pre-occupation with many other engagements and makes her sad.

3) *Svādhīnabhartṛkā (having the husband under subjection)*—She is a heroine whose husband is by her side as he is attached to her and thus has the great joy of her good luck.

4) *Kalahāntaritā (separated by quarrel)*—She is a heroine

whose lover does not turn up having left her due to jealousy or quarrel and hence she becomes intolerant.

5) *Khaṇḍitā* (*enraged*)—She is a heroine whose lover does not turn up when the conjugal union is due, owing to his attachment for other woman and thus she is distressed by his not coming.

6) *Vipralabdhā* (*the deceived*)—She is a lady whose lover does not come to her for a certain reason even though the appointment was made through the female messenger.

7) *Proṣitabhartṛkā* (*whose husband is on travel*)—She is a heroine whose husband has gone abroad on account of various duties; she wears her hair hanging loose.

8) *Abhisārikā*, is the woman who due to her love or infatuation is attached to the lover and gives up modesty in going out to meet him.

The eight types of heroines are to be represented thus—Khaṇḍitā, Vipralabdhā, Proṣitabhartṛkā, and Kalahāntaritā should gesticulate anxiety, sighs, dejection, burning of the heart, conversation with female friends, looking to one's own condition, weakness, depression, tears, appearance of anger, giving up of ornaments and toilet, sorrow and weeping.

Svādhīnapatikā should have gaudy and brilliant dress, face beaming with joy and excess of physical charm.

Abhisārikā—i) The courtesan should go to the lover with body beautifully decorated with various ornaments, walking slowly in the company of her attendants, with passion and joy, having delicate movements and intoxication; ii) the noble lady should go covering her face with a veil, walking timidly with limbs contracted, with face bent down (looking back often); iii) a maid should walk to her lover with uneven steps and eyes beaming with amorous joy and talking disconnectedly in intoxication. After going in this manner, if the lover is sleeping, the noble lady should awaken him with ornaments, the courtesan with cool scents and the maid by fanning him with her cloth. The superior and the middling types of women are not to gesticulate on the stage wearing of garment, bath, application of unguents and collyrium, tying of hair, use of meagre dress or one garment only and dyeing of the lower lip.

The inferior ones may do all this. But on certain occasions they too should not represent these.

The lying on bed should not be represented on the stage. The act should be ended by some meaningful speech. If due to some reason the lying down is to be represented, then kissing, embracing, tooth-bite, nail-cut, loosening the knot of the lower garment and pressing the bosom are not to be shown. Meals, watersport, and whatever is shameful should not be enacted on the stage as the play is to be witnessed by the father and the son, the daughter-in-law and the mother-in-law, i.e., the whole family together. The dealings with courtesans are treated by Bharata in detail in connection with the bāhyanāṭya. The courtesan is either in love or without love. After understanding the feeling or its want in women, one should approach them according to the methods mentioned in the science of love. The dealings with courtesans as described, should be used in Prakaraṇa and Nāṭaka in suitable proportions.

Citrābhinaya (Special representation of particular objects and ideas) :

The peculiarity required at times of the representation through gestures etc. which was not mentioned before is described under Citrābhinaya.

To indicate morning and evening, day and night, sky, seasons, clouds, large lakes, interiors of forests, directions, planets and the stars and anything that is slightly fixed (in the sky), both the hands are raised in Patāka and Svastika position and the head is upturned, using various glances. The objects on the ground are to be indicated with the same gestures of the hands and the head, by looking downwards. The moonlight, happiness, wind, flavour and smell should be gesticulated by gestures representing touch and horripilation. To indicate the sun, dust, smoke and wind, one is to cover one's face with clothes. Heat of the ground and of any other kind should be indicated by desire for shady place. The midday sun should be indicated by looking up with half closed eyes and the rising and setting of the sun by representing the sense of wonder. To indicate objects pleasant and happy, one should touch limbs, having horripilation and those of sharp nature one should not touch the limbs and show uneasiness and show narrowing of the mouth. The objects or the ideas which are grave and noble should be gesticulated with limbs having Sauṣṭhava and with pride and conceit. The Arāla hands kept in the place where sacred thread is held and then separated from Svastika position would indicate objects like necklace and garlands. The idea of entirety should be shown by moving the first finger, looking round and pressing the Alapadma hand. To indicate any thing audible or visible whether it relates to the person speaking or spoken to or anyone else, one should point to the ears and eyes respectively. Lightening, shooting stars, thunder and sparks of fire should be represented by frightened limbs and twinkling of eyes. To indicate anything undesired, hands should be in Udveṣṭita and Parāvṛtta, head bent, looking obliquely and avoiding[1] contact. Hot wind, darkness and lustre are to be gesticulated by covering the face and dust, rains, insects and bees are to be warded off by covering the face; lions, bears, monkeys, tigers and other beasts of prey are to be indicated by Padmakośa hands pointing downwards in Svastika position; in saluting the elders the Tripatākā hand should be in Svastika; and in holding up whip the hand should be in Khaṭaka and Svastika. The numbers upto ten should be indicated by fingers and multiples of ten, hundred and thousand by two Patāka hands. The umbrellas, banners, banner-staffs and various weapons should be shown by holding a staff; memory and meditation by fixed attention, downcast eyes, head slightly bent and the left hand in Sandaṁśa. The representation of offspring should be by head in Udvāhita and hands in Haṁsapakṣa held on the right side. The past, completion, destruction and words uttered in weariness should be indicated by taking left hand in Arāla to the head. Each season should be indicated by the characteristic, costume, activity or the scenery which is proper to it.

In the representation of their own nature men should assume Vaiṣṇava posture and women, Āyata or Avahittha. But due to special occasion the other postures may be used in the representation of the various states in different types of plays. The movements of men should be characterised by sportive and

1. Cf. NŚ. Vol. III, p. 268. F.N. 1 ज—असंस्पर्शात्तथानिष्टं–

patient physical actions and of women by delicate and sportive Aṅgahāras.

The parrots, sārikās and small birds should be indicated by the fingers of the Tripatāka hand moving and big ones like peacocks, cranes, swans, etc. by appropriate Recakas and Aṅgahāras; ass, camel, elephants, tigers, etc. by appropriate gaits and gestures; ghosts, demons, etc. by Aṅgahāras when absent (i.e., in narrating their actions) and when they are present, by fear, dismay and astonishment; gods when not present, by their characteristic marks, making obeisance or by movements suitable to the states: greeting a person who is not present, by touching the head with the Arāla hand raised up; the deities, superiors and ladies by Khaṭakā-vardhamāna or Kapota hand; gods and honourable persons when present by obeisance to them and by their deep influence; mountain and tall trees are to be indicated by lifting upwards the out-stretched hands. A swing should be indicated by swinging movements, agitation of limbs and holding the string. When the swing is directly present as fashioned by model work, the swinging should be done realistically, riding on the seat. The meaning of the words uttered in sleep (or dream) should not be represented by hands. The recitation in sleep should be with slow voice, the words, sometimes distinct and sometimes indistinct and the meaning of the word repeated twice depending on the recollection of the past. The recitation of the old people should be with faltering voice with some syllables dropped, that of children should have incomplete syllables and sweet voice.

Secret words are to be whispered in the ear; when some past incident is to be repeated due to necessity, it should also be spoken in the ear to avoid repetition.

Conventions of speech are four—

1. *Ākāśavacana* (*or Ākāśabhāṣita*)—It is the speech when the person addressed to is not on the stage. The dialogue is carried by uttering words in reply.

2. *Ātmagata* (*or Svagata*)—The words in the heart are given vent to. It is loud thinking.

3. *Apavāritaka*—The speech is connected with secrecy.

1. The Recakas are given in Appendix B.

4. *Janāntika*—The persons standing close by are not supposed to listen to the words spoken to some one else due to the need of the play.

Abhinava[1] explains the difference between Apavāritaka and Janāntika as follows—In the former, the speech is concealed from all others as it is intended to be listened to by the particular character, while in the latter it is concealed from the particular character only. It is 'aside' made to avoid a single character on the stage.[2] The Tripatākahasta is to intervene the speaker. Prakāśa, i.e., 'aloud' is not mentioned by Bharata. It comes after Svagata.

Prof. N. B. Purohit[3] has considered the difference in acting and stage effect of these conventions. He says that as regards Janāntika and Apavārita in the former, two of the many characters are talking apart and in the latter, care is taken to see that they are not over-heard. There would be modulation of voice and effort to conceal. The Apavārita makes a deliberate attempt to enlist the sympathy of the audience and becomes to that extent, a telling (kathana) of the private opinion (rahasya) to another (anyasya); and it differs from the Janāntika because it makes a deliberate attempt to avoid over-hearing or conceal the talk from another character on the stage and becomes, in that sense, a rahasyakathana.

Principal[4] Karmarkar has discussed the terms Janāntika and Apavārita. He says that when 'apavārya' is used the character has actually to turn away and the speech is heard by

1. NŚ. Vol. III, p. 281

'...सर्वेषां यन्निगूह्यते एक एव शृणुयादिति तदपवारितं जनान्तिकम्
एकान्तिकत्वं चैकस्यैव निगूह्यत इति विशेषः

2. Cf. DR.

'त्रिपताकाकरेणान्यानपवार्यान्तरा कथाम् ॥
अन्योन्यामन्त्रणं यत्स्याज्जनान्ते तज्जनान्तिकम् ।
रहस्यं कथ्यतेऽन्यस्य परावृत्यापवारितम् ॥

DR. I—65-66.

3. The Apavārita speech in Sanskrit Drama—by Prof. N.B. Purohit A.I.O.C. 1937, pp. 421-435.

4. Cf. The Dramatic Terms—जनान्तिकम् and अपवारितम्, by Principal R.D. Karmarkar.

A.B.O.R.I. Vol. XXXV, pp. 122-128.

one or more characters on the stage, excluding those to whom the 'turning away' refers. In Janāntika the persons on the stage are excluded by the raising of the hand with the three fingers stretched; the speech must be by way of interpreting the matter in hand and it must be addressed to a particular person by name and the speech must be replied to by the person addressed who also has to address the first, by name. In several editions of Sanskrit plays both these are seen used promiscuously. In Janāntika two speeches are involved. The stage direction may be used only at the beginning of the first speech but the idea in Janāntika becomes complete only when the second speech is uttered. In Apavārita the speech is addressed to no one in particular. Principal Karmarkar says further that the audience could not have as a rule considered the use of Tripatāka hand necessary for the purpose of understanding the Janāntika nature of the speeches concerned.

From the explanations given in the NŚ. it seems that in Apavārita the speech is concealed from all others on the stage, as it is connected with secrecy, while in Janāntika it is concealed from the particular ones only.

The dramatic composition which does not possess all the constituents and hence is defective like Prahasana need not be enacted with the conventions as per the Śāstra. Movements and gaits prescribed by the rules for a character who has entered the stage should be maintained by the actor, keeping up the temperament till he makes his exit.

Abhinava[1] mentions representation of some other objects and ideas like god Skanda, goddess Sarasvatī etc. according to the view of Kohala and others.

Āhāryābhinaya (the Extraneous Representation)—

The characters of the various types when indicated first by dress and make-up, accomplish the representation easily by means of gestures and the like. The production of the play depends on Āhārya. Abhinava[2] says that it is like wall for the painting in the form of the performance with all the representation. Even though all the other histrionic representation is

1. Cf. NŚ. Vol. III pp. 287-291.
2. NŚ. Vol. III p 109

absent, the particular character is determined by the special dress and make-up. Āhārya indicates something which is external. The other three forms of gesticulation are connected with the actor's physique but the Āhārya is something that is externally added.

It is four-fold—Pusta (the model work), Alaṁkāra (decoration), Aṅgaracanā (painting of body) and Sajjīva (living creatures)

Pusta is again three-fold:

1. *Saṁdhima* (*joined*)—It is the model work which is made up of birch, bamboo, skin, cloth and the like.

2. *Vyājima*[1] (*mechanically devised*)—It is made by means of a mechanical device.

3. *Veṣṭima*[2] (*wrapped*)—It is produced by wrapping. Hills, carriages, celestial cars, shields, armours, banners, elephants (or trees) which are constructed for use in a dramatic performance, are called model works.

Alaṁkāra includes flower garlands, ornaments and drapery. The flower garlands are of five types—

1. *Veṣṭima*—In this along with flowers, leaves and green grass are woven decoratively;

2. *Vitata*—In it many garlands are mutually put together.

3. *Saṅghātya*—In it the thread is woven through the flowers, or many bunches of flowers are woven together.

4. *Granthima*—In it the flowers are knitted together with knots.

5. *Prālambita*—It is long garland hanging down.

Ornaments—

1. *Āvedhya* (*to be pierced*)—the ear ornaments and the like, to be fixed by piercing the limbs;

2. *Bandhanīya* (*to be tied*)—girdle and arm band;

3. *Kṣepya* (*to be put upon*)—anklets and decorations of dress ;

1. NŚ. Vol. III. p. 109.

Abh. explains it as व्याज: सूत्रस्याकर्षादिरूप: क्षेपस्तेन निर्वृत्तो व्याजिमः, i.e., formed by pulling the rope etc.

2. NŚ. Vol. III, p. 110.

Abh. explains it as उपरि जतुसिक्थकादिना वेष्टस्तेन निर्वृत्तो वेष्टिमः, i.e. formed by wrapping over with lac, bee-wax, etc.

4. *Āropya (to be put round the neck)*—golden neck-chain and various necklaces.

The ornaments of men and women are to be used according to the fashion of the region and the caste.

Ornaments of the Divine and Royal males—

Ornaments of the head—Cūḍāmaṇi (crest-jewel) is to be worn on the top of the head, Mukuṭa (the crown), above the forehead.

Ornaments of the ear—Kuṇḍala (earring) to be worn in the lower lobe of the ear; Mocaka (ear pendant) in the central part of the ear and Kīlā, at the top of the ear.

Ornaments of the neck—Muktāvali (pearl necklace), Harṣaka (having the shape of a snake etc.), Sūtraka (golden neck-chain).

Ornaments of the fingers—Vetikā (golden ring) and Aṅgulimudrā (ring with various designs like bird, lotus etc.)

The ornaments of the forearm are Hastalī and Valaya; of the wrist, Rucaka (bracelet) just on the wrist and Cūlikā above it; of the upper arm, Keyūra (armlet) and Aṅgada (armband) to be worn above Keyūra; of the breast, Trisara (pearl necklace with three strings) and Hāra (necklace). The suspended pearl necklace and the flower garland are meant for the body. The Talaka (below the navel) and Sūtraka (still lower) are meant for the waist.

Ornaments for females—

Head—Śikhāpāśa, Śikhāvyāla, Piṇḍīpatra, Cūḍāmaṇi, Makarikā, and Muktājāla. Abhinava explains Śikhāvyāla as that in which the image of serpent was formed like the pericarp of the flower at the centre and round it the Piṇḍīpatra was formed by circular leaves like petals. Cūḍāmaṇi was to be worn at the centre of the head, then Makarapatra and then the pearlnet reaching the forehead. [Veṇīguccha appears to be an ornament to be tied to the braided hair.]

Ear—Kuṇḍala, Karṇikā, Karṇavalaya, Patrakarṇikā, Karṇamudrā (entwining the ear), Karṇotkīlaka (ear-top), Śikhipatra (ear ornament studded with multi-coloured jewels, in the shape of peacock feather), various kinds of Dantapatras (of ivory) set with jewels and Karṇapūra.

Neck—Muktāvalī (pearl necklace), Vyālapaṅkti (ornament

1. NŚ. Vol. III, pp. 112-113.

with snake motif), Mañjarī, Ratnamālikā (jewelled necklace), Ratnāvalī (bigger jewelled necklace), Sūtraka (the necklace with 2, 3 or 4 strings) as well as golden chain.

Upper arm—Aṅgada (arm band) and Valaya (arm ring).

Breast—Necklaces of artistic variety.

Bosom—Jewelled net.

Fore arm—Kharjūraka and Socchitika.

Fingers—Kaṭaka, Kalāpī, Śaṅkha, Hastapatra & Mudrāṅgulīyaka.

Hips—Talaka (set with network of pearls), Mekhalā (girdle with 8 strings), Kāñcī (girdle with one string), Raśanā (girdle with 16 strings) and Kalāpa (with 25 strings).

Pearlnecklaces of the divine and the royal females should be of 32, 64 or 108 strings.

Ankles—Nūpura (to be worn below the knee), Kiṅkiṇī (with small bells), Ghaṇṭikā, Ratnajālaka and gingling Kaṭakas.

Shanks—Pādapatra.

Toes—Toerings and Tilaka for the big toe.

There should not be a use of heavy ornaments. For, this would cause fatigue to actors. Hence, the golden ornaments should have only the thin covering of gold. The jewels should be studded in lac so that they would not cause exhaustion. Ornaments of the divine ones should be according to their will. In the case of human beings they should be worn with special attention.

The dress and decoration etc. of various females—

Vidyādharī—Hair tied in top-knot, decorated with ornaments of many pearls, clothes white.

Yakṣī and Apsaras—Jewelled ornaments with similar dress; the former should have only Śikhā.

Nāgī—Ornaments abounding in pearls and jewels. (The Nāgīs should have hoods over their heads.)

Munikanyā—A single braid of the hair, no use of ornaments, dress befitting the forest life.

Siddha women—Ornaments abounding in pearls and emeralds and dress, yellow.

Gandharvī—Ornaments abounding in rubies, lute in their hand and clothes of saffron colour.

Rākṣasī—Ornaments of sapphires, teeth white, dress black.

Goddesses—Ornaments of lapis lazuli and pearls, dress green like the colour of parrot's tail.

Divyavānarī—(divine female monkey) Ornaments of topaz and sometimes vaiḍūrya also, dress blue.

These are the dresses of celestial women in love making. In other conditions, the dress should be white.

Women on earth should be dressed according to their countries. Āvantī ladies should have curly hair; Gauḍī, mostly curls having Śikhāpāśa and braid of hair; Ābhīra women, two braids of hair and deep blue garment; women of northeast, Śikhaṇḍa held up and hair covered by garment; women of south, ullekhya,[1] kumbhi-bandhaka[2] and āvartalalāṭika.[3]

On the forehead tilaka mark with many artistic touches should be painted and the design above the eye-brows should have semblance of flowers. On the cheeks tilaka and patralekhā (drawing of decorative designs with scented pigments) should be there. Collyrium should be applied to the eyes and lips dyed red. The four front teeth should be white or dyed variously for when they are coloured, their beauty is enhanced. They should be coloured like pearls in the case of young girls or red like lotus leaves. When dyed in emerald colour the beauty of tender leaves is obtained by the lower lip.

The women whose lovers have gone abroad and those that are afflicted with calamity should have one braid of hair and the dress soiled. Those who are separated from lovers should have white dress, a few ornaments and disregard for cleanliness. Women's dress should be white in religious activity.

Male costume—

It is of three types—Śuddha (white), Citra (variegated) and Śyāma (soiled). Śuddha dress should be used when going to temples, while observing some auspicious rite or a vow, at the

1. Ullekhya seems to be tattoo.
2. Tying of hair in a small-jar-like shape?
3. Cf. Kumārasambhava. V. 55 ... 'ललाटिकाचन्दनधूसरालका ।'

Mallinātha explains ललाटिका as ललाटस्थालंकारः तिलकः ।

Śabdakalpadruma gives it as स्वर्णादिरचितललाटाभरणम् ।

It appears to be an ornamental mark made by sandal on the forehead, or an ornament to be worn on the forehead.

time of the conjunction of the particular day and the stars, at the marriage time and whenever any religious activity is to be performed. The Citra dress should be used in the case of gods, demons, yakṣas, gandharvas, nāgas and kings of amorous nature. Śuddha is meant for chamberlain, elderly Brahmins, merchants, ministers, priests, ascetics, kṣatriyas, vaiśyas and royal officers. Malina is meant for lunatics, intoxicated persons, travellers, and those in calamity. For Śuddha and Citra costume the lower and upper garments should be white and variegated respectively: and in Malina they should be soiled. The sages, Jain and Buddhist monks should have their dress according to their rules. Ascetics should wear tattered garments or bark or skin garments. Wandering ascetics & great sages should have kaṣāya (saffron-coloured) garment. Pāśupata should have variegated dress. The person guarding the harem and the lower people should wear saffron-coloured tailored garment. Warrior's dress should be suited for the battle, with brilliant weapons, armour, quiver and bow. Kings should have always variegated dress. When there is ominous appearance of any star or observance of auspicious rite their dress should be white.

Make-up—Aṅgaracanā :

The painting should be effected first and then the dresses according to the habitation and condition should be put on. The four original colours are, black, blue, yellow and red. The derivative colours are to be prepared by mixing them proportionately. They are Pāṇḍu (yellowish white); Kāpota (pigeon colour—white and blue); Padma (lotus colour—white and red); Harita (green—yellow and blue); Kaṣāya (violet—blue and red); Gaura (yellowish red—red and yellow). By mixing three or four colours many other shades may be prepared. In the mixture, the ratio of the strong colour to the weak should be one to two; in the case of the blue it should be one to four, for blue is the strongest of all colours. Thus knowing these rules of colours, the body should be painted. When one's own form is thus covered, with the change of dress, it is called vartanā, i.e., change of personality of the dramatic characters according to dramatic conventions. By the colours, together with the dress, one's original complexion is to be concealed and the form is so created that it resembles the particular character. Just as a creature enters another body giving up his own and resorts to the nature of the other one, so also the man covered with dress and make-up takes upthe role of the other whose dress he has put on. The different characters are to be painted as follows—

Gods, Yakṣas and divine nymphs are to be painted Gaura ; Rudra, Arka, Druhiṇa and Skanda, with golden colour ; Soma, Bṛhaspati, Śukra, Varuṇa, stars, Samudra, Himavat, Gaṅgā and Balarāma, white ; Mars, red ; Budha, Hutāśana (Fire), yellow ; Nārāyaṇa, Nara and Vāsuki, Śyāma; demons, goblins, mountains, Yama[1] and sky, dark blue. The men in six Dvīpas have colour of burnished gold but in Jambudvīpa, the men of various colours live. All but those who live in Uttarakuru should have golden colour. The people of Bhadrāśva should have white and Ketumāla, blue. Gandharva, Yakṣa, Pannaga, Vidyādhara and Pitṛs should be of various colours. In Bhāratavarṣa, the kings should have lotus colour, yellowish white or dark blue; happy men should be of yellowish red. Those practising wicked acts, possessed of evil spirits, diseased, engaged in penance, those whose work entails extreme physical work and those of inferior birth like Dhīvara, Ḍomba etc. should be painted black. The sages should have the colour of Badara (plum) and those engaged in penance should be black. The colour should be used according to the need of the situation, country and birth. Kirāta, Barbara, Āndhra, Draviḍa, Kāśī, Kosala, Pulinda and Dākṣiṇātya should be generally black. Śaka, Yavana, Pallava, Bāhlīka and those in the northern region should be generally Gaura; Pāñcāla, Śaurasena, Māhiṣa, Oḍramāgadha, Aṅga, Vaṅga, and Kaliṅga should be dark blue. Brahmins and Kṣatriyas should be Gaura ; Vaiśya and Śūdra, Śyāma.

The application of beards should be according to the region, condition and age. It is of four kinds—Śuddha (shaven), Śyāma (dark), Vicitra (smartly done) and lomaśa (hairy). The first should be in the case of religious mendicants, ministers and priests, those indifferent to sexual pleasure and those initiated for some vow. The Vicitra should be in the case of divine males, the kings, princes, king's officers, amorous persons and proud young persons. Śyāma should be employed in the case of those who

1. NŚ. Vol. III, p. 125. F.N. 5 इ यम आकाशं

are unhappy, struck by calamity and those that have not fulfilled their promises. Lomaśa should be in the case of sages, ascetics, men observing long lasting vows and those wearing tattered garments.

In the Furious[1] sentiment the body should be dripping in blood, mouth should be moistened with it and pieces of flesh in the hands. The demonic character should have huge physical frame with many heads and many hands, holding weapons of various kinds. In the case of the sentiment[2] of laughter, the Vidūṣaka should be covered with tattered clothes or skin or smeared with lamp black, ashes or reddish ochre. The teeth should be big ; hunch in the back, lameness, distorted face, baldness etc. may be employed. Lifeless objects, e.g., mountain, palace, mechanical contrivances, shield, armour, banner, rivers and various weapons should have bodily form according to necessity with suitable dress and speech as per the dramatic convention (e.g. weapons of Viṣṇu in Bālacarita of Bhāsa, rivers in Uttararāmacarita.)

Pratiśiras (*crowns and masks etc.*)—

Crowns should be used for Gods and kings. They are of three types : Pārśvāgata, Mastakin and Kirīṭa. The first is to be used in the case of Gods (in general), Gandharvas, Yakṣas, Pannagas and Rākṣasas ; second in the case of middling Gods and the third in the case of superior Gods. In the case of inferior Gods Pārśvāgata should be used. The Mastakin[3] should be employed in the case of kings. The Keśamukuṭa (with the locks of hair tied) should be used in the case of Vidyādhara, Siddha and Cāraṇa.

Masks should be employed in the case of Rākṣasas and Demons. They should have tawny hair and green beard. For the superiors amongst the Demons, Pārśvāgata should be used. Crowns are to be used when the head is shaven as in the case of sacrifice and when the hair are not long. Half crowns should be used in the case of commanders, princes and Mahāmātras. Ministers, Kāñcukīya, leaders of the guilds of merchants and priests should have turbans. The head of the goblins, mad men and ascetics

1. Cf. NŚ. XII 50-51.
2. *Ibid.* 138, 141.
3. NŚ. Vol. III, p. 132. F. N.5 भ—तथा मस्तकिनो

should have long hair. The heads should be shaven in the case of Śākya, Śrotriya, Nirgrantha, Parivrājaka and those initiated for vows or sacrifice. For other sects the head should be shaven or should have long or short hair according to their vows. The amorous people, rogues, and king's officers should have curly hair. The boys should have three tufts of hair. The sages should have matted hair. The Ceṭa (menial) should have triśikha (having three locks of hair on the head) or shaven head. Vidūṣaka's head should be bald or should have kākapada[1] (i.e., a hair-cut resembling crow's foot in shape).

Masks are to be used when characters with two or three heads etc. are to be represented, or when the character covering his own face manifests that of the other. As regards the artificial hands and legs, they should be prepared according to the necessity. The ghaṭī of the mask should be 32 aṅgulas in measure or of appropriate measure and should be prepared out of bilva paste and cloth or bark of trees etc. The mask should be made with ashes or husk of paddy mixed with bilva paste. Then it should be covered with the strips of cloth smeared with bilva paste. The ghaṭī should not be too thick nor too thin nor too slender. After drying it, the holes are to be made (for ear, nose, etc.) dividing it into two halves. The opening for forehead should be six aṅgulas by one-half aṅgula (or one ?) having angles at the two ends ; and for cheeks two aṅgulas by 1½ aṅgulas. The hole for the ear (and also for the mouth) should be three aṅgulas. The symmetrical portion of the neck should be 12 aṅgulas. Various forms of crowns set with jewels are to be fixed on them.

The different weapons like kunta, śataghnī, bow, etc. are described in details with their measurements etc. The details of jarjara also are given. The masks and crowns, chatra, cāmara, banner and bhṛṅgāra are described as the accessories.

Sajjīva means the entrance of the animals on the stage. They are four-footed, two-footed and footless. Abhinava[2] explains that when the Nāgāstra is to be used the image of serpent should be shown, in the Nṛsiṁhāstra the man-lion form should be represented etc.

1. Cf. Abhinava— काकपक्षवद्यत्र केशविच्छेदः । NŚ. Vol. III, p. 134.

2. NŚ. Vol. III, p. 135.

The accessories in the dramatic art are the imitation of the reality. The palaces, houses, or conveyances and various weapons cannot be prepared as they are found in the reality. The natural form is realistic, while the deviation from it will be conventional. The objects in the dramatic performance should not be made of iron or such other material. They would be heavy and would cause exhaustion. The objects should be light-fashioned out of wood, skin, cloth, lac and bamboo pieces. To represent the objects like shields, armour, banners, mountain, palaces, temples, horses, elephants, vehicles, aerial cars and houses, the skeletons should be made first of bamboo pieces. Then, covering them by appropriately painted cloth, the likeness of such objects should be produced. If cloth is not available then fine palm leaves or birch etc. should be used. Similarly, various weapons should be prepared with glass and bamboo slices and various forms with lac and bhāṇḍa. Imitation legs, heads, hands and skin should be fashioned with grass, birch, bamboo, bhāṇḍa[1] etc. Various articles may be prepared with clay. Various flowers and fruits should be prepared with bhāṇḍa, cloth, bee-wax and lac ; ornaments with bhāṇḍa, cloth, bee-wax, copper-sheets, mica-sheets and blue colour. The jewels should be fashioned with coloured mica sheet having the basis of copper (or bhāṇḍa).[2] The various crowns should be bright with mica sheets shining like jewels. All these should be used according to the direction of the expert teacher.

In battle, personal combat, dance and casting glances, a person burdened with heavy weight will feel fatigue and faint and thus the performance may be spoiled. One may even endanger his life with the difficult movements under the heavy weight. Hence, the ornaments should be made of bhāṇḍa, bee-wax, copper sheets and coloured mica sheets. The actual release of weapons should not be used on the stage nor cutting or piercing by weapon. It should only be indicated by gesture, or one may be allowed to

1. NŚ. Vol. III, p. 142. Abhinava—भाण्डैरिति अलाबुदलखण्डादिभिः । भाण्ड—fragment of gourd etc. ?

The other reading for भाण्ड is भेण्ड. In Marathi भेण्ड is a kind of frail light wood.

2. Cf. NŚ. Vol. III, p. 143; F.N. ९भ

release missiles on the stage if he has enough practice and skill (of course, causing no hurt).

Thus the NŚ. has treated the abhinaya in detail. The Sāmānyābhinaya and Citrābhinaya are dealt with in the NŚ. after the fourfold abhinaya is described. It is clear that in course of time the conventions regarding the gestures were multiplied and these additions were also included duly. To illustrate, in the Āṅgikābhinaya we have Śākhā, Nṛtta and Aṅkura as the three aspects. But in Sāmānyābhinaya, we have six aspects, e.g., Vākyābhinaya, Sūcā, Aṅkura, Śākhā, Nāṭyāyita and Nivṛttyaṅkura. Representation of the various ideas is treated in Citrābhinaya in addition to the earlier treatment. The conventional gained more prominence in the field of gesticulation. We find that in later works the uses of hand-gestures are much more in number. Whether every word is to be gesticulated or the purport of the sentence, depended on the nature of the character. Kallinātha [1] while describing the gesticulation of the nāndī verse in Vikramorvaśīya, in his commentary on SR., states the view that the gesticulation of the words as such only is enough, and by gesticulating the original word its termination is also gesticulated. I have illustrated in the Cākyār tradition the gesticulation of the various terminations also separately with the help of different mudrās. Of course, all such gesticulation becomes extremely conventional. It started from the imitation of the things and went on in a manner in which the likeness of the object became sometimes fainter. Such conventions came to be established which were based only on the interpretation of the expert. They included the gesticulation of abstract ideas as well.

I have described in detail the Abhinaya with the intention of making clear the various aspects of gesticulation. These details being used judiciously, were necessary for the performance of plays. The [2] NŚ. describes the dramatic representation as twofold.—Ābhyantara (regular) and Bāhya (not following the conventions). In the former, physical movements are not violent, hurried and complex. They are controlled by tempo, rhythm and the measurements of kalās. It has the words clearly uttered, without any harshness. The latter is of opposite type, i.e., the

1. SR. Ch. VII, p. 716.
2. NŚ. XXII. 75-80.

movements etc. are according to one's free will, unaccompanied by instrumental and vocal music. Thus the Ābhyantara follows the conventions laid down by Śāstra and the Bāhya does not follow them. Those who have not studied under teacher and thus are ignorant of the Śāstra perform Bāhyanāṭya.

Chapter III

MUSIC AND DANCE

Music

As music was an essential constituent of ancient Indian dramatic art, the NŚ. describes the theory and practice of the vocal and instrumental music in seven chapters beginning from Ch. XXVIII. Three Kutapas[1] are mentioned—Tata, Avanaddha and Nāṭyakṛta. In Tata group the vocal musicians and the players of the stringed instruments and the flutists were included ; in Avanaddha, players of Mṛdaṅga, Paṇava and Dardura were included and those that took part in the play comprised the Nāṭyakṛta. (Dr. Raghavan[2] says that Kutapa might have signi fied the rugs on which the orchestras were seated). Gīta (song), Vādya[3] (instrumental music) and the various Nāṭya were to be employed in the performance harmoniously in the manner of a fire-brand moved in a circle giving continuous impression.

1. Abh. explains कुतप as' कुतं शब्दं पाति, कुं च रङ्गं तपत्युज्ज्वलयति (वा) ।'

Kutapa maintained the sound (on the stage) or it brightened the stage.
NŚ. Vol. IV, p. 2

2. Cf. "Music in the Ancient Indian Drama", p. 4.

Cf. 'कुतपो मृगरोमोत्थपटे'—Amarakośa, N.S. Press, 7th Ed., p. 129.

3. Cf. 'न पुष्करविहीनं हि नाट्यनृत्तं विराजते ।'

'नन्दिमत quoted in Bharatabhāṣya, folio 205.

Cf. Pādatāḍitaka. When Bhaṭṭimaghavarman is entering the palace with striking gait, he is described by the Viṭa—'अनेन...अवीणममृदङ्गमेकनटनाटकं नाट्यते ।'

This implies that the playing of Vīṇā and Mṛdaṅga was essential for the dramatic performance

Śṛṅgārahāṭa, p. 183.

The music was called Gāndharva[1] as it belonged to Gandharvas[2] and was very dear to gods. The group of Gandharvas as Gandharva-gaṇa is mentioned in Taittirīya[3] Āraṇyaka. It seems that the Sāman-singers were connected with the sacrifice, while the Gandharvas were professional musicians. The word Gāndharva denoted music other than the Sāman-music. Of course, the Sāman-music must have given impetus to the Gāndharva music. Rāmāyaṇa refers to Gāndharva.

The NŚ. defines Gāndharva as based on Svara, Tāla and Pada and various musical instruments. Song, Vīṇā and flute give rise to Gāndharva. Dattila[7] defines Gāndharva similarly adding 'avadhāna' (i. e. सम्यग्बुद्धया दियोजन—conscious melodious employment of Svara, Tāla and Pada.[8]).

The songs were used in the Preliminaries; in the plays proper the Dhruvā-songs were employed. The instrumental music was used in the accompaniment of various songs and different movements. The instruments were of four classes—Tata

1. NŚ. XXVIII—9.

Cf. Abh. गां वाचं धारयतीति गान्धर्वम् . . . । NŚ. Vol. IV, p. 6.

2. Shri Bapat has given Sāyaṇa's explanation of Gandharva as one who maintains the speech in the form of songs.

Vaidika Saṁgīta, p. 8.

3. Taittirīya Āraṇyaka—I. 9.3, 'इति एकादश गन्धर्वगणाः ।'

4. Rāmāyaṇa Bālakāṇḍa IV 10, and Ayodhyākāṇḍa II 35.

5. In the inscriptions of Rudradāman (2nd century A.C.) and Samudragupta (4th century A.C.) we find the word 'Gāndharva' for music.

6. यत्तु तन्त्रीकृतं प्रोक्तं नानातोद्यसमाश्रयम् ।
गान्धर्वमिति तज्ज्ञेयं स्वरतालपदात्मकम् ॥

NŚ. Vol. IV, p. 5. Verse 8; F. N. 3ड..पदाश्रयम्:

7. Cf. Dattilam—Verse 3.

8. Nāradīyaśikṣā gives the etymology of Gandharva as—

गेति गेयं विदुः प्राज्ञा धेति कारूपवादनम् ।
वेति वाद्यस्य संज्ञेयं गन्धर्वस्य निरोचनम् ॥

1—4—12.

The commentary of Bhaṭṭaśobhākara explains it as—'ga' stands for song, 'dha' for the playing of Vīṇā by the skilful use of fingers and 'va' for the playing of (other) instruments.

(stringed), Avanaddha (percussion), Suṣira (wind-blown) and Ghana (cymbals).

The Vīṇā is described as wooden and human. The Svara in connection with the Vīṇā includes the seven musical notes (Svaras), two basic scales (Grāmas), fourteen derived scales (Mūrcchanās), the three voice registers (Sthānas), two Sādhāraṇas, Varṇas, Alaṁkāras, Dhātus, Śrutis and Jātis. Regarding the vocal music, Svaras, two Grāmas, Varṇas, Alaṁkāras, the three Sthānas, Jātis and two Sādhāraṇas are treated. Tāla has 21 subtopics connected with it. Pada is two-fold—Nibaddha and Anibaddha. The various metres with their language aspect form the treatment of Pada.

In the creation of Nāṭyaveda, it is stated that Brahman took song from Sāmaveda. The earliest source of Indian music being Sāman, the basis of Gāndharva was also Sāman-music. The seven notes of Indian music were already established in the Sāman-music. They are given in the Sāmavidhāna[1] Brāhmaṇa as Kruṣṭa, Prathama, Dvitīya, Tṛtīya, Caturtha, Mandra and Atisvārya. They were in descending order. They would correspond to Ma, Ga, Ri, Sa, Ni, Dha, and Pa of the Gāndharva music respectively. Prof. Sambamoorthy[3] says that the pure seven-note scale of ancient music is the scale of Sāman-music.

In the Ṛk-prātiśākhya[4] 'Yamas' are said to be seven notes. The commentary while explaining 'Pṛthag vā' refers to the notes other than these seven, due to sharpening or flattening. That means the intervals between the notes due to raising or lowering of them were also known.

The word 'Grāma' primarily indicates a group. In music, it would denote a group of basic notes, i.e., a scale.

The two Grāmas, i.e., Sa-grāma and Ma-grāma are given by Bharata as the two basic scales having fixed relation of Śruti-intervals between the different notes of the octave. Thus the

1. Cf. Music of Hindostan by Fox Strangways, pp. 258-259.

2. Cf. Nāradīya-Śikṣā : यः सामगानां प्रथमः स वेणोर्मध्यमः स्वरः। etc., according to which we get the order Dha, Ni.

Cf. Historical Development of Indian Music, pp. 410-416.

3. Cf. South Indian Music; Book IV, pp. 68-69.

4. Ṛk-prātiśākhya—XIII—43, 44, 45.

Sa-scale has the following Śrutis (i.e., musical intervals)—

Sa	Ri	Ga	Ma	Pa	Dha	Ni
4	3	2	4	4	3	2

The Śruti values of the intervals of the Ma-scale are as follows:

Sa	Ri	Ga	Ma	Pa	Dha	Ni
4	3	2	4	3	4	2

The Pa note of Ma-scale is one Śruti lower; consequently, the interval between Pa and Dha of Ma-scale is four Śrutis. The NŚ[2] has given the number of Śrutis in the Grāma[3], (i.e., basic scale) as 22.

Mr. Alain Danie Lou[4] states that within one Octave we cannot discern more than 22 groups of sounds having distinct expressions. The division of the Octave into 53 intervals is only necessary to make these 22 different expressions coincide with perfect harmonic relations in the different modes.

[According to the Śruti values given in cents, the interval of the two-Śruti note would be 112 cents (90+22), that of the three-Śruti note would be 182 cents (70+90+22); and of the four-Śruti note 204 cents (22+70+90+22).]

We do not get the names of the 22 Śrutis in the NŚ. The Śrutis are illustrated by the help of Vīṇā (most probably the 7 stringed one). Later when the Śrutis were tuned separately on 22 strings as has been explained by the Saṁgīta-ratnākara, the naming and the study of the musical effect of the Śrutis became well-established in musical practice. From the manner in which SR. asks us to get the Sa-scale on the 22 stringed Śruti-vīṇā, we find that the Śrutis were quite distinctly fixed in musical field.

The concord or the discord of the notes is also explained by

1. Ni Sa Ri Ga Ma Pa Dha Ni of the ancient pure Sa-scale would correspond to Sā Ri Ga Ma Pa Dha Ni Sā of the modern Hindustani scale respectively.

Cf. Bhāratīya Saṁgita by Mule, p. 131.

2. NŚ. Vol. IV, p. 19.

3. According to Mr. Fox Strangways, "Grāma' literally 'village' as opposed to Jungle (araṇya), means a civilised as opposed to an unsophisticated scale". Cf. Music of Hindostan, p. 106.

4. Cf. 'Introduction to the Study of Musical Scales', pp.245-246.

giving the Śruti intervals. The very pleasing concord of two notes in the scale is that of Sa and Ma and Sa and Pa having the intervals of 9 and 13 Śrutis respectively. The first is more prominent in vocal music and the second in the instrumental music. Ma stauds at the middle of the seven-note scale. For both Ma-scale and Sa-scale the position of Ma remains unchanged. Pa and Dha are changed into Ma-scale. Hence, for the distinction between the two basic scales, essential as the basis of melodies, Ma should not be disturbed. That is why it is said that Ma[1] is never to be dropped.

The distinction between the two basic scales was due to the principle of Saṁvāda (concord). In the Sa-scale the concord of the fifth was more marked (Sa-Pa, Ri-Dha and Ga-Ni); while in the Ma-scale that of fourth (Sa-Ma, Ri-Pa, and Ma-Ni).

The Svaras (i.e., the musical notes) are of four types according to the principle of consonance or otherwise. They are : (1) Vādi-Svara (Sonant), (2) Saṁvādi-svara (consonant), (3) Anuvādi-Svara (assonant), and (4) Vivādi-svara (dissonant). Vādin is the note which is responsible for the effect of the melody. As Vādin is repeated often, the other notes of the melody-type are used in relation to it, with the respective Śruti intervals. Consonance and the others are regulated by definite number of Śruti-intervals.

The musical notes having the interval of 9 and 13 Śrutis mutually are called consonant, e.g., Sa-Pa; Ri-Dha; Ga-Ni and Sa-Ma in the Sa-scale and Sa-Ma; Ri-Pa; and Ga-Ni in the Ma-scale. The interval of 20 Śrutis between the two notes makes them dissonant, e.g., Ri-Ga; Dha-Ni. This interval in the upward scale is two Śrutis. The notes having other Śruti-intervals than these would be assonant, e.g., Ri, Ga, Dha and Ni of Sa; Ma, Pa, Ni of Ri etc. in the Sa-scale; and Pa, Dha, [Ni, Sa,] Ri and Ga of Ma; Dha, Ni, Sa, [Ri], and Ga of Pa etc. in the Ma-scale.

1. न मध्यमस्य नाशस्तु कर्तव्यो हि कदाचन ।
सर्वस्वराणां प्रवरो ह्यनाशी मध्यमः स्मृतः ॥
NŚ. Vol. IV, p. 43.

2. Cf. NŚ. Vol. IV., p. 15 (Baroda Edition) and NŚ. Vol. II, p. 3. (Text), Edition by Dr. M. Ghosh.

Svara is defined by Mataṅga[1] as the sound which has musical quality that creates the melody. When the interval between the notes is lowered or raised, their musical quality gets affected. The interval between the notes is responsible for their musical quality of a specific nature. The musical sound is different from other sounds as the other sounds do not possess this nature. The interval of 2 Śrutis between the pure notes, is the smallest in the Indian scale. Then comes the interval of 3 Śrutis and that of 4 Śrutis. These notes correspond to Semitone, Minortone and Majortone respectively of the Western scale. One Śruti interval was clearly noticed when the Pa of Sa-scale and Ma-scale were compared. Starting from this smallest interval, Bharata gave a clear-cut idea about the definite Śruti intervals between the notes of the seven-note scale.

The distinction between Svara and Śruti given by SR. is as follows—Śruti is the sound first produced [when a string of Vīṇā is plucked] and the note produced afterwards continuously by resonance is Svara. When the seven notes were fixed in the scale of the Vedic period the increasing or lowering of pitch of any one of these musical notes was noticed in vocal music, and in the playing of Vīṇā or flute. Hence, the pure original notes which were the basis of the scale were fixed by the principle of Saṁvāda and the number of total intervals in the seven-note scale was decided. Bharata mentions Śrutis in the case of wooden Vīṇā, while in the case of Śārīrī Vīṇā he mentions Svaras only. (By Śārīrī Vīṇā we have to understand the human voice).

The two notes other than the principal seven, were also noticed as being used in the music. The longest interval (i.e., of 4 Śrutis) was between Ga and Ma, Ma and Pa and Ni and Sa in the scale. A two Śruti interval between Ga and Ma; and Ni and Sa added two more notes which are given as Svara-sādhāraṇa. Pa was already lowered by one Śruti in the Ma-scale, hence between Ma and Pa (though of 4 Śruti interval in the Sa-scale) there was no other note. These two intermediate

1. B.D. p. 12.
2. SR. 1-26.

to have notes of the two registers and the prominence of 21 stringed Vīṇā to get all the three registers, this 12 note Mūrcchanā system lost its importance.

We have seen that Antara Ga and Kākalī Ni are termed as Sādhāraṇa Svaras. They are called Sādhāraṇa because they neither give up their original nature fully nor resort to the nature of the next higher note. They stand in the midst.

The Sa-scale with Antara Ga and Kākalī Ni would be Ṣaḍja Sādhāraṇa and the Ma-scale with them would be Madhyama Sādhāraṇa. They are called Kaiśika as their performance is subtle.

Abhinava and the SR. explain Ṣaḍja Sādhāraṇa and Madhyama Sādhāraṇa as follows :

When Ni is raised by one Śruti (i.e., it becomes Kaiśika Ni) and Sa is lowered by one Śruti (i.e., it becomes Cyuta Sa) the Ni has 3 Śrutis, Sa 2, and Ri 4 Śrutis. This is Ṣaḍja Sādhāraṇa. By similar process when in the Ma-scale Ga has 3 Śrutis, Ma 2 and Pa 4 respectively, it is Madhyama Sādhāraṇa.

The NŚ. prescribes that the use of these Antara Svaras is to be made in ascending scale only and that too in small measure. If the Antara Svara[2] is used in descending scale in small or large measure, it would destroy the melody of the Jāti and the Śruti.

Jātis :

The NŚ. treats 18 Jātis. They were the modes of music with the rules about combinations of notes fixed for particular Jāti in the particular scale. Seven among them are named as Śuddha (i.e., the pure Jātis). These are defined as those which have the notes after which they are named as the Graha, Aṁśa and Nyāsa notes. To this, Apanyāsa is also added by Dattila, Mataṅga and Śārṅgadeva. The Nyāsa of pure Jāti is necessarily Mandra. The pure Jati has all the seven notes. When any one or more of these are dropped excepting the Nyāsa, the pure Jāti becomes Vikṛtā, i.e., modified. By the combination of two

1. NŚ. Vol. IV, pp. 33-34; SR. I. 5, 7, 8.
2. जातिरागं श्रुतिं चैव निहन्यादन्तरस्वर: । NŚ. XXVIII. 36.

Cf. V.L.जातिरागं श्रुति चैव नयन्ते त्वन्तरस्वरा:।

NŚ XXVIII—37, Ed. by Ghosh.

or more Jātis the Saṁsargaja-Vikṛtā Jātis would be formed. These are eleven in number. The rule about the Nyāsa being necessarily mandra is not expected in the Śuddha Vikṛtā Jātis. The ten characteristics of the Jāti are as follows :—

1. *Graha*—It is the note that is used in the beginning of the song. It is an alternative term for Aṁśa.

2. *Aṁśa*—It is the prominent note in the song. The peculiar charm, i.e., the melodic expression of the song depends on it. It is the basis for the limit of the employment of notes in the high and the low registers. It is perceived prominently (in many combinations of notes). It is used as the Graha, Apanyāsa, Vinyāsa, Saṁnyāsa and Nyāsa.

Mataṅga points out the difference between Graha and Aṁśa. The former may be the Sonant, Consonant, Assonant or Dissonant, but the latter is always, Sonant. The difference is understood also as Aṁśa being the principal and Graha, the subordinate. In pure Jātis Aṁśa is the Graha. In the modified Jātis Graha may be any other note.

3. *Tāra*—The limit of the notes to be used in the high register is the fourth note from Aṁśa (which of course belongs to the middle register) or the 5th note. According to the reading given by Mataṅga, it may be the seventh note also.

4. *Mandra*—The limit of the notes to be used in the lower register is the Aṁśa or the Nyāsa or the Apanyāsa note.

5. *Nyāsa*—It is the note with which the song ends.

6. *Apanyāsa*—It is the note with which the division of the song (Vidārī) ends.

The terms Saṁnyāsa and Vinyāsa occur in the definition of Aṁśa. When the note not Dissonant of the Aṁśa is used at the end of the first division of the song, it is called the Saṁnyāsa; and such a note used at the end of the parts of the divisions of song is termed as Vinyāsa.

7. *Alpatva*—It is the use of a note or notes in small measure. It is two-fold—by skipping over the particular note or notes, e.g., in hexatonic and pentatonic treatment; and by non-repetition. The non-repetition is to be made of the notes which are not the Aṁśa notes. Skipping over a note may also be carried out by not employing the note fully.

8. *Bahutva*—It is of two kinds—by using the note fully or by repeating it often.

9. *Ṣāḍavita*—Six notes are used omitting one note. (The consonant note of that note, which is dropped is employed).

10. *Auḍavita*—Five notes are employed dropping two notes having consonance.

The Madhyama note was never to be dropped in Ṣāḍavita and Auḍavita.

The term Antaramārga occurs in the NŚ. after treating Alpatva and Bahutva. It is the movement (Saṁcāra) relating to the strong Aṁśa and other notes and the reduction relating to the weak notes. Mataṅga[2] has given the illustration of Kārmāravī Jāti in which Gāndhāra is employed in combination with all notes. It is not the Aṁśa note hence it is Alpa; but it is used in large measure for Antaramārga.

The Aṁśa note being most prominent in the Jāti was often used in combinations with its Consonant and Assonant notes. This extensive use of the Aṁśa note gave the particular melodic expression to the Jāti, e.g., the notes Sa and Ri, as Aṁśas would give the Jātis the melodic expression conducive to the Heroic, the Furious and the Marvellous Sentiments. The use of Antaragāndhāra and Kākalīniṣāda, was to be had in the Jātis not having the use of Ga and Ni. Antara Ga and Kākalī Ni were not to be used as Aṁśa notes. The use of these Sādhāraṇa notes is given by Bharata in the Madhyamā, the Pañcamī and the Ṣaḍja-Madhyā Jātis, when Ga and Ni were dropped in their pentatonic treatment.

The pure Jāti with all its modifications had the basis of the Nyāsa that kept its character distinct. The Nyāsa of the pure Jāti in the low register being difficult to be sung was changed to the one in the middle register in the Mediaeval period, as is seen in the illustrations given by Saṁgītaratnākara.

The Jātis belonging to the Sa-scale are Ṣāḍjī, Ārṣabhī, Dhaivatī, Naiṣādī, Ṣaḍjodīcyavatī, Ṣaḍjakaiikśī, and Ṣaḍjamadhyā; while those belonging to the Ma-scale are, Gāndhārī, Madhyamā, Pañcamī, Gāndhārodīcyavā, Raktagāndhārī, Gān-

1. NŚ. Edition by Dr. Ghosh. Part II (Text), p. 15. Verse 97.
2. BD. pp. 59, 60.

dhārapañcamī, Madhyamodīcyavā, Nandayantī, Kārmāravī, Āndhrī and Kaiśikī. The general rule is given as, Ma and Pa should be used prominently in the Erotic and the Comic; Sa and Ri in the Heroic, the Furious and the Marvellous; Ga and Ni in the Pathetic and Dha in the Odious and the Terrible sentiments.

The use of these Jātis in relation to the sentiments is given in the NŚ. according to the prominent note.

Varṇas, or the musical exercises are of four types : Sthāyin :— Repetition of the same note or notes steadily.

Ārohin—Notes employed in ascending order.

Avarohin—Notes used in descending order.

Saṁcārin—Notes employed in ascent and descent in a mixed manner. The embellishments of music (Alaṁkāras) in connection with these Varṇas are also treated in the NŚ. The use of Varṇas and Alaṁkāras was made in singing the Gītis in combination with tempo. The four Gītis (i.e., types of songs) were meant to provide rhythmical varieties. They were not to be employed in connection with the Dhruvās and were to be used by the musicians in the Gāndharva only.

The music of the Jātis[1] with its many varieties gave rise to the later Rāga system. The tribal and the regional varieties of music were also studied. The musical science of the Mediaeval period incorporated all these in its scope. The definition of Aṁśa of the Jāti lays stress on Rāga—the particular pleasing effect of the melody which resided in the Aṁśa. Thus, the Rāga conception in the sense of charming melodious effect was already there, but as one of the characteristics of Aṁśa. It was not recognised as a separate entity to be the basis of the different melody types called Rāgas later, as the conception of Jāti was prominent. Rāga is so called because the presentation of the notes in the particular manner delights the minds of the listeners. Mataṅga takes the credit to himself of first defining and making clear the nature of Rāga system.

1. Cf. 'तथा चाह भरतमुनिः 'जातिसम्भूतत्वाद् ग्रामरागाणामिति' ।

Bṛhaddeśī, p. 87

"जातिभ्यो रागसंभव" इति मुनिवचनात् ।

Bharatabhāṣya, folio 28.

The melody types derived from the Grāma system are called Grāma-rāgas.[1] The sub-varieties Bhāṣā, Vibhāṣā and Antarabhāṣā are derived from the Grāma-rāgas which incorporated the different styles of the presentation of the Grāma-rāgas.

Mataṅga has given the use of the Rāgas in the dramas, e.g., Śuddha Ṣāḍava in the Preliminaries ; Śuddha Sādhārita in the Garbha-saṁdhi; Śuddhakaiśikamadhyama in the Nirvahaṇa-saṁdhi; Bhinna Ṣaḍja in the entry of the hero while on hunt; Bhinna Pañcama in the entry of the Sūtradhāra; Gauḍakaiśika in Karuṇa; Gauḍakaiśikamadhyama in Bhayānaka ; Sauvīraka in the entry of the ascetics, householders and sages ; Mālavapañcama in the entry of Kañcukin; Mālavakaiśika in love in separation; Bhammāṇapañcama in the case of those exhausted in travel in the hot season ; Gāndhārapañcama in Vismaya and Hāsya etc.

We get the use of music in relation to the junctures as Madhyama Grāma in the Mukha (the opening), Ṣaḍja Grāma in the Pratimukha (the progression), Sādhārita in the Garbha (the sprouting of the germ), Pañcama in Vimarśa (the pause over the germ that has sprouted) and Kaiśika in Nirvahaṇa (bringing together the objects of all the junctures). This is corroborated by Mataṅga also. This use of Rāgas seems to belong to that period in which Rāga-music was replacing the Jāti-music.

The Kuḍimiyāmalai[2] Pallava inscription of the 7th century A.C. mentions seven Grāma-rāgas (and Svarāgamas), namely Kaiśika-madhyama, Kaiśika, Ṣāḍava, Madhyama-grāma, Ṣaḍja-grāma, Pañcama and Sādhārita.

Abhinava[3] has given the use of the various Rāgas in detail,

1. Shri K.V. Ramachandran states that the ancient musical theory grouped Rāgas into three Grāmas according to their pitch level; the Rāgas of Saḍja Grāma had the range of the deep bass and barytone; those of the Madhyama Grāma that of the heroic tenor; and those of the Gāndhāra Grāma that of the lyric soprano. According to him the high pitched Ga Grāma was probably assigned on the stage to the Gods and heavenly beings, the Kinnaras and Gandharvas and characters like Nārada and Urvaśī— a circumstance that would explain the association of this Grāma with heaven, in later musical works.

Music and Dance in Kālidāsa, p. 3.

2. Cf. Epigraphia Indica, Vol. XII, pp. 226-237.

3. BK. pp. 544-546. NŚ. Vol. IV, pp. 72-78.

as stated by Kaśyapa and others. To give an idea a few illustrations are cited below:

Ṣaḍja—in miserable state and insult;

Trāvaṇī—in sorrow;

Bāhya-ṣāḍava—in Mati, Dhṛti and Avahittha ;

Bhinna-kaiśika—in secretly coveted love and righteous heroism;

Bhinna-kaiśikamadhyama—in wonder, energy, etc.

Paurālī—in exciting situations;

Ābhirī—in Narma-sphuñja;

Gāndhārapañcama—in wonder and joy of the inferiors.

Mālava-pañcama—in the anxiety and deliberation of women etc.

It becomes clear that when the Jāti-music was in vogue, the use of Jātis is given in connection with the music in the drama and when the Rāga system was developed, the Rāgas suited to the occasions owing to their emotional appeal are mentioned.

Dr. Raghavan has stated that a class of Rāgas was known as Kriyāṅga, in the classical period; and the name is explained in the musical treatises as referring to the dramatic use of the melody-types for emotional situations.

Instrumental Music :

The orchestra consisted of four kinds of musical instruments—Tata (stringed), Suṣira (wind-blown), Ghana (cymbals) and Avanaddha (drums). In the stringed instruments Citrā and Vipañcī are described as the major Vīṇās (Aṅga) and Ghoṣā, Kacchapī etc. as the subordinate ones (Pratyaṅga); in wind instruments only flute is the major one while conch and Tuṇḍakinī, the subordinate ones; in Avanaddha Mṛdaṅga, Dardura and Paṇava are the major ones and Zallarī, Paṭaha etc. as the minor ones; Ghana includes the cymbals.

1. Cf. Music in Ancient Indian Drama by Dr. Raghavan, p. 12.

Cf. करुणोत्साहशोकादिप्रबला या क्रिया ततः ।
जायन्ते च ततो नाम क्रियाङ्गास्तेन हेतुना ॥

Saṁgītasārāmṛta p. 65

1. *Tata*—Citrā Vīṇā had 7 strings for the notes of the scale while Vipañcī had 9 strings, the two additional ones being for Antara Ga and Kākalī Ni. They were harp-type Vīṇās. The NŚ. says[1] that Citrā was to be played by fingers while Vipañcī with Koṇa (plectrum). These Vīṇās are found in earlier sculptures of Sanchi, Bharhut (2nd century B.C. and 1st century B.C.), Amaravati, Nagarjunkonda (1st and 2nd century A.C.), Pawaya (5th century A.C.) and so on. The Rāmāyaṇa[2] refers to Vīṇā and Vipañcī. The Mahābhārata[3] calls Saptatantrī as well-known Vīṇā. Guttila[4] Jātaka also gives the idea that the Vīṇā (referred to as Sattatantī) had seven strings for the seven notes of the scale. It is described there that Bodhisattva broke the seven strings one by one and still the notes could be continued. In Vīṇāthūṇa[5] Jātaka the hunchback is compared to the Vīṇā-daṇḍa with broken strings indicating thereby that the Vīṇā was the bow-shaped harp. The Yāḷ (bow-shaped harp) is referred to in the Śilappadikāram.

This harp-typed[6] Vīṇā had a hollow belly covered with a board or stretched leather. The belly was broader towards the back where its end was rounded and tapered towards the front and then continued into an upstanding curved arm. The strings were stretched one above the other, from this arm to the belly. These strings varied in length. It was usually placed on the lap and played with fingers or a Koṇa. This harp-type Vīṇā had fourteen strings for the two Saptakas (as seen in the description of Yaḷ[7] with fourteen strings), and then twentyone strings for three Saptakas. This twentyone-stringed Vīṇā having all the notes of the three registers was called Mahatī and also Mattakokilā.

I am inclined to take the NŚ. Vīṇā as the seven-stringed one though Abhinava takes it to be the twentyone-stringed one.

1. सप्ततन्त्री भवेच्चित्रा विपञ्ची नवतन्त्रिका ।
विपञ्ची कोणवाद्या स्याच्चित्रा चाङ्गुलि-वादना ॥
(NŚ. Vol. II ed. by Dr. Ghosh, p. 32)
2. Rāmāyaṇa, Sundarakāṇḍa X, 40-41.
3. Mahābhārata, Vanaparva, 134.14.
4. Jātaka, Vol. II, p. 249.
5. Ibid, pp. 224-226.
6. Cf. 'The Parts of Vīṇā' by A. K. Coomaraswamy. Journal of American Oriental Society 1931, pp. 244-253.
7. See Śilappadikāram, p. 99, footnote.

Nānyadeva[1] has mentioned Mataṅga as Caitrika—the player on Citrā Vīṇā. Of course, the twentyone stringed Vīṇā became the principal Vīṇā in course of time as it could give all the three registers easily. On Citrā also it was possible to have other notes produced by stopping the strings and thus shortening the length.

The bow-shaped harp gave notes in ascending[2] scale when played downwards from the top, as the strings became more and more short downwards.

From the study of the sculptures in India it appears that the fretted Vīṇā came into vogue in musical practice in the Mediaeval period.

In connection with Vīṇā-playing, the NŚ. has treated the four dhātus (the methods of producing notes on Vīṇā by strokes), in detail with the subdivisions. They are as follows—

1) *Vistāra*—a) *Saṁghātaja*—using two strokes;

b) *Samavāyaja*—using three strokes;

c) *Vistāraja*—using[3] one stroke for the note (in all the three saptakas);

d) *Anubandhakṛta*—mixed playing by breaking up and combining the groups of strokes given above; hence it is of irregular type.

2) *Karaṇa*—Having varieties of strokes 3, 5, 7 & 9 ending in long measure.

3) *Āviddha*—Using 2, 3, 4 and 9 strokes gradually and slowly.

4) *Vyañjana*—Using the fingers variously.

In regard to the manner of Vīṇā-playing three modes are given—in Citrā-Vṛtti, the instrumental music was more prominent ; in Dakṣiṇā, the vocal and in Vṛtti, both equally prominent. In the accompaniment to the songs the Vīṇā-playing was of three types. In Tattva, the song and Vīṇā-playing followed

1. चित्रोक्ता सप्ततन्त्रीभिर्वक्ति सप्त स्फुटान् स्वरान् ।
मतंगो वादकस्तस्याश्चैत्रिको नाम नापरः ॥
See Bharatabhāṣya, folios 184-185.

2. Dattilam-9— (ध्वनिः) · · ·वीणायामधरोत्तरः ।
SR. VI. 131-132, pp. 492-493.

3. Kallinātha—एवमेकप्रहारभवो विस्तारजः ।

each other closely and simultaneously; in Anugata, Vīṇā followed the song and in Ogha, there was the fast tempo and hence forceful manner (Crescendo) played irrespective of the meaning of the song.

The Karaṇas[1] in connection with Vipañcī and other Vīṇās are given as six—

1. *Rūpa*—When the principal Vīṇā plays one long note, two short ones are played on Vipañcī and when one short note is played on the principal Vīṇā two drutas are played on the other. (Two drutas are equal to one short).

2. *Kṛtapratikṛta*—The Rūpa is performed in continuation in all parts.

3. *Pratibheda*—When on the principal Vīṇā two short notes are played one long note is played on the other etc.

4. *Rūpaśeṣa*—When the principal Vīṇā-player stops (at the end of the part of the song) the other continues.

5. *Ogha*—When the principal Vīṇā is played in slow tempo the other is played in very fast tempo.

6. *Pratiśuṣka*—The note other than the prominent and the consonant is played on the string of the principal Vīṇā and the other Vīṇā.

Bharata says that in the accompaniment of Dhruvā songs the Vīṇā should be generally played with Koṇa.[2]

Suṣira—The flute was the most ancient musical instrument. It was the leading instrument in ancient India. In many dance panels in the ancient Indian sculptures flute is seen though Vīṇā is absent. (In Khajuraho temple sculptures Vīṇā is seen with flute, drum, and cymbals in a few dance panels). The flute gave very sweet notes. Bharata says that the Vīṇā, flute and the vocal music should be in perfect harmony. As regards the flute-playing, the manner of producing different notes is described. The four Śruti notes were to be produced by keeping the hole fully open; the three Śruti notes, with fingers shaking; and two Śruti notes by covering half of the hole with fingers.

Thus the notes of Sa-scale and Ma-scale with the Sādhāraṇa

1. Cf. SR. VI. 113-120; and Abhinava—NŚ. Vol. IV, p. 123.
2. NŚ. XXIX. 117.

notes also should be produced on the flute. The flute was to accompany all the notes sung by the musicians.

3. *Ghana*

The cymbals supplied the rhythm. Tāla is derived from Tal in the sense of Pratiṣṭhā[1] (stability). Tāla is the foundation necessary for music. It is indicated by the clapping of hands also. The measure of time in the musical sphere is the one that suits the musical purpose. The Kalā as the time-measure in the musical field is not the same as is understood ordinarily. The Kalā of the medium tempo is the average one in musical sphere.

The Mārgas of rhythm were three—Citra, Vṛtti and Dakṣiṇa; in the first, the Kalā was of two Mātrās (Mātrā[2] being the time required for the utterance of five short syllables), in Vṛtti of four Mātrās and in Dakṣiṇa of eight Mātrās. Thus the Kalā was three-fold.

Tryasra and Caturasra were the two principal Tālas. The Tryasra was named Cācapuṭa, having the measure of Ga (i.e. Guru—two Mātrās), La (i.e. Laghu—one Mātrā), La and Ga and the Caturasra, Caccatpuṭa having the measure of Ga, Ga, La and Pluta (elongated i.e. three Mātrās). Each of these two was again three-fold—Ekakala,[3] Dvikala and Catuṣkala. In the case of Cācapuṭa, Ekakala was of six Mātrās, Dvikala of twelve Mātrās and Catuṣkala of twentyfour Mātrās; while in the case of Caccatpuṭa, Ekakala was of eight Mātrās, Dvikala of sixteen Mātrās and Catuṣkala of thirtytwo Mātrās.

The other Tālas were the Ṣaṭpitāputraka having Pluta, La, Ga, Ga, La, and Pluta ; Sampakveṣṭāka, having Pluta, Ga, Ga, Ga, and Pluta ; and Udghaṭṭa having Ga Ga Ga. The Miśra Tāla would be the mixture of Tryasra and Caturasra. The Saṁ-

1. See Abhinava— 'तले भवस्तालः——' NŚ. Vol. IV, p. 152.
2. NŚ. XXXI. 4. निमेषाः पञ्च मात्रा स्यात् ।
See Abhinava—पञ्च निमेषा ह्रस्वाक्षरपञ्चकं यावत् ।
NŚ. Vol. IV, p. 153.
3. According to Śārṅgadeva Kalā here means Guru i.e. two Mātrās. Elsewhere Kalā denotes Laghu i.e. One Mātrā.
Cf. Saṁgītaratnākara (Adyar Ed.), Vol. III, pp. 10-11.

kīrṇa (mixed) Tālas with 5, 7, 9, 10 and 11 Kalās were deemed unfit for Dhruvās.

The Tāla (as indicated by hands) was again Niḥśabda (without sound) and Saśabda (with sound), each being four fold—

1. *Niḥśabda*—(a) Āvāpa : Contracting the fingers with the palm turned upwards ; (b) Niṣkrāma : Spreading the fingers with the palm turned downwards; (c) Vikṣepa : Moving swiftly the hand as in Niṣkrāma to the right, and (d) Praveśa : Taking back the hand pointing downwards. When there would be four Kalās, these should be used in the order mentioned above and when two, Niṣkrāma and Praveśa should be employed.

2. *Saśabda*—(a) Śamyā : Clapping by the right hand, (b) Tāla : Clapping by left hand (c), Sannipāta : Clapping by both hands together, and (d) Dhruva : The movement of the hand with the snapping of the fingers according to the three-fold Kalā. The Tāla of the three fold Āsārita, Vardhamānaka and the seven Gītis is dealt with by Bharata in detail. The treatment of the Tāla of the ten Lāsyāṅgas also finds place. The songs have upohana in the beginning which contains notes of the song sung with meaningless syllables.

4. *Avanaddha*

The Tripuṣkara is mainly described in detail as it gives all the varieties of drum-playing. Puṣkara[1] is Vādyabhāṇḍamukha i.e. the face of the drum (which is covered tightly with hide). The tightening or loosening of the hide would change the pitch, as high or low. In the detailed treatment we get Mṛdaṅga (a drum with two heads), Paṇava (a drum with two heads, thinner in the middle part and fastened with strings) and Dardura (drum with one face) shaped like a ghaṭa (pitcher).

Tripuṣkara is a drum with three faces according to Dr. Raghavan.[2] He explains Mṛdaṅga as one having mud as its characteristic ingredient. This is corroborated by Śilappa-

1. 'पुष्करं वाद्यभाण्डमुखम् ।' Śabdakalpadruma Vol. III, p. 198.

2. 'Why is the Mṛdaṅga so called?' by Dr. Raghavan. J.M.M.A. Vol. XXIV 1953, pp. 135-136.
—do— XXVI 1955—p. 148.

dikāram. In the preliminaries preceding the dance of the Cākyār, vocal and instrumental music are described. The drum muzhavu (muraja or mukha in Sanskrit) is described as smeared with mud. He also quotes Mr. Talbot Kelly who says in connection with Burmese 'pwes' — "These (percussion instruments) are tuned by clay being squeezed on to the skin until the right pitch is reached." A drum with three faces is found in the Naṭarāja temple of Chidambaram in the Ūrdhva-tāṇḍava sculpture in front of the shrine of Naṭarāja and in one of the sculptures at Hampi.

Generally Mṛdaṅga is explained as one which has its body formed of clay. A drum with 4 faces is found in a dance sculpture at Delwara temple, which is played on the left, right and the upper faces. Similarly there is one with five faces in the Madras Museum which was played in temple music. But in many other ancient Indian sculptures and paintings the drum is usually with two faces and with one face as well. Prof. Kapadia[1] in his article on "The Jain Data about Musical Instruments" has referred to the commentary of Jinaprabhasūri on 'Ajiya-Santi-Thaya' a hymn composed by Nandiṣeṇa. The commentator has explained 'tiukkhara (tripuṣkara) as पुष्करमातोद्यमुखम् तच्च दर्दुरट (क ?) स्यैकं मुखम्, मुरजस्य च मुखद्वयमेतानि त्रीणि पुष्कराणि त्रिपुष्करमुच्यते। It seems that the drums with two faces and one face were more common than the drums with three faces.

The sixteen syllables which are produced by playing on the drum are given as ka, kha, ga, gha, ṭa, ṭha, ḍa, ḍha, ta, tha, da, dha, ya, ra, la and ha. How they are to be produced by playing and how the conjunct consonants are also to be produced is described by Bharata, e.g., 'ddham' is to be produced by striking simultaneously on the two faces of Aṅkika Mṛdaṅga (i.e. the two-faced drum placed on the lap).

The four Mārgas of drum-playing are : (1) Aḍḍita (playing on Aṅkika[2] Mṛdaṅga ; (2) Ālipta (playing on Vāmaka (left side drum) and Ūrdhvaka) ; (3) Vitasta (playing by quickly strik-

1. J.O.I. Vol. II, p. 385-386.

2. Aṅkika, Ūrdhvaka and Āliṅgya are the varieties of drums with two faces. Aṅkika was shaped like a myrobalan, Ūrdhvaka like that of a barley grain and Āliṅgya like that of a cow's tail.

ing with the span, on Ūrdhvaka and right face of Aṅkika) ; and (4) Gomukha (playing on all the drums with Āliṅgya-playing abundant). Aḍḍita is to be employed in the Erotic and the Comic sentiments ; Vitasta in the Heroic, the Furious and the Marvellous; Ālipta in the Pathetic ; and Gomukha in the Odious and the Terrible. Nānyadeva[1] states that Aḍḍita is to be used in the case of superior characters.

Even playing by both hands (i.e. by left hand on left side and right hand on right side) is called Sama, uneven playing (i.e. by the left hand on the right side and right hand on the left side, having Svastika of the hands) is Viṣama and mixed playing is Sama-viṣama.

Three Mārjanās are described. The Mārjanā would be effected by applying clay (suited for the purpose) to give the Sthāyī notes.

	Left face of the drum	Right face of the drum	Upper face of the drum
Māyūrī	Ga	Sa	Pa
Ardhamāyūrī	Sa	Ri	Dha
Kārmāravī	Ri	Sa	Pa

The Māyūrī was to be used in the Ma-scale, Ardhamāyūrī in the Sa-scale and Kārmāravī in the case of Sādhāraṇa.[2] The other notes should be produced by applying pressure on the face of the drums. According to Abhinava and Nānyadeva[3] the Mārjanās were to be employed as follows :

	Āliṅgya	Āṅg(k)ika	Ūrdhvaka
Māyūrī	Ga	Sa	Pa

Ma[4] should be produced on the other face of Āṅgika.

Ardhamāyūrī	Sa	Ri	Dha

The six Karaṇas[5] in connection with drum-playing are—

(1) *Rūpa* —When two long syllables are played on Mṛdaṅga, two short and one long are played on Paṇava;

1. Bharatabhāṣya—folio 209.
2. *Ibid.* ,, 'कार्मारवी च कर्तव्या साधारि(त) समाश्रयेत्(या?)' ।
3. NŚ. Vol. IV, p. 431; ibid.
4. According to Vema Ma was to be produced on the upper face of the drum in Māyūrī. Cf. BK, p. 484.
5. Cf. Bharatabhāṣya—folios 213, 214 & Abhinava—NŚ. Vol. IV, pp. 428-429.

(2) *Kṛtapratikṛta* — When one Karaṇa (particular combination of drum beats) is played on Tripuṣkara, it is followed afterwards by Paṇava and others ;

(3) *Pratibheda* — When one Karaṇa is played on Mṛdaṅgas simultaneously, a different one is played on Paṇava (e.g., when two short syllables are played on Mṛdaṅga, one long is played on Paṇava) ;

(4) *Rūpaśeṣa* — When Mṛdaṅga-playing is stopped Paṇava-playing continues ;

(5) *Ogha* — It is crescendo (like the flow of the stream) ;

(6) *Pratiśuklā* — Mṛdaṅga-playing is repeated by Paṇava and Dardura.

Yati[1] :

Yati is the regulating of the duration of words, Varṇas or syllables in relation to songs and instrumental music. It is of three kinds:—

(1) *Samā*—(Even): It has the same tempo in the beginning, the middle and the end. It has predominance of instrumental music.

(2) *Srotogatā*—(Current-like) : In it the playing is sometimes stopped and sometimes continued in a running manner, like the water-current.

(3) *Gopucchā*—(Like cow's tail) : It is playing having long and short syllables, extended towards the end ; it is mostly used in songs.

Pāṇi[2] :

(1) *Samapāṇi*—The instrumentation evenly follows the tempo (of the song), starting with it;

(2) *Avapāṇi*—The playing of instruments precedes the start of the tempo;

(3) *Uparipāṇi*—The playing of instruments follows the start of the tempo.

Laya—(Tempo) : It is of three kinds—Druta (fast), Madhya (medium) and Vilambita (slow).

In accompaniment, the close simultaneous manner would

1. Cf. NŚ. (Edition by M. Ghosh). Vol. II. XXXI. Verses 489-495 and SR. V. 50-55, pp. 366-367.

2. *Ibid.*

be Tattva, following afterwards would be Anugata and crescendo would be Ogha.

The NŚ. has described the eighteen rhythmic Jātis of drum-playing giving their uses in conformity with the type and the mood of the character. The various Toṭakas (striking beautifications) due to the combinations of the playing of different drums are treated and the instrumentation in regard to the Dhruvās is also given.

The drum-playing which should accompany the various types of characters in different situations is described by Bharata with the drum-beats in each case, e.g.,

Heroes in natural movement—

In the case of Gods—gham, drām drām drām ;

In the case of kings—ghem tām kem tām ;

In the case of Brahmins, middling characters—Kṛṇa kiṭi etc.

According to conditions—

In hurried gait—dham, dham ghe ghe ṭam

In the states of hurried movements—dhram ghem ghem ghem, etc.

The Ālipta Mārga is to be used in misery, disease, separation from the loved ones, loss of wealth, observance of vows etc. Thus the instrumentation is described in the case of movement of one going in a chariot, boat, aerial car, etc., in the movements of demons, lame, disabled, dwarf, etc., the servants, evil spirits, the shaven headed, eunuchs, Śākya, Pāśupata, Yati, aged Brahmin and Kañcukin, etc.

In the case of females also the drum-beats for the movements of divine females, queens, Brahmin ladies, middling type women like courtesans, and inferior type of females are given. When the drum should start playing and when it should exactly stop is specifically mentioned.

The making of different drums is treated in the NŚ. with their measurements.

Abhinava quotes Kohala while discussing the gaits and gives the specific Tāla and Laya in connection with the particular gait. He has given some Tālas which are not found in the

NŚ. and hence seem to be the later development. As their actual use is given it is certain that they were in practice. Some of them are described below—

Subhadra (Dhruvā Tāla)—Abhinava[1] states that it is to be used in secret love as per the view of Kohala and others. (It has the fifth, sixth and ninth short syllabic measures and the remaining seven long ; it is used in the Furious and the Heroic sentiments).

Jambhaṭikā—It has two[2] Laghus and then two Drutas (Druta = $\frac{1}{2}$ Mātrā) with stop and then the same repeated again; it is used in the Pathetic.

Khaṇḍadhārā—It has many[3] Drutas ending in Guru ; it is used in moving by chariot.

Dhārā—It has eight Drutas[4] in the beginning and eight in the end without stop ; it is used in the Terrible (in fast tempo, in the case of inferior characters).

Narkuṭa—It has two Gurus[5] two Laghus and two Gurus repeated; it is used in the case of Śakāra, Viṭa and Vidūṣaka, in laughter. Dvipadī[6] having four long syllabic measures was to be used in the case of the superior characters.

(Abhinava[7] has given the actual drum beats, i.e., Dham Dhak Tsuk Dhi, to be used in the case of the gait of the parasite Śekharaka in the Nāgānanda who comes reeling, with the glass of drink in his hand).

On occasions like festivities, royal march, auspicious incidents, marriage and fight, all the instruments, i.e., the major and the subordinate ones, should be played. In domestic scenes of normal nature instrumental music should be least, while in the poetic compositions having exciting nature, all the instruments should be played. The percussion instruments are to be played for the harmony of constituent parts, for covering a gap in the performance and for adding charm. (The sketches of

1. Cf. NŚ. Vol. II p 142 & footnote.
2. *Ibid.* p. 146 & footnote.
3. *Ibid.* p. 151.
4. *Ibid.* p. 148 & footnote.
5. *Ibid.* p. 158 & footnote
6. *Ibid.* Vol. II p. 133.
7. *Ibid.* p. 140.

various musical instruments are given by me at the end.

Dhruvās

The NŚ. has devoted one full and long chapter for the treatment of Dhruvās. These are the songs which are to be sung in the course of the play. Dhruvā is so called because in it the words, Varṇa, Alaṁkāra, Yatī, Pāṇi and Laya are harmoniously fixed. As Abhinava[1] suggests they are so called because they stabilise the production or their themes are of fixed significance. The Tāla for the Dhruvā songs was Tryasra and Caturasra of six and eight Kalās[2] respectively. The song with one Vidārī (i.e. part) was Ekaka, with two Vivadha and having three to six Vidārīs, Vṛtta. Vṛtta was to be employed in the case of the superiors, Vivadha in the middling and Ekaka in the inferiors.

The Dhruvā songs are of five types according to their place and the mood. (1) The Prāveśikī is the entrance song; (2) The Naiṣkrāmikī is the exit song when the character leaves the stage at the end (or in the middle) of the act; (3) The Ākṣepikī is the song which indicates the change of mood with the change of the medium or the slow tempo to quick tempo (or vice-versa); (4) The Prāsādikī[3] is the song which calms the audience that are experiencing a different sentiment due to Ākṣepa; it burnishes or reinforces the mood already introduced; (5) The Antarā is the song sung when a gap or a mishap in the performance is to be covered up or when owing to the overpowering feeling, there is a tense situation in the action as when one is in deep grief, loss of memory, sleep or has fallen down. (ND.[4] says that it should have meaningless syllables.)

The two-fold Sthāna (position) of Dhruvās is described as

1. Cf. Music in Ancient Indian Drama by Dr. Raghavan—Reprint, pp. 8-9.

2. Kalā is equal to Mātrā i. e. time required to utter five short syllables.

3. According to Abhinava and the Nāṭyadarpaṇa Prāsādikī should be used necessarily after Prāveśikī-Ākṣepikī.

See Abhinava. NŚ. Vol. IV. p. 361; ND, p. 173.

4. ND, p. 173.

Parastha and Ātmasaṁśrita. Abhinava[1] explains it as referring to the song that helps the sentiment and mood, e.g., when the Dhruvā song would refer to Rāma, suffering due to separation from Sītā, it would be Ātmasaṁśrita (i.e. concerned with the character proper) and the Dhruvā song employed in this context referring to Lakṣmaṇa's sorrow seeing Rāma's condition would be Parastha (i.e. concerned with the other character).

Bharata has treated the various metres of all these Dhruvās with illustrations. They are to be in Śaurasenī Prakrit. This ignores the later rule which prescribes Mahārāṣṭrī as the language of songs of ladies. Though most of them are in Prakrit, examples of some Dhruvās appear in Sanskrit. Dr. Ghosh[2] points out the illustration 'अधिकं विरहे । मदनो दहति ॥' and states that though Sanskrit song is enjoined in the case of divine ones, this illustration relates to Viraha (separation)—a human affair. He further says—"This example together with the definition of its metre constitutes one stanza. This may be the reason of its loss of Śaurasenī character and ultimate conversion to Sanskrit. In Śaurasenī it would be 'अधिकं विरहे । मदणो दहदि ॥' The transition from Śaurasenī to Sanskrit is easy. The language of the Dhruvās is simple. They deal with the sun, the moon, the stars, the clouds, the storms and typical sights in different Indian seasons. The important part is played by seasons which furnished themes for most of the Dhruvās which seem to have enjoyed a great popularity."

The Dhruvā compositions are full of long syllables (Avakṛṣṭā) or short ones (Drutā) or mixed. The Avakṛṣṭā is to be used in Pathos and when the character is fettered, thwarted, fallen, diseased, fainted and dead. Sthitā is the Dhruvā of slow tempo which is to be employed in the case of longing, dissimulation, anxiety, bewailing, exhaustion, loss of spirit, and dejection. Drutā should be employed when there is fall of meteors, confusion, intolerance, wonder, dejection, excessive joy, anger, excitement and in the Heroic, the Furious and the Terrible sentiments. Prāsādikī in medium tempo should be used in love

1. Abh. NŚ. Vol. IV. p. 362.

2. Cf. Prākṛta verses in the Bharata-Nāṭyaśāstra' by M. Ghosh. I.H.Q. Vol. VIII Supplement, pp. 1-52.

scenes, pacification, remembrance, speeches with excellence, first meeting of lovers, joy, entreaty and wonder. Antarā should be employed in the case of physical distress, in anger and in aiming (at the target). When the character enters singing (e.g. Malayavatī's entry in the first Act of Nāgānanda), crying in excitement, announcing anything, in wonder or calamity, Dhruvā should not be employed.

The Dhruvās should be symbolic; e.g., the moon, the fire, the sun and the wind are to used in the case of divinities and Kings; the cloud, the mountain and the ocean in case of the demons; elephant in rut and royal-swans in the case of the superiors; peacocks and beds of lotuses etc. in the case of the middling; cuckoo, bee, crow, etc., in the case of the inferiors; the night, the moon-light, lotus-plant, she-elephant and river (the Sanskrit words for all these being in feminine gender) in the case of queens; creeper, female swan etc. in the case of women of midding types and courtesans; female bee, female cuckoo etc. in the case of inferior women. The symbolism for different characters is dealt with in such details.

The entrance song is to be sung to indicate anything happening in the fore-noon and the exit song may be used (in general) to indicate anything happening by day and night. Gentle Dhruvās are to be sung to indicate the forenoon and the excited ones to indicate the noon; the pathetic Dhruvās are to be sung in the case of afternoon and evening.

The Dhruvās are to be used fittingly taking into consideration the theme, the performance, the type of the character, moods, season, age, place, time and condition. The NŚ. says that those things which remain to be expressed in speech should be presented in song; for, through songs only the strength and ripeness come to the meaning of the words.

The Dhruvā of short syllables and quick tempo should be used in the case of entries in chariot, in aerial cars and on elephants etc. When the movement is quick, the Dhruvā with short syllables should be employed and when it is slow (with wide steps), with long syllables. When there is Ākāśabhāṣita the Dhruvā should be significant of speech. The language of the Dhruvā should normally be Śaurasenī; the

Narkuṭa Dhruvā[1] should be in Māgadhī. In the case of heavenly beings the song should be in Sanskrit and in that of human beings in Ardha-Sanskrit.

In the Tryasra Dhruvā the steps should follow three Kalās and in the Caturasra they should follow four Kalās[2], which are respectively in the case of the middling and the superior characters. The Tryasra Narkuṭa should be used in the case of the inferior characters. In confusion, anger etc. the steps should follow a Kalā or half Kalā. When the steps would be of 1, 2, 3 or 4 Kalās, only the instrumental music should be used harmoniously and not the song. There should be no pause of one or two Kalās in the Dhruvā, in dramatic procedure and hence harmonious instrumental music should accompany and not song. The first round of the Dhruvā should be without the accompaniment of drum, which should accompany later. This is meant for the proper understanding of the theme of Dhruvā by the audience. The NŚ. has given in detail the starting of Tāla in connection with various Dhruvās. It has also stated the merits and the demerits of the singers and the instrumentalists. Generally women's voice is sweet, hence vocal music should be their province and the men have the vigour for instrumental music, hence instrumental music should be their sphere. The reverse of this would be of course, an exception.

The embellishments of music should not be used too much in the case of the Dhruvās, for their meaning is important; hence it should not be hampered by intricacies of singing. Nānyadeva[3] has mentioned Rāga, Tāla and the uses of the various Dhruvā songs given in the NŚ. A few examples are given below—

Dhruvā	Rāga	Tāla	Used in the case of—
Jayā	Kākubha	Cācapuṭa	Inferior characters.
Kamalamukhī	Pañcama	Caccatpuṭa	Superior characters.

1. NŚ. Vol. IV, p. 350—Abhinava—
नटोऽधमप्रकृतिः । तत्र भवानि नर्कुटानि वृत्तानि ।
अधमविषयाच्च त्र्यश्रोऽत्र तालः ॥

2. Kalā is equal to Mātrā i.e. the time required to utter five short-syllables.

3. Cf. Bharatabhāṣya, folios 147-166.

Kanakamālā	Ṭakka	Caccatpuṭa (Druta)	Fighting actions of the hero.
Siṁhākrāntā	Ṭakka	—	Fighting actions of the superior and the middling.
Kumudinī	Mālavakaiśika	Caccatpuṭa	Entry of superiors in love.
Bhūtala-tanvī	"	" and Cācapuṭa	Faltering gait of the superior.
Utkṛti	"	Caccatpuṭa (Druta)	The hero's entry accompanied by the beloved.

Abhinava[1] has illustrated the use of Ākṣepikī Drutā in the change of mood of Rāma in the Udāttarāghava from that of love to that of heroic after listening to the words of Rāvaṇa and Vilambitā in the change of mood of Aśvatthāman in the Veṇīsaṁhāra from that of heroic to that of pathetic, after listening to the speech from behind the curtain. The ND[2]. also has given illustrations of Dhruvās from the classical Sanskrit dramas, e.g., the Prāveśikī indicating the entry of Viśvāmitra in the Anargharāghava of Murāri in which there is the description of the sunrise; the Prāveśikī indicating the entry of Prince Candragupta in the Devī Candragupta of Viśākhadatta, (who gesticulates feigned madness) in which the moonrise is described; Naiṣkrāmikī indicating exit of Candragupta in the same play, leaving for the palace; Ākṣepikī, the same illustration from the Udāttarāghava cited by Abhinava. Rājaśekhara[3] has put in Dhruvās in his plays. He says[4] "It (the Dhruvā) announces or explains the respective characters, delights the hearts of the audience and establishes the emotional continuity." Dāmodarabhaṭṭa[5] in his Kuṭṭanīmata refers to the use of entrance and exit Dhruvās, while describing the enacting of

1. Cf. Abh. NŚ. Vol. IV, pp. 360-361.
2. Cf. ND, pp. 172, 173
3. Cf. Music in Ancient Indian Drama, pp. 9-10. by Dr. V. Raghavan. Bālabhārata 1-12. Bālarāmāyaṇa, pp. 10, 59, 60.
4. Bālabhārata, 1-14.
5. Kuṭṭanīmata, Verses 880, 883, 927.

the first Act of the Ratnāvalī. In Vikramorvaśīya[1]—Act IV we have the Prāveśikī (in the additional Prakrit verses given by Raṅganātha) indicating the entry of Sahajanyā and Citralekhā. The Prāveśikī at the entry of Purūravas is also given. Out of the remaining Anyokti[2] stanzas (17 in Prakrit and one in Sanskrit), from Vikramorvaśīya, Act IV, stanzas No. 4 and 75 are taken as Naiṣkrāmikī Dhruvās and the remaining stanzas as Ākṣepikī Dhruvās by Prof. H.D. Velankar.

Dr. K.K. Raja[3] has given some Dhruvās as employed in the Kūṭiyāṭṭam, e.g., the entrance Dhruvā in Sanskrit at the entry of Vasantaka in the Mantrāṅka of Pratijñāyaugandharāyaṇa; the Dhruvā verses, also called Akkitta (to be sung in Kaiśikī Rāga) on the introduction of Śāṇḍilya in Bhagavadajjukīya, (the last one of these verses being in Prakrit and the rest in Sanskrit); and the Dhruvā verse (in Sanskrit), in the Aṅgulīyāṅka of the Āścaryacūḍāmaṇi (describing the moonrise).[4]

I have described in the introduction, the performance of 'Daru' in connection with the present classical dance drama styles. The Darus are mentioned by King Tulaja of Tanjore in his Saṁgītasārāmṛta. The entrance song is very important and is the means to indicate the mood etc. of the character entering. It was applied even to the entry of Sūtradhāra in the preliminaries and it has survived to recent times. The Pātrapraveśadaru (entrance song) is sung and then the character enters in the Bhāgavatamela-nāṭaka of South India. In connection with Kathakali the Pātrapraveśa[5] Ślokas (verses indicating the entry of characters) are found.

1. Vikramorvaśīya, (N.S. Press, Bombay, 1925) Act IV—1.5.

2. See Vikramorvaśīya, (Ed. by Prof. H.D. Velankar) Act IV—2, 3, 4, 6, 12, 14, 19, 23, 28, 29, 35, 41, 43, 48, 54, 56, 63, and 75 and Editor's Introduction, pp. LXIV—LXXII. Sahitya Akadami, New Delhi.

3. Cf. 'Kūṭiyāṭṭam' by Dr. K.K. Raja, pp. 26-29.

4. In the Pratāparudrakalyāṇa Nāṭaka of Vidyānātha, the Naṭī sings Dhruvāgīti at the request of the Sūtradhāra.

5. Shri Krishnachandra Pisharoti of Trichur informed me that in Kirmīravadha a Pātrapraveśa Śloka is sung in the melody called Navarasa which is well-known only in Kerala; in the Kalyāṇasaugandhika, the Rāga Śaṅkarābharaṇa is used when Bhīmasena addresses Pāñcālī.

Dr. Raghavan[1] says that the Dhruvās were not written by the poet himself. To the original prose text, song verses were added when the play was enacted. Taking the suggestion from these song verses or Dhruvās, the poets themselves began to insert verses, wherever the emotion or idea reached a degree of pointedness and needed effective expression. In the great classical period, when the prose-verse dramatic masterpieces were produced, the stage-artists had their own composers who wrote the Dhruvā music, using the poet's contextual verses for guidance. According to him, the few cases seen in the classical plays are merely exceptions indulged in for novelty or to show the poet's knowledge of stage technique.

Prof. R.B. Athavale[2] has also discussed the topic of Dhruvās. He has pointed out that some Dhruvās used in the plays are in Sanskrit also; e.g., Prāveśikī Dhruvā in the Bālabhārata of Rājaśekhara; so also the Ākṣepikī in the Udāttarāghava referred to by the Nāṭyadarpaṇa. Thus the Dhruvās were composed in Sanskrit metres of the Gaṇa-kind also. He takes the Antarā as being sung behind the curtain always while the other four types were sung on the stage even by the main characters such as the hero and the heroine. He understands Mālavikā's song in the Mālavikāgnimitra as the Dhruvā of Prāsādikī kind, for it is Catuṣpadā (which is a variety of Dhruvā) and is sung in the medium tempo which is prescribed for Prāsādikī by the NŚ. Malayavatī's song in the Nāgānanda is also understood by him as Dhruvā of the Ākṣepikī type for there is the change of Śānta Rasa into Love. Prof. Athavale further says that as a rule the Dhruvā songs were originally verses from the texts of the dramas and as such were written by the poets themselves; the ND. refers to Kavidhruvā (the Dhruvā of the poet), (ND. page 172). The description of the performance of the 1st Act of Ratnāvalī given in the Kuṭṭanīmata, is also interpreted by him in his favour. Verse 927 of it is rendered by him as—"The king advanced beautifully to the charming tunes of the Niṣkrāmikī Dhruvā which he first sang

1. Cf. 'Music in Ancient Indian Drama', pp. 10-11.

2. 'Ancient Sanskrit Drama and Music' by Prof. R.B. Athavale, a paper read at the A.I.O.C. Srinagar (1961).

and then left the stage." (The last two verses of the first Act of Ratnāvalī are understood by him as constituting the exit Dhruvā.) Vatsarāja is played here by a girl. Bharata prefers women for vocal music.

Considering all this he concludes that the Dhruvā songs were composed both in Sanskrit and Prakrit. They were mostly sung by the characters on the stage. Sometimes, however, they were sung behind the curtain. Most of these Dhruvā songs were choice verses from the texts of the dramas to be performed on the stage. In rare cases, however, these songs were composed by composers attached to the dramatic companies in ancient India.

From the explanation of Nāṭyāyita (given in the Abhinaya Chapter) we know that when the Dhruvā song started the character gesticulated the mood etc. indicated by it. The singing of the Dhruvās by the musicians started behind the curtain and when it was removed the character entered. Dr. Raghavan points out that the concerned actor himself who had to identify with the theme of the song was in the habit of joining in a snatch or two of it.

With a few exceptions the Dhruvā songs given by Bharata are in Prakrit. The language of women was mostly Prakrit and according to Bharata the vocal music should be generally the province of women as their voice is naturally sweet. The symbolism of the Dhruvās with their meaningful content enriched by the melodious music served as the fitting background to the performance.

In the classical plays the Dhruvā songs are not embodied (with a few exceptions already cited) as they were the part of the stage-craft and as such the musicians were mainly concerned with their compositions. It is just possible that they might have got them composed from the playwrights themselves.

As regards the illustrations cited by Prof. Athavale it is seen that the stage direction "नेपथ्ये" (behind the curtain) is used in the two Prāveśikī Dhruvās in the Bālarāmāyaṇa of Rājaśekhara (page 10 and pp. 59-60). The ND. also in illustrating Ākṣepikī refers to the change of mood by listening to the "नेपथ्यवाक्य" (i.e. the speech behind the curtain). The description in Kuṭṭanīmata gives in verse 926 the purport of the last verse of the Act I of the Ratnāvalī (I.25) and the verse 927 starts with the words "एवमभिधाय" (speaking thus) and then tells that the hero left the stage with all, with the exit song. It can be understood that the verse 25 of the lst Act of Ratnāvalī need not be taken as the exit song. Malayavatī's song is a prayer to Goddess Gaurī. Mālavikā's song is in connection with the Chalita Nāṭya. It is possible to understand that the great dramatists like Kālidāsa and others introduced music in the plays to achieve greater effect by putting songs in the mouth of characters themselves.

As regards the use of songs actually referred to as sung on the stage in the classical plays we have the following illustrations—the song of Naṭī in the Prologue of Pratimā; the song of Naṭī in the Prologue of Śākuntala; the song of Haṁsapadikā in the 5th Act of the same play, (it is sung, of course, by the songstress behind the scenes); the song of Mālavikā (already referred to); the songs of the Ceṭī in the First Act of Ratnāvalī; Malayavatī's song in the Nāgānanda (Act I) (already pointed out); two songs of Āraṇyakā in the 3rd Act of Priyadarśikā etc.[1] Singing of songs in Prakrit in praise of Yama is referred to in the Mudrārākṣasa (Act I) when the spy Nipuṇaka is moving with the Yama-paṭa. King Bhoja mentions a further kind of music to be employed in the drama. Certain situations required a certain melodic background and to provide this melodic background, a song was sung in which Rāga alone mattered and not the words of the song. Bhoja[2] refers to the songs so used as Śravya or Ākṣepikī.

According to Dr. Raghavan,[3] the verses which are put in the mouths of the respective characters were sung. He says "The evidence of surviving practice, as well as some observations of Bharata, his commentator and other writers, shows that they were sung. The Pāṭhya[4] is to be sung properly, says

1. There is also the song of the King (the hero) in the 2nd Act of Viṇāvāsavadatta.
2. Cf. Music in Ancient Indian Drama, p. 13.
3. *Ibid.*
4. NŚ. XIX 77.

एवमेतत्स्वरयुतं कलाताललयान्वितम् ।
दशरूपविधाने तु योज्यं पाठ्यं प्रयोक्तृभिः ॥
Kashi Sanskrit Series, p. 226.

Bharata. Blossoming forth on the boughs of the dialogue like so many flowers, the verses of the Sanskrit drama would indeed appear to frustrate themselves if they are not to be sung and rendered in Abhinaya."

Shri Daji[1] Bhatavadekar who has staged the Sanskrit plays like Śākuntala, Uttararāmacarita and others very successfully maintains similar view. He says that the singing of verses in the Sanskrit plays in appropriate Rāgas helps to intensify the mood. He has illustrated the verse 'त्वं जीवितं त्वमसि मे' etc. (Uttararāma III—26) in support of his view. It is sung in the Rāga Pilu of the Hindustani music.

We have seen that Abhinava[2] while commenting on the use of the 7 notes, rejects their musical employment in Pāṭhya (recitation). He says that Pāṭhya is different from Gāna (song) which is the Dhruvā-song proper. According to him the Recitation should start with the Sthāyī note of the Jāti in which the particular Dhruvā is sung. Hemacandra[3] also distinguishes Pāṭhyarūpaka from Geyarūpaka. The Cākyārs (who only have the ancient tradition of staging Sanskrit plays) at least nowadays, recite the verses slowly, gesticulating them side by side. In their tradition there is the list of different Rāgas for different situations. Dr. K.K. Raja[4] says that these Rāgas are not the same as the Rāgas in music; but they are the Rāgas of recitation. The manuals giving the stage directions indicate the particular Rāgas to be adopted in each case. Thus Vasantaka in the Mantrāṅka is asked to hum and sing in Kaiśikī. The prose text of Unmattaka in that Act 'Modaā...' etc. is to be in Velādhūli. The verse 'Navakuvalayadhāmnoḥ...' etc. by Arjuna in the Subhadrādhanañjaya is in the Rāga called Arttana. One rule strictly observed by the Cākyārs is that when the Recitation goes on, the playing of drums is to be stopped. That means the recitation of the verses, when it adopted singing was not accompanied by the percussion rhythm. In the plays, when singing with the accompaniment is referred to we have

1. "Saṁskṛta Nāṭakātīla Abhivyakti (Marathi), by Shri Daji Bhatava dekar. Viveka Vijayādaśamī Viśeṣāṅka.

2. Cf. NŚ. Vol. II pp. 385-386.

3. Cf. Kāvyānuśāsana. Vol. I. VIII. 4, p. 447.

4. Cf. 'Kūṭiyāṭṭam' by Dr. K. K. Raja, pp. 38, 39.

the stage direction 'गायति' (sings) specifically. They are sung usually by famale characters.

If the verses are to be sung they must be fit for singing. Simplicity of expression is required so that they could be sung without sacrificing the meaning. Bharata is very emphatic regarding the recitation of the verses which must express the meaning prominently. As such the verses with very long compounds would not be suitable for singing. Abhinava's efforts to distinguish between the Recitation and the singing suggest that the use of music in the Recitation might have been resorted to.

Bāṇa[1] has referred to the recitation of Vāyupurāṇa in his Harṣacarita. It was accompanied by flute. Though the verb 'Papāṭha' (recited) is used, it is clear that it was recited musically.

I think as the Dhruvās supplied effective musical background there was no necessity of singing the verses again by the characters. What is meant by the employment of Svara and Tāla in the Recitation was the recitation with the specific notes prescribed for the mood (e.g. Ma and Pa for Love etc.) and the metrical rhythm. In the Uparūpakas the use of music was prominent while in the Rūpakas it was as the background. Moreover, Kāku (the effective modulation of voice) was very important in the Recitation. The modulation would not be so effective while singing a verse. Hence, where Kāku was necessary singing of verses must not have been employed. Some verses might have been chanted in suitable melodies for striking effects. But singing of verses with full accompaniment would not have been the practice as a rule in the presentation of classical Sanskrit plays. The musical plays were being developed separately. Of course, it was the expert director who was to decide to what extent the verses should be set to music to heighten their effect without losing their meaningful content.

Shri K.V. Ramachandran[2] states that the instrumental

1. Cf. 'गमकैर्मधुरैराक्षिपन्मनांसि श्रोतृणां गीत्या पवमानप्रोक्तं पुराणं पपाठ ।'

Edition by Gajendragadkar. Harṣacarita—III p. 6.

2. Cf. Music and Dance in Kālidāsa by K.V. Ramachandran, pp. 11-12.

music was set apart for the junctures, by which a few select Rāgas adumbrated the mood of a whole act through poignant instrumentation, that stirred the listener to the depths of his being. He has suggested that the use of Śuddha Sāveri (Guṇakari) at the departure of Śakuntalā and Maṅgalakaiśika for the re-union of Śakuntalā played on instruments might have been very much effective.

As pointed out by Shri Ramachandran the judicious use of suitable melodies played on flute and lute would have helped to create the atmosphere in the effective manner, in the performance.

DANCE

The classical dance of Karaṇas[1] and Aṅgahāras was used primarily in the Preliminaries. The use of dance is explained as 'it adds beauty and grace'. It is naturally liked by all and is auspicious. It should be employed on the occasions of marriage, birth, coming of the son-in-law with the bride at father-in-law's, festivity, prosperity, etc. It is the source of amusement. When something connected with love occurs between a married couple, dance should be used. When the lover is near and the sight of season (like spring) and time (like moon-rise) are observed, dance is employed. When the heroine is Khaṇḍitā, Vipralabdhā or Kalahāntaritā, dance should not be used. Likewise, when a conversation is going on with a companion or when the lover is not near or has gone abroad, dance should not be there. If during the performance of any part of the play, the heroine is gradually pacified, dance should be used till its end. When there is the adoration of a deity, the forceful Aṅgahāras of Śiva should be used, and when there is a song connected with the Erotic sentiment the gentle Aṅgahāras performed by Pārvatī should be employed. Thus, the NŚ. has mentioned the occasions for dance in the drama.

Abhinava[2] gives seven divisions of Nṛtta.

1. *Śuddha* — in which Recakas and Aṅgahāras are present ;

1. The 108 Karaṇas are given in Appendix B.
2. Cf. NŚ. Vol. I, pp. 182-183.

2. *Gītakādyabhinayonmukha*—in which there is the gesticulation of a song in a general manner ;

3. *Gānakriyāmātrānusāri-Vādyatālānusāri*—that following the song and the rhythm of the instruments accompanying it, having the various movements of the body ;

4. *Uddhata*—forceful ;

5. *Sukumāra*—gentle ;

6. *Uddhatasukumāra*—forceful-gentle ; and

7. *Sukumāroddhata*—gentle-forceful.

The first three are to be used in independent Laukika (that is popular) dance and in satisfaction of the Deities. The last four are employed in the preliminaries.

Harṣavārtika[1] finds no difference in Nṛtta and Nāṭya, as both Nāṭya and Nṛtta have the similarity of Anukāra (imitation), the constituents like sentiments, emotions, the movements of eyes, hands and head, being common. As the Karaṇas are used in the gesticulation of Nāṭya, Nṛtta is Nāṭya itself—this is the view of Kīrtidhara.[2] To illustrate : the use of Karaṇas Sūcīviddha and Ūrdhvajānu is found in the entry of Aśvatthāman, Alapallavasūcī (Ardhasūcī) in the entry of Purūravas, Garuḍaplutaka in the entry of Garuḍa; Rāvaṇa's Puṣkara (aerial car) is gesticulated by Vaiśākharecitaka and the confusion of Vatsarāja due to fire by Atikrānta etc.

These views quoted by Abhinava give us the idea that this classical dance was used in dramatic representations. Such uses would surely come under the conventional in the dramatic art. Once some features were adopted to make the imitative acting graceful, it was but natural that those who were experts in classical dance began to represent the roles in plays.[3] Here, naturally the dance element overpowered and we find even now how the classical dance-drama forms have maintained that tradition to the fullest measure.

1. Cf. NŚ. Vol. 1 p. 206.
2. *Ibid.*, p. 206.
3. A strikingly allied situation is presented by Marathi stage on which the introduction of classical music had a popular appeal for a number of years. During this period, musicians, expert in classical music became top-ranking actors.

Shri K.V. Ramchandran[1] says in this connection that in course of time, the classical playwright seeking to make his play visible on the stage seized readily these Karaṇas as the medium of visible expression. Thus the Karaṇa Līna was employed in situations where the heroine was entreating her lover; Apaviddha, in anger ; Valitoruka in the coy love of the mugdhā ; Svastikareçita in joy ; Nikuṭṭana in self importance, Kaṭichhinna in wonder ; Vakṣaḥsvastika in sympathy ; Unmattaka in the pride born of beauty-consciousness ; Mattalli in love etc. A less important purpose also was served by some of these Karaṇas, e.g., Samanakha announced the commencement of the dance ; Diksvastika indicated the change of music and Ākṣipta denoted the clown.

Abhinava has given the usages of many of these Karaṇas[2] connected with moods, situations and movements etc. of the different types of characters. It becomes clear, then, that the classical dance which was first employed in connection with the Preliminaries, gradually found scope in the dramatic performance. It imparted grace to the performance and served the purpose of gesticulation as well, in suitable proportions.

In the classical plays, we find dance actually employed, e.g., Hallīsaka in Bālacarita of Bhāsa, Chalita in Mālavikāgnimitra of Kālidāsa, the dance of the two maid-servants in Ratnāvalī etc. The ten Lāsyāṅgas also were allowed to be used judiciously in the plays of Love.

The dance without gesticulation is termed as Nṛtta and the one with gesticulation of the words giving rise to states (bhāvas) as Nṛtya. In the performance of Sanskrit drama, Nāṭya, Nṛtya and Nṛtta were employed suitably.

1. Cf. "Dance Traditions of South India" by Shri K. V. Ramachandran. Triveni, Vol. VII, No. 4, pp. 308-319.

2. The illustrations of all the 108 Karaṇas as found in the Naṭarāja temple at Chidambaram are given in the NŚ. Vol. I, Chapter IV.
II Edition, G.O.S. Baroda 1956.

In 'The Classical Dance Poses of India' (II Edition) by Gopinath & S.V.R. Rao, the Karaṇas, excepting Lalāṭatilaka, Avahitthaka and Viṣṇukrānta are illustrated and their uses given.

Chapter IV

THE THEATRE, THE TROUPE AND THE SPECTATORS ETC.

The Theatre

Chapter II of the NŚ. deals with the theatre. As the open-air performance met with disturbance from some dissatisfied members of the audience, closed theatres became a necessity. The very large size of the theatre was also a handicap as the facial expressions could not be observed properly by the spectators removed far away from the stage. The effective modulation of voice by the actors and the subtleties of music went unnoticed, in such a theatre.

The theatres were of three shapes—Vikṛṣṭa[1] (rectangular), Caturasra (square) and Tryasra (triangular). They were of three sizes—Jyeṣṭha, the large one, had the measure of 108 Hastas (one Hasta=one and a half feet); Madhyama, the medium, 64 Hastas and Avara, the small 32 Hastas. Thus, there would be, in all, nine types. If the measurements are taken to be in Daṇḍa (Daṇḍa = 4 Hastas) then there would be nine more types. Abhinava[2] remarks that all these would not be useful, but they are only mentioned to maintain the tradition. The theatre with the dimension of 108 Daṇḍas would be too large. While giving the details afterwards, the NŚ. gives measures in Hastas alone. Hence, Hasta-daṇḍa[3] should be understood as a Daṇḍa (a measuring rod) of one cubit (Hasta), as is done by Prof. Subba Rao[4] or it should be understood as Hasta or Daṇḍa[5], i.e., for 108 Hastas, 27 Daṇḍas may be measured.

1. Dr. P. K. Acharya takes Vikṛṣṭa as semi-circular or circular theatre, preferring the reading Vṛtta.
   Cf. Ancient Indian Theatre by Mankad, p. 22.
   Cf. 'The Playhouse of the Hindu Period' by P.K. Acharya.
   Dr. S.K. Aiyangar, Comm. Vol., p. 363.
2. NŚ. Vol. I, p. 49.
3. 'प्रमाणमेषां निर्दिष्टं हस्तदण्डसमाश्रयम् ।' NŚ. II-9.
4. NŚ. Vol. I, p. 427.
5. Cf. BK. pp. 869–870. Kumbha has given the dimensions 27 Daṇḍas in place of 108 Hastas etc.

The large theatre was for gods, middle-sized for kings and the small for the rest of the people. Abhinava[1] explains that the large one was meant for performances like that of Ḍima and others, in which gods were the heroes and Asuras, their rivals. Being full of Ārabhaṭī style, these required a large stage. The middle-sized one was meant for plays like Nāṭaka and others in which kings featured mostly and the small one for plays like Bhāṇa and Prahasana in which the rest of the people featured. As the NŚ. treats the three[2] types (the rectangular, the square and the triangular) with the dimensions 64 × 32, 32 × 32 and 32 Hastas respectively, it is clear that they were mostly in vogue. Rectangular type of medium size with the dimension 64 × 32 Hastas was the most suited and hence prominence is given to it. If a theatre is larger than this, the recitation and the music would not be properly heard and the facial expressions with the various glances (expressive of the moods) would not be distinctly visible.

Before commencing the construction of the play-house, the ground should be prepared and then on an auspicious day, after propitiating Brahmins and performing sacred rites, the lay-out should be started.

The Rectangular type

With a piece of white cord, a plot of 64 Hastas in length and 32 Hastas in breadth should be measured. This should be divided into two, making two halves of 32 × 32 cubits each. The rear half should be again divided into two parts of 16 × 32 cubits each. The Raṅgaśīrṣa should be fashioned in the half division of the front part (i.e. 8 × 32) and the green-room in the back part. After this, the Sthāpana (foundation) should be laid on an auspicious day, sounding all the musical instruments like conch, Mṛdaṅga, etc. and performing religious rites meant for the occasion. Then the construction of walls should be carried out and pillars should be raised under the asterism Rohiṇī or Śravaṇa. The four pillars at the four corners, i.e., South-east, South-west, North-west and North-east, should be

1. Cf. NŚ. Vol. I, pp. 51-52.

2. Prof. Subba Rao has explained that these dimensions of the three types are most proper for mortals.

Cf. NŚ. Vol. I, pp. 427-428.

named as Brāhmaṇa, Kṣatriya, Vaiśya and Śūdra respectively. Various rites are mentioned in connection with the raising of the pillars.

Thus, the pillars, doors, walls and the green-room should be constructed.

Regarding the construction of the stage proper, there are differences of opinion. Abhinava[1] says that the Raṅgapīṭha, i.e., the stage proper was 8 × 16 Hastas and to both sides of it, there were two Mattavāraṇīs 8 × 8 Hastas square. At the back of the Raṅgapīṭha, Raṅgaśīrṣa would be placed 8 × 8 Hastas square. It would be raised higher than the level of the Raṅgapīṭha in this type. The Nepathyagṛha[2] would be constructed in the remaining western part of 16 × 32 Hastas. The front half of 32 × 32 cubits was meant as the auditorium.

I shall discuss first all the different explanations of the terms Raṅgaśīrṣa, Raṅgapīṭha and Mattavāraṇī offered by different scholars.

Abhinava himself gives the other view about Raṅgapīṭha, i.e. 16 × 8 Hastas. But this 16 Hastas deep stage with only 8 Hastas in width would not be so suitable. Hence, the Raṅgapīṭha with 8 × 16 Hastas measurement seems to be more proper.

Prof. Subba Rao[3] has not accepted the two divisions of the stage as Raṅgaśīrṣa and Raṅgapīṭha. He takes Pīṭha as the base of the Raṅga and Śīrṣa as the top or the upper surface. He says that the Raṅgaśīrṣa was to be fashioned with Ṣaḍdāruka. That means, Ṣaḍdāruka made the Raṅgaśīrṣa. According to him, Ṣaḍdāruka is a frame with cross bracing (involving 6 pieces, 2 horizontals, 2 verticals and 2 diagonals) to combat a reversal of stresses due to heavy thumps in the performance of Nāṭya. This interpretation of Ṣaḍdāruka is not supported by the existing traditional theatres which have no such use of the wooden frame with a cross bracing. No Sanskrit commentator has explained Ṣaḍdāruka in this manner. The raised[4] stage was made by filling it with earth.

1. NŚ. Vol. I, pp. 56, 57, 60, 61.

2. Dr. Acharya has shown two green-rooms on both the sides of the stage in the sketch.

3. Cf. NŚ. Vol. I, pp. 423-454.

4. Cf. 'रंगपीठं सुकृष्णाभिर्मृद्भिरापूरितं दृढम् ।' BK., p. 322.

Dr. Ghosh[1] also does not take Raṅgapīṭha and Raṅgaśīrṣa as two different parts. According to him, the tiring room would measure 48′ × 12′, the stage with two Mattavāraṇīs (12′ × 12′ each) 48′ × 12′ and the auditorium 48′ × 72′.

I think that Raṅgaśīrṣa and Raṅgapīṭha were two different sections of the stage, the former used mainly for the orchestra and the latter as acting space.

Mattavāraṇī was to be fashioned to the side of the Raṅgapīṭha 1½ Hastas in height with four pillars, according to the measure of the Raṅgapīṭha. The word Mattavāraṇī is used in singular number by the NŚ. Prof. Subba Rao has understood Mattavāraṇī to be on the front of the Raṅgapīṭha. As it represents Airāvata he takes it to mean, "a line of intoxicated elephants" on the front side of the stage. He reads Stamba in place of Stambha and then explains it as the post to which the elephant is tied. This explanation given by Prof. Rao appears to be beside the point. It is prescribed in the Nāṭyaśāstra that iron pieces should be placed under the four Stambhas of the Mattavāraṇī. That means, they must be understood as regular pillars. Prof. Yajnik[2] understands Mattavāraṇīs to be a set of two side buildings or wings.

Scholars like Miss Ketkar, Dr. Raghavan, Shri Mankad, Prof. K.R. Pisharoti and Dr. C.B. Gupta have accepted Abhinava's explanation of Raṅgapīṭha, Raṅgaśīrṣa and Mattavāraṇī. Shri Mankad takes Raṅgaśīrṣa to be 8 × 32 Hastas (at least in the days of Abhinava). He suggests[3] that the back parts of both the Mattavāraṇīs had walls 8 Hastas each and the curtain 16 Hastas was placed in between the two back walls of the Mattavāraṇīs. Thus according to him the Vikṛṣṭamadhya would have these parts—auditorium of 32 × 32 Hastas, Raṅgapīṭha of 8 × 16 Hastas with a curtain at the back 16 Hastas long and two Mattavāraṇīs on the two sides of the Raṅgapīṭha each 8 × 8 Hastas; these Mattavāraṇīs would have

1. Cf. 'The Hindu Theatre' by Dr. M. Ghosh, I.H.Q. Vol. IX, pp. 591-592.

Cf. The Nāṭyaśāstra, Ed. by Dr. Ghosh, Introduction, p. LVIII.

2. The Indian Theatre by R.K. Yajnik, Chapter II, pp. 36-51.

3. Ancient Indian Theatre by Shri Mankad, pp. 16 and 39.

one side wall and one back wall. At the back of this (i.e. Raṅgapīṭha and Mattavāraṇīs taken together) there would be a space 8×32 Hastas called Raṅgaśīrṣa out of which, the central portion of 8×8 Hastas would be a raised platform one Hasta higher than the Raṅgapīṭha. At the back of this Raṅgaśīrṣa there would be the green-room 16×32 Hastas. In the front wall of this green-room on the side of the Raṅgaśīrṣa, exactly in the centre, there would be a decorative panel (the Ṣaḍdāruka) with four vertical pillars and two horizontal beams. Shri Ray Govinda Chandra[1] takes Mattavāraṇī as the entamblature fashioned on pillars over the Raṅgapīṭha. He says that as its arch was supported on wooden elephant heads it was called Mattavāraṇī. Strangely enough, he takes Raṅgaśīrṣa in front of the Raṅgapīṭha, lower than it. According to him, Raṅgapīṭha is adjoining the green-room.

To understand Raṅgaśīrṣa in the front of the stage, does not stand to reason. For, in that case, the musicians would be seated in front of the actors and some of them (e.g. the Mṛdaṅga players) would be facing the audience with their backs towards the actors. This arrangement would be quite improper. Hence, Ray Govinda Chandra's explanation of Raṅgaśīrṣa is out of question.

Later writers like Kumbha[2] and Vipradāsa, have understood Raṅgaśīrṣa and Raṅgapīṭha as two different parts of the stage. It seems that they have understood Mattavāraṇī (as the Uparibhūmikā ?) fashioned on the four pillars (two to the south and two to the north) of the Raṅgapīṭha, (decorated with golden Kalaśa). Both of them have explained the Ṣaḍdāruka as two columns on each of the two sides of the door in the front wall of the green-room and beams below and above them. They formed a decorative panel. (The two doors for the green-room are understood as one being in the back wall, for the troupe and the other in the front wall, to enter the stage). Miss Ketkar[3] has explained the Ṣaḍdāruka as two pillars on both the sides of the Raṅgaśīrṣa eight Hastas apart, adjoining the green-room wall, two in front at a distance of

1. Cf. भरत नाट्यशास्त्र में नाट्यशालाओं के रूप (हिन्दी), pp. 16, 17.
2. Cf. BK, pp. 320-322 and pp. 869-870 and 881.
3. Bhāratīya Nāṭyaśāstra, pp. 31-32.

four Hastas from the first two pillars on both the sides of the Raṅgaśīrṣa and the two beams over them: (according to her they would serve as the upper storey etc. in the plays). She understands two more doors on the south and north sides of the Raṅgaśīrṣa.

Prof. Diwekar[1] understands that there were two Mattavāraṇīs, enclosures with four pillars each on both sides of the stage. He has traced the history of the word Mattavāraṇī. According to him, at the outset, the word was connected with Matta-vāraṇas, i.e., intoxicated elephants. In the forest when two elephants are in rut and woo the same female elephant, they fight with each other and the winner is accepted as the lover. When elephants were tamed and employed in the service of great kings, the kings wished to witness the elephant fights. Such an elephant-fight witnessed by him is described in detail. A great enclosure was fenced off to keep away the spectators and protect them from the fighting elephants. In the centre of the enclosure there was prepared a raised rectangular space open in the middle, with pavilions of the same size at either end. In each of these two, an intoxicated elephant was shut up. The pavilions were curtained off so that the two elephants could not see each other, before the fight. The curtains were removed when the signal was given to start the fight. The elephants goaded by their tamers tried to drive the opponent out of the central place. The fight went on till one of the elephants was defeated and forced back to his pavilion. Prof. Diwekar thinks that from Raghuvaṁśa XII, there is reason to believe that Kālidāsa[2] must have seen such an elephant fight. He finally concludes that the middle ground was called Vedi and the two enclosures used for shutting up the mad elephants were called Matta-vāraṇīs. Later when the word became current, it was used for any two structures similar to each other at the two ends with common

1. Cf. 'Mattavāraṇī' by Prof. H.R. Diwekar. A.I.O.C., Vol. II, Part I, 1959, pp. 357-364.

2. विक्रमव्यतिहारेण सामान्याभूद् द्वयोरपि ।
जयश्रीरन्तरा वेदिर्मत्तवारणयोरिव ॥

Raghuvaṁśa XII—93.

ground in the middle. Each of the structures was called Mattavāraṇī, but the number always and necessarily suggested is two. This Mattavāraṇī, i.e., two enclosures of similar size may have any dimensions and any shape. In connection with the stage, Bharata says that they should have four pillars and they should be in proportion to the Raṅgapīṭha. The four pillars might have suggested the four legs of the elephants and there might have been an arch in the form of upraised trunks of the two elephants meeting each other at the centre as is depicted in the picture of Gajalakṣmī. The base of this arch might have been used for the drop curtain. Thus Prof. Diwekar has advanced his interpretation of Mattavāraṇī.

After consideration of all these views I would try to give the idea of Bharata's theatre. It is clear that the theatre was divided into three parts—the auditorium, the stage and the green-room. The green-room is called Nepathyagṛha indicating thereby that it was closed on the four sides by walls. The space at the back 16×32 Hastas was meant for the green-room. In the performance of the Nāṭaka and the Prakaraṇa etc., the most developed types of plays, the number of stage properties used was not large. Hence the whole space of 16×32 Hastas might not have been necessary for the green-room.

In this rectangular type, in the back wall of green room there might have been one door for the troupe to enter. There were two doors in the front wall of the green-room through which the characters entered the stage and made their exit. They were fixed for the entry and the exit of the characters according to their Pravṛttis. On the back side of the stage, between the two doors of the green-room, the musicians sat. The characters entered the stage through these doors but the entry was made effective by holding a curtain and then removing it. The wooden panel of six columns, as explained by Abhinava, decorated the green-room wall between the two doors. The central portion of the back of the stage was marked for the musicians which was afterwards raised up a little higher than the Raṅgapīṭha level to form 8 X 8 Hastas platform called Raṅgaśīrṣa. The[1] back part of the stage and the

1. उत्सेधेन तयोस्तुल्यं कर्तव्यं रङ्गमण्डपम् । NŚ. II-65.
Grosset reads रङ्गमण्डलम् in place of रङ्गमण्डपम्
Of. NŚ. Edition by Grosset, p. 20.

stage proper together formed a raised platform 1½ Hastas higher than the floor of auditorium. This was from the view-point of the convenience of the spectators. The stage had a roof supported by pillars (and perhaps possessed a decorative elephant motif).

(The word Raṅgāvataraṇa[1] in the NŚ. need not give us the idea that the stage was lower and that the actors came down on it. In ancient times, the Raṅga was a place where both sports and other entertainments took place. The Mahāraṅga[2] is described in the Harivaṁśa. Such an arena is unearthed at Nāgārjunkonda. The participants descended to the central[3] place for fights etc. The actors also used to descend to the stage which was of course lower when the Raṅga was of such type. The word Raṅgāvataraṇa was thus significant. Later, even though the stage was a raised platform in the theatres, the entry of the actors on the stage was denoted by the word Raṅgāvataraṇa).

The green-room was constructed in proportion to the requirements. Later on, on both sides of the stage, there were two Mattavāraṇīs (as has been pointed out by Abhinava) with four pillars, forming 8 Hastas square. There might have been an arch of the Mattavāraṇī like the upraised trunk of an elephant. The Mattavāraṇīs were also raised to the level of the stage. In the arrangement as given by Abhinava in the rectangular theatre of medium size, the two Mattavāraṇīs would also serve to check the audience from coming nearer the stage on both the sides.[4] In temporarily constructed theatres

I have understood Raṅgamaṇḍala in the sense of the stage proper accepting Grosset's reading. The meaning of the line would be then, that the stage proper would be raised up to the level of the two Mattavāraṇīs on both the sides. To understand Raṅgamaṇḍala as the auditorium as is done by Dr. Ghosh, is not proper. For, the auditorium was on a lower level than the stage and the Mattavāraṇīs. The word Raṅgamaṇḍala occurs in Chapter XII of the NŚ. where it means the stage. Cf. द्रुतैश्चूर्णपदैश्चैव गन्तव्यं रङ्गमण्डले ।

NŚ. XII. 90.

1. NŚ. XII—156, 158 and 165.
2. Harivaṁśa II. 29. 1-15.
3. Some of our wrestling grounds have the place of wrestling at the centre below and the spectators sit on all sides on the raised sloping ground.
4. Such a construction of two Mattavāraṇīs is not seen in the existing traditional theatres of Cākyārs.

a curtain behind the stage served to set off a green-room for the actors.

The Raṅgaśīrṣa and the Raṅgapīṭha were to have the floor as level as the surface of the mirror; it must not be like the back of a tortoise (i.e. high at the centre and sloping on all sides), or that of a fish (i.e. high along the centre and sloping on both sides). Jewels and precious stones were to be laid underneath this surface. The wood[1] work consisted of many artistic pieces such as decorative designs, carved figures of elephants, tigers, snakes, birds, creepers, etc. Many wooden statues also were to be set up. There would be latticed windows and windows with circular shape. There would be beams on the pedestals over the columns and the dovecots too. Pillars were to be fixed on the different levels of the theatre. No pillar, bracket, window, corner or another door was to come just opposite a door. The play-house was to be fashioned like a mountain cave. That means, it was covered with a roof sloping on both sides. The theatre was to have small windows and was to be free from wind; and hence it possessed good acoustic quality. The music would then be quite distinctly heard due to deep sounding. The play-house is described by Bharata as Dvibhūmi.[2] This is explained by Abhinava variously giving the different views—

1. The two floors, the bottom and the top of the Raṅgapīṭha;

2. The floor between the wall of the play-house (the outer side of Mattavāraṇī) and another wall, like the circumambulating path in the temple;

3. The roof of the stage in the play-house and the roof of the play-house itself or the upper storey;

4. With the reading 'Advibhūmi'—having one storey. Abhinava gives his teacher's view in the end explaining Dvibhūmi[3] in the sense of galleried seats in the auditorium.

1. Such decorative wood-work is seen in the Kūttampalams. The temple theatre at Irinjālakkuḍa offers a good example.

2. According to Yajnik the terrace in Ratnāvalī suggests that the stage itself had an upper building.

3. 'द्वे द्वे भूमी यत्र निम्नाते (निम्नोन्नते) ततोऽप्युन्नता इति निक्रमेण (निम्नोन्नतक्रमेण) रङ्गपीठनिकटात्प्रभृति द्वारपर्यन्तं यावद्रङ्गपीठोत्सेधतुल्योत्सेधा भवति ।' NŚ. Vol. I p.—64

It appears, as has been suggested by Dr. Raghavan, that the term Dvibhūmi referred to the two floors. i.e., that of the auditorium and the raised stage. The galleried seats are described in connection with the Caturasra type. It was convenient to have the galleried seats in the rectangular type also.

There were in all four doors in this rectangular type. Three in the green-room as mentioned before and one in the eastern wall of the auditorium, for the spectators. Abhinava records another view, according to which there were two more doors (in the northern and southern walls of the auditorium). Thus, according to this view there would be six doors in all.[1]

The walls of the play-house were to be plastered with mortar and were to have beautiful paintings of the pleasures of men and women and dance formations of Latā (or pictures of creepers, trees, etc.).

The Square type

After describing the construction of the medium Rectangular theatre, the Caturasra (square type) is dealt with. After carrying out all the auspicious rites duly, the ground should be measured 32 × 32 Hastas. The external wall should be built first with bricks and then the Raṅgapīṭha should be constructed. There should be ten pillars over it to support the roof. Outside the pillars, the galleried seats should be constructed with bricks and wood rising one Hasta higher gradually so that the spectators would be able to witness the performance comfortably. Then fourteen more pillars were to be erected. The Raṅgapīṭha should be 8 × 8 Hastas. Then the decorative wood-work should be carried out and the green-room should be constructed. There should be one door in the front wall of the green-room for the entry of the characters on the stage and the other (in the back wall of the green-room) meant for the troupe. The third door should be in front of the stage in the eastern wall of the play-house fo the spectators. Abhinava[2] understands two doors in this theatre as in the

1. NŚ. Vol. I, p. 70.
2. NŚ. Vol. I, p. 69.

case of the rectangular type, in the front wall of the green-room for the entry of the actors even though the singular number is used in the text. He has the support of Chapter XIII of the NŚ.[1] where the two doors of the green-room are referred to between which the musicians sat. Thus, he understands four doors for this theatre. The Raṅgapīṭha would be square and raised up having even surface. The Raṅgaśīrṣa would be of the same level in the square type. The number of pillars also is stated in connection with this type. Abhinava has explained the measurements of the different parts of this square theatre as follows—

The whole space 32 × 32 Hastas is divided into 64 squares of 4 × 4 Hastas each. The middlemost 4 squares would be the Raṅgapīṭha; behind it, the space of 12 × 32 Hastas remains. The Raṅgaśīrṣa (8 × 8 Hastas) would be in the space 8 × 32 Hastas behind the Raṅgapīṭha and behind that there would be the green-room. Regarding the pillars, he says, 10 pillars are in connection with the Raṅgapīṭha, then 6 more and again 8 more (in connection with the auditorium); thus in all, there would be 24 pillars. (The positions of the pillars are shown by me in the sketch). He has given the other view according to which the third set of 8 pillars was in connection with the green-room. There appear to be other views also in this connection but Abhinava has not mentioned them due to the fear of undue length of the book.

The Triangular Type

Regarding the triangular type the directions given are the minimum. Its stage was triangular, constructed in the centre. The dimension given is 32 Hastas each side. There was one door in one corner and the other door was at the back of the Raṅgapīṭha.

When[2] the performance was not to take place in the regularly built up theatre, i.e., when it was held in the temporarily constructed theatre, the eastern direction would be that to which the actors faced while performing. The drum players

1. NŚ. Vol. II, p. 197.
2. *Ibid.* XIII. 65, 66 and 67.

behind them would also be facing the east. There would be six doors for this theatre.

(The sketches of the three types of theatres described above are given at the end).[1]

Dr. Raghavan[2] in his article 'Theatre Architecture in Ancient India' has mentioned the theatres found in literature and Śilpaśāstras. I am stating them in brief. The Viṣṇudharmottara[3] refers to two types—Āyata (i.e. rectangular) and Caturasra (square). Saṁgītamakaranda[4] describes only the square type of theatre. It gives the dimension 96 × 96 Hastas and says that the theatre should be richly painted with the 84 Bandhas (formations) mentioned in the Kāmasūtra (or the dance Bandhas of the NŚ.), inlaid with innumerable gems of diverse colours and decorated with chowries, flags and festoons. It has mentioned four doors. The king's seat should be in the middle of the raised platform 24 × 24 Hastas which should be beautiful and perfumed. Bhāvaprakāśana mentions three kinds of theatres attached to the palace. It has Vṛtta (circular) in place of Vikṛṣṭa. The circular theatre was meant for the dance in which both the classical and the regional styles were mixed. The audience should be males. Besides the king there should be proprietors of other theatres and the chief citizens. In the square type, the audience should be the king, the courtesans, ministers, merchants, commanders of the army and the king's sons. In this theatre all sorts of mixed dance and music could be conducted. In the triangular theatre the audience included the king, priests and preceptors, king's harem and the chief queen. The dance conducted in this theatre should be of classical style only. Samarāṅgaṇa-Sūtradhāra of Bhoja mentions Gandharvaveśma among the various parts of the palace where Prekṣā (plays) and Saṁgīta (music and dance) were witnessed. Śilparatna of Śrīkumāra mentions the Maṇḍapas within a temple among which, the Nāṭyamaṇḍapa is one. The Nāṭyamaṇḍapa has 4 parts. The stage proper is

1. Raṅgadaivatapūjana is described in detail by the NŚ. in Chapter III.
2. Triveni Vol. IV 1931 No. 6. pp. 69-77.
   Triveni Vol. V 1933 No. 4. pp. 357-366.
3. Viṣṇudharmottara III—20 Verses 4 and 5.
4. Saṁgītamakaranda V—2 to 9.

square. At the back of the stage, there is place for drummer and other instrumentalists. Behind this there would be the green-room and in the front there would be the auditorium. (This would be the Kūttampalam of Kerala). Nāradaśilpa gives the three types as Daiva, Gandharva and Kṣatra. The first is to be built in the temple, second by the citizens in places where all people could witness the performance and the third in the king's palace. In the Daiva type, Daivikarasa is to be presented, in the Kṣatra the Heroic and in Gandharva all the various sentiments. The ground should be first divided into three parts—the stage should be in the central part; at the back of it there would be a curtain behind which there would be many rooms for keeping many things, (it was of course, the green-room) and there would be the auditorium. The seats of the Brahmins would be nearest to the stage and those of Kṣatriyas also. The audience hall would have storeys for women spectators. The Prāsādalakṣaṇa of Vāsudevasūri also mentions buildings for dance and dramatic performances.

Śilappadikāram[1] describes a small stage for dance performances. It was 8 Kols in length and 7 Kols in breadth and one in height. It had two appropriate doors. (Kol was a bamboo piece measuring 24 thumb-breadths, i.e., one Hasta). The stage is given as 20 Hastas wide and the green-room 1/3 of the whole theatre by Dāmodara.[2] I have mentioned Kumbha and Vipradāsa already in connection with the Raṅgapīṭha and Raṅgaśīrṣa. They have mentioned four types of theatres. Vipradāsa[3] has described the details as follows—The Rectangular theatre has the dimension of 108 × 64 Hastas. It is the largest one connected with temples. Caturasra is of two varieties—Dīrgha 64 × 32 Hastas for Kṣatriyas and Sama 32 × 32 Hastas for Brahmins. The Tryasra is meant for the lower castes. He has given the position of pillars as well. Another dimension of the stage as 16 × 16 Hastas in the Dīrgha type is also given. One point which Vīpradāsa has mentioned deserves notice. He says, that leaving 5 Hastas all round the playhouse a wall 3 Hastas high having one door for coming in and

1. Śilappadikāram—translation, p. 101.
2. The Eight Principal Rasas of the Hindus by S.M. Tagore, p. 60.
3. Cf. BK, pp. 320-322.

going out should be constructed. The attentive guards should protect it. This detail is found in the theatre unearthed at Nagarjunkonda, to some extent.

As regards the actual existence of the ancient Indian theatre, the earliest one that is found out is the cave theatre at Ramgarh. Shri Bidyabhusan[1] describes the Sitabengara cave as follows—The Sitabengara cave is six feet high inside or even less in some cases. At the far end of the cave, a high platform runs round the walls. Under this is a drain running towards the wall. Some holes have been carefully cut in the platform. The entrance to the cave is seventeen feet wide and the cave is fortyfour feet long all told. At the centre it is about 12 feet ten inches wide and about six feet high. The walls all around have been cut and treated and high stone-seats are set around the walls. On three sides there are two tiers of seats. The side with the double bench facing the entrance is eight feet six inches wide. The seats behind the entrance are set rather lower than the rest. There are small stone seats by the walls. Mr. Bloch[2] says that the Sitabenga cave on the Ramgarh hill evidently was not the abode of pious ascetics void of all worldly attachments but it was a place where poetry was recited, love-songs were sung and theatrical performances acted. In short, it may be looked upon as an Indian theatre of the 3rd century B.C. He further states that there is a sufficient space in front of the small rock-cut amphi-theatre for the creation of a stage, and the benches themselves might easily have seated fifty or more spectators. The two holes cut into the floor at the entrance might have been made to hold wooden posts to which the curtain was fastened which shut out the cold air of the winter nights when the audience retired to the interior. At such times, the spectators would be seated along the broad benches and the dancing party would perform in front of the curtain that closed the door.

There is some controversy regarding the use of this cave as a theatre. It is possible to understand that it might have been

1. The Theatre of the Hindus, p. 219.
2. Caves and Inscriptions in Ramgarh Hill by T. Bloch. Archaeological Report, 1903-4, pp. 123-131.

used for dance performances. For, the inscription in the Yogimara cave mentions a Devadāsī Sutanaka by name. We know that Devadāsīs are skilled in Nṛtva. Some of the ancient Indian caves were used for music and dance, e.g., Kailāsa, the rock-cut temple at Ellora, two caves in Pāṇḍavaleṇa at Nasik, Uparkot cave at Junagarh etc. No doubt the ancient Indian caves served as pleasure resorts also. But the study of these is not much useful to understand Bharata's theatre. There is a dance-scene in one of the Mathura sculptures on a railing pillar (1st Century B.C.) It has a stage where the dancer is exhibiting with the accompanying musicians. Among the audience, some are sitting and others standing. The stage has a roof sloping on both sides supported by four pillars at four corners. The theatre at Nagarjunkonda (3rd Century A.C.) gives us a good idea about the Prekṣāgṛha[1] of ancient times. It comprises a closed chamber on the west with its eastern limits abutting a pillared Maṇḍapa 55 feet square. There is an open courtyard around the Maṇḍapa on all sides except on the west. It is enclosed by a compound wall with a gateway at the centre of the eastern wall. The entire construction is in the brick masonry with mud mortar top plastered over. The Maṇḍapa is provided with limestone pillars having six rows of six pillars each, i.e., 36 pillars in all. The stage is 28 × 22 feet. A terra-cotta seal is also found near the theatre which might have been used for admission on different occasions.

The temple theatres of Cākyārs are described by me in detail in the chapter on Kūṭiyāṭṭam. Dr. Fabri states in connection with the ancient Indian theatre that all acting was done in front of a four-pillared little pavilion erected either in the open or inside a hall. Curtain on all four sides made this little pavilion into a Tiring room. Out of this entered the actors and into this they made their exit. From behind the curtain came the noises of divine utterances, shouts of the populace in the street, the call of the usherer announcing the approach of a king and the like. On two sides of this pavilion sat the

1. The detailed information with the sketch of the theatre at Nagarjunkonda is supplied to me by Shri Ramamurti, who was Asst. Superintendent of Archaeology, Nagarjunkonda, at the time when I visited that place. I am indebted to him for this information.

musicians. When the Tiring room was on a raised platform inside a hall there was an acting place in front of it suitable for dancing too. (Such a pavilion is seen in the Ajanta paintings in a dance scene.) Dr. Fabri[1] has also given the reconstruction of a presentation of Śakuntalā at Ujjain. Dr. Fabri's account of the ancient stage is not very much useful in understanding Bharata's[2] stage.

The Curtain :

Chapter II of the NŚ. while dealing with the theatre does not make a mention of the curtain. But in Chapter V[3] we get the word 'Yavanikā' behind which the first nine items of the preliminaries were performed. In Chapter[4] XII it is stated that the characters should enter when the Dhruvā is started and the Paṭa is removed. The words Yavanikā and Paṭa stand definitely for the curtain. The other variant for Yavanikā is Javanikā. Javanikā[5] occurs regularly in the lexicons.[6] Commentators[7] on Amara derive it from 'Ju' in the sense of speed or movement. The variant Yamanikā is also found. Hemacandra includes Javanī as a synonym for curtain and explains in the commentary as 'Javante asyām' (they move inside it). The word Javanikā occurs in the sense of a curtain in Harivaṁśa, Viṣṇudharmottara and Bhāgavata etc. The other words for the curtain are Pratisīrā, Tiraskariṇī, Paṭī, or

1. Five Thousand Years of Indian Theatre by Dr. Charles Fabri, Western Railway Annual 1955-56, pp. 63-79.

2. Shri T.N. Khazanchi, Superintendent of Archaeology and Museum, Srinagar, writes to me in his letter dated 8/4/59 that no theatrical structures as such have been located in ancient temples of Kashmir so far. However, there is one temple (situated far off from Srinagar) where there is a big pillared hall which might have served the purpose of dance performances etc.

3. NŚ. V—11 and 12.

4. NŚ. XII—3— ध्रुवायां संप्रवृत्तायां पटे चैवापकर्षिते ।

5. Cf. The Curtain in Ancient Indian Theatre, by Dr. S.K. De—Bhāratīya Vidyā, Vol. IX, pp. 125-131.

6. Amara. II 6.120; Abhidhānaratnamālā 2. 154; Kalpadrukośa verse 300.

7. "जवन्ति अस्यां जवनिका"—क्षीरस्वामिन्, Amara., p. 158.
"जवत्यस्याम् । जुः सौत्रो गतौ वेगे च ।...'यमनिका' इति वा पाठः । यमयति यम उपरमे ।..." व्याख्या सुधा Amara., p. 244.

Apaṭī. The word Yamnaī[1] occurs in the Vājasaneyisaṁhitā. Yamanikā is derived from 'Yam' to stop or restrain signifying a covering or a curtain. The Viṣṇudharmottara[2] lays down that all the entries should take place after removing the curtain. The holding[3] of curtain is mentioned in the commentary on Anargharāghava as a view of Mātṛgupta. Nāṭyasarvasva-dīpikā[4] also states the use of the curtain at the time of the entries of characters.

Abhinava[5] mentions the curtain between the Raṅgaśīrṣa and the Raṅgapīṭha. The NŚ. is clear as regards the use of a curtain. The entries were to be effected with the use of a curtain. Taking into consideration the present practice of classical dance, dance-drama and that of Cākyārs it is reasonable to understand that the curtain was held by two persons and gradually removed when the Dhruvā song started. The curtain is used in this manner in the classical theatre in the East and South East to make the entry effective.

The curtain mentioned by Abhinava seems to be a fixed one. In that case only the purposes of the back stage, stated by him as the concealment of the characters entering, and the resting place for them would be fulfilled. But if the curtain is all the while down, the orchestra and the decorative portion of the back stage would be concealed from the audience throughout. One curtain was there definitely before the dancer or the actor coming from the green-room. In the Mālavikāgnimitra,[6]

1. Vājasaneyisaṁhitā 14-22. The commentator Mahīdhara explains it as 'सर्वेषां नियमकारिणी' ।

2. Viṣṇudharmottara III. 9 ततो जवनिकाक्षेपैः प्रतिपात्रप्रवेशनम् ।

3. Anargharāghava p. 26, धृतिर्जवनिकायाश्च पूर्वरङ्गश्चतुर्विधः ॥

4. ततो यवनिका तत्र कर्तव्या शास्त्रनिश्चिता ।
अखंडममलं चित्रं विस्तीर्णं दीर्घमंशुकम् ॥
विस्तृतं पूर्वरंगेस्मिन् नैपथ्यं कल्पयेद्बुधः ।
नैपथ्यं तु विना पात्रं प्रविशेन्न कदाचन ॥

Nāṭyasarvasvadīpikā folio 24.

5. NŚ. Vol. I, p. 210. 'तत्र यवनिका रङ्गपीठतच्छिरसोर्मध्ये ।'

6. नेपथ्यगृहगतायाश्चक्षुर्दर्शनसमुत्सुकं तस्याः ।
संहर्तुमधीरतया व्यवसितमिव मे तिरस्करणीम् ॥

Māl. II.1

Cf. Kāṭayavema while commenting on this stanza explains नेपथ्यपरिगतायाः as यवनिकान्तरितायाः

Agnimitra refers to such a curtain. The curtain was removed and then the performer came in the full view of the audience. The later[1] commentators of the Sanskrit plays say while explaining the word Nepathya that it is the place set off by a curtain where make-up etc. is done. The word Nepathya[2] is explained as the curtain and make-up etc. also. In Mālavikāgnimitra the sound of the drum is heard from behind the Nepathya. This seems to be the curtain between the Raṅgapīṭha and the Raṅgaśīrṣa. In the fifth act of Śākuntala the beginning is with the entry of the king seated and Vidūṣaka. They listen to the song sung by Haṁsapadikā. The stage-direction is 'आकाशे गीयते' i.e. it is sung by one not on the stage. Knowing the arrangement of the musicians it must be understood as the song being sung behind the curtain.[3] The first entry of the King and the Vidūṣaka would be naturally after removing another curtain held by two attendants. The King and Vidūṣaka are sitting on the Raṅgapīṭha. Haṁsapadikā's song would be sung by the songstress behind the curtain between the Raṅgapīṭha and the Raṅgaśīrṣa [4]

It is clear then that for the dramatic purpose one curtain was necessary. As it was not fixed, being held by two attendants and then removed, we do not get its mention in the Chapter on the theatre. This was the earlier practice. (The entries by the two doors without the use of curtain might have been the earliest stage.) Later, another curtain was added between the Raṅgapīṭha and the Raṅgaśīrṣa. This might have been moved sideways it being held by rings through which a rope

1. Cf. त्रिपुरारिटीका on MM (N. S. Ed. p. 5)नेपथ्य: नाम पश्चाद्यवनिकान्तरितो वर्णग्रहणादियोग्यकुशीलवकुटुम्बावस्थानप्रदेशः। कुशीलवकुटुम्बस्य स्थली नेपथ्य इष्यते इति वचनात् ।

Similarly Vīrarāghava in his commentary on Mahāvīracarita and Jagaddhara in his commentaries on Veṇīsaṁhāra and MM.

2. Cf. Rāghavabhaṭṭa's commentary on Śāk. (Kale's Ed. p. 4) 'नेपथ्यं स्याज्जवनिका रङ्गभूमिः प्रसाधनम्' इत्यजयः ।

3. The other reading for आकाशे is नेपथ्ये.

Cf. Śāk. Edition I by Prof. R. D. Karmarkar, p. 116 footnote 4.

4. Cf. Kuṭṭanīmta 908—बभूवतुर्जवनिकान्तरिते' ।
and 909 'अपनीततिरस्करिणी'-

or a string passed. It was drawn aside when necessary. The entries through the doors in that case would be understood as from the South and the North sides of the stage. In the case of hurried entries the 'Apaṭīkṣepa'[1] would mean tossing the fixed curtain. When there would be only one curtain held by two attendants at the time of entries, the entry in excitement etc. would be without using the curtain, i.e., the character would enter the stage directly from the green-room doors.

The Acts of Sanskrit dramas end with the stage directions like 'निष्क्रान्ताः सर्वे' or 'निष्क्रान्तौ' or 'निष्क्रान्तः' etc. which indicate the absence of a fixed curtain in the front like the modern drop,[2] to mark the end of the Act. The nature of the endings of the Acts and the exit songs to indicate the exits, also point to the same conclusion.

There is a reference to three curtains in Śilappadikāram[3] as "the single screen and the screen between two pillars to the right of the stage beside the overhanging curtain." In the Jīvakacintāmaṇi,[4] three kinds of screens (Eḷiṇi) are mentioned. (Eḷiṇi appears to be the same as Yavanikā.) The Saṁgītacūḍāmaṇi[5] refers to the curtains as follows—There should be a thick and beautiful curtain in front; behind it there should be two very thin and beautiful curtains looking just like thin mist. The first curtain is the front 'drop' which is removed as soon as the

1. Dr. Bhat thinks that Apaṭī denotes a small curtain and that two such small curtains were hanging over the two green-room doors.

'Apaṭīkṣepa', by Dr. G.K. Bhat; a paper submitted to the A.I.O. Conference, Ujjain (1972).

2. Dr. M. Ghosh says in connection with the Yavanikā mentioned in the NŚ. V. 11, "It appears that the first nine items of the Preliminaries were performed on the stage covered with a front curtain much like the modern drop curtain. There were besides this, two curtains on the two doors of the tiring room. It seems that the front curtain came in to regular use in later times and especially at the end of each Act. Cf. Javanikāntara used as a synonym of 'act' in the Karpūramañjarī."

Cf. The Nāṭyaśāstra Vol. I Ed. by Dr. M. Ghosh, Translation, p. 77 footnote 10 on verses 8-11.

3. Śilappadikāram—translation, p. 101.

4. *Ibid.*—footnote 3, p. 102.

5. Theatre Architecture in Ancient India by Dr. Raghavan. Cf. The Theatre of the Hindus, p. 161.

show beings. Behind the mist like curtain, the danseuse performs the dance called Lāsya. Vema[1] also speaks of three curtains, the one thick and the other two thin like mist. They were to be held in order by women. The Yavanikā[2] is mentioned as 8 Hastas long and 5 or 6 Hastas wide. Jāyana[3] mentions three or more curtains according to one's choice in the dance hall. Shri S.M. Tagore[4] quotes verses according to which the colours of the curtains are given suited to the sentiment. The curtain was to be held by two beautiful women in the entries of the various characters. We do not, however, find the use of such curtains having different colours for different sentiments in existing traditions.

The painted curtains with scenes are not mentioned by any authority. Hence, it is definite that the curtain did not serve the purpose of painted scenery. In MM.[5] we have a reference to Citrayavanikā. This seems to be the curtain between Raṅgapīṭha and Raṅgaśīrṣa which was painted with different colours. The use of three or more curtains mentioned by the different authorities seems to have been in connection with dance performances which were made more effective by such practice.

Scenic appliances

There were no realistic settings. Some suggestive model works of animals, birds etc. were brought on the stage, e.g., the toy clay-cart in the Mṛch., the clay-peacock in the Śāk., an

1. BK., p. 819.
2. BK., p. 796.
3. BK., p. 514.
4. Cf. Eight Principal Rasas of the Hindus, p. 59, footnote :

कार्या यवनिका तत्र नीरन्ध्रा सूक्ष्मवाससा ।
धार्या सुरूपनारीभ्यां तत्तत्पात्रप्रवेशने ॥
शुभ्रवर्णा च शृङ्गारे पीता वीरा प्रशस्यते ।
धूम्रवर्णा च करुणे कर्तव्या कोपनादृते ॥
हास्ये विचित्रा कर्तव्या नीलवर्णा भयानके ।
बीभत्सके धूमला स्याद्रौद्रे रक्ता प्रशस्यते ॥
अद्भुते कृष्णवर्णा स्यादेतत्प्राचीनसंमतम् ।
अरुणापि सा सर्वत्र कार्या यवनिका बुधैः ॥

5. MM., p. 160. (N. S. Press 1915.)

elephant model in the Udayanacarita, the mechanical doll in the Bālarāmāyaṇa etc. The fashioning of mountains, carriages, aerial cars, palaces, houses, temples, horses, elephants, trees, etc., is described as Pusta, in Āhāryābhinaya. These objects were made of light material like bamboo-pieces, leather, cloth, etc. This means that they were only suggestive models and were not to be used realistically, e.g. ascending the palace or mountain would only be represented by gesticulation. It was not even necessary to prepare all these. Bharata[1] says that houses etc. should be fashioned as described in the Pusta[2] or they should be represented by gesticulation. Mounting the swing should be done realistically when the swing is fashioned according to Pusta, otherwise the swinging[3] should merely be gesticulated. We have seen that Abhinava[4] has described the use of Citrapaṭa with the paintings of horses in the hands of the charioteer to give the idea of the chariot. In Chapter XII of the NŚ. the various gaits and movements are described for climbing the mountain, the palace etc. and descending from them; so also for moving in chariots, on horses, elephants, in boats etc. That shows how the gesticulation was highly developed to give the idea of these to the spectators. The conventional was more appealing than the realistic on Bharata's stage. If such things are shown realistically, the acting is, sometimes put into the background. Movements through carriages and aerial[5] cars etc. by mechanical devices were not impossible for the ancients in India. There might have been some efforts to present them realistically on a sufficiently large stage. But such type of realism was not thought as very important for the drama, for the

1. NŚ. (Kashi Sanskrit Series) XX—41-43.
NŚ. XII. 106—संज्ञामात्रेण कर्तव्यान्येतानि विभ्रिपूर्वकम् ।

2. Prof. Siddheswar Chattopadhyaya holds the view that Pustas were very essential things in ancient Indian dramatic productions. Many of the dramas of poets like Bhāsa, Kālidāsa, Śūdraka and others cannot be staged at all without necessary models. In ancient Indian stage, Pustas, according to him, were used not to represent everything realistically but to suggest the dramatic situations, being miniature models of hills, cars, etc. 'Pusta in Sanskrit Dramaturgy'—Paper read at the A.I.O. Conference, Srinagar.

3. NŚ. XXV 83-85.

4. NŚ. Vol. II, p. 151.

5. Cf. 'Yantras or Mechanical Contrivances in Ancient India' by Dr. Raghavan. (Published by the Indian Institute of Culture, Bangalore.)

bare stage with minimum accessaries gave utmost .importance to the actor's skill.

Dr. G.K. Bhat,[1] in connection with Bhāsa's stage suggests compartmental stage. It is created by a wall of wood work or wooden framework with light painted canvas stretched across it. This facilitates the representation of the particular scenes. He says that the Mattavāraṇīs could be used to locate an apartment like that of Vasantasenā. Miss[2] Ketkar states that Kakṣyās were on both the sides of the Raṅgaśīrṣa and the divisions of Kakṣyā were made by small walls which could be changed when necessary.

According to the Kakṣyāvibhāga[3] convention (already described in Chapter II) we know that in the front, middle and back divisions of the stage, certain parts were understood as representing certain localities like the mountain, garden etc. When the actor, moved[4] round on the stage (as per the stage direction 'Parikramya'), he was understood to have come to different place which was mentioned by the dramatist. (It appears[5] that the Raṅgapīṭha and the Raṅgaśīrṣa were not separately marked in the earlier times and leaving aside the place for musicians, the remaining stage was divided into Kakṣyās.) There was no necessity of the compartmental stage as suggested by Dr. Bhat.

It is interesting to compare the ancient Indian stage with the Shakespearean stage. The description[6] of the Fortune theatre closely modelled on the Globe as given by Raymond Williams is as follows. It was shaped square, 80 feet each way over all and 55 feet each way in its interior. There were

1. 'Bhāsa's stage' by Dr. G.K. Bhat J.O.I. Baroda, Vol. II Parts I—IV 1953, pp. 339-345.

2. Bhāratīya Nāṭyaśāstra, pp. 39-40.

3. Cf. Sanskrit Drama and Performance by Dr. Raghavan, p. 20. The use of Kakṣyās is pointed out by me in Chapter V, while describing the staging of some scenes from Sanskrit plays.

4. This convention is used very effectively even now in the Marathi folk-theatre.

5. Cf. NŚ. Vol. II p. 197.

'तेन भाण्डेन यत्परित आक्रान्तं तद्विवर्ज्यं शेषे रङ्गपीठदेशे निष्क्रमण-
प्रवेशगत्याद्युपयोगी स्थानविभागो निर्देश्यः · · ·।'

6. See Drama in Performance by Raymond Williams, pp. 54-56

galleries in this theatre in three storeys running all around its walls. Within these galleries there was a yard into which the stage projected. The stage was some 40 feet wide extending into the middle of the yard giving a depth of some 26 feet. The spectators in the galleries and the yard surrounded the stage on three sides. The height of the stage above the level of the yard was about 4 feet. The galleries were roofed over with thatch but the yard was open to sky. Over the stage extended a cover beginning a little below the eaves of the top gallery and probably sloping forward and supported by two tall pillars towards the front of the stage. At the back of the stage was the Tire House. From this there were two doors, one on either side for the entrance to the stage. Between these doors there was a hanging curtain which, when necessary, could be drawn back to reveal an inner playing space which might be as much as 15 feet wide. Above this place and projecting slightly over the open stage was a gallery which was also available for the action of the play. It was some 10 or 12 feet above the stage. This gallery was accessible from behind by means of stairs from the Tiring Room. There was also perhaps a trap-door in it immediately above the inner playing space. On the main stage, there were trap-doors large enough for properties to be drawn up through them from the space below the stage.

Scenic representation was sparing but a painted black cloth could be used for the panorama of a city; battlements could be set up (the gallery was already available as the wall of a city or a castle); a window could be set up in the gallery (which was thus available for the upper room of a house); a hell's mouth could be set up in an open trap; alcoves, bowers, cells, tombs could be represented in the inner playing space; trees where necessary could be set on the stage and mossy banks; beds, tables, benches, stools were commonly employed. It was also possible by the use of hangings to set up tents and other enclosed spaces on the stage itself. But in general, all properties were used as the materials for an action rather than in the construction of any full representation. Place and atmosphere were largely determined by the dramatic action itself.

According to Prof. Thorndike[1] the main stage was conceived as unlocalised territory. The dramatist had the bare open platform in his view and he planned his play for that. The localization of scenes was provided by the use of the curtain and the inner stage. The inner stage was employed for presenting an inner locality, a discovery and scenes with heavy properties.

Ancient Indian stage differed mainly from the Shakespearean in not having a gallery.[2] There were no trap doors also. The musicians sat at the back of the stage. The gesticulation was highly conventional in Indian theatre. The stage conventions together with the poetic descriptions and the conventional gesticulation were sufficient enough to create the atmosphere before the imaginative audience. The Indian stage and the Elizabethan stage were alike in not having a drop curtain.

The Chinese classical stage is nearer to the ancient Indian stage due to its simplicity and conventionality. The theatre, in the East and the South East Asia, in general, is marked by these characteristics. (The account of the theatre in the East and the South East Asia in Appendix C will make this statement clear.)

The Troupe

The group[3] forming a dramatic company, as given by the NŚ. consisted of the following members—

Sūtradhāra—He was the director of the plays. His natural qualities were intelligence, good memory, generosity, steadiness in speech, good health, sweet nature, tolerance, self-control, sweet-tongue, calmness, truthfulness, politeness, and holiness. He was the knower of Sūtra (thread) which brings about the

1. Cf. Shakespeare's Theatre by Ashley H. Thorndike, pp. 104, 105, 108, 109.

2. That the ancient Indian stage had no gallery or upper storey will be made clear by the descriptions of the staging of some scenes from Sanskrit plays given in Chapter V.

3. NŚ. N.S. Press 1943, pp. 652-657.
NS. G.O.S. Vol. IV, Chapter XXXV, 21-28.
NS. Ed. by Dr. Ghosh, Vol. II., pp. 204-208.

unity of songs, instrumental music and recitation, with the application of āstric instruction. He was important in the Preliminaries. Sometimes he played the main role in the play. [Sthāpaka who resembled Sūtradhāra in his qualities used to carry out the Prologue. He is not mentioned separately in the troupe.]

[*Pāripārśvaka*—He was of middling type possessing the qualities of Sūtradhāra in a lesser degree. Sometimes he assumed secondary role in the play. He is also not mentioned separately in the troupe].

Taurika—He was expert in playing on all the musical instruments (*Tūra*—a musical instrument).

Kuśīlava—He arranged the various musical instruments properly and was an expert player of musical instruments.

Nandī[1]—He praised all the world by sweet words of praise and salutation, with auspicious rites. He pleased people in the performance of the play in various ways with Sanskrit and Prakrit recitation.[2]

Nāṭyakāra —He created the different roles of different types, as directed.

Bharata—Through him the play was raised up with various types of roles; he was like a leader and his representation was accompanied by instrumental music.

Naṭa—He gesticulated the life of the people endowed with sentiments and states.

Vidūṣaka—He was ready-witted and humorous, adorned by Cheda (stripes of colour). [He gesticulated being short, curved, hunch-backed, with deformed face, bald and tawny-eyed].

Nāyaka—He was the hero of the dramatic representation, expert in the dramatic art.

Nāṭakīyā—She was extremely beautiful and had mastery over tempo, rhythm and sentiments.

The Mukuṭakāra fashioned various types of crowns; Ābharaṇakāra prepared ornaments; Mālyakṛt, garlands; Veṣakara dresses. Citrakara was the painter and Rajaka the

1. Barodo edition of the NŚ. reads Vādī.
See. NŚ. Ed. by Ghosh, Vol. II. Chapter XXXV. 97.

2. Nandī is given separately in the Baroda edition. See NŚ. (Baroda edition). Vol. IV. XXXV. 29.

dyer. Kāruka fashioned objects by means of lac, stones, iron and wood.

Thus the dramatic company had the actors and actresses for the various roles in the play. There were musicians and other craftsmen. It is to be noted that the Nāṭyakara is also a member of the troupe. From the prologues of the plays we know Naṭī as the wife of Sūtradhāra.

Sometimes there were competitions among the rival troupes.

The producers were expected to know thoroughly Samatva (co-ordination, i.e., the harmony of the movements of major and minor limbs accompanying song and instrumental music), charm of limbs, recitation, roles, sentiments, instrumental music, songs, dress and make-up.

There were Nāṭyācāryas (the teachers of the dramatic art) who instructed the pupils in Nāṭya. They enjoyed patronage of the masters like kings etc. The teacher was an expert in vocal and instrumental music and the movements following the rhythm. He was to know what is reasonable. He was intelligent, steady-minded and he possessed good memory.

Roles[1]

The impersonation in the play was of three types—

1. Anurūpā, i.e., similar, e.g., when women act female roles and the men, the male roles, of same age and condition.

2. Rūpānurūpā, i.e., imitating the role, befitting the form, e.g., when the male actor takes the female role and the woman the male role, skilfully.

3. Virūpā, i.e., dissimilar—when the child enacts an old person or an old person, the role of a child etc.

The roles of gods should be enacted by actors who are young, graceful, lustrous, and faultless in appearance. They should have sweet voice. The roles of Rākṣasas, Dānavas and Daityas should be presented by tall and large-bodied actors, who possess thunder-like voice, fierce eyes and naturally crooked eye-brows; those of princes and kings by actors having beautiful eyes, eyebrows, forehead, nose, lips, cheeks, face, neck and

1. Cf. NŚ. Ch. XXVI & XXXV.

other limbs and graceful appearance; they should be tall, proportionate in body, learned and of good character. The roles of commanders and ministers should be taken by actors with faultless body, with clarity in speech and action. They should be neither too tall, nor too fat and should be skilled in perfect reasoning. They should be bold and capable of proper decision at the right time. Chamberlains and the learned Brahmins should be enacted by actors, short or tall, with tawny eyes and long nose. The servants should be presented by actors who are short, slow, hunch-backed, deformed, ugly-faced, squinted in eyes, fat, flat-nosed and ill-tempered. The roles of those[1] with many faces and arms and of beasts, Gajānana etc. should be effected by the instructor with the use of clay, wood, lac and leather. The actors who do not possess the physique and the nature meant for the roles, should be employed as per the instruction of the teacher.

The delicate type of performances having love as its principal sentiment should be enacted through women. The forceful type having military and complicated actions should be enacted through men.

Generally in the temples and the mansions of kings, commanders and other important personalities, the performance would be enacted by women with male roles also. The dramatic representation is found to be enacted in heaven by Rambhā, Urvaśī and others. Hence, the preceptors should teach it with efforts to the ladies.

In the Mahābhāṣya we have the term Bhrūkuṁsa for the male actor taking woman's role. In the Priyadarśikā, Manoramā was to enact the role of Vatsarāja in the Garbhanāṭaka in Act III. In Kuṭṭanīmata, the enacting of the first act of Ratnāvalī is described from which we know that the females took male roles also. In Mālatīmādhava, the nun and her pupil (Parivrājikā) are enacted by the Sūtradhāra and his assistant, (this seems to be the necessity due to their being nuns). Though the practice of assuming male roles by males

1. Cf. NŚ. XXVI 3-4.
Cf. Prabodhacandrodaya the commentary Candrikā, p. 14.
सजीवपशुपक्ष्यादिप्राणिनां रूपधारणम् ।

and female roles by women was preferred, we find ladies acting male roles also in the troupes of ladies as described in Kuṭṭanīmata.

The social status of the actors

The NŚ. is raised to the status of Nāṭyaveda in the first chapter which shows that the Nāṭya was regarded highly. From NŚ. Chapter XXXVI, we know that due to the excesses indulged in making fun of the higher people, the actors lost their original status. Śailūṣa, a synonym of Naṭa, is called as Jāyājīva also. This term signifies that he found his livelihood through his wife. From Rāmāyaṇa we know that Śailūṣa used to offer his wife to others.[1] The Arthaśāstra[2] lays down among the duties of the Śūdras the work of artesans and Kuśīlavas (who are described in the NŚ. as connected with music). Manu prohibits Brāhmaṇas from becoming actors. He[3] imposes a minor penalty for illicit connection with the wives of actors. Manu and Yājñavalkya[4] lay down that the testimony of a Kuśīlava is not valid and no Brāhmaṇa should accept food from the actors. This fact is corroborated by the Sūtradhāra in the prologue of the Mṛcch.[5] when he says how he should find a brahmin in Ujjayinī befitting people like him to accept his invitation for dinner. The Viṣṇu[6] code assigns the profession of actors to the Āyogavas, the illegal progeny born of Śūdra and a daughter of Vaiśya. Baudhāyana[7] enumerates Raṅgopajīvana (living on the dramatic art) as a lesser sin (Upapātaka).

It seems, then, that due to the loose morals, the actors as a class suffered the loss of their respectable position in the society. When the actresses were often courtesans, it was but natural that their moral standard was low. But the art was great. Hence, in spite of the prejudices, the actors received

1. Rāmāyaṇa II, 30-8 शैलूष इव मां राम परेभ्यो दातुमिच्छसि ।
2. Arthaśāstra I. 3.
3. Manusmṛti VIII. 362.
4. Yājñavalkyasmṛti, I. 6. 161; II.5.70, Manu, IV. 214-215. VIII. 65
5. Mṛccha. Ed. by Prof. R.D. Karmarkar 1937, p. 8.
6. Viṣṇusmṛti XVI 3-8.
7. Baudhāyana II, 2, 5.

affection and favour of kings. Bāṇa has enumerated actors and actresses among his friends. Bhartṛhari refers to the friendship of the actors with kings. Bhavabhūti's natural affection for actors is mentioned in the MM. Kulaśekhara Perumal, the Kerala King, himself acted in his own play. In the Cākyār tradition the satire on the society by the temple actors cannot be challenged by anybody. Thus even though the actors suffered a setback in their social position, still for all practical purposes they won the hearts of the great and small alike in the society. The Nāṭya being a very powerful means of enjoyment and instruction, was considered important and hence the actor enjoyed popularity for his skill in the dramatic art.

Spectators,[1] *success in the performance, judges etc.*

The true spectator becomes possessed of the states represented in the play. Normally the young people are pleased with love, the old with Purāṇic legends and tales of virtue, the learned with religious or philosophical instruction, seekers of money with the topics of wealth, the brave with the Heroic, the Furious and the personal combats and fights and the passionless with salvation. The children, women, and the uncultured are pleased with the laughter and the costume.

Spectators express their appreciation of a successful performance by such exclamations as 'well done', 'how pathetic'. 'how wonderful' etc. Smile and laughter according to propriety, and swelling uproar at times, manifested their approval. Signs of success expressed physically are horripilation, rising up from the seat, giving away clothes (or waving garments)[2] and moving up fingers (raising the hand). The success is divine when the performance abounds in temperaments and states and is not marred by any untoward incident. Sometimes there would be obstacles due to supernatural powers like strong wind, rain, fall of the pandal etc. There would be obstacles created by professional enemies due to jealousy etc. such as excessive laughter and crying, (clapping at wrong

1. NŚ. Vol. III, Ch. XXVII.
2. Cf. Abh. 'चेलादिप्रक्षेपं चेलाद्यभावे चोर्ध्वांगुलिकरणादिभिः
NŚ. Vol. III, p. 308.

places),[1] throwing cow-dung, clods of clay etc. The entry of an intoxicated person or a lunatic would also disturb the performance. Sometimes the actors also become responsible for the failure. For example, unnatural acting, absence of proper movements, expression of temperament suited to another's role, loss of memory, recitation of other character's speech, falling of crown or ornaments etc. would lead to such a disaster. If the vocal music is out of tune and rhythm or the percussion instruments are wrongly played the performance would receive a setback. The defects in the recitation like repetition, the use of words with wrong meaning, the confusion of long and short vowels and the wrong stops etc. would definitely come in the way. The irreparable obstacles are—

1. Those due to natural calamity;
2. Incompletion of work on time—(Abhinava[2] explains it as inappropriateness of time, the performance suited for one time, presented at the other).

Abhinava[3] says that the preliminaries also should be critically judged. The judges should be of good character and high birth, learned, dutiful, middle aged, proficient in drama, alert and impartial. They should be expert in playing four kinds of musical instruments. They should also be expert in arts and crafts, the four kinds of histrionic representation and know the subtlety of Rasa and Bhāva etc. In the dramatic representation nothing is completely perfect or devoid of blemishes; hence, the blemishes should be marked from the viewpoint of the dramatic art.

When there is a conflict about the merits of a performance the assessors to be referred to are those expert in sacrifice when sacrifice is represented, the dancer-actor in histrionic represen-

1. Cf. Tālikāpāta in place of Nālikāpāta;
NŚ. Kāvyamālā, Edition 1943, p. 421.
2. Cf. Abh. NŚ. Vol. III, p. 316
'शेषोदकनालिकया काल उपलक्ष्यते । तस्य शेषत्वमन्यकालव्याप्ति-योग्यता तेन यत्र काले यदनुचितं तत्र तन्निबन्धनं यथा प्रभाते सङ्गीतकदर्शनादि राज्ञः ।'
3. 'जर्जरमोक्षस्यान्त इति पूर्वरङ्गप्रयोगोऽपि परीक्ष्य इति दर्शयति ।'
NŚ. Vol. III, p. 317.

tation, prosodist for metrical compositions, grammarian for extensive recitation, the expert in missiles and archery for the grace of a pose, painter for costumes and make-up, courtesan in enjoyment of love, Gāndharva for musical notes and royal servant for etiquette. In case of a dispute regarding the knowledge of Śāstra the decision should be made on the basis of Śāstra. The decision about the award of the banner for the best performance should be given impartially. For this purpose the merits and demerits of the performance should be recorded with the help of writers and enumerators who should carry out their work attentively. The judges should sit 12 Hastas away from the stage. They should note merits and defects in the performance. The defects originating from the supernatural power or enemies' efforts should not be recorded. If due to the excellence of the performance both the contesting dramatic groups are equal in merit, the banner should be given to both with the approval of the king.

Time of the performance and occasions etc.

The plays could be performed in the morning, afternoon, evening and at the dawn. The performance, pure or mixed, pleasant to the ear and relating to a story of virtue should take place in the morning, the one rich in instrumental music, having the story of strength and energy in the afternoon; that having Kaiśikī style and the Erotic as the main sentiment in the evening[1] and the one relating to the greatness of a hero and which is full of pathos should take place at dawn. Dramatic performance should not be presented at the midday, the midnight, the twilight prayer and the meal time. But if the patron so desires, the rules about time and place need not be considered.

The ND.[2] says that the maximum time limit of enacting an Act (with all the embellishments) would be 30 Ghaṭikās and minimum two Ghaṭikās. (Ghaṭikā is equal to twentyfour minutes).

1. The Prologue of MM. indicates morning time.

2. 'चतुर्यामो मुहूर्तंत इति मुहूर्तादारभ्य यामचतुष्टयं यावत् सर्वापकर्षेण घटिकाद्वयाभिनेयः । सर्वोत्कर्षेण त्रिंशद्घटिकाऽभिनेयः ।'

ND., p. 31.

According to the living tradition in the temple theatres of Kerala, the scenes from Sanskrit plays are staged at night. Only the Third Act of Abhiṣeka Nāṭaka (i.e. Toraṇayuddhāṅka) is[1] staged in the forenoon as it is the Cākyārs' convention. According to Bharata the nature of Rasa of the scene is the criterion to decide which scene is to be staged when and how long.[2]

From the prologues of the plays we know that the plays were performed by the troupes during the religious festivals in temples before the public. At the courts of the kings also the dramas were produced before the appreciative audience. Festive occasions like the Spring Festival were the most common for the performance. Special occasions like marriage, birth of a prince etc. were celebrated by arranging dramatic performances. The patron or the temple authorities used to bear the expenses and arrange the performances.

The lighting was provided by torches or lamps. In connection with the Pūjā of Raṅga the word Dīpikā occurs. It is stated[3] that the master of the dramatic art should illuminate a ll the Raṅga with a lighted torch.

1. Cf. 'The Time of staging a Sanskrit Drama' by K.R. Pisharoti, I.H.Q. June 1950. pp. 146-148.

2. Prof. H.R. Diwekar states in connection with the timing of dramatic representation that the merits of drama were marked from Sūtradhāra's beginning of Tripadī called Āmukha before which he handed back the Jarjara to the attendant (Jarjaramokṣa). He has explained the verse जर्जरमोक्षस्यान्ते सिद्धेर्मोक्षस्तु नालिकायास्तु etc. (NŚ. XXVII. 41) 'सिद्धिमोक्ष' was the commencement of noting down the merits and 'नालिकामोक्ष was placing the Ghaṭī in water. He further says that in the points of failure 'शेषोदकनालिकत्व' is mentioned by Bharata. He understands it as the performance remaining unfinished in the time measured by Nālikās. (Nālikā is the same as Ghaṭikā.)

Cf. 'Timing of Dramatic Representations in India' by Prof. H.R. Diwekar. J.R.A.S. G.B. & I. 1928, pp. 893-896,

3. Cf. NŚ. III. 90.

'प्रगृह्य दीपिकां दीप्तां सर्वं रङ्गं प्रदीपयेत् ।'

CHAPTER V

THE PERFORMANCE

A. *Pūrvaraṅga—the Preliminaries* :

Before the actual performance of the play started the Preliminaries were gone through for the propitiation of the deities and the appeasement of evil spirits. In the concluding part, the audience was entertained and the drama and the dramatist introduced. The Pūrvaraṅga was so called because it was performed prior to the actual commencement of the play. It was simple in the beginning. Lord Śaṅkara gave the classical dance to make it more striking. Thus the Śuddha (pure) Pūrvaraṅga was carried out in a simple manner and Citra (striking) in an elaborate way. The Preliminaries were marked by instrumental and vocal music, dance and recitation. Of course, the NŚ. enjoins that the music and dance should not be carried on for too long a time lest the spectators feel bored.

In all, nineteen items are mentioned in the NŚ. in connection with the Preliminaries. The first nine were to be performed behind the curtain and the remaining, after the curtain was removed. These nineteen items were as follows—

1. *Pratyāhāra*[1]—It was the arrangement of the instruments.
2. *Avataraṇa*—In it, the musicians took their seats.
3. *Ārambha*—It was the commencement of vocal exercise for singing, (the singing of musical notes for the melodious adjustment of voice).

1. Kutapavinyāsa —

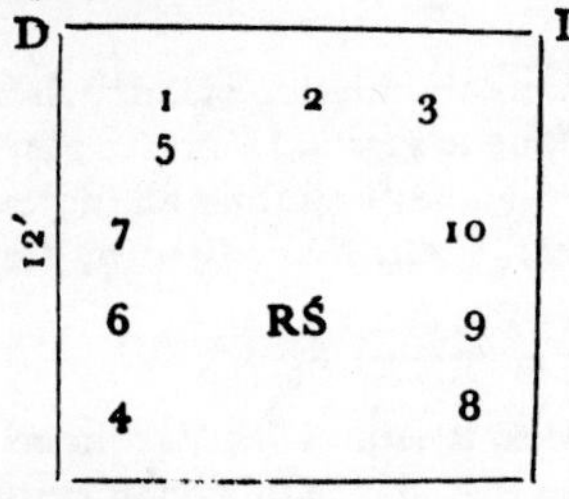

1. Mrdaṅga-player.
2. Paṇava-player.
3. Dardura-player.
4. Songster.
5. Vīṇā-player.
6. 7. } Flute-players.
8. 9. 10. } Songstresses.

D—Green-room door.
RŚ.—Raṅgasīrṣa.

4. *Āśrāvaṇā*—It was the adjustment of the musical instruments in proper tune.

5. *Vaktrapāṇi*—The different styles of playing musical instruments (effected by the hand) were rehearsed.

6. *Parighaṭṭanā*—The strings of the instruments were played upon duly.

7. *Saṁghoṭanā*—In it there was employment of hands in different manners to indicate the time beats.

8. *Mārgāsārita*—It was the playing together harmoniously of drums and stringed instruments.

9. *Āsārita*—It was of three types, i.e., long, medium and short, and meant for the distinction of Kalā and Pāta (in regard to Tāla).

These nine items[1] were mainly connected with the instrumental music and were performed behind the curtain, hence they were called Bahirgītas. Then, after removing the curtain, dances and recitals were presented accompanied by the playing of all instruments. The remaining ten items were—

10. *Gītavidhi*—The song in praise of God, of Madraka[2] or other class or Vardhamānaka[3] was sung, along with the class-dance.

11. *Utthāpana*—The reciters of Nāndī started the performance first of all.

12. *Parivartana*—All the guardian deities of different worlds,

1. Of these items, 3 to 8 are described in all details in Chapter XXIX of the NŚ. Vol. IV, pp. 105-118.

2. The Gītas are seven—Madraka, Aparāntaka, Ullopya, Prakarī, Ovenaka, Rovindaka & Uttara. The treatment of their Tāla is given in NŚ. XXXI.

3. The Vardhamānaka is a combination of four Āsāritas. In it there is a gradual increase of Kalās, due to gradual increase of syllables and an increase of Laya, instrumental music, gestures, and an increase in the number of dancers (in successive phases). Cf. NŚ. edited by Dr. Ghosh. Vol. II Text, XXXI—98-99.

See NŚ. (Baroda) Vol. IV. XXXI 69-159.

As stated by Dr. Raghavan, the songs like Vardhamānaka, Āsārita etc. were made part of an interpretative dance involving gesture. These songs were composed by Brahman and contained praise of Śiva.

Cf. Bhoja's Śṛṅgāraprakāśa by Dr. Raghavan, p. 585.

were saluted by (the Sūtradhara) walking (all over the stage) in all the four directions.

13. *Nāndī*—It included the blessings of Gods, Brahmins and Kings ; it was to be recited without exception.

14. *Śuṣkāvakṛṣṭā*—It was the Avakṛṣṭā Dhruvā with meaningless syllables in it ; it indicated the verse for Jarjara (the bamboo pole worshipped by the Sūtradhāra).

15. *Raṅgadvāra*—It was so called because with it the verbal and physical gesticulation started.

16. *Cārī*—It consisted of movements delineating the Erotic sentiment.

17. *Mahācārī*—It had the movements delineating the Furious sentiment.

18. *Trigata*—It was the conversation between Vidūṣaka,[1] Sūtradhāra and Pāripārśvaka.

19. *Prarocanā*—It was the address to the audience by the Sūtradhāra, suggesting the (theme of the) play, to be presented with proper reasoning.[2]

Nirgīta or Bahirgīta was the music in which there were no words or songs but only combinations of sounds having no meaning. The rhythmic syllables which were played on the instruments mainly constituted the Nirgīta. Dr. Raghavan[3] mentions that it was the contribution of the Asuras to the Sanskrit theatre and even now, the memory of this ancient tradition survives in a high degree of instrumental proficiency being claimed in musical parlance as "Asura-sādhakam".

After employing Gītaka and Vardhamānaka, Utthāpanī[4] Dhruvā was to be sung, having eleven syllables in each foot with the first two, 4th, 8th and the 11th long. It was to be

1. Abhinava remarks that this Vidūṣaka is one of the two Pāripārśvakas adopting the dress and speech etc. of Vidūṣaka.

NŚ. Vol. I, p. 219.

2. Prof. Kalikumar Datta states the list of 22 elements of Pūrvaraṅga as given by Bharata. He has in this list, three kinds of Āsārita, Śuṣkā and Avakṛṣṭā separately. He has also mentioned the list of 22 items as given by Bhāvaprakāśana and has referred to the views of Sāgaranandin and others in this connection. Cf. Prologues and Epilogues in Sanskrit Drama, by Kalikumar Datta—Our Heritage Vol. V, Pt. I, 1957.

3. 'Music in Ancient Indian Drama' by Dr. V. Raghavan, p. 14.

4. See NŚ. Vol. I., p. 256.

sung in Caturasra Tāla. Four Parivartas (with all the details of the Tāla prescribed) were to be resorted to. One Parivarta was made of four Sannipātas, each Sannipāta being of 8 Kalās. The first Parivarta was to be in slow tempo and at the end of the third Sannipāta, the drums were to be played. When the second Parivarta commenced in the middle tempo, the Sūtradhāra together with two Assistants was to enter with flowers in hand, purified, clad in white, of good mind, initiated and casting glances in wonder. His standing posture was to be Vaiṣṇava, with the Sauṣṭhava, (naturally graceful position) of the body. The Assistants were to be on both the sides of the Sūtradhāra, carrying Bhṛṅgāra (gold pitcher) and the Jarjara. The Sūtradhāra was to go five steps (as prescribed) and then offer flowers saluting Brahman. Then in the third Parivarta, in quick tempo, after first sipping and then sprinkling himself with the water, the Jarjara was to be taken up. After taking the Jarjara, the Sūtradhāra was to mutter some Mantras (incantations) and then approach the musical instruments. This fourth Parivarta also was to be in quick tempo. In the Tryaśra type of the Preliminaries, the movements would have twentyfour Kalās while in Caturaśra, thirtytwo Kalās.[1] Sprinkling with water is not prescribed in the Tryaśra type. Thus the Utthāpana was to be performed. In Parivartana, the Parivartanī[2] Dhruvā, having thirteen syllables in each foot with only the last syllable long, was to be employed. During the singing of this Dhruvā, the Sūtradhāra was to salute different deities towards the directions to which they belong. At the end of Parivartana, the fourth man was to enter with flowers in his hands. He was to worship the Jarjara, Kutapa and the Sūtradhāra duly. He was to move, accompanied by the drum only. There would be no song but chanting of meaningless syllables. He was then to leave the stage. After this, Avakṛṣṭā[3] Dhruvā was to be sung, consisting mostly of long syllables, with Sthāyivarṇa. Then the Nāndī, with eight or twelve Padas (subordi-

1. The movements of hands and feet were sixteen in the Caturaśra type and twelve in the Tryaśra type. Each movement (Nipāta) was of two Kalās.

See NŚ. Vol. 1., p. 232; Abhinava— 'कलाद्वयेनैकं पतनमिति यावत् ।'

2. See NŚ. Vol. 1., pp. 256, 257.

3. See NŚ Vol. 1., pp. 257, 258.

nate sentences) was to be recited by the Sūtradhāra in the Madhyama note. (The Pada in connection with the Nāndī appears to be not a word or the foot of the verse but the subordinate sentence of the Nāndī for, after each Pada, the two Assistants were to say "Let this be so".) After this, the Avakṛṣṭā Dhruvā, with meaningless syllables indicating Jarjara was to be employed. In Raṅgadvāra, after Devastotra[1] (hymn of praise of God) a verse was to be recited in praise of the deity whose worship is the occasion, or the deity worshipped by the King or Brahmin. Then another verse, in praise of Jarjara, was to be recited and honouring it the Cārī was to be performed. Aḍḍitā[2] Dhruvā in medium tempo was to be employed. The Sūtradhāra was to have Avahittha posture and placing his left hand with its palm downwards, with breast in Udvāhita and the head Añcita and taking Jarjara with the other hand, he was to have Pañcapadī. He was to recite a Cārī verse with love as its subject matter and move back with the same steps as before, facing the west. Then placing the Jarjara in the hands of the Assistants he was to perform the Mahācārī. The Dhruvā to be employed was Caturaśrā in quick tempo. The verse expressing the Furious sentiment was to be recited. Then he was to call the Assistants and while they were coming, Narkuṭa song was to be sung. Then the Trigata was to take place in which Vidūṣaka spoke irrelevant things causing Sūtradhāra's smile. Lastly, the Sūtradhāra was to praise the audience and invite them (to witness the play), mentioning the subject of the play. Then all the three were to leave the stage. In the Tryaśra type, the measure of Tāla would be abridged suitably, e.g., instead of 16 Kalās there would be 12 etc.

In Citra variety, the class-dance would be performed in

1. Abhinava says, 'देवस्य विष्णोः स्तोत्रं...'

NŚ. Vol. I, p. 238.

2. In the interpolated portion of the Fifth Chapter of the NŚ. (G.O.S.), the treatment of these Dhruvās is seen. The Parivartā is given as having fifteen syllables in each foot, with the first two, fourth, eighth, tenth, fourteenth and fifteenth long; Avakṛṣṭā, having sixteen syllables in each foot, with the third, sixth, fifteenth, ninth, eleventh, and sixteenth long; Aḍḍitā, having thirteen syllables in each foot, with the third, sixth and thirteenth long.

Cf. NŚ. Vol. 1., pp. 256-258.

between two Padas of Nāndī. When the Utthāpana and Parivartana were carried out and the worship by the fourth person was offered, and sublime songs sung by expert musicians the Dundubhis (large kettle-drums) were played repeatedly. The female dancers (dressed as goddesses) scattered clusters of flowers all over the stage, performing delicate and graceful Aṅgahāras. The class-dance with Piṇḍīs,[1] Recakas and Aṅgahāras etc. was to be performed in between the Nāndī Padas, separately. Of course, the dance and music were not to be prolonged in excess for that would make the audience lose their patience.

After the Preliminaries (Tryaśra, Caturaśra and again Śuddha or Citra) were performed in this manner, the Sūtradhāra made the exit together with his assistants and the Sthāpaka similar in form and qualities to the Sūtradhāra entered in the same manner. In his entry, the Dhruvā would be meaningful and in middle tempo. Then he was to perform Cārī in praise of Gods and Brahmins with the recitation of verses containing sweet words, and various sentiments and states. Thus pleasing the spectators, he was to announce the name of the playwright and start the Prologue. He was to have recourse to God in a divine play, a man in human play and God or man in a play where there is union of God[2] and man. He was to indicate the subject of the play by alluding to its Mukha (opening) and Bīja (seed). After thus introducing the play, he left the stage.

In describing the Preliminaries, I have pointed out the main things. All the movements are described by Bharata in details with the respective Cārīs etc. Abhinava[3] has described, according to Kīrtidhara, who followed the view of Nandikeśvara, that four female dancers were to perform class-dance during the first Āsārita ; then again four during the second Āsārita etc. But he says that it is not witnessed by him.

The items of the Preliminaries behind the curtain, consisting of instrumental music mostly, were meant to create the atmosphere also. Then after the curtain was removed we find the offering of worship to the deities, the worship of Jarjara,

1. See Appendix B for Piṇḍīs etc.
2. Abh. 'दिव्यमानुषो रामादिः ।' NŚ. Vol. I, p. 249.
3. BK., p. 416.

the recitation of Nāndī and the humorous conversation in Trigata etc. The movements of the Sūtradhāra and the Assistants were prescribed with different Cārīs accompanied by instrumental music. Thus, together with the propitiation of deities, the interest of the spectators was also attracted. The use of dance created a very pleasing atmosphere. The elaborate Preliminaries have survived in the classical theatrical forms like Kathakali, Yakṣagāna Aṅkiyā Nāṭ etc. to certain extent, in which dances, music and recitation are employed before the actual commencement of the play and the deity is propitiated.

Abhinava[1] remarks that some items of the Preliminaries may not be resorted to daily but the Nāndī must be. He also says that this Nāndī is called Prarocanā when it occurs as an element of Bhārati Vṛtti. In the definition given by Bharata "Kāvyārtha-sūcakatva" (suggesting the purport of the play) is not mentioned. It is found in the definition of Ādibharata[2] as quoted by Rāghavabhaṭṭa in his commentary on 'Śākuntala'. ND.[3] adds to the definition the praise of the merits of good men. The Nāndī[4] should have the mention of the moon and the auspicious objects like conch, lotus, etc. and should contain 8 or 12 Padas. According to Abhinava, Pada means either a word or a subordinate sentence. There would be 4, 8 and 16 Padas for Caturaśra type and 3, 6 and 12 for Tryaśra type. The NLR.[5] gives two views—Pada as the foot of the verse, hence there would be 2 or 3 verses, and Pada as a word. The ND. says that the Nāndī may be composed by the poet or the troupe manager and it may be recited by the Sūtradhāra, Sthāpaka or the Pāripārśvaka. Śāradātanaya[6] gives the explanation of Nāndī as derived from Nandin. The dance of Nandin (Śiva's bull) became worthy of representation. Its worship in that form is called Nāndī. Nāndī is explained from 'Nand' 'to please' also. Miss Dave[7] thinks that Prarocanā and Nāndī

1. NŚ. Vol. I, p. 217.
2. Śāk., p. 4.
3. ND., pp. 171-172.
4. SD. VI. 25.
5. NLR., pp. 46-47.
6. Bhāvaprakāśana, VII, pp. 196-197.
7. Cf. 'Nāndī in Theory' by Urmila Dave, I.H.Q. XVII pp. 359-369.

were taken as benedictory verses one time or the other. She states that when the remark 'Nāndyante,'[1] etc. precedes the benedictory verse, the verse is Prarocanā and when the remark follows it, the verse is Nāndī. Thus there were two practices.

Prof. R.B. Athavale[2] says that when the Preliminaries were carried out formerly in full, by the Sūtradhāra, the Sthāpaka sang the dramatist's benedictory verse and carried out the Prologue. Sūtradhāra singing the dramatist's Nāndī also was perhaps the introduction of Bhāsa. According to him, at the time of Viśvanātha only one person, i.e., the Sūtradhāra sang the benedictory verse of the dramatist and presented the Prologue.

We know that the NŚ. mentions Sūtradhāra for the Preliminaries and the Sthāpaka for the Prastāvanā, (the Prologue) the concluding part of the Preliminaries. This Prastāvanā was not the contribution of the dramatist[3] in the pre-classical period. It seems that the elaborate Preliminaries were not performed in detail in the later period of the Sanskrit drama. Instead of Sūtradhāra and Sthāpaka both, the Sūtradhāra alone remained in the practice of the Preliminaries and carried out the prologue composed by the dramatist. The propitiation of the deities was also carried out by him. Some instrumental and vocal music was employed behind the curtain. The Sūtradhāra entered after the curtain was removed and presented the Prologue. The music served the purpose of entertaining the audience. The Nāndī was very important since the very first performance of drama, as is seen from the first chapter of the NŚ.

The introduction of the play and the dramatist was necessary in the olden days as there was no other effective way of providing this information to the audience. In the Trigata, the indication of the play was given through humorous conversation

1. Cf. Bhāvaprakāśana, p. 200. 'Nāndyanta' is explained as Tatpuruṣa compound and Bahuvrīhi compound.

2. "The Problem of Nāndī and Pūrvaraṅga". A paper read in the A.I.O. Conference, 1953.

3. See Abhinava—NŚ Vol. I., p. 249.
"द्विविधा प्रस्तावना भवति—पूर्वरङ्गस्याङ्गभूताऽन्यस्य वा । तत्र पूर्वरङ्गाङ्गेऽस्याः कविरुदासीनः ।"

of Vidūṣaka who asked such questions as, "who stands?" "who has won?" etc. The nineteen items of the Preliminaries were not the concern of the dramatist. The Sthāpaka presented the Prologue of the play in which the name of the poet, of the play and the introduction of the play were given. We find that the classical playwrights have their own Prologues having in the beginning, a benedictory verse or verses. That is why, we have the stage direction —'नान्द्यन्ते' after the benedictory verse or verses. In Bhāsa plays, we have 'नान्द्यन्ते तत: प्रविशति सूत्रधार: ।', and then the Sūtradhāra recites the benedictory verse of the Sthāpanā, and carries out the Prastāvanā which was the work of Sthāpaka. There must have been another benedictory verse sung before the entry of Sūtradhāra. Such a practice is seen in some other plays of the later period as well, e.g., Subhadrā-Dhanañjaya, Tapatī-saṁvaraṇa, Bhagavadajjukīya, Padmaprābhṛtaka, etc. In the plays of Kālidāsa, Śūdraka, Harṣa and Bhavabhūti etc. we have the benedictory verse or verses in the beginning after which the stage direction, "नान्द्यन्ते", occurs. These two practices seem to be due to the original two-fold division of the Preliminaries. In the practice as found in the Bhāsa plays and some others, the benedictory verse which belonged to the work of the troupe was sung when the items before this Nāndī were carried out. After completing the Preliminaries,[1] the Sūtradhāra entered again and carried out the Prologue after reciting the benedictory verse of the Prologue. In the second practice, after some instrumental and vocal music was gone through, the benedictory verse or the verses of the dramatist were sung and gesticulated giving scope for dance, and then the Sūtradhāra started the Prologue. The dancing and singing were not to be prolonged too much.

In the Prologue of the Sanskrit plays, we see the Sūtradhāra entering first alone and then calling his wife or assistant. Some-

1. The three verses put into brackets between the first and second line of stanza 161 of chapter V, give us the idea that the Sūtradhāra recited the Nāndī and re-entering the stage, carried out the Prastāvanā.

Cf. NŚ. Vol. I Second Edition, p. 247.

See Abhinava—"सूत्रधार एव स्थापक इति सूत्रधार: पूर्वरङ्गं प्रयुज्य स्थापक: सन् प्रविशेद् इति न भिन्नकर्तृकता ।" NŚ. Vol. I., p. 248.

times, the Sūtradhāra asks his wife to sing a song relating to the season so that the interest of the audience is fully aroused. At the end of the Prologue, the Sūtradhāra introduces the first scene of the play in an effective manner and leaves the stage. Sometimes, the Sūtradhāra and his assistants appear in the main or subordinate roles of the play e.g., the Sūtradhāra and the Pāripārśvaka take the roles of Kāmandakī and Avalokitā in the Mālatī-Mādhava or, the Director[1] takes the role of Buddha as referred to in the Avadānaśataka in regard to the performance of a Nāṭaka in the city of Śobhāvatī.

B. Presentation of plays :

Some scenes from the Acts of Sanskrit plays are discussed here from the view point of staging[2] them.

(The fixed curtain between the RŚ. (Raṅgaśīrṣa) and the RP. (Raṅgapīṭha) is mentioned as the back curtain. The curtain held by the two attendants is mentioned simply as the curtain).

Pratimā Act III : The main scene begins with the entry of Bharata in a chariot, with the charioteer. The charioteer would be in front of Bharata with the picture of horses in one hand and whip in the other. The posture assumed would be Samapāda. The speed of the chariot is gesticulated by both with quick steps. Their movements would be atthe centre of the stage. They come near Ayodhyā. A soldier comes, and tells them that Bharata is to enter Ayodhyā after one Nāḍikā (Nāḍikā = 24 minutes) in the Rohiṇī asterism. The speed of the chariot must have been shown as slowed down by slow movements. After this message Bharata decides to take rest in the Devakula nearby. The chariot is stopped, that means, Bharata and the Sūta stop and the former gesticulates descending from the chariot. The charioteer, asked by Bharata to rest the horses, leaves the stage. Then Bharata would move round indicating going to the Devakula (temple). (Before the entry in the Devakula, the curtain covering the statues would

1. Cf. The Indian Theatre : p. 149.

2. The technical details of the Abhinaya given by the NŚ. and the commentary of Abhinava relating to them are made use of while describing the staging of these scenes. The use of music is given with the help of Abhinavabhāratī, Bṛhaddeśī and Bharatabhāṣya.

be removed so that the four statues would come into view). The man in charge of the Devakula enters. He tells Bharata who is about to salute the statues not to do so as they are those of Kṣatriyas. Then through the statues Bharata is made to understand Daśaratha's death. He faints. (The words of the attendants 'move away' would be uttered in the green-room). Then there is the entry of the Queens i.e., Bharata's mothers and Sumantra.

Mālavikāgnimitra Act II :

The orchestral arrangement is complete and then enter the King, the Vidūṣaka, Dhāriṇī, and Parivrājikā with the attendants. The King and Vidūṣaka would be seated on the right side of the stage while the Queen and Parivrājikā on the other. This entry would be effected by holding the curtain and then removing it. The entry of Mālavikā would take place after drawing aside the back curtain, by the Northern door of the green-room. The orchestra would be now in full view, arranged properly on RŚ. Mālavikā's performance would take place in front of the RŚ. In the performance Mālavikā first sings the song and then gesticulates it with the physical and temperamental gesticulation. The stage direction before her performance is 'उपवहनं कृत्वा चतुष्पदं वस्तु गायति', (after first having Upavahana i.e. the singing of the notes of the melodytype, she sings the song of four lines). The Prakrit song is sung expressing love in separation. After this, the stage direction is, 'इति यथारसमभिनयति' i.e., after singing the song she gesticulates it according to the sentiment. In this performance of Mālavikā the physical gesticulation i.e., Śākhā is gentle as the subject is love. The tempo prescribed is medium.

Vikramorvaśīya Act III.

After the Viṣkambhaka, Kañcukin enters, who is sent by the Queen with a request to the King. He describes the atmosphere of the palace at the evening. Then he looks towords the curtain behind and indicates the entry of the King, who is coming with Vidūṣaka, surrounded by female attendants carrying torches in their hands. He stands on one side of the stage. Then after the back curtain is drawn aside, the entry of the King would be effected standing in the back part of the stage. After his speech to himself, Kañcukin would approach him and telling the request of the Queen, would leave the stage. (The King, with the attendants would step round showing, proceeding to the Maṇiharmya palace terrace where the Queen is waiting for him.) All of them gesticulate ascending the staircase. The King looking up describes the moon-rise. After Vidūṣaka's speech he salutes the divine moon with folded hands. The King sits and asks the attendants to leave as there is no necessity of torches due to moonshine. The back curtain is drawn to cover the stage. There is some time for the arrival of the Queen. The King expresses the suffering of his mind due to his love for Urvaśī. Then there is the entry of Urvaśī dressed as Abhisārikā and Citralekhā by aerial path. The King and Vidūṣaka are in the central part of the stage. When the back curtain is drawn aside, Urvaśī and Citralekhā would enter performing aerial Cārīs to show that they are moving through the sky. They gesticulate descending to the palace terrace and listen to the conversation between the King and Vidūṣaka, concealed i.e. simply standing on one side of the stage. Listening to the love-lorn condition of the King, Urvaśī approaches at once and finds that the King is indifferent though she is standing in front of him. In haste she has forgotten to give up the Tiraskariṇī i.e. the invisibility which she has secured due to the miraculous power. The King would gesticulate not seeing anything. (The King while saying that his one shoulder which was pressed by her shoulder due to the jolt of the chariot when it came down on the ground, is only 'blessed one' and the rest of his body is simply a burden to the earth, would point to his shoulder and while doing so turn his look a little bent towards it. Thus Urvaśī's presence would go unnoticed by him). At this moment, the Queen enters. Behind the back curtain (which would be drawn to cover the back stage), the words are heard, "This way, this way, your ladyship". The back curtain is removed and the Queen would come on the stage on the opposite side of Urvaśī. The Queen with the maid would move round and then approach the King. The Queen is made to sit near him by the King. Urvaśī and Citralekhā are there standing in full view. (The spectators are to imagine that their presence is not known to the other characters on the stage). After the Pūjā (worship) the Queen leaves the stage. Urvaśī then goes to the back of the King and fulfills his expectation expressed by him in a verse, by closing his eyes from behind. Citralekhā makes a sign to Vidūṣaka not to speak. The King gesticulates the feel of the happy touch and understands Urvaśī's presence.

Śākuntala Act VI:

Sānumatī's entry would be effected after removing the curtain. She would perform the aerial Cārīs casting downward glances to gesticulate moving in the sky. The descent would be gesticulated by assuming Samapāda posture and moving with quick steps. Sānumatī would be on the front division of the stage. Then the two maids enter. They would be on the middle part of the stage. Kañcukin enters by tossing the back curtain. When the maids are told about the spring festival forbidden by the King, they inquire about the reason. The Kañcukin informs them that the King has been repenting since the day he got the ring, remembering all about Śakuntalā. Behind the back curtain, the words are heard, "May Your Majesty advance" uttered by Vidūṣaka. The maids leave the stage. The King and Vidūṣaka then enter when the back curtain is drawn aside. When they proceed to Mādhavī Maṇḍapa by moving round on the back part of the stage, Sānumatī also follows. Her remarks heighten the situation very effectively, throughout the Act in which the King's repentance is depicted powerfully. She admits that he has in every way wiped off Śakuntalā's grief caused by her repudiation. Sānumatī's exit would be gesticulated by upward jumps to indicate that she is going up in the sky.

Mudrārākṣasa Act III :

The King Candragupta has ascended the Sugāṅga palace. He is in the back part of the stage. When he knows that Kaumudī festival is prohibited by Cāṇakya, he sends the Kañcukin, to call him. The King would be seated at the centre in the front part of the RŚ. The next entry is that of Cāṇakya seated in his house. This entry would be effected by holding the curtain and then removing it. He would be in the middle part of the stage. There are two verses of Cāṇakya referring to the efforts of Rākṣasa and one expressing his plan. Then there is the entry of Kañcukin, who would be in the front portion of the stage. He recites one stanza, moves round and comes to Cāṇakya's house. Then, he recites one stanza describing the very modest abode of Cāṇakya and two more stanzas describing his greatness. There is some conversation between him and Cāṇakya. Afterwards, both of them step round to show that they are on way to the palace. Cāṇakya gesticulates ascending and approaches the King.

It can be seen that all this time, i.e. from the departure of Kañcukin to the arrival of them near the King there is much recitation. During all this time the King is seated in the front part of the RŚ. The back curtain would be drawn to cover him, so that the scene at Cāṇakya's home etc. would be facilitated. (I understand in this manner, the purpose of Viśrānti (i.e. rest) for the actors, served by back curtain.) Afterwards when Cāṇakya and Kañcukin are moving round in the middle part of the stage, the back curtain would be drawn aside.

Veṇīsaṁhāra Acts IV and V :

At the beginning of the Act IV, there is the entry of Duryodhana fainted, in the chariot. The banner of the chariot is cut off in the battle. The charioteer is taking away the chariot. He takes it under the shade of a banyan tree. Duryodhana regains consciousness and asks the Sūta to take the chariot to the place where Duḥśāsana is. The Sūta tells that the horses are unable to carry the chariot. Duryodhana gets down from the chariot and says feelingly and with pride that time should not be wasted by going in a chariot (i.e. bringing in another chariot and then going, hence the delay). In this scene, the chariot fashioned according to Pusta would be used and it would be moved by the Sūta. In act V, we have the entry of Dhṛtarāṣṭra, Gāndhārī and Sañjaya in a chariot. Here the movement of the chariot would be shown by gesticulation only. When Sañjaya requests the other two to get down slowly, the stage direction is, 'उभाववतरणं नाटयत:'—'both gesticulate getting down'.

Mālatīmādhava Act VI :

The nuptial dress and decoration are sent by the King for Mālatī. Kāmandakī asks Makaranda to wear the nuptial dress of Mālatī and to go to marry Nandana, disguised as Mālatī. She hands over the box to him. Makaranda then says that he would wear the dress going behind the variegated curtain. He goes behind the curtain and after three very short speeches of Mādhava and Kāmandakī enters smilingly, dressed as Mālatī. The veil would be there to effect the disguise. (The Antarā Dhruvā would be employed while Makaranda is getting disguised behind the curtain.).

Mṛcchakaṭika Act I :

Vidūṣaka and Cārudatta are inside Cārudatta's house. Vasantasenā enters pursued by Viṭa, Śakāra and Ceṭa on the royal path. The time is late evening. Cārudatta is engaged in meditation. Vasantasenā understands from the words of Viṭa that Cārudatta's house is to the left. After moving round, she gesticulates touching by hand and says that this is a side-door which is closed, indicated by the touch of the wall and the panes. Then there is a conversation between Cārudatta and Vidūṣaka. Cārudatta has asked Vidūṣaka to take the offerings to the mothers. Vidūṣaka is not willing to go alone. Cārudatta asks the maid Radanikā to accompany him. Vidūṣaka gesticulates opening the door. Radanikā has the offering and a lamp in her hands. Vasantasenā puts out the lamp by the end of her garment and gesticulates entering the house. When the lamp is put out, Cārudatta asks Maitreya what it was. Vidūṣaka tells that the lamp is blown off by the gush of the wind. He asks Radanikā to go out by the door and he goes inside to light the lamp. Radanikā goes out and is held by Śakāra by her hair mistaking her to be Vasantasenā.

This scene has the interior part of Cārudatta's house, side-door in the wall of the house and the road. When the pursuit of Vasantsenā is going on, on the road, they (i.e. Śakāra and others) would be moving about on the middle part of the stage. Cārudatta would be sitting on the front part of the RŚ. at the centre. The back curtain would be drawn when the pursuit scene goes on as it is fairly long. Vasantasenā would move round and come near the curtain to the left side which she would touch by her hand to gesticulate touching the wall. The curtain would be drawn aside to reveal Cārudatta, Vidūṣaka and Radanikā. Vidūṣaka would gesticulate opening of the door and Vasantasenā would gesticulate entering the house. (Afterwards during the scene between Viṭa, Vidūṣaka and Śakāra, the back curtain would be again drawn to cover Cārudatta and Vasantasenā).

I am now describing the staging of some scenes in detail bringing out the salient points.

i) Svapnavāsavadattam Act I :

(There is no back curtain).

After the entrance song sung in the melody[1] with Dha as the starting and prominent note and Pa as the ending note, the two guards enter when the curtain is removed. While speaking "Move away, move away gentlemen", they indicate the same by the movement of the hands. The curtain is held again. The entrance song is sung in Ṣaḍjamadhyā Jāti in slow tempo. The curtain would be removed gradually and Yaugandharāyaṇa in the garb of a recluse and Vāsavadattā in the costume of a lady of Avantī, enter the stage by the northern side. The guards are behind them. The dress of both is soiled. (Vāsavadattā gesticulates fatigue of the journey.) Yaugandharāyaṇa gesticulates listening and says, "How here also people are asked to move away". He recites the verse, 'धीरस्य…' etc. (I-3). Vāsavadattā asks "Who is this man that is driving away people ?", pointing her hand in that direction. During this conversation, the two guards would be moving on the stage. After Yaugandharāyaṇa's verse, 'पूर्वं त्वयाप्यभिमतं' etc. (I-4) the guards would repeat, "Move away, move away" looking at them. Then the Kāñcukīya enters after the entrance song in Ṣāḍjī Jāti and asks the guards not to clear off the people, moving the Tripatāka hand. The guards then leave the stage. Yaugandharāyaṇa looks at the Kāñcukīya and says to Vāsavadattā that they should approach him. While he is moving the drums would be played upon appropriately. Kāñcukīya is at

1. 'अधमानां प्रयोक्तव्या का (क) कुभेन जया सदा ।'
Bharatabhāṣya—folio. 148.

'ककुभः पञ्चमन्यासो धैवतांशस्तु निर्मितः ।' BD, p. 100.

the back. Vāsavadattā would be standing on the left side. Yaugandharāyaṇa knows from him that Princess Padmāvatī is coming there to visit her mother. Then the curtain would be held. After the entrance song in Ṣaḍjodīcyavatī Jāti in medium tempo, she would enter with her attendants by the right door while the curtain is being lowered and then removed. They would move round in the back part of the stage. The entry of the Tāpasī would be effected by using the curtain, as usual. She would be seated at the centre of the back part of the stage. After the conversation between the Tāpasī and Padmāvatī etc. Yaugandharāyaṇa requests the princess to accept his sister as Nyāsa (deposit). This is accepted by Padmāvatī. Next is the entry of Brahmacārin. Now, all are in the back part of the stage. After the removal of the curtain when the entrance song is sung in the melody of the Śuddhamadhyā Jāti, the Brahmacārin would be seen in the front part of the stage looking up, gesticulating fatigue and the heat of the sun. He looks in search of a place to take rest. He moves round and describes the penance forest gesticulating the verse, to create the sight of the penance grove. Afterwards, he gesticulates entering the hermitage. He would look at the Chamberlain first, then at the ascetic and lastly at the ladies etc. Afterwards the great sorrow of Udayana at the death of Vāsavadattā is narrated by the Brahmacārin very effectively. The tunes of Naiṣādī Jāti played on flute and Vīṇā would be used as effective background. This account of the Brahmacārin has a very great effect on Vāsavadattā, Yaugandharāyaṇa and Padmāvatī. Due to the great love of Udayana for Vāsavadattā, attraction for the King is produced in the mind of Padmāvatī.

After the exit of Brahmacārin and then of Yaugandharāyaṇa, the Kāñcukīya recites the verse, 'खगा वासोपेताः' etc. (I-16) describing the sunset with gesticulation and all exit with the exit song sung in the Ṣāḍjī Jāti.

ii) Śākuntala Act IV :

(The back curtain is employed).

In the main scene of this Act the departure of Śakuntalā is depicted. Kaṇva has returned from his journey and an aerial voice informs him of Śakuntalā's marriage with Duṣyanta and her pregnancy. He has approved of Śakuntalā's marriage.

Kaṇva immediately decides to send Śakuntalā to Duṣyanta. A hearty pathetic send-off is given to Śakuntalā by the inmates of the hermitage including animals and even trees. Śakuntalā leaves for the capital escorted by two pupils and Gautamī. Kaṇva feels greatly relieved like a person who has returned the deposit kept with him on sending Śakuntalā over to her husband.

The stages of this main scene can be set out as follows :

1) The entry of the pupil who is asked by Kaṇva to ascertain the time.

2) The entry of Anasūyā. She blames the King for his immodest behaviour towards Śakuntalā. At this time, the pupil leaves to tell Kaṇva that it is day-break. Anasūyā's speech is continued. She says that the King had not even sent a letter for so long a time. She is sorry for her friend but understands that it would be the effect of the curse of Durvāsas. She thinks of sending the ring as recognition but none from the ascetics could be requested to go as a messanger. She cannot inform Kāśyapa also about Śakuntalā's marriage and pregnancy. Priyaṁvadā enters and hastens her to be ready to perform the customary rites at Śakuntalā's departure. She tells that she knew from Śakuntalā how revered Kāśyapa knew everything through an incorporal metrical speech when he entered the sacrificial fire chamber. Both of them proceed towards Śakuntalā with the auspicious decorations.

3) Śakuntalā is seated bathed over the head and is being congratulated upon by the hermit ladies who leave after giving the blessings. Now, Priyaṁvadā and Anasūyā approach Śakuntalā. They arrange for her toilet with decorations available in the hermitage. The ornaments and the silken garments are brought by two hermit boys offered by the trees in the forest. The boys leave the stage. Śakuntalā is to be dressed up with the rich costume and ornaments.

4) Kāśyapa enters after bath, uneasy at heart due to the thought that Śakunta ā is to leave today. Śakuntalā puts on the two silken garments. All move round the sacrificial fires. Kāśyapa calls for Śārṅgarava and others. They come. He asks them to show the way to Śakuntalā. He requests the trees in the penance forest to permit her, who is proceeding to her hus-

band's place. This permission is understood through Cuckoo's notes. The words are heard in the air that the journey would be quite safe and good. The whole Tapovana (penance-forest) is distressed at the separation of her as she was one with it. She goes to her sisterly creeper Vanajyotsnā to take her leave. All of them again step round. Śakuntalā requests her father to send a word when the doe who is carrying would be safely delivered. The fawn that was brought up by her, clings to her garment again and again. The whole atmosphere is surcharged with pathos. Kāśyapa gives his message to the King. Śakuntalā falls at the feet of her father, embraces her friends, and looks back at the hermitage. Gautamī asks her to send back her father. She again embraces her father and leaves. When she disappears with the escort behind the row of trees, the others return to the hermitage, which is, at it were, vacant. Kāśyapa expresses the mental peace he is experiencing as he has fulfilled his duty towards his daughter.

The enactment would be as follows :

1) This scene takes place in the precincts of the hermitage. The pupil has gone out in the open to ascertain the time. He would come after stepping round, in the front part of the stage and looking up in front, would say that it is dawn and recite the two verses (IV-2,3). His entry would be effected by using the curtain.

2) Anasūyā enters the stage by tossing the back curtain, on the other side. Then the pupil would leave, and afterwards Priyaṁvadā would enter in joy and haste. Hence, she would also come on the stage without the entrance song. Afterwards both proceed to meet Śakuntalā by moving about on the stage. Priyaṁvadā would look towards the back curtain (with Vilokita glance).

3) Śakuntalā would be seated at the centre in the front part of the RŚ. with the lady ascetics and Gautamī by her side. She is supposed to be in the hermitage. By drawing aside the back-curtain she would be revealed to the audience. (The entrance song would be in medium tempo and the melody type would belong to Ma scale with Sa as dominant and ending note, Dha used scarcely and with Kākalī Ni). The three lady ascetics utter the blessings and leave the stage. Gautamī is there with Śakuntalā. The two friends come near Śakuntalā

and say, "Friend, may this be your happy bath". Śakuntalā now looks at them. Her glance is expressive of the mixed feelings of sorrow and joy. She welcomes them and tells them to sit down. They sit near her with the auspicious vessels and ask her to be ready to get decorated. Śakuntalā would gesticulate shedding tears, for the decorations at the hands of her friends would be difficult to obtain henceforth. The friends try to console her by saying that it is not proper to cry on the auspicious occasion. They wipe out her tears with the 3rd finger of the Tripatāka hand. They gesticulate decorating her. Then the silken garments and ornaments are brought by the two hermit boys. The friends know how to wear these ornaments due to their practice of drawing pictures. They enact decorating her. The application of the lac dye to feet would be effected by Kartarīmukha hand pointing downwards; putting the ear-ornament by Bhramara hands; fixing ring by Haṁsāsya and putting pearlnecklace by Khaṭakāmukha hand etc.

4) While the gesticulation of decorating is going on, Kāśyapa would enter. A curtain would be held by two persons and the entrance song would be in slow tempo with the melody in which Sa is the starting and dominant note, Pa ending note and Ni Kākalī. The curtain would be removed and he would come in full view. He would recite the verse, 'यास्यत्यद्य…' etc. (IV. 6) with the notes Ni and Ga expressive of the pathetic mood. He would be in the front part of the stage while reciting the verse. Then he would step round towards Śakuntalā. The two friends have finished decoration and they ask Śakuntalā to put on the two silken garments, lower and upper. The garments would be handed over to her. She would go in the green-room and come out after wearing them. (Antarā Dhruvā would be sung here.) (If the putting on of the garments also is gesticulated by pantomimic action, there would be no necessity of going to the green-room.) When all of them step round in the back part of the stage they would be understood as circumambulating the sacrificial fire. When the two pupils who are to escort Śakuntalā enter, all of them would move about coming to the middle part of the stage. Śārṅgarava would be in front of them. (The cuckoo note indicating the permission given by the trees would be produced on the flute. For all the movements

there would be appropriate drum-beats.) The verse, 'रम्यान्तरः...' etc. (IV. 11) would be recited in the green room. All would listen to it gesticulating wonder by the Vismita glance. Śakuntalā salutes looking towards the back with Añjali Hasta and moves about. She expresses her mind to Priyaṁvadā turning to her (and with the Tripatāka hand also to indicate Janāntika) that she is eager to see her husband but at the same time her feet proceed forward with great difficulty, while leaving the hermitage. (The eagerness to meet Duṣyanta and the distress at the separation from the hermitage where she was brought up from childhood and with which she had become one all this time, would be very effectively gesticulated by facial expressions by Śakuntalā.) Priyaṁvadā says that the penance grove is also experiencing the same distress at her separation; "The does are with the Darbha mouthfuls dropped down, the peacocks have given up dancing, the creepers with the yellowish leaves cast away are shedding tears as though." (IV-12). By facial expressions and the bodily gestures of other limbs the actions of the doe, peacock and the creepers would be very effectively presented by Priyaṁvadā. Śakuntalā gesticulates remembering by moving the head and raising the eye-brow. She takes leave of Vanajyotsnā which is to the right. She would turn to the right, go a little distance and gesticulate embracing the creeper. Kāśyapa says that he is free from anxiety towards her and the creeper as both are united befittingly. Śakuntalā has got a befitting husband and the creeper has resorted to the mango tree. Śakuntalā says to her friends that this is a deposit placed by her in their hand. She would look at the friends pointing to the creeper. The friends shed tears saying, "In whose hands are we now placed ?" Kāśyapa asks them to be calm for they are to console their friend. They move round to show that they are going ahead. Śakuntalā requests to send a word of safe delivery of the doe who is carrying and as such can move only near the hermitage. She would look feelingly back. She would gesticulate impediment in the movement as the fawn is clinging to her lower garment which was brought up by her with great care as her adopted son. She has a semiturn and a look full of affection and would gesticulate fondling the fawn. She tells to it that her father would take its care when separated from her. She proceeds weeping. The gait is faltering due to continuous tears. They have come to the bank of the lake which is the limit upto which the beloved person is to be followed while departing. Kāśyapa and others have to return to the hermitage. All of them would move round now and are supposed to stand in the shade of the Kṣīra tree. Kāśyapa stands thinking, facing the audience with down-cast eyes, about the message to be sent to Duṣyanta. Śakuntalā and Anasūyā have a small 'aside' expressing the sorrow at separation from the lover, referring to the yelling of the Cakravākī not seeing her mate. Now Kāśyapa's message is ready. It is given in the verse, 'अस्मान् साधु…etc'. (IV-17). He advises Śakuntalā about the duties of a housewife in the verse 'शुश्रूषस्व…etc'. (IV-18). Kāśyapa asks her to embrace him and her friends because they are not to follow her as they are also to be given in marriage and hence their going to Hastināpura is not proper. She embraces her father and asks how she would be able to sustain her life separated from him. He consoles her by telling that due to her manifold duties as wife and mother she would not feel the sorrow of separation from him. She falls at his feet. He blesses her. She asks both her friends to embrace her simultaneously. The friends tell her that if per chance the King becomes hesitant about recognition, she would show the ring to him engraved with his name on it. Śakuntalā says, "By this suspicion of yours I am made to tremble all over." She would gesticulate the nervousness at this time by shaking all the body. They tell her not to be afraid. Excessive affection suspects evil. Śārṅgarava asks to hasten and Śakuntalā stands looking to the hermitage. They would have come now to the right side of the stage. Śakuntalā says, "When shall I see possibly the penance grove again !" Kāśyapa tells her that she would come to the peaceful hermitage with her husband after being for a long time the co-wife of the earth bounded by four oceans and after bringing about the marriage of her son and then transferring the burden of the family life over to him. Śakuntalā again embraces her father and proceeds towards the right door of the green-room, with the escort. Her steps would be slow and she would often look towards her father, friends and the hermitage. The exit song would be appropriately employed in the melody having the notes Ga and Ni and with Pa as the dominant note. When they disappear the friends say that Śakuntalā has gone out of sight by the rows of trees. Kāśyapa and the friends then move round to indicate that they are going back towards the hermitage. The verse, "अर्थो हि कन्या etc." (IV-22) would be recited by Kāśyapa in slow tempo. All the three would leave the stage through the left door of the green-room with the exit song sung in Kaiśikī and Ṣaḍjamadhyā Jātis combined.

Ratnāvalī Act III :

From the conversation of the two maids in the Praveśaka (interlude) we know the plan of Vasantaka and Susaṅgatā which was overheard by (Kāñcanamālā) the maid of the Queen. The plan was to bring about the meeting of the King and Sāgarikā who would be dressed as Vāsavadattā and accompanied by Susaṅgatā in the disguise of Kāñcanamālā. The meeting was to take place in the Mādhavī bower in the darkness of evening. The main scene has the following stages of action :

1) The King expresses his love-sickness—Vasantaka comes to him and tells his plan.

2) They proceed to the Mādhavī bower, reach it and wait for Sāgarikā. The King asks Vasantaka to hurry up. Vidūṣaka goes to bring her.

3) The Queen comes to the same place along with Kāñcanamālā knowing from her about this meeting. Vidūṣaka comes covered with a veil and listening to the sound of the footsteps he thinks that Sāgarikā has come. Kāñcanamālā makes a sign to him by snapping the fingers. Vidūṣaka approaches them and they come to the King. The King addresses Vāsavadattā mistaking her to be Sāgarikā. She removes her veil, facing the rising moon. The King becomes dumbfounded. He prostrates at her feet but she leaves him in anger.

4) Then enters Sāgarikā dressed as Vāsavadattā She is just on the point of killing herself by hanging lest she should be disgraced by the Queen when her engagement affair is known to her

5) The King is proceeding towards the Queen to propitiate her. Vidūṣaka hears the sound of foot-steps (of Sāgarikā) and

guesses that the Queen might be returning in repentance. The King asks him to ascertain. Vidūṣaka goes and sees that Sāgarikā is placing the noose of creeper round her neck. He thinks her to be the Queen and shouts for help. The King rushes and takes away the noose and finding her to be Sāgarikā, is happy.

6) Then comes Vāsavadattā along with Kāñcanamālā for reconciliation with the King and finds that the King is about to embrace Sāgarikā. She asks Kāñcanamālā to arrest Vidūṣaka by the noose and takes Sāgarikā in front. The Queen goes looking at the King, along with Sāgarikā, Vidūṣaka and Kāñcanamālā. The King leaves crestfallen and dejected, finding no other way than to enter the harem and propitiate the Queen.

The staging :

1) The entry of the king seated gesticulating love-sickness, would take place after the curtain is removed. He would be in the back part of the stage. The entrance song would be in the Rāga Mālavakaiśika sung in middle tempo. Vidūṣaka's entry in joyful mood would be in the front part of the stage. By stepping round, he would approach the King.

2) The King and Vidūṣaka would move round and come to one end of the back part of the stage which would be understood as Mādhavī bower. Then Vidūṣaka would exit. The King would sit on a seat supposed to be the stone slab. (While proceeding to the garden in the darkness, their coming near the garden would be indicated by gesticulating fragrance i.e., by slightly narrowing down the eyes, expanding the nostrils and by inhaling. By the difference in fragrance, the King knows the row of Campaka trees, Bakula trees etc. They would show groping for the path in the darkness. Their movements would be accompanied by appropriate drum beats. The pitchy darkness is also gesticulated in this manner. Vidūsaka, while moving through the Makaranda garden would have his feet drawn over the ground and hands groping for the way. Thus, by the description and gesticulation, the same zone of the stage would be Makaranda garden.).

3) The entry of Vāsavadattā and Kāñcanamālā would be

after the back curtain is drawn aside and the entrance song is sung. They would be on the other side of the stage. They would move round to show that they have come near Citraśālikā. Vidūṣaka enters and stands near them. After the snapping of fingers is heard, he would approach them. They would step round and come to the King. The description of the moonrise gives the idea of the moonshine. When Vāsavadattā removes her veil in anger, the King looks at her and knows his mistake and gesticulates embarrassment. Sitting on the knees and folding his hands in Añjali he requests the Queen to be gracious. She turns her face towards him and sheds tears. Not minding even his prostration she leaves.

4) Sāgarikā would enter by the same side of the greenroom, when the curtain is removed and the entrance song is employed.

5) The King and Vidūṣaka step round. The King rushes to help Sāgarikā. The noose would be fashioned as a model work. The king has her hands placed round his neck.

6) The Queen with her maid would enter. They move round. Kāñcanamālā gesticulates listening to the words of the King. The Queen becomes joyful and thinks of going at the back of the King and embrace him. But hearing Vidūṣaka's words addressed to Sāgarikā she knows of her presence. When she hears the King saying that his real love is for Sāgarikā alone and the Queen commands only service from him, she understands the facts and approaches them. The King caught redhanded gesticulates helplessness. The Queen would angrily leave the stage having in front of her Kāñcanamālā, in whose front there would be Vidūṣaka and Sāgarikā. The King would exit with the exit song.

iv) Uttararāmacarita Act VII:

The scene of the Act is laid in the neighbourhood of the hermitage of Vālmīki. A play written by Vālmīki is performed before Rāma and Lakṣmaṇa in the presence of the citizens of Ayodhyā and the denizens of the three worlds. This play within a play is meant to convince the subjects of Sītā's chastity and of the wantonness of the scandal spread among them about Sītā. The Act closes with the happy re-union of Rāma,

Sītā and their two sons Kuśa and Lava. The stages of the action would be as follows—

1) Lakṣmaṇa enters and informs about his being ordered by Rāma that as they are invited to witness the performance of the play composed by Vālmīki and enacted by the divine nymphs, he should go to the theatre on the bank of the Ganges and seat the spectators. He has done his job.

2) Rāma enters and asks whether the judges have taken their seats. He tells that Kuśa and Lava should also be treated with the respect due to Candraketu. He sits on the seat arranged for him.

3) The play then commences. Sūtradhāra enters, carries out the prologue and leaves the stage. This small play depicts Sītā's abandonment by Rāma, her throwing herself into the Ganges when the pangs of delivery began, her giving birth to two sons in the water, the consolation given to her by the Ganges and the Earth, the Jṛmbhaka missiles entering the boys, the Ganges taking upon her the work of entrusting the boys to Vālmīki and Sītā's request to the Earth to take her in her bosom.

4) Arundhatī and Sītā enter and the former testifies Sītā's chastity.

5) Vālmīki, Kuśa and Lava enter. Śatrughna's arrival after killing Lavaṇa is reported by Vālmīki. All ends in happiness.

The staging :

1) Lakṣmaṇa would enter when the back curtain is drawn aside. The entrance song would be in the Rāga Śuddhakaiśika in medium tempo, belonging to 'Ma' scale, having Kākalī Ni and with Tāra Sa as the starting note and Pa as ending note. Rāma's entry is suggested by the verse (VII-1) recited by Lakṣmaṇa.

2) Rāma would enter when the other curtain is removed. Rāma and Lakṣmaṇa are seated on the front part of the stage slightly turning towards the back curtain which is drawn.

3) Sūtradhāra then enters when the back curtain is drawn aside and tells about the play which is composed by Vālmīki and is full of the Pathetic and the Marvellous sentiments. Rāma's speech would be recited, facing the spectators. From the green-room the words of Sītā would be heard. These are

uttered in Pathetic desperateness expressing her decision to throw herself into the Ganges. Lakṣmaṇa says to himself, "Alas, this is something quite unexpected." Sūtradhāra recites the verse, meaning that Sītā throws herself in the Ganges, in the throes of child birth and then leaves the stage. Then the back curtain would be drawn. Rāma speaks with emotion, "Oh Queen, have care for Lakṣmaṇa." Lakṣmaṇa tells him that this is a play (being enacted). The entry of Sītā supported by the Earth and the Ganges who have a dummy boy on the lap of each would be effected by drawing aside the back curtain, when the entrance song is sung. Rāma asks Lakṣmaṇa to support him. Sītā knows from the two Goddesses that she has given birth to two sons. Lakṣmaṇa falls at the feet of Rāma at this good fortune and sees that Rāma has fainted. Rāma would enact fainting by sitting stiff indicating loss of consciousness. Lakṣmaṇa fans him by the end of his upper garment. The Earth and Sītā embrace each other and faint. The Earth blames Rāma for his behaviour. When Sītā says that she is reminded of her husband, the Earth says, "What is your noble lord to you now?" Then Sītā exclaims, "Or rather it is as my mother says." She utters these words with tears in her eyes which are turned down in bashfulness. The Ganges tells the Earth not to be angry for she knows Rāma very well. In the green-room the verse would be recited about the two boys securing the missiles, which would wait upon them. The Ganges tells that she would hand over the boys to Vālmīki. Lakṣmaṇa thinks that Kuśa and Lava are these two boys because they have the missiles with them from the birth. Similarly, both are with Vālmīki, have form similar to Rāma and are twelve years old. Sītā requests the Earth to take her with her. The Earth asks her to wait until the two sons are weaned and then she would do what seems proper to her. The Ganges says, "So be it". The two goddesses would then leave the stage with Sītā, with the exit song. Rāma again faints as Sītā disappears. From the green-room the words are uttered, "Remove the musical instruments.........A holy miracle is to take place ordained by the great sage Vālmīki." (The back curtain would be drawn). Lakṣmaṇa would look towards the green-room and recite the verse, 'मन्थादिव...' etc. facing the audience, gesticulating the miraculous sight, i.e. the waters of the Ganges agitated, the sky crowded with divine sages and Sītā rising from the water together with the Ganges and the Earth. In the green-room, again the words of the Ganges and the Earth are uttered, requesting Arundhatī to do a favour and offering Sītā, her daughter-in-law, to her. All this time, Rāma is unconscious.

4) Then enter Arundhatī and Sītā when the back curtain is removed. Sītā touches Rāma who recovers consciousness at the touch. The words of the Ganges and the Earth come again from the green-room that they have fulfilled their duty. Arundhatī now addresses the citizens (facing the audience) asking them whether Sītā whose innocence is thus proved should be received or not. Lakṣmaṇa tells that the subjects and the whole collection of creatures are doing obeisance to the Queen etc. Arundhatī asks Rāma to appoint his beloved as fellow worshipper with him in the sacrifice. Sītā says to herself that her lord knows how to remove her grief. Afterwards, Arundhatī (looking towards the green-room) says "Revered Vālmīki, let Kuśa and Lava, the sons of good Rāma, born of Sītā's womb, be presented now." She then leaves the stage.

5) Then enter Vālmīki, Kuśa and Lava. The happy union takes place. The news of Śatrughna's victory is told by Vālmīki. The Bharatavākya is recited by Rāma and the play ends by the exit of all, with the exit song.

D. Bharatavākya :

The performance of the plays ended with a verse of benedictory nature. It is placed generally after some such words as किं ते भूयः प्रियमुपकरोमि । अतः परमपि प्रियमस्ति । तथापीदमस्तु । (भरतवाक्यम्) We have a verse called Praśasti[1] in the Nirvahaṇa juncture. Rasārṇavasudhākara identifies Praśasti with Bharatavākya which is found at the end of the plays. It[2] defines it as "the wishing of welfare of the world by the actors." According to Shri Chintaharan[3] Chakravarti, the Bharatavākya was a

1. NŚ. XIX—104. 'नृपदेशप्रशान्तिश्च प्रशस्तिरभिधीयते ।

2. 'भरतैश्चराचराणामाशीराशंसनं प्रशस्तिः स्यात् ।' III, 74.

3. Cf. A note on the Bharatavākya by C. Chakravarti, I.H.Q. Vol. V 1929, pp. 549-552.

business of the Bharatas (actors). Bharatavākya was so called because it was chanted by the actor divested of his dramatic character. According to Shri Vibhutinath[1] Zha, the Bharatavākya at the end is a necessity in a drama. It is so called as it is after Bharata, 'the father of Indian drama'. Dr. Ghosh[2] says that the Saṁdhyaṅga (the part of Juncture) which immediately precedes the Praśasti is Kāvyasaṁhāra i.e. the end of the (Dṛśya) Kāvya. This term loses its significance if the Praśasti is considered as a part of the play written by the playwright. This Praśasti might have been composed by the author in some cases. The Bharatavākya is a function of the Bharata or the Naṭa.[3] Prof. Kali Kumar Dutta[4] says that the interpretation of Kāvyasaṁhāra given by Dr. Ghosh is not corroborated by the writers on Dramaturgy. He states that Praśasti is really an Aṅga (part) of the last Saṁdhi (Juncture) and from the earliest time it was in vogue; but it was not a compulsory Aṅga. The Aṅga preceding Kāvyasaṁhāra is Pūrvavākya or connecting the previous matters with the end. So, the expression like 'किं ते भूयः'... etc., comprising the Kāvyasaṁhāra was a dramaturgical sanction and even in the fragments of Aśvaghoṣa it is seen that there is the expression 'अतः परम्' just before the Praśasti. He holds that 'Bharatavākya' is only a stage-direction.

We find that the Praśasti is given as the last Aṅga (part) of the Nirvahaṇa juncture in the NŚ. The Saṁdhyaṅga (the part of the Juncture) Kāvyasaṁhāra,[5] just before it, is defined as 'वरप्रदानसंप्राप्तिः'. The total number[6] of the Saṁdhyaṅgas mentioned by Bharata is 64. The Kāvyasaṁhāra is treated by Abhinava as the 64th Saṁdhyaṅga. He has illustrated Praśasti by the last verse of the Ratnāvalī (IV.21) which is placed after the remark 'तथापीदमस्तु'.[7]

1. Bharatavākya by Vibhutinath Jha, I.H.Q. Vol. VI 1930, pp., 175-176.
2. The Bharatavākya by M. Ghosh, I.H.Q. Vol. VI 1930, pp., 485-486.
3. Cf. Śāk.—Arthadyotanikā p. 203
भरतवाक्यं नटवाक्यम् । नाटकाभिनयसमाप्तौ सामाजिकेभ्यो नटेनाशीर्दीयत इत्यर्थः ।
4. Prologues and Epilogues in Sanskrit Drama — Our Heritage Vol. V 1957, pp. 61-80.
5. NŚ. XIX. 103.
6. NŚ. XIX. 67.
7. NŚ. Vol. III, pp. 60-61.

It appears then that just as there was benedictory verse in the beginning, so also there was generally one at the end of the play, called Praśasti[1]. As it was concerned with Bharatas i.e. the actors, the term Bharata-vākya is found later on. It was usually recited or chanted by the main actor (or in some cases by the actors) in the assumed role. The change of dress was not significant.

1. NŚ. Vol. III, p. 56. Abhinava—'अन्ये तु त्रयोदशाङ्गत्वेऽप्यस्य निर्वहण-सन्धावपि प्रसक्ते (प्रशस्ते ?) रितिवृत्तान्तभूतत्वेन गणनमन्याय्यमिति त्रयोदशाङ्गत्वात् चतुःषष्टिसंख्यां समर्थयन्ते।

It appears that some critics did not admit Praśasti as an Aṅga of the Nirvahaṇa Juncture.

Chapter VI

KŪṬIYĀṬṬAM

The staging of Sanskrit drama according to ancient dramatic technique is current in Kerala even now. The actors who enact the Sanskrit plays are called Cākyārs. They belong to an intermediate caste—Ambalvāsis (temple dwellers' caste) between the Brahmin and the Nāyar. The services of the Ambalvāsis are dedicated to the temple. The Cākyārs form a separate sub-caste within this fold. They are the temple[1] artists. Their social status is next to the Brahmins. They cannot learn the Vedas not being Brahmins. But they are to study the Nāṭyaveda and their vocation is Kūttu or Nāṭya—the theatrical art. They were the sacred thread and chant Gāyatrī.

The Tamil epic 'Śilappadikāram' refers to Cākkaiyan.[2] The derivation of the word Cākyār is not so certain. It is either from Śakti, (Cakkī in Bhāṣā) or Śākya. But according to Shri K.P.N. Pisharoti it seems to have been derived from Śākya rather than from Śakti for the Cākyārs are not the devotees of Śakti. The late Shri K.R. Pisharoti[3] explained it as a corrupt form of Ślāgyar, a man of respectability, a respect due to his wisdom and learning. It is[4] said to be corrupt form of Ślāghya-Vākkukār (those gifted with excellence in words) or Ślāghya-Kulakkār (men of respectability). Cākyārs are, it is said, the descendents of Sūtas. Shri K.R.

1. Shri K. Bharatha Iyer states that when a Namputiri woman is suspected of adultery, she is at once placed under 'suspension' till her guilt or innocence is proved. A trial is conducted by competent judges drawn from the members of the Namputiri society. When the guilt is proved she is out-casted. The judges decide the period which is the interval between the date of her offence and the date she is out-casted. An issue, during this period, if a male, becomes a Cākyār, if a female—Naṅyār.

Cf. 'Kathakali' by K. Bharatha Iyer, Ch. II Kerala Stage.

2. See Appendix E (i).

3. The Theatre of the Hindus, p. 194.

4. The Cochin Tribes and Castes Vol. II, p. 128. by L.K. Anantakrishna Ayyar.

Cf. Bhagavadajjukīyam—Introduction, p. XVIII, Footnote 7. Ed. by Anujan Achan.

Pisharoti[1] has given the traditional account as follows—A particular Sūta with his family came over to Kerala with one of the Perumal Kings, as his courtier. When his family was about to become extinct it was allowed to adopt into it the children of Brahmin women born of criminal intimacy. This procedure continues even today. Such children, if invested with the sacred thread become Cākyārs, if not Nambyārs. The girls are taken into either section indifferently.

The Cākyārs in their acting are helped by Pāṇivādas i.e. Nambyārs, and their women-folk, the Naṅyārs, in vocal and instrumental music. The Nambyār plays on the Miḷāvu—a close-necked metalic jar having its mouth tied up with a piece of leather. The Naṅyārs act as actresses and also sound cymbals and sing the verses which the actor gesticulates.

The Kūttu has religious character. The Actors are under fast[2] till the performance is over. The performance is to be held only in temples. The caste Hindus alone are allowed to witness it. It is a visual sacrifice to please the deity.

Certain innovations were added to the staging in the 9th century A.D. which are current till now. Kulaśekhara Perumal (about 900 A.D.) wrote two plays Tapatīsaṁvaraṇa and Subhadrā-Dhanañjaya. He was not only a good playwright but also a good actor. Tolan, his Brahmin minister, wrote Āṭṭaprakāra, a guide to Nāṭya, designed to help actors. Many innovations were introduced in the stage practice to make the acting more realistic and the stage more popular. Cākyārs enjoyed absolute freedom of speech on the stage. Tolan used this as a powerful weapon of social reform through Vidūṣaka. The Vidūṣaka used Malayāḷam words also together with Sanskrit, thus giving rise to the style called Maṇipravālam, which could be followed by the masses. [See Appendix E (iii).]

There are three varieties of Kūttu[3], In Prabandham Kūttu, the Cākyār has the dress and make-up of Vidūṣaka. The Vācikābhinaya (verbal gesticulation) is prominent. The Nambyār plays on the Miḷāvu and Naṅyār sounds the cymbals. The Cākyār recites a verse from a prabandham (composition) dealing with a story from Rāmāyaṇa or Mahābhārata and

1. Cf. The Theatre of the Hindus. p. 194.
2. See Appendix E (ii).
3. See Appendix E (iv).

afterwards proceeds to expound it. There are many apt analogies introduced, annecdotes told, and references to present situations made. The Cākyār must be a great ready-witted scholar to do this effectively. Prabandham kūttu is generally acted in the afternoon. In Naṅyār kūttu,[1] the Naṅyār is there instead of the Cākyār. Here, there is pure acting and no scope for satire. Accompaniment of Miḷāvu and cymbals helps her. The Naṅyār is dressed in a queer way. She first recites a verse and then acts it in pantomime. It is generally acted after night fall. Naṅyār kūttu[2] is very rare these days. The most important variety for my purpose is Kūṭiyāṭṭam, which I am going to deal with in detail.

In Kūṭiyāṭṭam, Sanskrit plays are staged. The term is composed of two words, kūṭi meaning—combined and āṭṭam—acting. According to Dr. S.K. Nayar 'āṭṭam' is derived from 'āḍu' to move, hence āṭṭam is dance. In Āṭṭam, Nṛtta, Nāṭya and Nṛtya are combined.

The difference between kūttu and kūṭiyāṭṭam is quite evident. In kūttu we have one character with the dress and make-up of Vidūṣaka and predominance of Vācikābhinaya. But in kūṭiyāṭṭam all the four-fold abhinaya is used effectively. There are different characters with different dresses and make-up which provide the 'visual charm' in the art, while the recitation and the use of music combined with the proper expression of different emotions, helped by bodily gestures, bring to us the full-fledged dramatic representation.

In olden days the Sanskrit plays were wholly staged by the Cākyārs. But this art is not thriving these days. A few acts only are enacted in the traditional manner by a small group of Cākyār families.

Nowadays, we get the presentation of the first act[3] of Tapatīsaṁvaraṇa and Subhadrādhanañjaya; the Mantrāṅka of

1. Cf. The Theatre of the Hindus, p. 196 and 'Kūṭiyāṭṭam' by Dr. S.K. Nayar, Annals O.R.I. Centenary Number, p. 18.

2. According to Dr. K. K. Raja, the Naṅyār kūtta is not a distinct type. It is mono-acting by a Naṅyār, representing through gestures alone the story of Kṛṣṇa and is part of the Nirvahaṇa of the Ceṭī in the Praveśaka scene of Subhadrādhanañjaya, Act. II.

See 'Kūṭiyāṭṭam' by Dr. K. K. Raja, p. 20.

See Appendix E (v).

3. See Appendix E (vi).

Pratijñāyaugandharāyaṇa; Śūrpaṇakhāṅka, Aṅgulīyakāṅka, Udyānapraveśāṅka and some part of the last act of Āścaryacūḍāmaṇi; some part of the Kalyāṇasaugandhikavyāyoga; some part of Mattavilāsaprahasana; second Act of Nāgānanda; and Toraṇayuddhāṅka and Vālivadhāṅka of Abhiṣekanāṭaka.

Works[1] in Malayāḷam and Sanskrit dealing with the representation of Sanskrit dramas are still in possession of the Cākyār families. Amongst these, some deal only with the explanation of the meanings, others with dance, music, vocal and instrumental, dress and make-up, manner of recitation, gesticulation etc. Similarly, there are various conventions regarding the entry and exit of characters, the different parikramas etc. which are traditionally handed down.

The theatre, Kūttampalam, is situated in the courtyard of the temple. It is constructed on the right-hand side of the main temple so that the actors would be facing the idol when they act. When there are no such permanent structures some place suitable for acting is turned into a stage, inside the courtyard (surrounded by walls) and the representation is carried out.

The theatres are rectangular and of three sizes—small medium and large. The medium one at Irinjālakkuḍa is supposed to be the best from the view point of Cākyār performance. The large one is that belonging to the Trichur temple, and the small type which I studied belongs to that of Guruvāyur temple. The construction is basically similar in all these three types. The stage is square, higher than the auditorium. The auditorium again has two levels. The raised floor just in front of the stage is meant for higher caste Brahmins while the lower one for others. The stage has a roof with ornate ceiling supported by wooden pillars. There is exquisite wood carving on the ceiling but it is spoiled by the smoke of the brass lamp and hence not clearly visible in details. The Guruvāyur and Irinjālakkuḍa Kūttampalams have stage roofs supported by four pillars each at the four corners. But the Trichur stage has twelve pillars. Naturally, such a large number of pillars causes some inconvenience to the actors and at times the pillars come in between the actors and the spectators. Just behind the stage and adjoining it is the green-room. There are two doors in the front wooden wal

1. See Appendix E (vii).

of the green-room through which the actors come out on the stage or go back to the green-room. There is one door in the back wall of the green-room meant only for the actors to enter the green-room for make-up etc. In between the two doors in the front wall, the instrumentalists are placed. There is a wooden structure to support the Miḷāvu. At Trichur we find two such structures for two Miḷāvus. At Irinjālakkuḍa also there is an arrangement for the other Miḷāvu. To the left of this, the other instrumentalists stand. The auditorium has two doors on the left and the right hand side. There is one more extra door in the front wall just opposite the stage for the entry of terrible or devilish characters like Śūrpaṇakhā etc., when they enter through the audience[1]. (I have given sketches of these three types of temple theatres with all their details and actual measurements, at the end).

The roofs of these theatres are wooden and highly decorative. The kutapa (orchestra) consists of Miḷāvu (big one-faced drum), two wind instruments called kulal and kompa, the former being the chief one, cymbals and Iḍakka[2]. In Iriṅjālakkuḍa and Trichur, as it is already pointed out, the sitting arrangement is provided for two Miḷāvu. The Milāvu is generally made of copper. It is placed with its close-necked face turned upwards and is played by hands. Sitting upon a raised seat the player plays upon it. It serves as the main musical instrument used in staging the drama. Sometimes, conch and maddaḷam are added in specific entries like those of kings, royal personages, etc. The player on the Milāvu sits and to his left, the other instrumentalists stand. To the right hand side one or two Naṅyārs sit on a piece of cloth spread on the stage. They indicate the rhythm by playing the cymbals. On one Miḷāvu the player uses different kinds of drum-beats (karaṇas) to suit the representation. On the other again, the rhythm is prominently indicated. The player of wind-instrument gives tunes just in conformity with the particular occasion. The Naṅyār does the whole work of singing or reciting the verses. Nowadays, the vocal music used by these Naṅyārs is reduced merely to the status of recitation.

1. See Appendix E (viii).

2. Iḍakka is a delicate, sensitive small drum; it is played by a small stick. The Iḍakka-player stands near the left Milāvu.

See Appendix E (ix).

There is one big brass lamp in front of which all the acting is presented. The lamp is kept brightly burning with big wicks and a proper supply of oil from time to time.

There is no other equipment on the stage but for a stool or two. The curtain, (not very large) is used before the first entry of every character. This curtain is held by two persons in their hands and is removed after its work is over.

What to us appear as most complicated scenes to be represented in the absence of suitable settings, are presented on the Cākyār stage in a very simple manner by the use of this curtain.

In the Verbal gesticulation, the dialogues consisting of prose and verse are recited clearly and slowly so that each word would be audible to the audience. The speeches are recited with the proper emotions. The high, middle and low accents are used to heighten the effect. For example, when Rāma addresses Sītā as 'Vaidehi', he utters 'vai' with the vowel 'ai' prolonged and then 'de' with prolongation of 'e' in 'de' and finally 'hi' with elongated accent. The peculiar manner of recitation in which the utterance is thus prolonged and hence very slow is explained by the Cākyārs as due to the necessity created by the Physical gesticulation. Each word is to be gesticulated and the mudrās for the original word (prakṛti) and the termination (pratyaya) are also different. The gesticulation in the first instance is simultaneously done with the utterance of each word. Unless the recitation is sufficiently slow it would not be possible to express each word by mudrās. And hence this typical manner of utterance is used. It is seen that formerly, in the recitation of verses different Rāgas were used to make the recitation fully effective.

The conventions regarding the recitation of Sanskrit and Prakrit in the Sanskrit drama are the same. Each character uses the particular language of his or her own speech. Vidūṣaka speaks Deśabhāṣā i.e. Malayāḷam mainly. He first utters his original Prakrit speech and then gives the Sanskrit rendering of it followed by its explanation in Malayāḷam. This Vidūṣaka also explains the meaning of the speeches of other characters, first enacting as if listening to them with the words meaning 'What do you say?' in Malayāḷam. Such terrific characters like Śūrpaṇakhā also use Prakrit Malayāḷam in their 'asides' as occasion arises. In the recitation of verses which are rather difficult to understand, the recitation takes place in detail according to the construction of the sentences; first the main sentence, then the clauses, different adjectives of subject, object, etc. so that the understanding would be as clear as possible.

The Cākyār actor is expert in expressing different moods by facial expressions alone, in which the particular eye movements play a very important role. They gesticulate quite effectively such Temperamental states as stupefaction, horripilation, swoon etc. When there are stage directions like 'सस्पृहम्' (with longing) 'सरोमविक्रियम्' (with horripilation)'सरोषम्' (angrily) before the speech, they are never gesticulated with hastamudrās (i.e. hand-gestures). These are technically called kriyās. They fully reveal the import of the speech before it is uttered and thus serve to heighten the effect of the speech. When we have the stage-direction 'सरोमविक्रियम्' it would be enacted by the throbbing of all the body-hands, chest, head etc. but when the Verbal gesticulation goes on, the word 'रोमाञ्च' will be gesticulated by hastamudrā, with the thumb touching near the tip of the first finger and moving it upwards on both the hands from the wrist, then in a circular motion around the chest to indicate the hair standing on end. The convention that in these kriyās hastamudrās are never to be resorted to, is strictly followed.

In Āhāryābhinaya (i.e. dress, make-up etc.) the paste of rice, charcoal powder, turmeric powder, red lead, red chalk, red arsenic, indigo and ghee are used in make-up. The different kinds of grass and flowers, bamboo stumps mica and betelnut-leaves etc. are used to prepare decorations for head and body. The material is quite cheap and the ornaments and decorations are prepared for the particular act only for the temporary use.

I shall now give a detailed description of the dress, make-up etc. of some characters who appear in the Aṅkābhinaya (i.e. enacting of one Act) which is in existence these days. The dress and make-up of the hero in general is almost the same. A dhoti and a full-sleeved shirt form the dress. There is one upper garment, neatly folded aud twisted with flower-like formations at each end, worn right over the left shoulder and from under the right arm. This is worn by almost all the characters including the heroine with the exception of Vidūṣaka, maid-servants etc. The ornaments consist of pairs of bracelets, worn on the wrists and the upper part of arm, necklaces, rings and the karṇakuṇḍala—the ear-rings hanging from the head-dress. There is kirīṭa[1] i.e. crown on the head. This crown has slight variations according to the type of the hero. The different types are individualised by minor changes in ornaments and other decorations such as the mark on the fore-head etc. The facial make-up consists of Cuṭṭi i.e. facial border which is prepared of rice-paste and lime. The basic colour applied to the face is light green, over which there are other patches of colour over the cheeks, round the eyes and so on, to make the expression of the particular character more effective. The head is decorated with a crown. As a rule, the king alone would wear a crown. Arjuna is Kirīṭin, that is why he always has a crown; Sūgrīva would wear one only when he becomes the king after the death of Vālin. All heroines share similar dress and make-up. A sari, blouse and the upper garment form the dress. Bangles, necklaces and ear-rings are the chief ornaments used. The head-wear is beautifully decorated. The clown wears only a dhoti and his upper body is bare and marked by white stripes of colour upon it and red spots on arms and chest. He wears a pair of bracelets upon his wrists. His facial make-up consists of red marks over the cheeks, nose and chin and white stripes over the face, prominent moustache and the eyes smeared over thickly with collyrium. On the fore-head three white stripes are painted with a dark tilaka-mark at the centre. Besides the sacred thread, he has an upper garment, which he uses at times. He has a simple type of head-wear provided with an artificial tuft of hair. Vidūṣaka has the same dress and make-up in different plays. Vālin has a red beard just below green cheeks and chin. The green patch over the red one makes the face more effective through the bright colour contrast. This beard is formed of particular crimson flowers. Over the green patch comes a white one over which the red is repeated. All round the eyes dark black is applied in the shape of a bird. The fore-head is marked with three dark red vertical lines at the centre and there is some decoration on either side of these. Sugrīva has only a head-dress till the death of Vālin. Both Hanumat and

1. See Appendix E (x).

Sugrīva are painted with basic red. However, the beard of Hanumat is made of cotton and hence is white, (being of good omen). A tail is added to the monkey-type.

Rāvaṇa has no beard but there is a white border along the cheeks and the chin upon the basic green. Just below nose and all along the lower part of the eyes red is applied. The eyes are bordered all around with dark colour. Over the eyes, comes green followed by red on the fore-head. On the tip of the nose a white knob is fixed. The basic green colour forms the make-up for Sāttvika or divine personages. Bibhīṣaṇa has his make-up like Arjuna with basic green and on the fore-head, possesses a Vaiṣṇava mudrā.

The role of Śūrpaṇakhā, the demoness is always presented by a male actor. The basic colour used for her make-up is black with five trident marks in white upon the chin, tip of the nose, two cheeks and the centre of the fore-head. Huge, pointed and ugly artificial breasts are tied up. Crude type of bracelets and ear-ornaments are also there. A crude and fantastic head-wear is worn as a decoration. She wears anklets made of silver or plated brass.

Garuḍa has artificial beak and feathers. But no mask is used.

Lips are always painted crimson in the case of all characters including even a demoness like Śūrpaṇakhā.

Mythologically Rāvaṇa is supposed to be Daśamukha, a ten-faced demon King. However, the daśa-mukhatva i.e., the possession of ten faces is shown by gesticulation, e.g., in the Aṅgulīyakāṅka of Āścaryacūḍāmaṇi Rāvaṇa, whose passion is excited by the rise of the moon, is standing near Sītā and recites the verse, the gesticulation of which produces the effect of his being ten-faced.

Durgā (Kātyāyanī) wears a crown even though a female. There is a dark facial border in her make-up. She has bow and arrow in her hands. The rest of the dress is like that of the heroine

Music and Dance :

The instrumental music consists mainly of two Miḷāvus, two wind instruments, one Iḍakka and cymbals. The sound of Miḷāvu is rather high-pitched. When the body gestures are going on, the instrumental music is used all the time. As soon as the recitation is to begin, the character gives a signal by the hand to stop the music and then begins the speech. According to different movements, the instrumental music changes to heighten the effectiveness of the action of the character. At the entry of the hero, the conch is blown to indicate the royal grandeur of the character. The verses of the text are recited in a particular manner to make the meaning clear and to express the mood appropriately.

The oldest Cākyār Śrī Cāccu said that formerly different melodies were used. The list of different Rāgas indicative of various situations and moods is traditionally handed down e.g., the Muḍḍa[1] melody is desirable in the love in union of demonesses, while Muralīndala is proper in the love in union of Rāma. In the description of rainy season, Puranīra is to be used, while at the end of act and the destruction of the wicked ones Śrīkaṇṭhī is to be used. The use of specific Rāgas in the recitation of verses was meant to heighten the effect. In this manner of recitation instrumental music was not used. At present, of course, the verses are recited expressing the emotion but there is no noticeable use of musical melodies.

In no case instrumental music is to be played when recitation is going on. The singing is to be done by two Naṅyārs, sitting on the right-hand side of the stage. They also play the cymbals to indicate the rhythm. Full-fledged singing with the accompaniment of orchestra is, nowadays, nearly nil. The different karaṇas (rhythmic beats) are used by the Pāṇi-vāda, the Miḷāvu-player to suit the movements in Tryasra or Caturasra Tāla.

In Bhagavadajjukīya Prahasana we get verses which are called the Akkittā Gānas (songs). First we have two verses in salutation of Lord Gaṇapati, the auspicious deity. The musical quality of the verses is quite evident. On the first day after the entry of Sūtradhāra the dance marks the end. During the dance the Akkittā song is used. There are songs at the end of the performance. When after the entry of Śāṇḍilya, the dance begins we have Akkittā songs. These verses are to be sung by the songstress and Śāṇḍilya is to enact them. Generally they are expected to be sung in

1. See Appendix E (xi).

Indala. The direction is 'Indalena gātavyā' (to be sung in Indala melody). [See Appendix E (xii)].

Dance :

Dance is also occasionally employed. Vidūṣaka has his peculiar dance called Cārī Nartana, just after his entry. It consists of going four steps. At the end of one cārī he has one bhramarī i.e. moving in four directions, just to form a square. When Śūrpaṇakhā (in charming form) decides ultimately through frustration, to devour Rāma and Lakṣmaṇa, she performs a Vikaṭa i.e., a fierce dance. Arjuna too dances vigorously when he is preparing to employ the Āgneyāstra (the fire-missile) against the demon.

Starting of Kūṭiyāṭṭam :

The stage is well decorated with the green leaves of coconut and plantains and red silk. A big lighted brass lamp is kept at the centre in the front part of the stage. The actors pay homage to Gods and teachers in the green-room, with great reverence, lest any slight mistake may incur the divine displeasure. While this preliminary item goes on in the green room there is no instrumental music. At the end of this the Nambyār beats Miḻāvu and Naṅyār sings verses in praise of God Gaṇapati and the Goddess Sarasvatī and Lord Śiva. Then the Nambyār brings some holy water from the green-room, sprinkles it on the stage and recites the Nāndī verse of the act that is to be staged. (These Nāndī verses are the Maṅgalaślokas specially composed for the use of Cākyārs.) The Nambyār appears on the stage in ordinary dress and without any makeup. Then the curtain is held by two persons and with the instruments being played upon, the main character stands behind the curtain. As the curtain is removed the character makes his appearance. The preludes, which we find in the text are dropped and the first entry is that of the main character i.e., generally, the hero. Perhaps the idea behind this is that the beginning of the Act should be made through the principal character alone. [See Appendix E (xiii)].

On the next day the Nirvahaṇa starts, in which the hero, only through bodily gestures expounds the earlier portion of the story leading to the incidents in the Act about to be presented. This Nirvahaṇa consists of Anukrama, Saṁkṣepa and Vivaraṇa.

In the Anukrama, the parts of the story leading to the present condition of the hero are shown through gesticulation in the reverse order. Here, if the portion of the story which precedes the actual plot of the play is expected, then that is also included. To take an illustration, in the Nāgānanda, after the introduction the hero enters and he expounds the meaning of the first verse in brief, and concludes the first day's acting. On the next day, Nirvahaṇa starts. This is carried out by the player whose dress and make-up are the same as that of the hero. This is essential, for the presence of the hero is necessary quite often. In the words of Prof. K.P.N. Pisharoti, the stage manager with the dress and make-up of the hero, carries out the Nirvahaṇa i.e., establishing the content of the play. "Who is the father of Jīmūtavāhana, the hero ? What is his capital ? Who are his parents ? What is their life history ? What is the occasion for this waiting upon them ?" Such queries are raised in the minds of the spectators and are answered.

In the Anukrama, the explanation of the present condition of the hero is first given, then the occasion for his service of the parents, then the earlier incident of bringing the desire-yielding tree from heaven and planting it on earth for the suppliants, then his birth history, after that the marriage of Jīmūtaketu and Mahāpuṇyā (his parents), then the creation of the capital of Vidyādharas and afterwards the creation of Himālaya. In this way the former story is expounded in the reverse order.

The Cākyārs have a collection of verses, not embodied in the play, for such purposes.

Afterwards, we have the Saṁkṣepa. In this, the story is gesticulated beginning right from the creation of the world upto that of Himālaya in brief. After that, the story from the creation of Himālaya upto the present condition of the hero is told in due order through gesticulation. This forms Vivaraṇa. When Nirvahaṇa is complete, actual staging of the Act begins. In the Aṅgulīyakāṅka of Āścaryacūḍāmaṇī there is very large scope for Nirvahaṇa. The actor, with the dress and make-up of Hanumat gesticulates the whole story of Rāmāyaṇa together with other stories connected with it in the course of Nirvahaṇa.

For this the Cākyārs have collected nearly five hundred verses from Rāmāyaṇa or in some cases, from other works also. Hence from the view point of gesticulation this Aṅgulīyakāṅka is prominent.

In Toraṇayuddhāṅka, the third Act of Abhiṣekanāṭaka when the curtain is taken away we have the entry of Śaṅkukarṇa. He is frightened to death. All of his body is trembling. Turning here and there he looks in fear, holds his head by both hands, cries, shows jaws some times, runs helter skelter and finally turns round in suspicion that somebody is following him. In this way Śaṅkukarṇa behaves just in a manner, a man when caught in a whirlwind would behave. This striking beginning thus becomes very effective.

When Vidūṣaka is present in the Act he also carries out Nirvahaṇa i.e. telling his former story, but it is narrated in Malayāḷaṃ.

Now I shall present a description of the staging of the Act II of Āścaryacūḍāmaṇi and then that of Act I of Subhadrā-Dhanañjaya in sufficient details so that a concrete idea of the method of enacting the Acts of Sanskrit plays by the Cākyārs would be given.

The Nambyār in his ordinary dress, appears as Sūtradhāra and recites the following verse, which indicates the second Act.

गोदावर्यास्तटान्ते मृदुपवनचलत्पङ्कजामोदहृद्ये
सेव्ये वैखानसानां सहजसहचरीसंयुतो वर्तमानः ।
आविर्भूतस्मरार्तां दशमुखभगिनीं दर्शयन्तीं रिरंसा-
मारादालक्ष्य रामः स्मितरुचिरमुखो व्याहरन् वः पुनातु ॥

The Nambyār then retires to the green-room. The instrumental music commences for the entry of Rāma. The curtain is held and after the removal of the curtain Rāma is visible seated on a stool. He gesticulates the story beginning from the entrance in the hermitage of the sage Agastya, till the arrival at Godāvarī region. He then takes a full view of the entire land-scape and enacts the trees, creepers, animals, birds etc., which are seen there. In this abhinaya the original word and the terminations have also different mudrās[1] (hand-gestures). Thus after the gesticulation of seeing the region of Godāvarī, he wants to convey the feeling in which there is no room for the expected sense of wonder and he addresses Sītā as Vaidehi etc. This entry is with Sītā. But according to convention the role of Sītā is never enacted here and hence Rāma, again by gesticulation creates the impression of the presence of Sītā sitting upon his lap. From the next day the Nirvahaṇa starts and it goes on for three days. On the fifth day we have the whole Act presented to us. After the first entry the curtain is not used. The player enters covering his face by the end of his upper garment, stands near the brass lamp and slowly removes the veil. Taking a full view of the audience he sits on the stool. The entry is of course with Sītā, sitting on his lap though Sītā is actually absent. First we have Anukrama, in which the story upto the arrival at the hermitage of Agastya is gesticulated in the reverse order ; then there is Saṁkṣepa beginning with the birth of Rāma upto the arrival at the hermitage. Then Vivaraṇa begins in which the incidents preceding the second act are enacted. Rāma calls Lakṣmaṇa and tells him to build a cottage. Lakṣmaṇa obeys. The actor ties up the two ends of the lower garment and by this action the audience has to understand that he is now Lakṣmaṇa. Then we have the verse from the first Act enacted by Lakṣmaṇa by bodily gesttures alone. This enacting is an elaborate affair, that goes on for an hour or even more. The verse[2] is as follows—

ज्याघोषेण निराकरोमि भयदान् पर्यन्तभाजो मृगान्
पर्णैः सद्म समापयामि शयनं बध्नामि पुष्पच्छदैः ।
वेत्राणामुपपादयामि वलयैरायामिनां विष्टरं
सिञ्चामि क्षितिमार्द्रपङ्कजरजोविद्धैरपां रेणुभिः ।।

The actor comes to one end of the stage and gesticulates the twang of the bow. Of course, there is no bow in his hands actually. He simply enacts it. The effect of the twang is produced on the Miḷāvu. Then the actor goes to the other end and

1. This hastābhinaya is carried out according to the work 'हस्तलक्षणदीपिका'.

2. Āścaryacūḍāmaṇi, Act I, V. 5

gesticulates in fine details the fearful flight of the various animals after hearing the twanging of the bow. In this gesticulation a very minute study of animal behaviour is displayed which creates a semblance of the presence of these animals. It would be interesting to illustrate the point. The behaviour of the lordly elephant would give a sufficient picture. The royal gait, the flapping of the ears, lifting up of the trunk, flapping of the left ear simultaneously with the movement of the right leg and vice versa are imitated realistically. The elephant is now in front of us thus undisturbed and enjoying his security. Suddenly, he hears the twang, gets frightened and runs away hastily in the manner, befitting an elephant. In this way the flight of a lion, tiger and other beasts is presented by gesticulation. Here, the gesticulation of the first quarter of the stanza ends. The other three quarters are also enacted with all details. In the construction of the cottage, the firm planting of four pillars, then fixing of the beams, tying them with strong creepers, preparing of the roof with leaves etc., are all clearly shown. Then he collects green tender leaves and flowers quite fresh, and prepares a bed with them. In the end, the ground is sprinkled with water mixed with the fragrant filaments of full blown lotuses. Thus in a very striking manner, the meaning of the verse is made clear to us without actually uttering the words.

Now the cottage is ready and Lakṣmaṇa proposes to report the same to Rāma. The actor then assumes the role of Śūrpaṇakhā. For this transfer of role, he simply puts in the two ends of the lower garment at the knot where the lower garment is tied to the waist. Śūrpaṇakhā is told by her brothers to choose her own husband. First she goes to heaven, but finding out some defect or other in the various Gods, comes down on earth. She looks at Rāma and is at once struck by his beauty. Her love-stricken condition is enacted e.g., looking slantingly, bashfulness etc. Her moving through the sky is shown by standing on the stool and then jumping up again and again. In the end, she descends from the sky simply by alighting from the stool. When she looks at Rāma she is dejected with the thought of her own ugliness contrasting it with the beauty of Rāma. (There are two verses at this stage from the collection of Cākyārs, which are recited by the Naṅyārs to bring out this difference clearly.)

In this Nirvahaṇa, next we have Śūrpaṇakhā in the graceful form. To show this the actor has the right end of the lower garment fixed at the knot and takes the posture of drooping shoulders. She looks at Rāma and is infatuated, for Rāma is as handsome as Madana (cupid). Rāma sees her. She requests him to accept her. Rāma tells her 'I am here with my wife so please go to Lakṣmaṇa, my younger brother who is alone'. She goes to Lakṣmaṇa. He is with bow and arrow and looks like Madana himself with his lotus-like eyes. She is fascinated and struck by love. The actor now becomes Lakṣmaṇa and gesticulates looking at her. Seeing her charming form, his mind is disturbed. 'Is she from heaven or earth ?' He ponders. Here we have the gesticulation of her beauty by him, through Pañcāṅgābhinaya (the representation of the five limbs). The hair, the eyes, the face, the breasts, and the feet—these five form the subject of Pañcāṅgābhinaya which offers a clear-cut idea of the most ideal form of a young beautiful woman. (In the case of men we have the gesticulation of broad chest in place of lofty bosom in the Pañcāṅgābhinaya.) Lakṣmaṇa then shows the effect of love on him. All the stages of love-stricken condition are enacted ending in swoon. After regaining consciousness he obtains control over his own mind with the thought, 'I am the younger brother of Rāma who is always dutiful and who has taken to the forest life to obey the words of his father. When I am under his power now how is it that I am overpowered by cupid ?' He asks her to go back to Rāma.

All this is conveyed without the use of words. The language of mudrās is, of course, highly conventional and unless there is some one with you to explain the meaning of the different mudrās it is not possible to understand this method of conveying the story.

On the last day the whole of the Act was enacted. As Rāma comes and sits upon the stool, the stage direction is, 'then enters Rāma with Sītā' (ततः प्रविशति रामः सीतया सह).

I shall first give a summary of the plot of this Act in brief. Rāma and Sītā are conversing about their forest life. Then Śūrpaṇakhā (in graceful form) appears. Rāma asks her whether she had been to Lakṣmaṇa. She tells that she was repudiated and requests Rāma once again to accept her. Rāma says that he has his wife, 'sahadharmacāriṇī' with him. Śūrpaṇakhā declares her determination to die there and then. Sītā pleads that this determination should not be ignored. Rāma asks her to go to Lakṣmaṇa once more. Unwillingly, she gets ready to do so and thinks that if Lakṣmaṇa rejects her this time also she would have her own demon form again. She leaves. Rāma and Sītā resume their conversation. Sītā inquires, "Why is that poor girl sent to Lakṣmaṇa ?" Rāma tells her that such immodest women do not deserve to be in contact with householders and adds that Lakṣmaṇa would never accept her. While they are further conversing in this train, they hear the wild cry of Śūrpaṇakhā and the words of Lakṣmaṇa 'Oh', flesh-eater, stop, stop' etc.

Then Lakṣmaṇa enters, sword in hand with Śūrpaṇakhā in her original demonic form. Sītā is frightened. Rāma is ready to attack her but Lakṣmaṇa tells him that he alone would do the work. Lakṣmaṇa and Śūrpaṇakhā fight, and in the end, she carries him into the sky. Rāma censures himself and prepares to attack her when the voice is heard 'I am fallen, please help.' Rāma understands that the demoness has been defeated by his brother and has fallen down on earth. They go in search of Lakṣmaṇa. He returns. All are happy. Then Śūrpaṇakhā comes there, all in blood, crying loudly and calling upon her brothers Rāvaṇa, Bibhīṣaṇa and Kumbhakarṇa to protect her. Her nose and ears have been cut by Lakṣmaṇa. She warns them that they would see the fruits of their immodest behaviour and she goes to show her condition to Khara and Dūṣaṇa. Then Rāma asks how Lakṣmaṇa had recognised her real form. He answers—'How would the heat be concealed from the fire?' Now Rāma declares that the enmity with the demons is started and it would be for the good of the world. For, the destruction of all the demons would be effected. Sītā draws the attention of Rāma to the red rays of the setting sun. The day is at its end. With the description of the sunset, the act ends.

Now I will try to deal with the salient points in the presentation of this Act.

Rāma gesticulates that Sītā is sitting on his lap and looking towards that imaginary Sītā, addresses 'वैदेहि ! विदूरे सर्वं

विस्मयनीयतया श्रूयते ।' 'Oh Vaidehi, all that is heard afar is full of wonder.' The word 'Vaidehi', is uttered slowly, every letter separated from the other with sufficient lengthening of the vowel and the last vowel is so prolonged that at the end, it almost appears that the speaker is out of breath. The sentence is also uttered slowly to form one unit. Every word is simultaneously, gesticulated by 'hastamudrās.' In reciting the verses too, the utterance is slow. First, the verse is recited quarter by quarter accompanied by 'hastamudrās.' At the end of each half, there is a slight drum-beating. Next, the utterance is according to the sentence construction i.e., the subject with its attributes, the object and its attributes, and verb etc. For example,

'पञ्चवटी त्रियामाचरैः सेव्या इति मे मतिः ।'

Every word, every attribute, is then followed by detailed gesticulation. Then in the end, the latter half of the stanza is recited once more and the gesticulation of the verse ends. In the last quarter, 'श्रोतुर्विस्मयनीयवस्तुविषयाः शैलाटवीसागराः ।'— 'the mountains, forests and oceans are the objects of wonder for the listener' the word 'शैलाटवीसागराः' would be uttered first, then the word श्रोतुः and lastly 'विस्मयनीयवस्तुविषयाः'. (For the gesticulation of 'विस्मय' see photo 1).

The speeches of Sītā in Prakrit are uttered by the Naṅyār. Rāma would pose as Sītā, enacting bashfulness, drooping shoulders etc. (see photo 2). Thus Sītā's speeches would be recited by the Naṅyār and Rāma would only show the gestures. The entry of graceful Śūrpaṇakhā 'ललितसुकुमारवेषा शूर्पणखा' would then follow. Śūrpaṇakhā comes out of the green-room and stands to the left. Rāma looks at her and says 'सुंदरि किं दृष्टः त्वया लक्ष्मणः ।' (see photo 3). She answers 'yes'. When Rāma learns from her what has happened —that Lakṣmaṇa has rejected her—he says to himself 'तस्य अनेन वचनेन भवितव्यम् ।' 'His speech is bound to be so'; the stage direction is 'सस्मितम् आत्मगतम्'. First he gesticulates his thought and then utters the speech. When the stage direction is 'प्रकाशम्' he looks at her and says, 'भद्रे पुनरपि भवतीं परिश्रमपथे नियोक्ष्यामि ।' 'Oh, good girl, I am going to ask you to try again'. She answers that she would stay there only and wait upon him. Sītā remarks that the girl is revealing proper discrimination for the merits by her affection towards her husband. Rāma looks at Śūrpaṇakhā and tells 'भद्रे तवायं व्यवसायः मयापि प्रार्थनीयः ।' 'Oh, good maid, this your resolve is to be desired by me also'.

After the first utterance of this speech Śūrpaṇakhā goes into the green-room. For, now the gesticulation of the verse is to go on. In the verse Rāma tells that in the presence of sacred fire he has married Sītā by the order of the elders for the dutiful sacred life. As she is there he is really bound by duty. So he requests her to think of his responsibilities. (As the gesticulation of important verses takes place for a long time the other character retires to the green-room.) In this verse the word 'सन्नाह' (preparation) was elaborately enacted ; (पर्णशालां निर्माय, जटामाबध्य, देहपीडां संवर्ध्य, तपः कृत्वा इ.). At the end of the verse Śūrpaṇakhā reappears from the green-room.

Afterwards, when Śūrpaṇakhā decides to take her original form in case Lakṣmaṇa rejects her once again, she provides the spectacle of a fierce dance (see photo 4). Of course, Rāma has gone to the green-room before this. At the exit of Śūrpaṇakhā, Rāma and Sītā are once again seen in conversation.[1]

We have the stage direction 'सीतां निरीक्ष्य' i.e., 'observing Sītā'. Here the actor gesticulates the beautiful form of Sītā—her long dark hair, beautiful fore-head, curved eye-brows, long eyes, blooming cheeks, earrings, round bosom, delicate arms, girdle, garments etc. After this, he feigns being affected by love through the arrow of Cupid and in the end swoons. The sentences or verses which are simple for understanding are first uttered accompanied by gesticulation then followed by gesticulation alone and finally by simple utterance once again. Only when the speeches are difficult to understand we have the padānvaya i.e., the difficult words separately and elaborately enacted.

When the words 'तिष्ठ तिष्ठ पिशिताशने तिष्ठ' are spoken in the green-room, at the time of loud cries of Śūrpaṇakhā the instrumental music is very vigorous.

Rāma hears this and says that the voice resembles that of Lakṣmaṇa. He at once prepares for fight. He has his loins girt, two ends of the lower garment tied and he gesticulates an animated fighting mood. He is quite ready with the bow in the left hand and an arrow in the right (see photo 5). Laksmaṇa then enters, repeating the speech 'तिष्ठ तिष्ठ' etc., and goes to the green-room. Śūrpaṇakhā as a demoness enters

1. See Appendix E (xiv).

with the use of the curtain as we find in Kathakali[1] style. The curtain is held. The orchestra goes on vigorously. The actor comes and stands behind the curtain. The face of Śūrpaṇakhā is first visible over the curtain, then gradually the curtain is lowered and then taken away disclosing Śūrpaṇakhā in her hideous form on the stage.

She enacts her pitiable condition arising out of her ugly features as a demoness. She utters her speech in a rhythmic manner accompanied by the drumming. She is ready to devour the delicate preys Rāma and Lakṣmaṇa and present Sītā to Rāvaṇa. Sītā is full of fear to look at her. Rāma asks her not to be afraid. Then Śūrpaṇakhā goes to the green-room and comes again on the stage. Now she is all alone on the stage. Her earlier story is told and enacted. Here the actor explained this story in Prakrit Malayāḷam. This was a very interesting scene as the great actor revealed his best in it. The moving through the sky was enacted by standing on the stool and moving the hands, as it were, in the swimming position. Alighting from the stool meant descent to earth. She has already found fault with all the Gods. On the arrival on earth she moved here and there in search of an eligible husband. References to some members from the audience were made by pointing towards them and then rejecting them as of no worth. The boys who were sitting on the stage were also picked up and then summarily rejected as being mere children. Thus the search of Śūrpaṇakhā for a bride-groom was enacted in a very lively manner. Then Śūrpaṇakhā goes to the green-room. Now Lakṣmaṇa enters to describe her in a verse and full scope for his gesticulation of this verse becomes a dramatic necessity. Rāma enters and when his gesticulation of the verse describing her begins, Lakṣmaṇa retires to the green-room. At the end of this all the three assemble on the stage. Śūrpaṇakhā gives out oft-repeated wild cries. Lakṣmaṇa takes upon him the task of fettering her (photo 6). Then Rāma goes in the green-room and we have a fight between Lakṣmaṇa and Śūrpaṇakhā (photo 7). It goes on for some time to create the appearance of heroic mood. The instrumental music is forceful. The speeches between the two are also befitting the fighting mood. Lakṣmaṇa threatens, 'I shall cut you now in pieces for the birds'. Śūrpaṇakhā says 'I shall first devour this cruel-hearted

1. The use of the curtain found in Kathakali is a tradition borrowed from Kūṭiyāṭṭam.

one in a solitary place'. Then she seizes him and carries him in her flight into the sky. The stage direction is 'खमुत्पत्य निष्क्रान्ता'. Śūrpaṇakhā stands on the stool (which is handy) with Lakṣmaṇa, holding his hand; they get down and go back, to the green-room. When Rāma gets ready to go and help, Sītā asks, 'Who would protect me?'. Rāma, in turn questions 'By whom would Lakṣmaṇa be protected?' Then Sītā's answer is that he possesses a weapon in his hand. Rāma is dejected and remarks, 'What is the use of a weapon for one who is caught in the hands of a demoness?' He defies the helplessness of human life, for he can see only the things on earth (see photo 8). The demoness disappeared snatching Lakṣmaṇa with her in his very presence. Sītā also feels sorry. Rāma enacts taking out his arrow from the quiver to employ it at the bow. At this time the words of Śūrpaṇakhā are heard, coming from the green-room, 'हं पादिदह्मि, अज्ज सरणं सरणम् ।'; and Rāma confidently says that the demoness is surely vanquished by Lakṣmaṇa. He goes in search of Lakṣmaṇa (the stage direction is 'उभौ परिक्रामतः'—both move round). After moving round Rāma looks about and utters the verse 'जगतीधर...' etc. at the end of which he leaves for the green-room. Then the stage direction is 'ततः प्रविशति लक्ष्मणः।' The curtain is held, when it is removed Lakṣmaṇa is seen standing on the stool. He is supposed to be on the aerial path. He feels sorry for striking a woman but consoles himself in a verse that he only cut the nose and ears of the demoness seeing her wickedness. After this verse he comes down from the stool and goes to the green-room saying, "Now I shall go near Rāma." Both the brothers emerge from the green-room. The stage-direction is 'सहर्षम् आलिङ्ग्य' Rāma embraces Lakṣmaṇa in joy (see photo 9). When Rāma inquires the whereabouts of the demoness, Lakṣmaṇa stands with his face downcast. At this stage, the stage direction is 'ततः प्रविशति साक्रन्दा शूर्पणखा'—"then enters Śūrpaṇakhā crying." This entry being very interesting the audience is extremely alert. The instrumental music is going on in full force. As has already been noted in the description of the temple theatre, there is one door at the back of the audience in the centre of the front wall. We hear the fierce cries and right through the audience Śūrpaṇakhā enters. The torch-bearer ahead provides flashes of light by throwing explosive powder in the flame of the torch. Really the disgustful terror is now incarnate. Śūrpaṇakhā is all wet bathed in blood with her ears and nose lopped off (see photo 10), and shouts pitiably with most terrific force "Oh noble Rāvaṇa, Oh noble Kumbhakarṇa, Oh noble Bibhīṣaṇa, save me, Oh, save me from the immodest behaviour of these men concealed under the guise of ascetics." Rāma describes her aweful appearance in a verse. Rāma acknowledges that the punishment given is quite appopriate. Indeed, this is the punishment to be given to women for whom death is the penalty. He then reports that it is so heard that this is Śūrpaṇakhā living in the Daṇḍakāraṇya, the elder sister of Khara and Dūṣaṇa and younger sister of Rāvaṇa. After the verses are recited Śūrpaṇakhā gradually goes to the stage shouting "Remember well, Oh men, this your wicked act. You will see its fruit henceforth". Lakṣmaṇa shouts "Go away first". She exits saying that she will show this condition of hers to Khara and Dūṣaṇa. Then the remaining Act is enacted in the usual manner. At the close of the Act, the day has come to an end and the enacting is closed by the verse of Rāma describing the sunset. All exit.

At this stage, the Cākyār comes out, washes his feet and sips the holy water. He then takes a burning wick from the lamp and extinguishes it. He lights it once again and places it in the lamp. There is no Bharata-vākya, but in the place of it, this method forms the vidhi (item) of ending of each Aṅkābhinaya (enacting of the Act).

I witnessed the enacting of the First Act of Subhadrādhanañjaya in 1958 as it had the character of Vidūṣaka also. I am describing some important pieces of gesticulation of this Act. [See Appendix E (xv)].

[At the end of his pilgrimage Arjuna has come to the Prabhāsatīrtha.]

Dhanañjaya enters after the curtain is removed. The stage direction is—'ततः प्रविशति धनुर्बाणपाणिः धनञ्जयः'। (Then enters Dhanañjaya with the bow and arrow in his hands.). But the actor represents the bow and arrow by gesticulation only.

A very striking gesticulation is presented in the case of the ollowing stanza :

शिखिनि शलभो ज्वालाचक्रैर्न विक्रियते पतन्
पिबति बहुशः शार्दूलीनां स्तनं मृगशावकः ।
स्पृशति कलभः सैंहीं दंष्ट्रां मृणालधिया मुहु-
र्नयति नकुलं निद्रातन्द्रीं लिहन्नहिपोतकः ॥

Arjuna has come in the vicinity of penance forest. He looks around and observes the extraordinary sacred life in the penance grove based upon peaceful co-existence. The wonder of this life is described in the above quoted stanza. After looking all round (according to the stage-direction 'समन्तादवलोक्य') Arjuna is struck by the sight. The moth which is hovering in the midst of the fire-flames is not affected by the multitude of flames, the young one of a deer sucks the bosom of many a tigress, the young one of an elephant touches the jaws of a lion again and again thinking that they are lotus fibres and the young serpent lulls the mongoose to sleep by licking.

Before the stanza, he utters, "Oh, the high-souled nature of the sages due to their greatness !" The stage direction which precedes this, namely of looking all around, (technically called kriyā by the Cākyārs), is primarily gesticulated through facial expressions in which the expression through eyes dominates, coupled with physical movements also. But there is no gesticulation by hands. Arjuna stands with his hands crossed over his chest. Gradually, he takes a view of the surroundings—he looks in one direction—expresses wonder at what he sees and gesticulates that wonderful sight. The fire is burning ablaze. A moth hovers round and falls in it. Its wings are not burnt. By the upward, downward and sideways movements of the eyes he is able to show the hovering round of the moth. The actor's eyes are expressive of immense wonder. Then he turns to the other direction. He gesticulates the tigress (see photo 11) and then the deer sucking her breast (see photo 12). This he does with many tigresses. Similarly, looking towards another direction he gesticulates the young elephant touching the jaws of a lion thinking them to be lotus-fibres; and lastly the young serpent giving up the natural enmity, lulling the mongoose by licking. All these unusual scenes are presented to the audience vividly by powerful facial expressions and appropriate physical movements. Herein we see the greatness of the actor in bringing out the whole picture with such minute details.

In order to give a clearer idea of the nature of the gesticulation by hands, I shall illustrate the first half of this stanza. (The numbers refer to the s ketches of the Mudrās.) 'शिखिनि' i.e., 'in the fire'—The fire is gesticulated by spreading out the palms and shaking them simultaneously upwards up to the chest creating the appearance of rising flames. (The hands are moved only upto the level of chest so that the eye-movements would not be obstructed.)

The locative[1] is denoted by the mudrā in which the tips of the thumb and the first finger touch each other to form a circle and the remaining three fingers straight.

'शलभ:' the moth[2] is presented by keeping the first finger straight and moving it up and down while the other fingers are bent inside with the thumb touching. To show the hovering movement the hand in the "śalabha-mudrā' would be moved as in the figure of eight horizontally.

ज्वालाचक्रैः:—'by the multitudes[3] of flames'—The left hand with fingers stretched and thumb separated is placed just below the chest indicating fire and the right hand turned upwards with fingers stretched and the thumb separated is held just above the left hand to signify the flame. The right hand moved round would represent the cakra (multitude). The plural is shown with the first finger of the right hand stretched and turned round from inside and then moved up while the other bent fingers touch the thumb. Then the instrumental would be denoted by the mudrā used in the locative. (To indicate हेतु i.e., the cause, the hand is moved round from the left. The dative. ablative and genitive also have the same mudrā).

'न विक्रियते'—'is not destroyed' is shown with loose fists of both hands brought together with thumbs stretched up and shaking slightly to indicate the negative.

'पतन्'—i.e., 'falling'[4], is gesticulated by eye movement together with that of hand in which the first two fingers of both hands are stretched, the remaining touching the thumb, are moved first inward and then outwards in the same continuous motion.

'पिबति'—i.e. 'sucks'[5], is shown by circular motion of the eyes as well as by hand movement. All the fingers of each hand touching one another are placed near the mouth and slowly turned out from inside in one motion.

'बहुश:'—'frequently', is presented by the repetition of the action of sucking.

'शार्दूलीनाम्'—'of the tigresses'[6] is represented by first denoting a tiger, with palms of both hands crossing, with fingers spread; to indicate[7] the feminine gender the left hand would be in kaṭaka-mudrā, in which the wrist of the left hand is held by the two middle fingers and the thumb of the right hand with its first and last fingers straight. The fingers of the left hand are stretched and joined together. The plural is described earlier.

'स्तनम्'—'bosom'[8], is shown by the mudrā which is formed by touching the tip of the first finger of the right hand with that of the second finger of the left hand and vice versa in a crossed position and the last finger of each hand touching the third finger of the other hand.

'मृगशावक:'— i.e. 'the young one of a deer'—The deer[9] is shown by the right hand, thumb touching the two middle fingers at the ends and stretching the first and last fingers; the young[10] one is presented by the left hand with the first three fingers touching each other and the last finger straight, brought down to indicate the diminutive.

(The dual[11] is shown by the left hand with the thumb touching the third finger and stretching out the first two fingers and with the first finger of the right hand turning inwards and letting it out in the same motion.)

Vidūṣaka comes on the stage on the fourth day. At the removal of the curtain he dances the 'चारीनर्तन.' After this, he cleans his sacred thread, then his hair, and then throws down those that come out in the process of cleaning, in the midst of the audience. The garment, wet with perspiration, is then wrung to ooze out the water. And then he gesticulates exhaustion caused by the fatigue of the journey and the heat of the midday sun. We find him with a begging bowl (made of plantain leaf) in his hand.

For five days Vidūṣaka[1] expounds the four purposes of human life, while narrating his former story. A good many interesting anecdotes are told and references made. He has full scope for humour and satire. Instead of the usual Dharma, Artha, Kāma and Mokṣa, he advocates Vinoda, Vañcana, Aśana and Rājasevā as the four aims of life suited for the present age. He presents them in the order mentioned above. In Vinoda and Vañcana all topics dealt with in Erotics (the Kāmaśāstra) find place. In Aśana, the eatables and non-eatables, the varieties of food, dishes and everything connected with eating is brought in. Lastly in the Rājasevā he describes the qualities of good kings and bad ones, good servants and bad ones etc. And ultimately he connects his presence in the service of the hero and the story of the play which was held up, is again recommenced by Vidūṣaka uttering his speech in the play proper.

Arjuna comes on the stage and gesticulates the pangs of separation from his beloved. Then by mudrās he enacts big trees, creepers, flowers, foliage, beasts like deer and others. A big banyan tree is gesticulated and Arjuna enacts that he is taking shelter in the shade of this tree. As he stands there, from the green-room, the words of Vidūṣaka "O revered great sages, give me alms" are heard. Arjuna shows listening to them and remarks that, it is the voice of his friend Kauṇḍinya who is begging alms. Vidūṣaka then enters from the green-room and repeats his speech. First he recites his 'Prakrit' speech, then gives the Sanskrit rendering and afterwards its explanation in Malayālam. (This process of Vidūṣaka's speeches goes on till the end. Not only that but he also explains in Malayālam the verses and difficult speeches of the hero too).

When Arjuna gets ready to employ the fire-missile against the demon, we have his forceful movements accompanied by vigorous instrumental music for about five minutes or so. The heroic atmosphere is easily created. He gives the challenge, "Either leave the girl or go away. Otherwise I shall kill you".

1. For the detailed treatment of Vidūṣaka's role, see my article—'The Vidūṣaka in the Kūṭiyāṭṭam', published in Indian Antiquary Vol. II No. 4, October 1967.

Vidūṣaka also tries to help his friend. But again he misunderstands the word 'सद्यः' 'at once' as सद्या 'the feast'. The stage direction after the verse is शरं सन्धत्ते—'fixes the arrow'. But Dhanañjaya only shows it by gesticulation. There is neither bow nor arrow in his hands. And now Vidūṣaka, as usual, explains the verse for a long time and tries to show his own bravery. When Arjuna challenges, he too challenges. As he is a Brahmin he shows his sacred thread to frighten the demon. He has his loins girt. With the upper garment he tries to strike the demon. He recites a 'Maṇipravālam' verse. When the demon runs away he takes the credit as belonging to them both. "We both protected the girl by our bravery" he says. While the girl is falling down he makes a mark on the ground to ascertain as to whom the girl should belong. If she falls on Arjuna's side she would belong to Arjuna and if on his side of the mark, to him. But if she falls on the mark, then he suggests that she be divided between the two. (This comic relief actually tries the patience of the other character who is standing in the position of one with arrow ready for shooting during all this time.) Now Arjuna gesticulates taking back his arrow. From the green-room come the words of the maiden "Save me ! Please save me !" Arjuna is ready to receive her, with his hands spread out. Then Arjuna and Vidūṣaka go to the green-room. The stage-direction is 'ततः प्रविशति पतन्ती कन्यका'—"then enters the maiden falling down". A curtain is held. The instrumental music goes on fast to create excitement for this entry. The girl comes out from the green-room and stands on the stool behind the curtain. With the atmosphere of astonishment thoroughly awakened by the instrumental music, the curtain is removed and the heroine is seen on the stool looking down in a frightened manner and showing by her bent head and the position of her arms that she is falling down, reciting her speech "Save me, Oh, please save me". (See photo 13).

Next day this entry is repeated. Arjuna then comes from the green-room with Vidūṣaka, holds the maiden and helps her down from the stool. The girl looks at Dhanañjaya slantingly, with her fear and nervousness still there, enacted by the shivering of her body. She utters her speech accompanied by gesticulation and then followed by mudrābhinaya. Both are attracted to each other. Vidūṣaka observes this and comments. (See photo 14). (When this snap was being taken by me the flash exploded and the readywitted Vidūṣaka enacting terrible fright cried out "Oh, the lightening has fallen on me". All the audience could not but laugh.)

When Arjuna stands thinking about the maiden, lost in himself, Vidūṣaka tries to address him. He says, "Oh friend, tell me this". But when he realises that his words are not heard he goes near him and ascertains whether he is asleep or awake, but on seeing his love-stricken condition he tries to console him. (See photo 15). Later, when Vidūṣaka mistakes the Gātrikā for a serpent he enacts fear in a very effective manner (photo 16). Even when Dhanañjaya tries to convince him of the truth he is still not quite sure. He moves forward to take it but comes back. This goes on for some time and then in the end he cautiously lifts it up and knowing the truth now, laughs at himself. Dhanañjaya takes it with reverence, holds it to his bosom and gets consolation. He decides to secure the maiden and hands back the Gātrikā to Vidūṣaka.

With the description of the setting sun the Act closes. All go to the green-room. Then the final item is performed by the Cākyār acting as the hero.

I am describing some more scenes from other plays to explain the role of Vidūṣaka.

In the second Act of Nāgānanda, when the hero points to the moon-stone slab (photo 17) and says[1] "This is the moon-stone slab, where resting her very pale face on her sprout-like left hand, deeply sighing and weeping, my beloved, while I was delayed, was seen by me divulging her (inner) feelings by the slightly throbbing lower lip and (somehow) checking the anger of her mind"; Vidūṣaka has also something to say, "This[2] is the

1. Nāgānanda II-6.
शशिमणिशिला सेयं यस्यां विपाण्डुरमाननं
करकिसलये कृत्वा वामे घनश्वसितोद्‌गमा ।
चिरयति मयि व्यक्ताकूता मनाक्स्फुरिताधरा
नियमितमनोमन्युर्दृष्टा मया रुदती प्रिया ॥

2. उरलटिषिला सेयं यस्यां विजृम्भितमासनं
पुरकरतले कृत्वा वामे बहिः श्वसितोद्‌गमा ।

slab of mortar, where I saw my beloved, squatting upon it and sighing out, with her face placed upon the palm of the left hand, manifesting her distress by using the abusive words and showing her angry mind, when I was delaying."

(There are more than fifty such verses to the credit of Vidūṣaka in this Act.)

In the Svapnāṅka of Svapnavāsavadattā Udayana is remembering the joys of his secret love and says "When[1] I was instructing her frequently, she was looking at me and with her hand, from which the playing stick had been dropped, only played the lute in air."

Vidūsaka says, "She[2], who was winnowing the rice (to remove chaff) by the winnowing basket, looking at me, with her hand, from which the winnowing basket was dropped, did the work of winnowing in the air."

In the Tapatīsaṁvaraṇa, Vidūṣaka's first entry is with his body disabled, having fallen off a horse, with his legs and hands broken. In Nāgānanda, he enters waiting upon the hero. The Mantrāṅka of Pratijñā is important from the view point of the expansion of speech.

In Vālivadhāṅka of the Abhiṣeka the combat between Vālin and Sugrīva is actually shown. Vālin stands on one side of the stage and Sugrīva on the other. Vālin looks at his opponent with an angry look and holding his fist ready to strike, runs towards Sugrīva and gesticulates giving a hard blow on the chest of Sugrīva. (The sound of the blow is produced on the Milāvu). Then Sugrīva turns round, runs to the other end and enacts in the same fashion striking Vālin. Thus with the help of Milāvu the actual combat is shown very effectively, heightening the speed of the blows gradually, for about ten minutes or so. In the end, Vālin enacts being shot by Rāma's arrow, (Rāma is not on the stage at all, only the two combatants are there), and gesticulates falling down. Then the curtain is held. The

चिरयति मयि व्यक्तोद्वेगा दुरुक्तिविकत्थनै:
प्रकटितमनोमन्युर्दृष्टा मया चेरुमीप्रिया ॥

1. बहुशोऽप्युपदेशेषु यया मामीक्षमाणया ।
हस्तेन स्रस्तकोणेन कृतमाकाशवादितम् ॥

Svapnavāsavadatta V-6.

2. बहुशोऽप्युमि चेरुंबोल्ल मया मां नोक्कमाणया ।
हस्तेन स्रस्तशूर्पेण कृतमाकाशचेरितम् ॥

actor goes to the green-room and comes out fixing an arrow in his chest. When the curtain is withdrawn he is seen fallen on the ground, with the arrow pierced in his chest. Sugrīva, Rāma and Lakṣmaṇa are standing just near him. Vālin dies on the lap of Sugrīva. Before dying he gives the hand of Sugrīva into that of Rāma and places round the neck of Sugrīva, the golden necklace (the royal emblem). Then the curtain is held to indicate the end.

While gesticulating the words, the full stories indicated by the particular words were gesticulated in details. For example, the prologue in Bhagavadajjukīya was enacted for seven days. The whole Bhagavadajjukīya was enacted for fortyone days. Some scenes were also presented realistically in former days e.g., the flight[1] of eagle in Nāgānanda. Preparing the ground with all the sacred ceremonies, the stage was constructed in the open space of the temple. A raised structure was built. On its top the actor with the make-up of Garuḍa (Eagle) stood. Ropes were tied to the different parts of his body, which would of course be unnoticeable. These were wound together and manipulated by the Nambyār. By loosening the tight rope the descent was effected and by tightening it the ascent. That place called 'kūttuparampu' is seen even now near the Śiva temples. The story goes that once due to some confusion in handling of the ropes the actor met with an accident. Since then this experiment is never attempted.

In Nāgānanda, the heroine decides to put an end to her life by hanging herself from the red Aśoka tree with the noose of creepers. She puts the noose round the neck. But the maid who was ordered by her to go and see whether Mitrāvasu has gone far away or not, apprehending danger does not go away but is standing concealed. She runs in haste and cries for help. The hero approaches hurriedly and snatches away the noose of creepers. This scene is enacted thus. Removing a plank from the ceiling, a long piece of cloth is tied to the roof. Then twisting it round and round, its length is reduced. Holding this piece the heroine gesticulates preparing the noose and climbing on the stool she enacts placing the noose round her

1. It is called Parakkum Kūttu or Flying Dance. Cf. 'Kūṭiyāṭṭam' by Dr. K. K. Raja, p. 37.

neck. Of course, the noose is not placed round the neck at all but under one arm-pit and on the other shoulder. But in her standing position, the appearance of hanging herself is created in a very good manner.

In Tapatīsaṁvaraṇa the heroine plunges into the stream of a river and is wafted by the flow. To achieve this effect, the appearance of river is created by white threads. One end is raised and the other kept at a low level. On the raised part of this river the heroine plunges and then goes to the other side, enacting as it were, being carried away with the stream.

When the transformation of one person into the other is to be shown on the stage as in Māyāsītāṅka of Āścaryacūḍāmaṇi, it is presented as follows. Rāvaṇa himself shows as Rāma and then manifests his own real appearance. Actually the actor as Rāma is first there and then the actor dressed as Rāvaṇa comes and stands behind Rāma facing towards him. Afterwards both of them move round speedily. In the end, the actor dressed as Rāma goes to the green-room and Rāvaṇa remains on the stage.

As for the scenes where actual aerial vehicle etc., are to be shown, it is learnt that such entries were effected by stretching forward and backward the ropes etc. presenting the ascent or the descent of the aerial car actually. Such aerial car or the flight of eagle etc. was shown realistically only outside the closed theatres, when the stage was constructed in the open. Otherwise inside the closed theatre these are enacted only by gesticulation.

In the second act of Nāgānanda the heroine and the maid gesticulate being concealed behind the Aśoka tree (photo 18). They simply stand a little away to the right hand side of the hero and listen to the speech. Then they utter their own speeches. After their speech they go back to the green-room just before the gesticulation of the verse by the hero. Thus, the bifocal or trifocal scenes are enacted. The characters simply gesticulate that they are concealed etc.

When the actor has his abhinaya for a long time, the other characters retire to the green-room. If a verse is to be enacted for an hour or so, the presence of other character on the stage would be unwanted from the view point of the audience and also from that of the characters themselves, who would suffer a feeling of tediousness undoubtedly.

In Cākyār tradition there are rules regarding the performance of plays in the morning, by day or at night according to the type of the play. But nowadays the performance takes place generally at night from 9 p.m. onwards to suit the convenience.

I have tried to give information regarding the method of presentation of Sanskrit plays by the Cākyārs. They claim that their tradition is over a thousand years old at least. They have also met with unflinching criticism due to such an elongated process of presentation. They are subject to very harsh criticism in the work Naṭāṅkuśa. The attack runs as follows—"The Cākyārs have incorporated many things in their art which are obstacles to the production of sentiment. These must be removed. Now it can be said that in gesticulation, things not mentioned by Bharata are also to be resorted to as in the gesticulation of wonder, 'placing the finger on the tip of the nose'. That is not mentioned by Bharata—moving of the finger alone is mentioned. But this can be answered by saying that the word ādi includes that. The gesticulation of the other character by one character who has the dress and make-up of his own role is another point to be examined. Hanumat has the make-up of a monkey with a tail attached. The abhinaya must be four-fold. Then it is proper Nāṭya. Hanumat gesticulating as Rāma is something highly improper. What would be the position of sentiment in this ? Further than this, when Hanumat enacts also the graceful movements of Sītā it becomes extremely ridiculous. The dress and make-up imitate one and the gestures another. It should not be thought of as the highest skill of the actor. In enacting one role, the gesticulation of another is not a matter of skill."

I have observed that the ample scope given to Vidūṣaka in the Kūṭiyāṭṭam sometimes becomes detrimental to the spirit of the play, when he indulges too much in parody-making.

Chapter VII

CONCLUSION

I have tried to give the idea of the performance of Sanskrit drama as can be reconstructed from the NŚ. and the living traditions available in India. It is very clear that the ancient Indian dramatic performance[1] employed the three arts of drama, dance and music harmoniously.

Sanskrit plays of the great dramatists like Bhāsa, Kālidāsa, Śūdraka, Harṣa, Bhavabhūti etc. are being staged in India by colleges, universities and other institutions, like Sanskrit Associations. Competitions in the performances of Sanskrit plays are also arranged by the states like Maharashtra. In these performances some groups use the accessories in the form of suggestive models while others employ realistic settings. Some verses from the plays are sung in proper Rāgas with full accompaniment in the plays staged by the Brahmana Sabha of Bombay. These efforts are really commendable at this time when the cinema has captured the public mind overwhelmingly. New plays are also written and staged. Recently, the play Kālidāsacarita written by Dr. Velankar was staged successfully by the Brahmana Sabha of Bombay. In Calcutta, some Sanskrit Professors are trying their best to interpret the NŚ. and stage Sanskrit plays accordingly. In Madras, there are valuable efforts in this direction, under the able guidance of scholars like Dr. Raghavan, which are very important in regard to the performance of classical Sanskrit drama.

1. I-tsing (7th century A.D.) refers to the staging of the Nāgānanda in this manner. "King Śilāditya versified the story of the Bodhisattva Jīmūtavāhana, who surrendered himself in the place of a Nāga. The version was set to music (literally string and pipe). He had it performed by a band accompanied by dancing and acting and thus popularized it in his land."

'A Record of the Buddhist Religion' by I-tsing; Ed. by Takakusu, Oxford, 1896, p. 163 f.

Cf. Kūṭiyāṭṭam by Dr. K. K. Raja, p. 50, note 10.

Dr. Raghavan[1] has pointed out that in the performance of Sanskrit plays we have to evolve a distinct Indian style based on an idealised technique which would depend more on the actor's art rather than on the external mechanical aids in imitation of the Western technique of production.

Some Western critics also now-a-days favour the union of dance and music with drama.

It seems that the efforts to bring realism by employing huge sets have exhausted their appeal. Mr. Raymond[2] Williams says regarding the text and performance that a far greater variety of rhythm should be used. In performing such arrangements of rhythms, use can be made of the various degrees of formality in speech itself and also of recitative and song. A song for example can be used not as a separate piece of atmosphere nor as an interlude but as a means of creating a certain kind of feeling. The extension to more than one voice is also possible. A dramatist who wants to use a singing chorus can draw at once on a rich and available skill. The rhythm made by the dramatist must be communicated by the performer not only with his voice but also with his body. A rich expressive means of communicating dramatic emotion in physical movement is found in the ballet. Dance, in itself, can be openly used at certain points. As a normal rule, music would be one of the means of expression which, the play as a whole, and where necessary, can command. In regard to the element of design also in place of realistic setting the interestingly stylized conventions would be welcome. He finally says that the greatness of drama lies in its capacity to unite the rhythms of the human voice, of the human body and of instruments in a moving form and so to embody the deepest and farthest reaches of human feeling.

Mr. Henry[3] W. Wells says that the main influence of the East on the West in the dramatic fields springs from the ancient texts and the theatrical traditions which these represent.

1. Cf. Sanskrit Drama and Performance, by Dr. Raghavan, pp. 27-28.
2. Cf. Drama in Performance, by Raymond Williams, pp. 116-123.
3. Cf. Eastern Drama and the Western Stage, by Henry W. Wells, The Illustrated Weekly of India, Feb. 11, 1962.

In connection with dance and music in drama, Balawant Gargi[1] states that European producers have sought to discover new forms and a fresh approach. Producer Bertolt Brecht drawing richly from the Eastern theatrical traditions has used music, mime and stylization and by mixing them with the vigorous realism of the West, has created his epic theatre. My Fair Lady, an adaptation of Shaw's Pygmalian inter-weaves Shaw's pithy, aphoristic dialogue with honeyed melodies. Many times, the actors directly speak to the audience. In the most serious moments and emotional peak points songs are used. When the arguments take a serious turn the clownish antics break the tension. The chorus appears suddenly from the wings and sings a lusty song commenting on the action and forecasting the events. Some times, the song sums up the situation while, occasionally it serves to bridge time and space.

Śākuntala[2] was produced successfully in New York by Lee Morgan and his associates. From the photographs in the Illustrated Weekly it is seen that the suggestive model of a tree is planted on the stage behind which Duṣyanta stands and observes Śakuntalā and Priyaṁvadā watering the plants. Watering of plants is shown by gesticulation. The departure scene of the fourth Act is enacted on the bare stage. Actual deer fondled by Śakuntalā is brought on the stage.[3]

We find that while producing the classical Sanskrit plays on one hand the efforts to use settings and curtains with painted scenery are there to bring on realism on the stage, while on the other hand, only some suggestive models are used or none. I offer my humble suggestions in regard to the performance of Sanskrit plays at present. One thing is to be made clear, at the outset, that instead of Prakrit speeches of the classical Sanskrit plays, their Sanskrit Chāyās (renderings should be used for the sake of convenience. If the actor-

1. "Dance and Music in Drama" by Balawant Gargi, The Illustrated Weekly of India, Feb. 7, 1960.

2. 'Shakuntala in New York', The Illustrated Weekly of India, March 6, 1960.

3. The Hindustani theatre produced Miṭṭī kī Gāḍī (the Hindustani version of Mṛcch.) in absolute simplicity on a bare stage using song, speech and mime for effect.

dancers are available, stylized conventional gesticulation can be used profitably. The stage should be bare having only one curtain at the back. The entrance and exit songs should be composed in simple Sanskrit when they are not indicated by the verses in the text. The Rāga-Rasa relation and the Rāga-time relation should be employed while using the music. I am pointing out a few examples of the use of Hindustani music. The Rāga Bhairava or Toḍī etc. should be employed in devotional mood and morning time; Jogī or Kāliṅgaḍā for Pathos; Aḍāṇā for the Heroic; Māṇḍa, Khamāja, Kāmoda, Kedāra etc. for love; Bahāra, Basanta for the glory of the spring season or in the descriptions of gardens etc. The slow tempo should be used in the Pathos, medium in love and fast in the Heroic. The instrumental music of lute and flute should be used playing suitable Rāgas to accentuate the mood. The Mṛdaṅga should accompany the movements with the various appropriate Bols. In this, drumming used in Kathak and the Cākyār tradition would be of great help. The musicians should be placed at the back or on one side of the stage. Thus, harmonising the graceful movements of dance with music, the play should be produced. Some verses may be appropriately sung, e.g., the verses indicating the entry or exit or those expressing the emotions, or those containing beautiful poetic descriptions. When the plays are performed by the actors who are not dancers, the emphasis should be laid on effective recitation and chanting of verses with appropriate gestures so that the situation would be brought to life powerfully. Some suggestive models may be used, when necessary, on the back stage which would be revealed to the audience by drawing aside the back curtain. The pantomimic gestures should be used with masterly skill to create the location, wherever possible. Some of the simple verses should be sung in proper Rāgas by the characters themselves without making the meaning suffer due to music. This would help the performance greatly. The use of settings or painted scenery should be avoided. The instrumental music should be used amply, particularly the Mṛdaṅga or Tablā and the stringed instruments like Sitār or Violin so also flute and Shehnai. There is great scope for the use of the instrumental music with the various melodies and rhythm patterns in the performance of Sanskrit plays. India has achieved superb skill in playing these instruments due to the development of hundreds of years. Different sounds also necessary for dramatic effect might be produced on drum and other instruments. If the stringed instrument like Sitār or Violin is played making it suddenly out of tune, the terror or pathos can be effectively suggested. The skilful drumming on Tablā with the fingers moving very fast would accentuate agitation.

I think the ideal performance of classical Sanskrit drama would be that when the actor-dancers expert in classical dance would produce the Sanskrit plays on the simple stage using the vocal and instrumental music to the utmost advantage.

APPENDIX A

Sculptures suggested to be the representations of scenes from Sanskrit plays :

(i) Bhita Medallion[1] :

As to the scene depicted on the medallion, Dr. Vogel[2] has suggested a comparison with the scene in Kālidāsa's famous drama 'Śākuntala', in which King Duṣyanta with his charioteer is being entreated not to kill the antelope which has fled for refuge to Kaṇva's hermitage.

This medallion is supposed to be of Śuṅga period. Prof. V.V. Mirashi[3] rejects the suggestion that this is a scene from 'Śākuntala'. For, there are two deer in the medallion and they appear as not running in fear but sporting. The peacock which is near them seems to be dancing, spreading its feathers. He says that this would be better understood as a scene from the life of Gautama (Buddha) which depicts Gautama going out for sport and meeting on the way an old man and getting the idea of old age for the first time.

If we study the medallion (see plate 1) we find that in the upper half, a King is going in a chariot with his charioteer. The chariot has four horses. An asceticlike person is seen in front of the horses, with his hands stretched out as if in a request to stop. The horses also appear to have checked their speed, from their raised front hoofs. At the back of the chariot there is a female figure standing near a tree. Behind her there is a small cottage. In the lower part of the medallion there is another figure on knee which appears to be holding a lotus. There are two deer, out of which one has its neck turned back. In front of the deer there is a peacock.

It cannot be made out clearly whether the figure in the chariot has a bow in his left hand or not. In the Śākuntala,

1. Terracotta plaque No. 17—The sketch of this plaque is reproduced double the actual size in the Archaeological Report 1911-12 by Sir John Marshall on plate XXIV.

2. Cf. Ibid, page 36.

3. Cf. Kālidāsa (Marathi) by V. V. Mirashi, pp. 24-25.

we know Śakuntalā was with her two friends watering the trees. It is very difficult to find out the exact details in this small medallion and with all that it cannot be called a stage representation of the scene from the first act of the play.

(ii) Another sculpture[1] is from the National Museum, New Delhi. (See plate 2). It belongs to Kuṣāṇa period (About 100 A.D. or beginning of the second century A.D.). Shri C. Sivaramamurti[2] understands it as depicting a scene from the first Act of the Mṛcchakaṭika in which Vasantasenā is followed by Viṭa, Śakāra and Ceṭa.

The lady to the right, in this sculpture, is looking sideways, slightly turning her face. She has pulled up her anklets upto knees. The maidservant near her is holding the umbrella and her anklets are in the normal position. There is a man to the left who is fully visible. The right leg of the other man behind him is clearly seen while the left leg is partly visible, in between the two feet of the person in the front. This other fellow has placed his right hand just below the right shoulder of his companion and the left hand on the left shoulder.

Shri Sivaramamurti understands the lady as Vasantasenā, the fellow to the left as Viṭa and the person hiding behind him as Śakāra.

In the play, when Śakāra can't see Vasantasenā due to pitchy darkness, he confesses to his friend that he hears the scent of her flowers but does not see quite clearly the jingling sound of the ornament, with the nose choked with the darkness. Viṭa takes pity on Vasantasenā and at his suggestion she removes the jingling anklets and the flower-garland.

Shri Sivaramamurti states that the Sculptor has restricted the men to Viṭa and Śakāra omitting Ceṭa. He has similarly minimised the attendants of Vasantasenā to one, so that the sculpture should not be crowded. Instead of removing the anklets, they are shown as pulled up suggesting thereby that the jingling has stopped. The flower on the braid is also not removed; but the maiden is shown as covering it with an upper

1. I was able to get a full size photograph of this sculpture through the courtesy of Shri Sivaramamurty, Keeper, National Museum, New Delhi.

2. See—'Sanskrit Literature Illumines Art' by Sivaramamurti—A.B.O.R. Institute, Poona, 1972, Vol. LIII, Parts I-IV, pp. 11-15.

garment, which is almost a veil, to subdue the perfume arising from the flowers.

We know from the play that in this scene Vasantasenā is separated from her attendants. The maid with the umbrella (Chatradhāriṇī), accompanying Vasantasenā is found in the Fifth Act. Hence, we can at the most say that the incident in the play is used by the sculptor as the motif for this sculpture. This sculpture can't be identified as being an exact stage-representation of the scene in the First Act of the Mṛcch. and as such it does not help us in giving a clearcut idea of the stage.

(iii) A third sculpture[1] from a temple at Nalanda (6th or 7th century A.D.) is suggested to be depicting a scene from Śāk. Act VI. This panel has a banana tree near which a man is sitting with something like a board in his left hand. In his right hand there is something like a pen or a brush. There is another man sitting near him. It is suggested that this is a scene from Śāk. Act VI in which the King accompanied by Vidūṣaka is sitting in the Pramadavana, having a picture board in his hand on which Śakuntalā with her two friends is painted. The stick-like thing in his hand is understood to be a brush.

But we know that in the play the King wanted the painting brush to give finishing touches to the picture. He asks the maid to get it. The maid goes and while coming with the brush-box, is met by the queen, who takes the brush-box from the maid to hand it over herself to the King. But seeing the Pratīhārī going to the King with a letter, the queen goes back deciding not to disturb the King in his royal duties. Thus the King does not receive the brush at all. There is Sānumatī also present in the play. Hence there is difficulty in understanding this sculpture also as depicting a scene from Śāk. Act VI.

1. I am grateful to Shri S. V. Sohoni. I.C.S. Patna who pointed out this sculpture to me.

APPENDIX B

Class Dance

The classical[1] dance was added to the preliminaries to make them more striking. The beautiful Aṅgahāras were taught to Bharata by Taṇḍu at the word of Śaṅkara. The Aṅgahāras are 32 in number. They are based on combinations of Karaṇas which range between 6 and 9. The Karaṇas are the basic dance units with graceful hand movements (Nṛtta-hasta) and a corresponding foot movement (Cārī) preceded and followed by rhythmic and harmonious attitude of the body (Sthāna). There are 108 Karaṇas[2] defined by the NŚ. and their descriptions and usages are given by Abhinava and Śārṅgadeva. They[3] are given here with the help of Abhinava's commentary and Saṁgītaratnākara.

1. Talapuṣpapuṭa—The hand in Puṣpapuṭa is held on the left side and the foot is in Agratalasañcara and the side Nata. This is used hy Sūtradhāra in scattering flowers on the stage.

2. Vartita—The hands are in Vyāvṛtta and Parivartita, bent at the wrist and then placed on thighs. It is used in gesticulating jealousy with upturned Patāka hands, and anger, with downward Patāka hands.

3. Valitoruka—The thighs are Valita and the Śukatuṇḍa hands are in Vyāvṛtta and Parivartita. This is used in the case of a Mugdhā (a coy pretty maiden).

4. Apaviddha—The right hand is in Śukatuṇḍa falling on the thigh and the left hand is held on the breast. It is used in gesticulating jealousy and anger.

5. Samanakha—The feet are Samanakha and joined, hands hanging down and the body in natural pose. This is used in the first entry of the dancer.

6. Līna—The two Patāka hands are in Añjali placed on the breast, the neck stretched and shoulders bent; it is employed in request to the beloved.

1. NŚ. Chapter IV.
2. Cf. Tāṇḍavalakṣaṇa by Naidu and Pantulu.
3. For the illustrations of these Karaṇas see NŚ. (Baroda Ed.). Vol. I (Second Revised Edition) Plates I-XVIII.

7. Svastika-recita—The hands in Recita and Āviddha gesture are held in Svastika; then separated and held on the hip; it is used when dancing is the main object and when the purpose of the dancer is simply to express great joy.

8. Maṇḍalasvastika—The hands with their palms turned upwards pointing in front and Sama, are moved in Svastika position and the posture is Maṇḍala; it is used in indicating insult.

9. Nikuṭṭaka[1]—Each hand is moved near its respective shoulder, having Alapallava gesture, accompanied by the movement of the respective leg, with Udghaṭṭita foot; it is used in self-adulation.

10. Ardhanikuṭṭaka[2]—One hand is moved near its shoulder having Alapallava gesture, accompanied by the movement of the respective leg, with Udghaṭṭita foot; it is employed in self-adulation.

11. Kaṭicchinna—The waist is turned alternately and both hands in Pallava are held on shoulders repeatedly. This is used in wonder.

12. Ardharecitaka—The hand moving in Sūcīmukha (touches the other), the foot is moved up and down and the side is bent; it is employed in ill-conceived movement.

13. Vakṣaḥsvastika—The legs are in Svastika and the Recita hands are brought on the breast which is bent; it is used in repentance and sense of shame.

14. Unmattaka—The foot is in Añcita and the hands are in Recita; it is used in pride due to extreme good luck.

15. Svastika—Hands and feet are in Svastika; it is used in indicating secrecy and avoiding search skilfully.

16. Pṛṣṭhasvastika—The legs come together in Svastika with Apakrāntā and Ardhasūcī Cārīs and the arms are thrown up and down and brought together in Svastika; its use is similar to that of Svastika.

17. Diksvastika—With Svastika of hands and feet, the dancer turns in all the four directions; it is employed in the movement of the body while singing.

1. Cf. Abhinava—NŚ. Vol. I. p. 101 and 102; SR. VII. 609-612.
2. *Ibid.*

18. Alātaka—Making Alātā Cārī, the right hand is moved from the level of the shoulder and then the Ūrdhvajānu Cārī is performed. This is used in graceful dance.

19. Kaṭīsama—After Svastika, foot is separated, the two hands are on the navel and the waist respectively and the side in Udvāhita; used by Sūtradhāra at the incantation of the Jarjara.

20. Ākṣiptarecita[1]—The left hand is on the breast and the right in Recita thrown up and sideways (and brought near the breast ?) and then the other in Recita and Apaviddha; it is employed in series of accepting and giving up things.

21. Vikṣiptākṣiptaka—Hands and feet are first thrown out and then drawn near; it is used in going and coming.

22. Ardhasvastika—Legs are in Svastika, the right hand in Karihasta and the left on the breast.

23. Añcita—The Karihasta hand is in Vyāvṛtta and Parivṛtta alternately and then bent upon the tip of the nose; it is used in elation due to one's own superiority or excellence, in the presence of others.

24. Bhujaṅgatrāsita—Raising up the Kuñcita foot, the thighs should have an oblique movement, the waist and the knee should be turned.

25. Ūrdhvajānu—Throwing up a Kuñcita foot, the knee is held up to the level with the breast and the hands are moved in harmony.

26. Nikuñcita—Moving the foot in Vṛścika Karaṇa, the (left) hand is bent at the side and the right is held at the tip of the nose; it is used in moving in the sky, guess and in deep meditation.

27. Mattalli—A whirling movement is made with the feet turned alternately and the hands are in Udveṣṭita and Apaviddha; it is used in intoxication.

28. Ardhamattalli—The feet are moved from Skhalita, the left hand is in Recita and the right placed on the waist; it is used in medium intoxication.

1. The description of this Karaṇa is not clear to me. Cf. Abhinava—NŚ. Vol. I, p. 107 and SR. VII. 589, 590.

29. Recitanikuṭṭita—The right hand is in Recita, the right foot in Nikuṭṭita and the left hand in Dolā; it is used in swinglike movement.

30. Pādāpaviddhaka—The two Khaṭakāmukha hands are placed with their back touching the navel and the feet are in Sūcī and Apakrāntā Cārīs.

31. Valita—With the hand in Apaviddha and foot in Sūcī, the trika is turned round.

32. Ghūrṇita—The right hand is moved round in Vartita and the left in Dolā and the foot is moved from Svastika.

33. Lalita—The left hand is in Karihasta and the right hand is moved variously and the foot is moved up and down repeatedly; it is used in graceful dance.

34. Daṇḍapakṣa—Performing Ūrdhvajānu Cārī, the hand in Latā is placed on the knee.

35. Bhujaṅgatrastarecita—After performing the Bhujaṅgatrāsitā Cārī the hands in Recita are placed on the left side.

36. Nūpura—The trika is turned round gracefully with the hands in Latā and Recita respectively and the foot in Nūpurapādā Cārī.

37. Vaiśākharecita—Hands and feet are in Recita and so also the waist and the neck; the posture is Vaiśākha. This is used in carrying one forward.

38. Bhramaraka—With the Svastika foot in Ākṣiptā Cārī and hands in Udveṣṭita, the trika is turned round; it is employed in haughty movements.

39. Catura—The left hand is in Añcita (i.e. Alapallava), the right hand in Catura and the right foot in Kuṭṭita; it is used in the Sūcī gesticulation of Vidūṣaka indicating wonder.

40. Bhujaṅgāñcitaka—The foot is in Bhujaṅgatrāsitā, right hand in Recita and the left hand in Latā.

41. Daṇḍakarecita—The hands and feet are thrown freely on all sides like a staff and are moved in Recita; it is used in the case of haughty persons or great joy.

42. Vṛścikakuṭṭita—Vṛścika Karaṇa is performed with the hands in Nikuṭṭita; it is employed in wonder and desire for going in the sky.

43. Kaṭibhrānta—After performing Sūcī Cārī the right foot is placed at the side and the waist moved round; it is used in gaits.

44. Latāvṛścika—The foot in Añcita is turned backwards and the left hand is in Latā with its palm and fingers bent and turned upwards; it is used in falling down from the sky.

45. Chinna—The Alapadma hand is placed at the waist, which is Chinnā by turn and the posture is Vaiśākha; it is employed in movements of the limbs and breaking of the Tāla.

46. Vṛścikarecita—The foot is in Vṛścika and the two hands in Svastika to be moved in Recita and Viprakīrṇa; it is used in moving through air.

47. Vṛścika—The two hands are bent and held near the shoulders and the leg bent and turned towards the back; back is bent; it is used in aerial movements and to indicate Airāvaṇa.

48. Vyaṁsita—In Ālīḍha posture the two hands are in Recita and held on the breast, then moved up and down in Viprakīrṇa; it is used in moving round on the stage in confusion or hurry.

49. Pārśvanikuṭṭaka—The hands in Svastika are held on one side and the foot is in Nikuṭṭita; it is used in concealing or revealing (something).

50. Lalāṭatilaka—After performing Vṛścika Karaṇa, the tilaka sign is made on the forehead with the toe of the foot; it is used in the movements of the Vidyādharas.

51. Krāntaka—The Kuñcita leg is bent behind the back and Atikrāntā Cārī is performed and the two hands are thrown; it is employed in haughty movements.

52. Kuñcita—The foot is in Añcita and the left hand in Kuñcita held at the left side with palm upwards; it is used to indicate greatly delighted deities.

53. Cakramaṇḍala—Aḍḍitā Cārī is performed, with the arms hanging and the body bent; it is used in haughty movements.

54. Uromaṇḍala—Fect ~~are~~ drawn away from Svastika and Aḍḍitā Cārī is pcrformed; the hands are in Uromaṇḍala.

55. Ākṣipta—The hands and the feet are thrown about swiftly; it is used in the gait of Vidūṣaka.

56. Talavilasita—The foot with the toe and the sole turned upwards, is extended high on the side and the palms

of the hands are bent; it is used in the movements of Sūtradhāra.

57. Argala—The leg is stretched backward two tālas and a half apart from the other and the hand is moved in confirmity with it in front; it is used in the movements of Aṅgada and others.

58. Vikṣipta—The hands and feet are thrown backwards or sideways in the same way; it is used in gaits of the haughty.

59. Āvarta—After extending the Kuñcita foot, it is moved again quickly and the hands are moved in conformity with the foot movement; it is employed in movements of heroes in moving forward (to save etc.).

60. Dolāpāda—Throwing up the Kuñcita foot, it is moved in the swinging manner from side to side; the hands are moved in conformity with the foot movement.

61. Vivṛtta—Hands and feet are first thrown out and then the trika is turned round and the two hands are in Recita; it is used in haughty gait.

62. Vinivṛtta—Performing the Sūcī Cārī, the trika is turned with the hands in Recita; it is used in gaits of the haughty.

63. Pārśvakrānta —Performing the Pārśvakrāntā Cārī, the foot is made to fall in front, the hand is kept in conformity with the foot movements; it is used in the movements of Bhīmasena and others in the Furious sentiment.

64. Nistambhita (or Niśumbhita)—The foot is bent towards the back, the breast raised high and the hand is at the tilaka mark (i.e. at the centre of the forehead); it is used in the gesticulation of Śaṅkara.

65. Vidyudbhrānta—The foot is turned backward and extended on all sides close to the head in a circular manner; it is used in haughty gait.

66. Atikrānta—After performing Atikrāntā Cārī, the foot is extended in front with the hands in conformity with the foot; it is employed in gaits.

67. Vivartitaka—The hand and foot are thrown out and the trika is turned round and the other hand is in Recita.

68. Gajakrīḍitaka—The left hand is bent and brought

near the ear, the right hand in Latā and the Dolāpādācārī is performed.

69. Talasaṁsphoṭita—The leg is lifted up quickly (in Atikrāntā or Daṇḍapādā Cārī) and then made to fall in front, with the hands in Talasaṁsphoṭita[1] (i.e. the hands with palms striking each other as in clapping).

70. Garuḍaplutaka—The leg is extended at the back, one hand is in Latā and the other in Recita and the breast is raised up; it is used in the flight of eagle.

71. Gaṇḍasūcī—The foot is in Sūcī position, the side bent, one hand placed on bosom and the other bent touching the cheek; it is used in the decoration of the cheek.

72. Parivṛtta—The hands are raised up in Apaveṣṭita and with the foot in Sūcī trika is turned round.

73. Pārśvajānu—One foot is in Sama position and the other placed at the back of the thighs and the hand in Muṣṭi is held on the breast; it is used in fights and personal combats.

74. Gṛdhrāvalīnaka—One foot is extended backwards with the knee slightly bent and the hands are outstretched; it is used in the gesticulation of birds.

75. Sannata—After a jump, the two feet are put forward in Svastika and the two hands in Dolā; it is employed in forward movements due to the words of the inferior.

76. Sūcī—Raising up a Kuñcita foot, it is placed on the ground in front, and the hands are in harmony with the foot movement.

77. Ardhasūcī—The Alapadma hand is held on the head and the right foot is in Sūcī.

78. Sūcīviddha—One foot in Sūcī is put at the heel of the other and the hands are placed on the waist and bosom respectively; it is used in anxiety.

79. Apakrānta—After making the Valita thigh Apakrāntā Cārī is performed with the hands moved in harmony.

80. Mayūralalita—With the foot in Vṛścika (i. e. performing the Vṛścika Karaṇa) and the hand in Recita, trika is turned.

1. Cf. SR. VII. 701.

81. Sarpita—Feet are moved from Añcita, the head is in Parivāhita and the two hands are in Recita; it is used in intoxicated walk.

82. Daṇḍapāda—After performing Nūpurapādikā Cārī Daṇḍapāda should follow and the hands should be in Āviddhavaktraka quickly; it is used in moving about in pride.

83. Hariṇapluta—After Atikrāntā Cārī the foot falls with a jump and the shank is bent and thrown up.

84. Preṅkholita—After performing Dolāpāda the foot falls with a jump, and the trika is turned round.

85. Nitamba—Arms are thrown up and then have fingers of hands facing each other; Baddhācārī is to be performed.

86. Skhalita—After performing Dolāpāda, both hands, following the foot movement should be in Recita or turned round.

87. Karihastaka—One hand is on the breast and the palm of the other in Udveṣṭita and the foot in Añcita.

88. Prasarpitaka—One hand is in Recita and the other in Latā and the feet[1] moving slowly with the soles rubbing the ground; it is used in movements of those going in the sky.

89. Siṁhavikrīḍita—After performing the Alātā Cārī, the other foot is moved quickly, with the hands following the feet; it is used in the gait of the furious.

90. Siṁhākarṣita—One foot is extended backwards and the hands are Nikuñcita[2] (i.e. Padmakośa or Ūṇanābha); in the movement of the second foot again the hands are Nikuñcita; it is used in gesticulating lion and others.

91. Udvṛtta—The foot, the hand and the whole body should be moved violently and Udvṛttā Cārī be performed.

92. Upasṛtaka—With one foot in Ākṣipta and the hands in harmony, the body is bent; it is employed in approaching with modesty.

93. Talasaṁghaṭṭita—After Dolāpādā Cāri the hands have the palms clashing each other and then the left hand is in Recita; it is used in compassion.

94. Janita—With one hand on breast and the other hanging loosely, the foot is moved in Janitā Cārī.

1. Cf. Abhinava—NŚ. Vol. I., p. 131; SR. VII. 718.
2. Cf. Abhinava—NŚ. Vol. I., p. 132; SR. VII. 724, 725.

95. Avahitthaka—After performing Janitā Cārī the hands have fingers facing each other and dropped down slowly; it is used in secrecy.

96. Niveśa—The two hands are on the breast, the bosom is Nirbhugna and the posture is Maṇḍala; it is used in elephant-ride.

97. Elakākrīḍita—Jumping with Talasañcara feet the dancer comes to the ground with body bent and turned; it is used in the gait of inferiors.

98. Ūrūdvṛtta—The hand is in Vyāvartita and then bent and placed on the back of the thigh, the shank is in Añcita and Udvṛtta; it is used in amorous anger, jealousy, request etc.

99. Madaskhalita—With the hand hanging down and the head in Parivāhita, the feet are turned in Āviddhā Cārī; it is used in intoxication due to wine.

100. Viṣṇukrānta—One foot is stretched forward and bent as if rising upwards and the hands are in Recita; it is employed in the gait of Viṣṇu.

101. Sambhrānta—Hand in Āvartita is placed on the thigh which is in Āviddhā Cārī; it is used in movements in confusion.

102. Viṣkambha—The (right) hand is moved in Sūcīmukha (touching the other), the left placed on the bosom and the foot is in Nikuṭṭita.

103. Udghaṭṭita—The feet are in Udghaṭṭita and hands ready for clapping and the side bent; it is used in excessive joy.

104. Vṛṣabhakrīḍita—Performing Alāta first, the hands are in Recita and afterwards they are in Kuñcita and Añcita.

105. Lolita—The hands are in Recita and Añcita and the head Lolita and Vartita on both the sides.

106. Nāgāpasarpita—The foot is moved from Svastika, the head is in Parivāhita and the hands are in Recita; it is used in medium intoxication.

107. Śakaṭāsya—After having the body at rest the Talasañcara foot is extended and the breast is in Udvāhita; it is used in sportive movements of the child, in Bhāṇikā etc.

108. Gaṅgāvataraṇa—The feet have the soles and the toes turned upwards and the hands are in Tripatāka, with fingers pointing downwards and the head bent; it is employed in the descent of the Ganges on earth.

The Aṅgahāras, the harmonious combinations of Karaṇas, are described in detail in the NŚ. (Ch. IV-verses 174-247).

The term 'Recita' means moving the limb round separately or its movement of any kind separately. The four Recakas are described, as follows.

1. Pādarecaka—Going from side to side with wavering feet or with differently moving feet, is called their Recaka.

2. Kaṭirecaka—In it trika is lifted up and the waist is turned as well as drawn back.

3. Hastarecaka—Raising up, throwing out, putting forward turning round and extending the hand, constitute Hastarecaka.

4. Grīvārecaka—It is the raising up, lowering and bending sideways and moving round of the neck.

The Piṇḍībandhas are the different dance formations in dance. The Piṇḍīs of various gods and goddesses are mentioned. According to Tāṇḍavalakṣaṇa[1] Piṇḍībandha is made by imitating the form of Piṇḍa (i.e. mass). According to it Piṇḍī is explained in detail as follows.

Piṇḍī literally means the cavity in the plinth of an idol into which the latter's lower portion fits snugly for stability. In the end, it indicated prime attribute, the root cause etc. Piṇḍībandha meant, at first, the concrete symbol which was created in the course of Deity's dance and therefore came to be associated with and to signify that Deity e.g., Liṅga. Piṇḍī may also mean the Aṅgahāras and Karaṇas introduced in the dance to signify a particular Deity. The meaning now expands to include Vāhana, weapon and other implements of that Deity. Piṇḍi also means the favourite Karaṇa of a Deity with which it is appeased e.g., Īśvarī with Talapuṣpapuṭa karaṇa. Whenever any Deity is to be indicated the dances appropriate to its nature are to be performed. In the interval between one such dance and another the dances suited to its Piṇḍīs are to be danced. Finally Piṇḍī appears to stand for any characteristic attribute of a Deity e.g. personal beauty for Lakṣmī, continuous flow for Gaṅgā etc. Shri K.V. Ramachandran[2] takes it to be a tableau based on Aṅgahāras

1. Cf. Tāṇḍavalakṣaṇa, pp. 105-106.
2. Cf. "Dance Traditions of South India" by Shri K. V. Ramachandran. Triveni Vol. VII No. 4, pp. 308-319.

in which one or more than one dancers took part. From the explanation given by Abhinava[1] of the various Piṇḍīs mentioned in the NŚ. it becomes clear that the Piṇḍībandha is the formation indicating the characteristic of that particular Deity.

The form of Śivaliṅga for Śaṅkara, the lion-riding for Caṇḍikā, eagle for Viṣṇu, lotus for Brahmadeva, Airāvata for Indra, fish for Madana, peacock for Kārttikeya etc. are the formations mentioned.

The Piṇḍībandhas[2] are executed by one or more female dancers. The Pattern which is formed by one dancer is Piṇḍī due to its being like a Piṇḍa (lump). The formation by two dancers is Śṛṅkhalikā[3] on account of its being like a Gulm (cluster); it resembles two lotuses on one stalk or a lotus-stalk with the lotus, held by a swan with its beak. The Pattern formed by three dancers is Latābandha due to being held together like Jāla (net). The pattern to be executed by four dancers is Bhedyaka[4] having Nṛtta (i.e. the other three dance formations). According to Bhāvaprakāśana Bhedyaka is the dance of each one of the dancers, separately, outside the group.

The Piṇḍībandha (i.e. Piṇḍī) is to be formed in the first (shortest) Āsārita, the Śṛṅkhalikā in the change of tempo, the Latābandha in the middle Āsārita and the Bhedyaka in the longest Āsārita.

1. NŚ. Vol. I, pp. 167-168.
2. Cf. Śṛṅgāraprakāśa by Dr. Raghavan, p. 588.
3. See Abhinava; NŚ. Vol. I. p. 191.
"नर्तकीयोज्य: परस्परसंबन्ध एव पिण्डीबन्धद्वयप्रकार: सजातीयो वा एकता-(ना) लावबद्धकमलयुगलवत् विजातीयो वा हंसवदनपरिगृहीतनालनलिनवत् गुल्मः शृंखलिकाशब्दवाच्यः ।"
4. *Ibid.*
"चतुष्टयप्रयोज्यस्तु । स तूक्तविधैस्त्रिभिः नृत्तैः सह वर्तते ।"
Bhāvaprakāśana; p. 246—एकैकस्य बहिः संघान्नृत्तं यत् स च भेद्यकः ।
Bhoja—भेदेन भेद्यको जातः—Śṛṅgāraprakāśa, by Dr. Raghavan, p. 588.

APPENDIX C

THE THEATRICAL ART IN THE EAST AND SOUTH EAST ASIA

CHINA :

The close relationship of dance, drama and music in the classical Chinese theatre is most probably due to the influence of Indian theatre. The basic form of the Chinese dance-drama was established during 7th and 9th centuries A.D. Some of the basic movements of this dance-drama have now been incorporated as an integral part of the pantomime and gestures of the ordinary drama in which dancing as such does not take place. That is why the training of the actor does not only consist of voice production and acting but also dancing and acrobatics.

The stage is five feet in height and almost like the Elizabethan stage. There are columns on each side, about twenty feet high which support the canopy. The play house has a roof sloped in two sections, over heavy beams with a row of windows that provide light by day. Four acetylene lamps provide lighting for the theatre. There are square tables and chairs for the rich, in half of the floor space in front of the stage and in the other half, benches for the middle class spectators. On the sides of the stage there are narrow benches which are meant for the cheapest seats. There is a gallery around the three sides, having boxes, which used to be reserved for ladies in former times.

The stage is not to face West which is an inauspicious quarter. There are two doors at the back of the stage for entrance and exit. They are covered by smaller curtains. The green-room is at the back of the stage. Scenery is not used for the creation of illusionary effect of reality. The imagination of the spectator is roused by the use of stage properties. A few illustrations will give an idea as to how the locality etc. are indicated on the stage.

If the appearance of a city is to be produced, two attendants, in front of the character who is sitting on a chair placed on a table, hold up a bamboo frame which supports a screen painted with a city gate in a brickwall about five feet in height. When this scene is over the attendants remove the wall, roll it up and take it away. When the table is brought to the centre of the stage, and chairs are placed on its sides, which are covered with fresh embroideries, the stage is then a council chamber. The entry of a character, in chariot is indicated by two attendants preceding him, each holding horizontally a square flag on which a wheel is painted. At the end of the battle the slain protagonist exits at a run. A chair serves as a prison. The actor who is to show his being imprisoned, stands behind it and looks through the back supports to suggest looking through a barred window. A chair can become a well also. To indicate jumping into the well and get drowned, the actor jumps upon it and then down on the other side and exits hurriedly. To indicate armies, the attendants carry banners each signifying one or two thousand men. Storm is suggested by black banners. A whip indicates a horse. The ideas of night and boat are suggested by lamp and oar respectively.

The Sheng (males), the Tan (females), the Chou (clowns) and the Chin (the painted characters), are the four important character types. The Sheng and Tan have heavy make-up, still their natural lines are retained. In the case of Tan, Chinese ink is dropped into the pupil of the eye to make the eye large and brilliant. The eyes and eye-brows of a young hero are drawn up by the use of adhesive tape, to give noble slant. Artificial braids are added to the Tan's head-dress. The Chou's costume is often fantastic. In his conventional make-up as a military type comedian, he has a smudge of white on his face, bright red cheeks and highly powdered white nose. A mask-like thick make-up is used in the case of the Chin. The major character of this type is the warrior. He wears a magnificent head-dress. The other Chin types are the black-faced god types and the white powdered-faced evil types. There are various mythological types like Gods, Demons or animals in semi-human forms with their symbolic dresses and make-up.

The symbolism of colour and form is elaborate; e.g. loyalty and uprightness are represented by red colour; simplicity and straightforwardness by black; obstinacy and ferocity by blue;

craftiness by yellow. Gold and silver are the colours of dignity and hence are used on the faces of Gods and fairies. Green indicates wicked ghosts, devils etc.

Laughter is divided into twentyeight types, such as happy, cold, flattering etc. The Tan actor is trained in atleast fifty kinds of sleeve-movements. A few illustrations are given here. A turning sleeve movement indicates a signal for the orchestra to get ready; when the sleeve is held before the face, it indicates embarrassment; it also indicates the actor's being hidden from the other characters on the stage.

The movements of fingers and arms are also equally symbolical. The opening or closing of a door is shown by the graceful stylised pantomime. Mounting and dismounting from an imaginary horse is also shown by conventional movements. In every case music led by the time-beater controls the rhythm of the actor.

The symbolism of colour is seen in the dress also. Costumes are based mainly on ancient models. Though a beggar's clothes indicate poverty and rags, they would be of rich silk or satin. The square hat is used by good officials and a round one by scoundrels. The skirt is used by the female character. It indicates a poor distressed woman when fastened over the chest. Resplendant armour is worn by military characters on state occasions, or on the battle-fields. This is the most spectacular costume. Four flags rising like wings from their backs are worn by the Generals. The feather movements in dancing have symbolic meanings, e.g. anger or determination is indicated by winding the feather.

The orchestra sits on the left of the stage. The man with a wooden clapper beats a steady time, punctuating recitation or the rhythm of the dances. There are cymbals, drums, gongs, trumpets, flutes and Hu-Chin (a Chinese Violin).

At the beginning of a performance, a pair of comedians provide a witty conversation. The next item is a real play and not just a dialogue, yet still a comedy. Nobody minds eating and tea-drinking that goes on among the spectators. The comic play is followed by a mythological one having brilliance of costume and dance, and a martial play in which magnificently dressed warriors walk across the stage on high boots with flags at their backs and display duels and fights in battle scenes, that are the occasions for expert acrobatics. After all these, the drama proper begins.

As each character enters he tells the spectators himself who he is and what part he has to play in the coming drama. The words are delivered in high pitched recitative, varied by bouts of chanting in passages where special stress is required for the heightening of emotion. There is, as a rule, one particular character who breaks at intervals into song and fulfils in some degree the functions of a chorus. A change of scene is indicated by a pantomimic action or by all the dramatis personae walking rapidly in single file round the stage.

Music is an integral part of the performance. Plays are distinguished by the type of the music they employ. Music accompanies the songs and dances. It intensifies and forms a frame-work of sound for action and gestures. Some passages are, however, decorative. They give the actor time to rest his voice to prepare himself because of the falsetto style of singing.

The actors all belong to the guild and are extremely jealous of their customs and traditions. It is the clown who lights the incense which burns in every green-room before the icon of the patron god to whom obeisance is made before and after every performance.

Japan :

Gigaku, a dance from China was introduced in the 7th century in Japan in which masks were used. After some time, it was included in Buddhist services. During the period of 8th to the 12th century A.D. Gigaku was superseded by Bugaku, which was of Chinese, Hindu and Corean origin. It became popular as court entertainment as well as Buddhist ritual dance. At the end of this period Dengaku, a simple and more acrobatic type was developed. At the same time, another form Sarugaku, from original cosmic mimic dance developed into new serious forms. This Sarugaku became the basis of the 'Nō' drama which was perfected in the 14th century. The 'Nō' plays are serious dramas. The 'Nō' play is not concerned with action. It expresses a situation in lyrical form. Both prose and verse are used. The language is archaic. The words are intoned by the actor in the manner of a chant. A chorus sitting at the side of the stage accompanies him, and sings the actor's part while he is dancing. The chorus also narrates the course of events throughout the play. The orchestra sits at the back of the stage. The instrumental music consisting of flute, stick drums and two hand drums, supplies a back-ground for the recitation, song and dance. It controls the timings of the actor's movements. Before the beginning of the play, at the climax and towards the close of the play, the flute is used which has a high shrill pitch. The 'Nō' dance relies to a great extent on the mime, which is far removed from the realistic imitation and is idealised to the extreme limit of symbolism; e.g. merely touching the eyes with the hand indicates weeping; covering the head with the sleeves indicates looking far into depths etc. There are five positions of the 'Nō' dance—standing erect, moving left, right, forward and backward. Each motion of hand and foot is controlled by fixed rules. There are special names for changes of movements. A kimono lying on the stage will represent a sick person. A smile is indicated by a lift of the mask and the tear by a downward glance.

The 'Nō' actors were treated with honour at all times. There are no female players. Child actors take parts of princes, young emperors etc. Actors use masks of painted wood. They are of five types—the aged, the male, the female, deities and Buddhas, and monsters. There are also masks other than these meant to be used in special plays. Faces are covered completely by masks, which have small eye-openings.

The dress is derived from the official dress of former times, adopted for dramatic purposes. There are outer garments, garments worn indoor, the lower garments in the nature of a divided skirt or an elongated trousering worn in ancient Japan and head-dress of different types. There is no attempt at realism.

The stage is square in shape $19' \times 19'$, and made of highly polished and seasoned cypress. It has slight decline towards the front. The ornate roof of the stage is supported by pillars at each corner which is the integral feature, even though the stages are built within the auditorium these days. (The former performances took place in the open-air). The four pillars have special names and they serve as the direction points for the dancing. A conventional pine-tree is painted on the wall of the back stage. There is a small sliding door at the right of this, through which the chorus and the stage assistants make their entry and exit. The chorus take their place on the balustrated extension of the stage to the right of the audience. The orchestra is in front of the pine tree. There is a roofed balustrated passage connecting the stage platform with the green-room. The actors make their entry along it. The entrance to this is covered by a curtain. At the time of actor's entry or exit, the attendants seize the poles attached at the bottom on the inner side, with swift movements. Behind the curtain there is the mirror room i.e. the green-room. The audience sits on the three sides. In the 'Nō' theatre there is no use of scenery.

A fan, a sword, occasionally a spear and a wooden stand $3' \times 6'$ and one foot high serve as stage properties. The wooden stand may represent a palace, a fort, a mountain or a bed-chamber. A frame-work of light bamboo carried by an actor who represents a sailor, indicates a boat. An important role is played by fan in Japanese dance, as it is used to express different ideas symbolically. It represents heaven or elements or going to the other extreme or a wine cup or a sword. Riding a horse or shooting an arrow from the bow are also symbolized by it.

It may indicate the rising moon, opening a sliding door, the falling of cherry blossoms or the waves of the sea. A cylindrical black lacquered tube serves as a seat or a throne for the actors. In the comic interlude the lid is often used as a wine cup of an extra large size.

[Kyogen are comic pieces. 'Nō' and Kyogen are acted on the same stage. 'Nō' actors wear masks, Kyogen are never masked and are without the musical accompaniment to the dances in it. The actor in Kyogen who has a special seat assigned to him merely explains the general meaning of the dance or the pantomime. The Kyogen actors wear yellow tabi, the 'Nō', white. The former jest at the nobles, the clergy, the blind and the maimed; the mediocre are ridiculed. Kyogen are a recent introduction which provide comic relief in between the ponderous and the grave 'Nō' plays.]

Kabuki theatre : This theatre arose in the early 17th century. The settings here are most complicated and elaborate. Some sets are huge boats that extend to the entire length of the stage. Sometimes the stage becomes a house, a lake and a forest at the same time. Some sets are three storey places in which a counter part of action takes place on all the three levels. All stages revolve facilitating quick changes of time and place. The most celebrated feature is a raised gangway which connects the stage to the rear of the auditorium. On this the actors make entries and exit and perform dances. Trap devices in both, the stage and this gangway, allow the actors to appear and disappear at will. The Kabuki actors must be very good dancers. The costumes are gorgeous and follow authentically each period of Japan's history. A dancer will change costume so many as nine times in the course of one dance. The greatness of Kabuki is seen in its actors, and its manifold skills of stylisation of imitating puppets and animals. Kabuki is a synthesis of the three arts—dance, drama and music. Women's parts are traditionally played by men. The orchestra is seated on the stage. On both, the Chinese and the Japanese stage, the orchestra is responsible for the control of timing the actor's dancing, gestures and poses. In China, the orchestra also accompanies the actor's singing which is an important feature of the plays. But in Japan the Kabuki actor does not sing at all. It is done by the orchestra which speaks the actor's dialogues also on occasion.

Cambodia :

The most important element in the literature of Cambodia is its drama. The royal theatre of Phnompenk is called Rangram. The stage is open on all sides except at one end where there is a green room separated by partitions from the stage and the public. The stage is a sort of huge scaffolding raised on poles with a thached roof. The theatre is very simple in decoration and is lighted by oil lamps. The musicians sit on the stage at the end opposite to the green room. Members of the chorus are seated along the side between the green room and the orchestra. The actors and singers, except in the case of Rāmāyaṇa, are always women. The conductress who sits on a mat, in front of the chorus has before her the text of the piece, on a primitive reading desk. The plays are a combination of music, dance and pantomime. According to Cambodian notions, the principal characters must be a king, a prince or a princess. The pieces are divided into acts and scenes but the intervals are so short that the performance is practically continuous. Cambodian drama owes much to its Indian prototype.

The postures and movements are achieved only after a long strenuous practice. The pupils start with the exercise of the hands. The legs too have their special exercises. The basic posture of the Cambodian dance is, hips held back firmly, knees spread widely apart, feet turned outward, toes up and the angle of the hand on the wrist asymmetrically balanced by the sharp break in the elbow. From this stance, all positions and movements of the dance develop and to it they must return. The young dancer, howsoever clever she may be, must play minor roles of hand maids and attendants until she is older. If the size of the mature girl is large she plays men's parts; if small, those of women. Two men attached to the palace troupe play all demon, comic and animal roles. Nearly all Cambodian dance tells a story which is graphically depicted both by the action and hand movements. The walk is highly formalised, executed with knees bent and toes out while the hands, holding the basic position of extended thumb and forefinger sway forward and backward. A majority of plots is based on scenes from Rāmāyaṇa or on Hindu influenced traditional literature or Buddhist classics.

Siam :

Khon and Lakon are the classical dance and drama of Thais. The former is a masked play or a masked pantomime. It is the most ancient theatrical form which reminds one of its connections with India. The actors themselves are mute and the dialogue is sung by a set of musicians who sit with the accompanying orchestra. The gestures of the dancers interpret the meaning with perfection.

The themes of Khon dance are adopted from Rāmāyaṇa or Siamese Rama Kian (The Fame of Rāma). Their texts are highly Sanskritised. The names of some gestures and dance movements are akin to those in ancient Indian theatre. There are songs to be sung on the occasion of going through the sky, shedding tears, receiving and giving caresses and going out quickly, similar to the Dhruvās.

Lakon means a theatre and Lakon Ram means 'theatre dances'. Nowadays the word Lakon signifies the dance-drama performed by women who act male roles as well. It is staged with or without scenery and consists either of a plot or has merely meaningless abstract movements with music and some traditional conventions coming from the older Khon. The gestures that express the various meanings of the songs form a language of their own which is common to Khon and Lakon. It is necessary to express themselves through hand movements as the faces are masked in Khon and a heavily powdered mask like make-up is used in Lakon. Hence, all through the dance, not a single face muscle moves. These gestures are classified in three types—(a) those that express general emotions like love, hate, anger, joy, sorrow etc. (b) those that impart grace to ordinary movements like standing, walking, sitting etc. and (c) those that signify intentions like refusal, acceptance, calling etc.

Music is an indispensable element in the performance. In fact, the classical theatre of Siam is referred to as 'Saṅgīta' (the Sanskrit word meaning "playing of musical instruments, singing and dancing"). The five musical instruments used are of Indian origin—suṣira (the flute), ātata (dardura), vitata (one-faced drum), ātata vitata (mṛdaṅga) and ghana (the cymbals). Musical terms referring to the tempo are also similar.

Laos :

Many of the features of the Cambodian theatrical practices are found in Laotian theatre. The patronage, as in Cambodia, comes from the king who has private troupe of dancers. The king imported Thai trainees and got the troupe trained in the Thai style. Dance and music enjoy highest popularity and as such every girl of a good family is expected to know these arts.

All their dances consist of four fundamental steps at some point—salutation, making-up, flower-taking and walking. All these are exactly on the pattern of the Cambodian style. The making-up and flower-taking are both pure pantomime. Here also we have the Twilight and Dove dance as in Cambodia and a similar tradition of animal dances to interpret the actions of love-sick human beings.

There is only a distant relationship between Laotian and Indian dance. The angularities, energetic rhythmic pulsations and hand gestures of India are so softened and become so dreamlike that their symbolism transforms into a fleeting, momentary mood. The mythological stories of India too have undergone subtle changes. Everything has a happy ending and everyone has a good time even in adversity.

Java:

The chief entertainment of Java is provided by the Topeng where the performers wear masks except when it is presented before the sovereign and the wayang which is persented by shadows.

Panji is the favourite hero of Topeng and his adventures form the theme. There are distinct masks for him and other historical characters. The Dalang or the manager of the entertainment recites the speeches while the performers have only to 'suit the action to the word'—they are merely living puppets. It is the Dalong who furnishes the dialogue extempore. Besides him four persons form the gamelan (i.e. the band of musicians) and six persons act. But when the show is in front of a sovereign the performers themselves repeat their speeches with a previous rehearsal. The music of the band accompanies the piece throughout and varies in expression according to the nature of the action or the emotion expressed. The actors are splendidly dressed after the ancient costume and perform their parts with grace, elegance and precision. But on the whole, the show is more like a ballet than a dramatic performance.

Buffoonery is sometimes introduced to increase the zest of the entertainment and this extraneous character, whether he represents a dog, a monkey or an idiot, unfailingly excites considerable mirth often in the most interesting part of the performance. There is also a kind of pantomime called Barungan in which men dressed as various animals appear in procession or combat and their performance is accompanied by the beats of the gong and drum. It is an exciting amusement for children.

The most favourite themes of the dramas (Topeng) and the shadow plays are exploits of Panji who reigned in the 12th century. Another source of stories is the Javanese version of the Epics, Rāmāyaṇa and Mahābhārata. In the presentation of the plays there is no line of division between dancing and acting. The action is rhythmic throughout and matches with music. Changes of scenes are given by the entry and exit of actors.

Bali:

There is no regular stage as such in Bali where all the performances take place in open-air. In some dances the floor is covered with palm matting. As there is no stable stage, there are no fixed stage properties. But there are some essential accessories. There is curtain used in some types of performances. Lances, umbrellas and tall curved banners are employed in certain types. Sometimes the lances are used as gates through which the hero passes out of his spirit world into the world of human dance and drama.

There is no change of scenery at all. Whether the characters are in a forest or on sea-shore or in a palace court or journeying from one place to the other, the scene is suggested only through their conversation. A king or a guard would probably denote a palace. The process of the journey is suggested by words and glances and movements, over the very restricted space of the dance ground. The comic attendants always balance each other or balance their master by allowing him to lean upon them.

The lighting is provided by small lamps of cocoanut oil or kerosene. The soft light of these lamps shows faces and the glittering head-dress to the best advantage.

The drum is always in close relation to the dancer; and the melody of gender (an instrument with metal keys placed transversely on upright bamboos), continuously keeps time depending on the drum-beats. The cymbals too keep time in accordance with the dancer. The drum is the leader of the orchestra. Very complicated varieties of rhythmical elements combined with different varieties of tone are found in the drum-playing. The drum gives the signal for the entry of the dancer.

The dance-technique clearly shows the influence of the Indian dramatic code (NŚ.). The entry of each character is accompanied by his or her melody. The gestures and the step etc., are all in keeping with the rhythm and music. Many kinds of obeisance, sixteen types of accents, many manners of dropping to the ground or lifting or touching the dress etc., are used. There are many movements of feet in combination with arms and hands, movements of the head in all positions and for every type of character, and movements of cheeks and mouth. There are various glances of eyes e.g. angry, violent, fixed on an imaginary foe, sweet, sleepy etc. The ceremonial umbrellas are viewed in different ways which change their nature according to the character. If a beautiful lady is out of favour temporarily, there is provision for kicking her or whipping her with leaves. There are various movements of women, such as drooping of head and eyes, shedding real tears and the like. According to the type of character the style of talk differs. Each play has a different style of recitation. In Ardja, (which is largely sung), the intonation is very typical with extra-ordinary pitch-variations.

The principal lady is of any rank. She may be a queen, a princess, a demoness, or a modern girl. These roles were played by men formerly and in certain forms of dance-drama they are even now played by men. The beautiful appearance and the sweet voice of the leading lady are taken for granted. The men who play these roles look sometimes very effeminate even off the stage.

The female attendant of the principal lady always appears before her and calls her to come out. Her dress is similar to that of her mistress having some modifications. She dances in the same refined manner having different steps. As regards the male roles, the heroes are of two types—refined and coarse or strong. The king as hero is always manis, i.e., sweet and his enemies are kras, i.e., rough. This difference between the types does not exist in the mask-play like Baris. The principal character, he may be a king, a priest, a god, a demon or a magic monkey, is always played (with certain shades of difference) in a violent demonic way. In Ardja, the manis type of king and the mad gentleman (parodic type) may be played by girls.

Penasar and Kartala are two attendants of the hero. The Penasar is a secondary minister, the chief attendant of the principal person who happens to be on the stage and is always a step lower than this person even if the latter is of fairly low rank. The Penasar is the interpreter and hence his role becomes very important. He is conceived as lively and vigorous and rather foolish. Kartala is the clown and Penasar falls always in the verbal pit dug by Kartala (who is the younger brother to him). The Penasar dances if he can dance. These two are the most popular actors of the play as they speak in vernacular and provide comic element both in dialogue and dancing. They are generally very good acrobatic dancers and parodists.

Before the beginning of the actual play, the Penasar gesticulates signs of listening and waiting. The two start conversation of what has gone before. 'The king has decided such and such a thing; there is none so wise and so great as he is; now the king is coming.' They describe his beauty, costume and bearing. They may sit down, often balancing each other and watch him dance. A Raja melody is played to introduce the king.

In Wajang Wong, which dramatizes the Rāmāyaṇa, except the noble male and female characters, all others are masked. Śūrpaṇakhā appears as a refined lady and has no mask in the Rāmāyaṇa. Monkeys look terrible having supernatural powers like that of demons. The head-dress of Rāma is majestic. It is fashioned on the model of that of Viṣṇu or Kṛṣṇa found in the temple relics in Java and Bali. The head-dress of Rāvaṇa is the same but there are wing-like side pieces and it is decorated at the back with Garuḍa bird. The head-dress of Lakṣmaṇa has upward and inward curving horns. The head-dress of Bibhīṣaṇa has small downward curving horn curling inwards. Sītā's head-dress is a flower-covered crown with wing-like side pieces and Garuḍa behind. Her attendant's head-dress is smaller one. Rāma and Sītā wear long hair strewn with flower-petals. All noble characters dance in fine style and noble demons in boisterous style. The dance of the attendants is peculiar to them—it is of a grotesque type. Animals dance in a fantastic style with certain individual peculiarities like the variety of the leaps, bends, darting glances etc.

In the Dramatic Baris themes are taken from the Kavi version of the Rāmāyaṇa and the Mahābhārata. Rāma, Arjuna and Kṛṣṇa are all presented in a fiercely heroic mould of the demon Baris dancer. The heroic atmosphere infects Penasar and Kartala also. The heroine is necessarily refined. The full Balinese orchestra (which consists of gamelan gong, two big gongs, four drums, and a great number of metal-keyed or metal-knobbed instruments) accompanies the Baris.

In the Topeng play there is complicated and varied use of masks. The number of actors is never the same as that of the masks; it varies from 5 or 6 to sometimes 2 or 3 only. (In the oldest form one actor wore all the masks in succession.).

The sight of the dancing feet which indicates the coming of a dancer and the shaking of the curtain by invisible hands are the dramatic elements connected with every entry till all the cast has come out.

In certain Balinese dances we find movements which remind us of animals and they have animal names also showing that the resemblance is a conscious one. In Wajang Wong, there are the monkey dances in which monkeys, birds, deer, dogs and all the variety of animals which figure in the masks worn by Hanumat's monkey host gambol, hop and coil according to their kind. As regards the monkey technique each movement has its name and each monkey keeps within the role of its mask. When Sugrīva with his monkey band comes to Rāma, all the monkeys pay their respect to Rāma, with an infinite variety of beautiful dancing steps, slow posturing and saluting him with careful mudrās.

Ceylon :

Siṁhala Nāṭyam[1] is the medium of expression of Saṁhāra Tāṇḍavam, one of the twelve Tāṇḍavas. The link between dance in Ceylon and India is thus quite clear. A number of

1. See "Traditions and Chronicles of the Dance in Ceylon", by M. D. Raghavan.

common elements may be seen in the several forms of the dance of Ceylon e.g. 'the whirl'. In the Ves we see Nṛtta at its best. One of the Tāṇḍava dances of God Śiva is Ūrdhva-tāṇḍava danced with rapid whirling movements. This is among the remarkable features of the Ves in Kohomba Kankariya. J.E. Sederaman regards the Ves as a form of 'Vedic sacrificial dance' introduced into Ceylon by the early immigrants. On the soil of Siṁhala this was blended with indigenous elements and developed into the Ves as seen in the Kohomba Kankariya and in Kandyan dances today. There is the other dance in the cult of the Yakkas and spirits impersonated in the colourful costumes special to each, danced by the kaṭṭādiya. Kaṭṭādiya comes from kaṭṭu (disguised in the particular mask and costume) and āḍi (the dancer from āḍuka to dance), thus meaning, the disguised dancer. Dances in the cults of gods and the yakkas and spirits are all accompanied by vocal music and the rhythmic beating of the drums. The dances of Ceylon fall into two main groups—those using no masks and practised by the Vaddas and those using masks of varying characters practised by the Simhalese. The masked dances of the Simhalese seem to show more clear connection with the Indian Nāṭya. The Kolamnaṭima performance of the Simhalese begins with an invocation of gods chanted by an unmasked dancer. It is a kind of prologue in which the chief characters and the substance of plot are mentioned. There is the king, the queen and the Brahmin minister. But the Kolamnaṭima does not develop its plot by means of the dramatis personae. Different scenes are connected with one another by the narrator who introduces every new character coming on the stage. This narrator is known as tora-taru kathākāraya (kathākāraka) or the interpreter of affairs. His duty is to explain the characters coming, their acting and their words in prose. The leading characters are the king and the queen. The king is characterised by his gorgeous dress and big mask very carefully covered and painted, having a halo round its crown. The word kolam is derived from Tamil and means costume, guise or representation. As the kolam masks are very heavy and tall they are not suited for talking and hence the form of the performance might have been orginally in pantomime.

Simhalese masks are distinguished as in the cases of masks mentioned in the NŚ., by the headgears attached to them e.g. when turbans are attached to them, they are to represent ministers and a mask with a short-sized crown is meant for a prince. In these masks white is used to paint the faces of gods and goddesses and other divine beings and blue for the faces of foreign demons. To the accompaniment of drummers and musicians, who sing out the story in short melodies, the masked characters make their appearance successively. Each except the king and the queen (who scarcely move) performs an introductory dance; then they leave and reappear only when the course of the play requires their presence. A blessing is pronounced by some character at the end of a performance.

Musical instruments in Simhalese orchestra are classified into ātata (drums played with hands), vitata (drums played with stick), vitatātata (drums played with sticks and hand), ghanaya (cymbals) and susiraya (wind instruments), mainly flute.

That the fundamentals of Nāṭya in Ceylon are essentially the same as those of India is clear from the elementary hand gestures in Kandyan dances and to a less extent in the masked dances e.g. the kolam. The Kandyan dances are artistically more important; like Kathakali, they are energetic, almost violent and performed exclusively by men who are bare-footed. Terms such as Karaṇam, Aḍāvu and Kastīram occur in the Kandyan dance. Aḍāvus are the dance steps; Karaṇa is the co-ordination of the movements of the hands and the feet; Kastīrams are a combination of musical tunes in Kandyan music.

Burma :

In the Burmese performance also song, dance and instrumental music are indispensable elements. A jester is present in most of the plays. Unity of place is not cared for. Thagya Nat is the representative of the king of Thagya, and lives on the summit of Myimmo-daung (Mt. Meru). The well known water festival held in the Burmese New Year's Day when Thagya Nat is supposed to make his annual visit to the earth from heaven, may be thought as a variant of the Indradhvaja festival. According to Ridgeway, Thagya Nat is no other than Indra whose name Śakra became Thagya in Burmese. There are thirtyseven important Nats and Thagya stands first among them. Each of these is served by a medium who represents dramatically on the occasion of his or her festival. The medium imitates the dress, tastes and employment of each and some times alludes to his or her fate. Of course, this was the simplest form from which the Burmese drama has evolved. Yet it has not advanced beyond the purely lyrical stage consisting of dancing, singing and instrumental music. The modulation of the vocal expression is much more subtle and intense than the expression of the features, while gesture is restricted to the conventional posture of the dance. The special name for the dramatic performance is 'Zatpwe'. The play may be performed by men and women actors or by marionettes (yotthe). There are also shadow plays and puppet performances.

The stage is the ground generally spread with mats. In the middle of the stage area, always there is a small tree that is either planted or fastened to one of the poles supporting the roof. The Burmese temporary theatre is built with bamboo and its roof is covered with straw or dried grass. But the interior of it is covered with gorgeously covered silk and other stuff. On the two sides of the stage and in front, bamboo platforms are raised for distinguished spectators. The stage is illumined with lights consisting of earthen pots full of cotton seeds soaked in petroleum and occasionally replenished with oil. The orchestra is accommodated in the back portion of the stage behind which there is the tiring room.

The overall theme of the plays is the progress of the happiness of the leading characters through separation and hardship. The ending, however, is always a re-union and gladness prevails. At intervals, each character sings a song to emphasise the mood of the action which has just taken place. The costume is gorgeous and exotic with the kings and nobles. The full Zatpwe (pwe means any theatrical entertainment; something that is shown hence a show; Zatpwe is a classical performance) orchestra consists of about a dozen different instruments. The two chief instruments are extremely ornate.

One is a circle of twentyone small graded drums ranging in sound from low to shrill high pitch; each is tuned by placing a globe of moist rice paste in the centre of the hide covering to keep it taut. The scale is septatonic. The drums are encased in a sort of circular picket fence of gold painted slats studded with bits of sparkling mirrors. The performer sits at the centre of the circle on a small stool and swirls around while he plays. The other special instrument is the pole from which hang two large gongs of heavy metal. The frame is shaped like a mythological beast—actually five animals in one. Altogether, the instrument looks like a slender dragon. The deep reverberating resonance of the gongs punctuates the main pulses of the music and determines the basic tuning of the orchestra. Besides these two, there are ornately carved teak wood xylophones, several large drums, ivory horns and some other percussion instruments including the cymbals. Due to the varied instruments of this orchestra a rich variety of instrumental music is provided for the accompaniment. The orchestra plays constantly to announce the scene as one of gladness or sorrow, to lay its setting in a court or a forest, to indicate the tone of prowess or dalliance and to subtend the overall mood. It accompanies each dance in a pulsating, vibrant, explosive symphony of sounds. In the play, on the occasion of a festival at the court or a marriage feast, the main dance scene is provided in which two foremost stars of the troupe dance their most brilliant numbers. Sometimes an interlude, having no connection with the plot is introduced to provide for the dance.

All dance in Burma is based on the classical Zatpwe. It is invariably energetic and designed to excite, agitate and stimulate. In the Burmese dance, the dancer sings a short phrase, its words determine the rhythm; the drums repeat the rhythm. Then as the full orchestra repeats the same passage of melody and rhythm the dancer springs into dance. At the end of several of these phrases which altogether form a poem, and in which the whole procedure of song, drums and dance with full orchestra is repeated each time, a particular dance is completed. The basic starting posture for Burmese dancing is close to a crouch. The emotional range is limited. Dance in Burma is dynamics of poses. It is a series of gesticulations specified and determined by the aesthetic pleasure it gives.

Another type of pwe Burma offers is the Natpwe or the spirit dance. There are fighting dances also like sword dance and fire dance.[1]

1. Information regarding this appendix is collected from the following sources :-

(1) The Chinese Theatre by Jack Chen;

(2) The Kabuki Theatre of Japan by A. C. Scott;

(3) Theatre in the East by Faubion Bowers;

(4) The Dramas and Dramatic Dances of Non-European Races by William Ridgeway;

(5) Dance and Drama in Bali by Beryl de Zoete and Walter Spies;

(6) Contributions to The History of Hindu Drama by Dr. Manomohan Ghosh;

(7) Traditions and Chronicles of the Dance in Ceylon by M. D. Raghavan, separated from Spolia Zeylanica Vol. 28 Part II.

I am greatly indebted to the authors and publishers of these works.

APPENDIX—D

Ancient Indian Costume:

The details[1] of the male and female costume are given in this appendix with a view to help the understanding of the dresses of different characters described in the Āhāryābhinaya by the NŚ. Up to the 4th century B.C. ancient Indian literature is the only source for us to get the knowledge of the ancient Indian dress; but afterwards ancient Indian sculptures and paintings become more helpful to have a concrete idea of ancient Indian costume.

Up to the fourth century B.C. :

Vāsas was the lower garment worn by males. It was pleated properly for religious functions. The bunched pleats were generally tucked in at the navel. For the upper part of the body, there was a loose garment. Atka or Drāpi referred to in the Vedic literature, seems to be a mantle or a long cloaklike overcoat, which was embroidered with gold thread. The head-dress (Uṣṇīṣa) found earliest in connection with the Eastern people, had cross-winding and was tied with a tilt. It appears that a turban was not worn habitually by the Vedic people. It was compulsorily worn at the performance of the great sacrifices like the Rājasūya proclaiming sovereignty. The head-dress was thought to be a sign of dignity and authority.

Females had their lower garment similar to that of the males. Some ladies wore a single garment to cover the whole body. To cover the upper part of the body, there was a loose garment. In addition to this loose upper garment, there appears to be a close-fitting tailored garment embroidered with gold thread, worn by some women. In the case of women, head-dress was not common; it was rarely in use.

1. See : a) Indian Costume—by Dr. G. S. Ghurye;
b) Prācina Bhāratīya Veśabhūṣā (Hindi) by Dr. Motichandra.
I am greatly indebted to the authors of these books, from which the matter in this Appendix is mostly collected.

Fourth century B.C. to the Fourth century A.C. :

Western Region:

Males wore the lower garment (dhotī) with pleats in front. The surplus portion of it was worn on the left side by men in the extreme North-West. The manner of wearing the 'dhotī' by the archer was with Kāsoṭā i.e., the upper ends of the pleats were tucked in at the navel and their lower ends were taken behind between the legs and tucked in at the back center. A belt or a string held the dhotī in position at the waist. The upper garment was folded loosely. The more common manner of wearing the upper garment was, with its one end folded loosely, and thrown at the back side over the left shoulder and the remaining portion taken from the left shoulder over the chest to the right side and then over the back of the left shoulder, where the end was thrown over it to the front side. The upper garment was worn in a number of varieties. Royal personages might take the loose garment off the shoulders and wrap it over the buttocks. By turning the front ends, sometimes the left shoulder and the arm were covered. It was often tied round the waist fashionably. The upper parts of the body might be covered by the servants and common people with the garment spread out. The fact that men of certain classes did not use the head-dress is indicated by the lack of turbans. The dress of the foreigner consisted of tight trousers and a close-fitting tunic, with tight and tapering full sleeves. Loose upper garment was also worn on occasions. On the head-less statue of Kaniṣka, a long coat which is open-fronted and reaching the calves is seen over the tunic.

In the case of the females also there were two garments, the upper and the lower. The lower garment was generally without hind pleats. The front pleats were arranged in different ways. A girdle with clasp having one, three, five, or seven strands was worn on the waist by ladies. The loose piece of cloth (dupaṭṭā) used as an upper garment was worn in many ways. The 'sārī' was worn with the sakaccha manner (i.e. kāsoṭā) also. The lower and upper garments with or without the head-dress formed one variety of the costume. In the other variety there was the dhotī with ample front pleats and a tunic. In the third variety, there was 'dhotī' with ample front pleats and long-sleeved open-fronted coat. In another variety, there were baggy trousers and tunic. In one variety there were skirt (ghāgrā) and the dupaṭṭā. Double skirt was there in the case of the milk-maid. One wrap reached the ankles and the other over it above the knees. A close fitting bodice was also used. The purpose of veil was served by the scarf. The dhotī was worn in the manner of a Lungī (the dhotī worn round the waist without pleats) also. In the case of the foreign females, the scarf was there and the effect of 'sārī' was achieved by two pieces.

The Central Region:

The lower garment in the case of males was often a narrow 'dhotī' with a band or flat belt at the waist. It was worn in a more fashionable manner by royal persons and high officials. The standard manner was that the surplus portion pleated breadth-wise, tucking one end of the bunch at the navel and the other dangling between the legs. The lungī-type was also there sometimes. The dhotī was generally pleated neatly and tucked at the back. A dupaṭṭā or a scarf was the upper garment worn with many varieties.

(The charioteer and the king in the Bhita medallion appear to have full-sleeved coats.) The head-dress was a turban, sometimes a loaf-like cap, and a conical cap also. (In Bharhut sculptures, the turban of pheṭā type, with one side rising high is seen.) Sometimes both the ears were partially or completely covered by the head-wear.

The 'dhotī' was worn by women exposing large part of the abdomen. The girdle had strands from one to seven. There was flat belt also. Sometimes a broad lower garment was worn with hind pleats. The use of skirt also was made at times. The manner of wearing 'dhotī' without hind pleats was also in vogue. 'Dupaṭṭā' did not form a necessary part of the dress. The females of the Western region adopted the use of tailored garments first and then those of the Central region. Generally there was some kind of squat head-covering. A veil was also in use to cover the head and the back. Sometimes the head had no covering.

Eastern Region:

There was double Lungī as the lower garment for the males. Somewhat narrow 'dhotī' with a belt was also used. Sometimes both the ends of the upper cloth were thrown at the back by placing it about the neck. A turban with a ball-like projection in the front centre was the head-dress. There were other varieties also.

The 'dhotī' and 'dupaṭṭā' were worn in a delightful manner by women. In some cases there was a kind of skirt. The sārī-type with a fan-like arrangement in the front was also there. The surplus portion in the sārī type was bunched into a roll and tucked just below the navel creating a barrel-shaped protuberance. The head-dresses of women used to be more elaborate than those of men.

Deccan and Southern Region:

The lower garments were of two types:—simple wider 'dhotī' with flat belt having the front pleats arranged breadthwise and tucked in and the narrow 'dhotī' ending above the knees and the Lungī type. Dupaṭṭā was tied round the buttocks. Sometimes the scarf was not used. The head-dress was voluminous.

The lower garment of the females was a narrow 'dhotī' or a Lungī type. It was common to expose the whole abdominal region. Generally the body above the waist was not covered by ladies.

In the Southern region males wore broad or narrow type of 'dhotī' with flat belt. In the case of the broad 'dhotī' there were pleats hanging in the front. Some used close-fitting trousers also. The scarf was tied round the loins. A tunic with long sleeves was also in use. The head-wear was of many varieties. The close-fitting cap was not in vogue. Narrow 'dhotī' and a head-dress were worn by the males of Tamilnad.

Ladies rarely wore a narrow 'dhotī'. They had a heavy girdle zone and also the flat belt. The scarf was tied round the loins. The mode of wearing 'dhotī' with hind pleats was not unknown. There was 'sārī' type also. The head-dress of women had a greater variety. The Tamilnad ladies had their lower garment extended to the ankles.

4th to the 11th Century A.D.:

In this period, in the case of males, we get the high cylindrical cap of Sūrya and Viṣṇu, the four-cornered cap of Indra and the conical cap of the Pallava kings. There was squat 'pagaḍi' also. The head-dress was worn necessarily at the time of worship. The voluminous turban seems to be not in use. The 'dhoti' served as a lower garment. There were tight trousers also. A belt was used round the waist. A fairly close-fitting tunic short or long slipped into position over the head, with full length tapering sleeves or short or none was much more common in this period. (The Sun god shows the Northern dress with a double breasted coat fastened with string at the side. Gupta emperors used in the house, a coat which was a modification of the Kuṣāṇa coat.) The dancer in the Bagh painting wears trousers and tunic of printed cloth having long tapering sleeves. In the case of females the head-dress was rare and seen in special case. Head-dress in general was a speciality of the Eastern people and was seen in other place through their cultural influence. Its disappearance was due to the practice of drawing one portion of the scarf over the head (Avaguṇṭhana). Cut and sewn garments to cover the female bosom were generally used. There were two varieties—one fastened at the back common in North India and the other, knotted centrally just below the breast common in the Deccan and the South. A bodice and a short jacket were also there. The short 'dhoti' as well as the 'dhoti' worn as 'sāri' type was current. In the Eastern region the females wore the 'dhoti' in such a manner that the tucking of the bunched pleats did not give rise to protuberance at the navel.

We find the dresses of different people from the Ajanta paintings as follows—

Kings and feudatory chiefs generally have 'dhoti' and an upper garment worn on the left shoulder and under the right arm. Some times Kūrpāsaka (jacket) and a cap are worn. Kūrpāsaka is occasionally with half sleeves. The 'dupaṭṭā' is tied at the waist. The full sleeved tunic made of printed cloth is worn while riding a horse. The 'dhoti' is short one. In one case the 'dupaṭṭā' is seen flapping behind. In war, the use of half sleeved tunic and costly 'pagaḍi' is seen. The tunic reaching upto waist is worn while hunting. The pyjama and boots reaching upto knee are also seen. The Kañcukin has a flat turban, full sleeved tunic and chaddar worn slantingly. The tunic of the minister is white and full-sleeved. He also wears boots and a shawl going on the left shoulder and the end hanging over the left hand. The dignitaries wear an under-garment over which 'dhoti' also is tied. 'Dupaṭṭā' is loosely tied round the waist. Door-keepers have a tunic and some times a cap. Royal servants have a tailored garment or a 'dhoti'. The queen wears 'dhoti' reaching upto ankles or some times 'ghāgrā' also. Tailored garments are often used. The dancer has a tunic of printed cloth, with long tapering sleeves. Generally the maid servants use a 'sārī' and belt. Many have 'ghāgrā' and bodice also. They have generally full sleeved white tunic reaching upto knees. A cap is seen in some cases. Middle class women use tunic of printed cloth and 'dupaṭṭā'. There is no head-dress ordinarily for the ladies in the Ajanta paintings. But the queen or other nobilities have some times crowns. The village women have narrow 'sārīs'. Their head is either covered by a scarf or tied with ribbons.

There are many references[1] to dress in classical literature made by Dr. Ghurye, out of which a few (mostly from Sanskrit plays) are given below—

Dress of males:.

Head-dress—Yaugandharāyaṇa is described as wearing a turban (Uṣṇīṣa))Bhā. p. 99); Śakāra wears a diadem (Paṭṭa) (Bhā. p. 208).

Upper garment—Duryodhana in the Dūtavākya is described as wearing a white silken cloth as his upper garment (Uttarīya) (Bhā. p. 442). Vidūṣaka in the Ratnāvalī uses his upper garment to cover the picture-board under his armpit (Rat. Act. II, p. 101). Mantle (Prāvāra) is mentioned in the Mṛcch. (Act I, p. 36.) Kañcuka, long coat or robe, was used by the Kañcukin.

Lower garment—Dadhīca's lower garment was short enough to expose a third part of his thighs which was tightly tied. It was green in colour. (Harṣacarita 1, p. 37)

1. See—"Indian Costume", Appendix: pp. 227-301.

Dress of females :

Veil (Avaguṇṭhana)—In the Pratimānāṭaka, Rāma asks Sītā to take off her veil (Bhā. p. 263) ; Vasantasenā is asked by her mother to put on veil (Bhā. p. 237); a married lady was expected and entitled to use a veil in the public, (Mṛcch. Act IV p. 97); the Queen Dhāriṇī put the silken garment as veil over Mālavikā before offering her hand to the King (Māl. Act V p. 116).

Upper garment (Uttarīya)—The heroine makes use of her upper garment to hang herself in Avimāraka (Bhā. p. 167). The breast garment of Urvaśī fell in excitement due to anger (Vik. Act. IV p, 98): it must have been a small scarf thrown over the upper part of the body. Śakuntalā had a breast garment tied to cover her breasts (Śāk. Act I, p. 20). Bodice (Kañcuka)—Bāṇa tells us that the ladies of Sthāṇvīśvara used to wear bodice (Harṣacarita III p. 25).

Lower garment: Nīvī was the knot of the lower garment worn by women. Lower garments of varied colours were worn by Gopa maidens for festive dance (Bhā. p. 539) ; Purūravas fancies a foaming river as if it were Urvaśī dragging her white garment got loose in excitement (Vik. Act IV p. 108). The Queen in Ratnāvalī wears a garment whose ends were dyed orange with saffron for the Madanapūjā (Act. I, p. 42).

The marriage dress of males was red garment. Victims also were dressed in red garments. (Mṛcch. Act X p. 250). The female dress of marriage is described as two white silk cloths and an upper garment (MM. Act VI p. 146). Mālavikā's silken garment was not hanging too far when she was wearing the wedding attire used in Vidarbha (Māl. Act V, p. 101). The Queen wears white silken garment on religious occasion (Vik. Act III, p. 79). The chief queen was alone entitled to tie round her head the fillet (Paṭṭabandha) (Harṣacarita II, p. 39). The silken garment worn by Atithi had the figures of swans on it. (Raghuvaṁśa, XVII. 25).

APPENDIX E

More about Kūṭiyāṭṭam

(i) Dr. K.K. Raja states that the Koṭṭicceta dance performed by Parayūr Kūttaccākkaiyan is referred to in the Śilappadikāram. Kūtta is a Dravidian term meaning "dance or drama" and Cākkaiyan means a dancer or actor. (Kūṭiyāṭṭam p. 19) In the note 19, he points out that many scholars consider this as a reference to Kūṭiyāṭṭam in its earlier form.

(ii) Shri L.S. Rajagopalan informs that the actors are under fast on special occasions. When a Cākyār boy first performs he may fast. Also in some temples like Mūḷikkulam (the deity here is Lakṣmaṇa), the entry of the Sūtradhāra has to be done at the time of Saṅkrānta (change over from one month to the other). The performance may start at 12 midnight or even later. The Sūtradhāra here is to fast till the performance is over. In the case of the performances that are not part of a temple ritual, the actors do not fast.

(iii) The Vyaṅgyavyākhyā commentary on the Subhadrādhanañjaya by a Brahmin scholar of Paramésvaramaṅgalam gives us the account that the king himself explained to the Brahmin in detail the method of acting each role, pointing out the suggested ideas in the text to be brought out by the actor. The commentator says that it was on the basis of this explanation, he wrote the commentary.

(iv) Nārayaṇa Bhaṭṭa wrote prabandhas specially for the use of Cākyārs, for the presentation of Kūttu. Apart from the high literary merit, they are composed with a view to help the Cākyārs to bring in various topics without giving the impression that they are extraneous matter.

(v) Shri. L.S. Rajagopalan informs that the Naṅyārkūttu is performed during daytime. Actually Naṅyārkūttu is only the Ceṭī-pravéśa at the beginning of the IInd Act of Subhadrādhanañjaya. The Ceṭī enacts the story of Kṛṣṇa as a Nirvahaṇa (flash back). Somehow it got separated as a separate performance. He also says that originally there was no Prabandhakūttu.

Actually it was only the Nirvahaṇa of Vasantaka in the Pratijñāyaugandharāyaṇa. Later it also got separated.

(vi) Only the first half of the Ist Act of Tapatīsaṁvaraṇa is performed now-a-days. In the second half of this Act, a number of female characters are required and hence it is avoided.

(vii) The works dealing with the presentation of drama are known as Kramadīpikā and Āṭṭaprakāram. The former written either in Sanskrit or Malayalam or in both deals with the sequences, the costume to wear, the songs, the Rāgas etc. The latter gives in detail in Malayalam, the meaning of the passages and verses, how they are to be presented, the verses on which the Nirvahaṇa is based etc. Some of these texts are of a mixed nature.

(viii) The acoustics of the Kūttampalams is very good. There is no need for the amplification of sound. The position of the actor before the oil lamp is almost at the dead centre of the theatre and so the sound is heard equally well at all points in the theatre.

(Shri Goverdhan Panchal has made a thorough study of the Kūttampalams in his book—"Kūttampalam and Kūṭiyāṭṭam".)

(ix) The Miḷāvu originally used to be fashioned out of mud and hence in the Sanskrit writings in Kerala, it is referred to as Mṛdaṅgam and the Nambyār is even referred to as Mārdaṅgika. Only later the Miḷāvu started being made of copper. A few Miḷāvus of mud are still extant. The tonal quality of a Miḷāvu made of mud is softer than that made of copper. The copper instrument is more resonant. Dr. K.K. Raja has stated that there are two wind instruments in the orchestra of Kūṭiyāṭṭam, namely Kompa (trumpet) and Kuḷal (pipe) (Kūṭiyāṭṭam p. 23). But Shri L.S. Rajagopalan informs that Kompa is not seen being used any where. Probably the Maddalam and even the Timil are used in the Paṭṭābhiṣeka scene when Rāma is crowned. He further states that in Kūṭiyāṭṭam there are always two Miḷāvus. The rhythm only is produced on one and the vinyāsa of the Tāla is played on the other. The conch is used normally for the entry of major characters.

(x) Shri L.S. Rajagopalan states that there is only one type of kirīṭa and it is used by all kings and also by Arjuna as he is Kirīṭin. Śrīrāma etc. use a special kind of head-dress known as Vasikam. Bibhīṣaṇa has his make-up like that of Arjuna, but he does not have a crown. Only the facial make-up is same.

Vidūṣaka does not have a stick in his hand. In the Pratijñā, however, Vasantaka comes in the disguise of a travelling story-teller. His costume is different and he carries a stick. He is called Kuḷukkottu Unni in Malayalam.

(xi) The Muḍḍa melody is used by Demons also. Many of Rāvaṇa's ślokas relating to Sitā are recited in Muḍḍa Rāga. For special occasions there are also tālas for Khaṇḍa and Miśra.

(Shri L.S. Rajagopalan has given in detail the Rāgas and the Tālas used in Kūṭiyāṭṭam in his article on—'Music in Koodiyattam' which appeared in 'Sangeet Natak' No. 10.)

(xii) Shri L.S. Rajagopalan says that Akkitta songs are there in other plays also, but probably they appeared first in the Bhagavadajjukīya. They can hardly be called songs in the modern sense of the term. They are chanted in a sing song manner.

Dr. K.K. Raja states, while describing the Preliminaries, that there are songs sung by the Naṅyār invoking the deities Gaṇapatī, Sarasvatī and Śiva which are called Akkitta songs and the playing on the Miḷāvu is called Akkitta Koṭṭuka. He has given the various details of the Preliminaries. (Kūṭiyāṭṭam—pp. 24-29.)

(xiii) When the Nambyār comes to sprinkle water, he is supposed to wear Dhoti in the same manner as the Nambutiri pujāris wear it. It is called Tattu Utukkaka. The sprinkling of the water is done only after the Araṅgu Taḷi (cleaning of the stage by sprinkling water) śloka is recited. During that recitation, the Nambyār holds the water in his palm. As regards the main character appearing first, it is seen that in some plays the Sūtradhāra comes first. In Tapatīsaṁvaraṇa, the Vidūṣaka enters first.

The preliminary rites and the introduction of the main character are over on the first day. Then from the 2nd day onwards the Nirvahaṇa of the hero begins.

(xiv) Of course Sītā is not present on the stage. Her role is enacted by Rāma. The words of Sītā are uttered by the Naṅyār sitting on the stage playing cymbals.

(xv) The enacting of the Ist Act of Subhadrādhanañjaya takes 11 days.

Dhanañjaya enters and enacts the verse "ambāstanya" etc. (I.7). He performs the nityakriyā (the salutation to the guardian deities of the quarters) etc. and the performance ends on the first day. The verse "śikhini śalabhaḥ" etc. is enacted on the third day.

Shri L.S. Rajagopalan has given some details of the Netrābhinaya in his article "Eloquent Eyes—Netra-Abhinaya" in the Journal of the Music Academy, Madras, Vol. XLV, pp. 93-108. After showing the mudrās for ths śloka etc. the whole verse is reacted with the eyes alone. The actor stands with folded hands and with the eyes and facial expression only he enacts the whole verse. This is considered to be the forte of the Cākyārs.

I am greatly obliged to Shri L.S. Rajagopalan and Prof. K.P.N. Pisharoti of Trichur for their valuable suggestions in regard to Kūṭiyāṭṭam.

BIBLIOGRAPHY

General Works

Acharya, P.K. — A Dictionary of Hindu Architecture, Allahabad, 1927.

Agrawala, V.S. — Harṣacarita-Eka Sāṁskṛtika Adhyayana, (Hindi) Bihar Rashtrabhasha Parishad Patna, 1953.

-do- — India as known to Pāṇini, University of Lucknow, Lucknow, 1953.

Aristotle — Poetics and Rhetoric, J.M.Dent & Sons Ltd., London, 1953.

Bandopadhyaya, Shripada — The Origin of Rāga Delhi, 1956.

Banerjee, Gauranganath — Hellenism in Ancient India, Calcutta 1920.

Bapat, Dhundiraj Shastri — Vaidika Saṁgīta (Marathi) Bharat Gayan Samaj, Poona.

Bhat, G.K. — Vidūṣaka (Marathi), Maharashtra Granth Bhandar Kolhapur, 1959. Sanskrit Nāṭyasṛṣṭi, Continental Prakashan, Poona, 1964.

Bowers, Faubion — Dance in India, Columbia University Press New York, 1953.

-do- — Theatre in the East, Thomas Nelson & Sons Ltd. London, 1956.

Brihaspati, K.C.D. — Bharata kā Saṁgīta Siddhānta (Hindi) Prakashana Shakha, Suchana Vibhaga U.P. 1959.

Chen, Jack — The Chinese Theatre, Dennis Dobson Ltd. London.

Clements, E. — Introduction to the Study of Indian Music, Longmans Green & Co. 1913.

Coomaraswamy, A. The Dance of Shiva (Third Printing), Asia Publishing House, Bombay, 1956.

Culver, Charles A. Musical Acoustics, Edition Fourth, McGraw Hill Book Company Inc. New York 1956.

Dandekar, V.P. Marathi Nāṭyasṛṣṭi, Baroda.

Danielou, A. Introduction to the Study of Musical Scales, The Indian Society London, 1943.

-do- Northern Indian Music,
Vol. I, Visva Bharati, Calcutta, 1949.
Vol. II, Halcyon Press (Barnett) Ltd., Hertfordshire, G.B. 1945.

Dasgupta, H.N. The Indian Stage,
Vols. I and II Calcutta, 1934 and 1938.

Dasgupta, S.N. and De, S.K. A History of Sanskrit Literature, Classical Period, Vol. I, University of Calcutta, 1947.

De, S.K. History of Sanskrit Poetics, Second Edition, Calcutta, 1954.

-do- Some Problems of Sanskrit Poetics, Firma K.L. Mukhopadhyay, Calcutta 1959.

Deshpande, G.T. Bhāratīya Sāhityaśāstra (Marathi) Popular Book Depot, 1958.

Deval, K.B. The Hindu Musical Scale, Arya Bhushan Press, Poona, 1910.

Dikshitar, V.R.R. Śilappadikāram (English Translation), Oxford University Press, 1939.

Ghurye, G.S. Indian Costume, The Popular Book Depot, Bombay, 1951.

Framji, Phiroj Bhāratīya Śruti-Svara-Rāga Śāstra, Poona.

Gupta, C.B. Indian Theatre, Motilal Banarasidas, Banaras, 1954.

Ghosh, Manomohan Contributions to The History of Hindu Drama, Calcutta, 1957.

-do-	The Nāṭyaśāstra, Vol. I (Chapters I-XXVII), The Royal Asiatic Society of Bengal, Calcutta, 1950.
-do-	The Nāṭyaśāstra, Vol. II (Chapters XXVIII-XXXVI); The Asiatic Society, Calcutta, 1961.
Gopinath and Nagabhushan	Abhinayāṅkuram, Natana Niketan Publications, Madras, 1946.
Gopinath and Ramana Rao, S.V.	Classical Dance Poses of India, Natana Niketan Publications, Madras.
Iyer, K. Bharatha	Kathakali—The Sacred Dance-Drama of Malabar, Luzac and Co. Ltd., London, 1955.
I. Shekhar	Sanskrit Drama: Its Origin and Decline, Leiden, E. J. Brill, 1960.
Karanth, Shivaram	Yakṣagāna Bayalāṭa (Kannad), Harsha Mudrana, Prakatanalaya, Puttur, South Canara, 1957.
Keith, A.B.	The Sanskrit Drama, Oxford University Press, 1954.
Ketkar, Godavari	Bhāratīya Nāṭyaśāstra (Marathi), Arya Bhushan Press, Poona, 1928.
Levi, Sylvain	Le Theatre Indien, Paris, 1890.
Luders, H.	Bruchstucke Buddhistischer Dramen, Berlin, 1911.
Mainkar, T.G.	The Theory of the Saṁdhis and the Saṁdhyaṅgas, Pratibha Press, Poona, 1960.
Mankad, D.R.	The Types of Sanskrit Drama, Urmi Prakashan Mandir, Karachi, 1936.
-do-	Ancient Indian Theatre, Charutar Prakashan, Vallabh Vidyanagar, Anand, 1950.
Mirashi, V.V.	Kālidāsa, Suvichar Prakashan Mandal Ltd., Nagpur, 1934.

Motichandra — Prācīna Bhāratīya Veśabhūśā (Hindi) Bharati-Bhandar, Prayag, Saṁvat 2007.

Mule, K.G. — Bhāratīya Saṁgīta (Marathi) Part I, Bombay, 1940.

Naidu and Pantulu — Tāṇḍavalakṣaṇa, G.S. Press, Madras, 1936.

Nicoll, A. — Theory of Drama, George G. Harrap & Co., London 1937.

-do- — The Development of the Theatre, George G. Harrap & Co. London, 1948.

-do- — World Drama, George G. Harrap & Co. Ltd., London, 1954.

Pandey, K.C. — Comparative Aesthetics, Vol. I, Indian Aesthetics, 2nd Ed. Chowkhamba Sanskrit Series, Varanasi, 1959.

Panum, Hortense — Stringed Instruments of the Middle Ages, Their Evolution and Development, English Edition by Jeffrey Pulver, The New Temple Press, Norbury, London.

Parikh, J.T. — Sanskrit Comic Characters, The Popular Book Store, Surat, 1952.

Popley, H.A. — The Music of India, Second Edition, Y.M.C.A. Publishing House, Calcutta, 1950.

Raghavan, V. — Music in Ancient Indian Drama, (Reprinted from The J.M.M.A. Vol. XXV Parts I-IV.)

-do- — Sanskrit Drama and Performance, (Reprinted from The Madras University Journal, Vol. XXIX No. 1 July 1957).

-do- — Some Concepts of the Alaṅkāra Śāstra, The Adyar Library, Adyar, 1942.

-do- — The Number of Rasas, The Adyar Library, Adyar, 1940.

-do- — Yantras or Mechanical Contrivancea in

Ancient India, The Indian Institute of Culture, Bangalore.

-do- Bhoja's Śṛṅgāraprakāśa, Punarvasu, 7, Śrī Krishnapuram Street, Madras 14, India, 1963.

Ramachandran, K.V. Music and Dance in Kālidāsa, (Reprinted from the J.O.R. Madras, Vol. XVIII, Part II)

Ray, Govinda Chandra Bharata Nāṭyaśāstramem Nāṭyaśālāoṃ ke Rūpa (Hindi), Kashi Press, Varanasi.

Ridgeway, W. The Dramas and Dramatic Dances of Non-European Races, Cambridge University Press, Cambridge, 1915.

Sacks, Curt History of Musical Instruments (India) Norton.

Sambamoorthy, P. South Indian Music Book IV (Second Ed.) and Book V, The Indian Music Publishing House, G.T. Madras.

Sathe, V.D. Marathi Nāṭyaracanā, Venus Prakashana, Poona, 1955.

Scott, A.C. The Kabuki Theatre of Japan, George Allen and Unwin Ltd., London, 1955.

Sinha, Lalitkishor Dhvani aur Saṁgīta (Hindi) Bharatiya Jnanapitha, Kashi, 1955.

Strangways, Fox The Music of Hindostan, Clarendon Press, Oxford, 1914.

Swami Prajnanananda Historical Development of Indian Music, Calcutta, 1960.

Tagore, S.M. with Murtti and Vrindaka, The Eight Principal Rasas of the Hindus, Calcutta, 1880.

Thakur, Omkarnath Praṇava-Bhāratī, Prathama Vīṇā (Hindi) 1956. N. M. Tripathi and Co. Ltd. Bombay

Thorndike, Ashley H. Shakespeare's Theater, The Macmillan Company, New York, 1943.

Varma, K.M. Naṭya, Nṛtta and Nṛtya, Their Meaning and Relation, Orient Longmans, Bombay, 1957.

Wells H.W. — The Classical Drama of India, Asia Publishing House, Bombay, 1963.

-do- — The Classical Drama of the Orient, Asia Publishing House, 1965.

-do- — Six Sanskrit Plays, Asia Publishing House, Bombay, 1964.

Williams, Raymond — Drama in Performance, Frederick Muller Ltd. London, 1954.

Wilson, H.H. Raghavan and others — The Theatre of the Hindus, Susil Gupta (India) Ltd. Calcutta, 1955.

Yajnik, R.K. — The Indian Theatre, George Allen and Unwin Ltd. London, 1933.

Zoete, Beryl de and Spies, Walter — Dance and Drama in Bali, Faber and Faber, London, 1955.

Original Texts

Amarakośa 7th Ed. — N.S. Press, Bombay 1918.

Amarakośa with Vyākhyāsudhā 6th Ed. — N.S. Press, Bombay 944.

Amarakośa with Kṣīrasvāmiṭīkā — Poona Oriental Series No. 43, 1941.

Agnipurāṇa — Anandashram Press, Poona, 1952.

Anargharāghava with the commentary of Rucipati Upādhyāya — N.S. Press, Bombay 1937.

Abhijñānaśākuntala of Kālidāsa, with the commentary of Rāghavabhaṭṭa — Gopal Narayan & Co., Bombay, 1934.

Abhijñānaśākuntala — Ed. by Prin. R.D. Karmarkar Poona, 1952.

Abhinayadarpaṇa of Nandikeśvara, Second Edition (Revised) — Ed. by Dr. M. Ghosh, Calcutta, 1957.

Abhinavabhāratī of Abhinavagupta — The MS. in B.O R.I. Poona No 41 1925-1926.

Āścaryacūḍāmaṇi of Śaktibhadra	The Sri Balamanorama Press, Mylapore, Madras 1933.
Uttararāmacarita of Bhavabhūti, with the commentary of Ghanaśyāma, 3rd Edition	By P.V. Kane, Bombay 1929.
Karpūramañjarī of Rājaśekhara, (with Bālabhārata) 4th Edition	N.S. Press, Bombay 1949.
Kāmasūtra of Vātsyāyana	K.S.S. No. 29, 1929.
Kāvyānuśāsana of Hemacandra, Vol. I and II	Sri Mahavira Jain Vidyalaya, Bombay 1938.
Kuṭṭanīmata of Dāmodaragupta	Ed. by Madhusudan Kaul, Royal Asiatic Society of Bengal, Calcutta, 1944.
Kumārasambhava of Kālidāsa (Cantos I-IV)	Ed. by R. D. Karmarkar, Poona 1923.
Gītālaṁkāra, (MS.)	B.O.R.I. No. 977 / 1887—91
Caṇḍakauśika of Kṣemīśvara	Calcutta, 1931.
Jātakatthavaṇṇanā—The Jātaka together with its commentary	Ed. by V. Fausboll and T. W. Rhys Davids, London.
Tapatīsaṁvaraṇa of Kulaśekhara	T.S.S No. XI, 1911.
Dattilam	T.S.S. No. CII, 1930.
Daśarūpaka of Dhanañjaya with Avaloka of Dhanika	N.S. Press, Bombay 1941.
Dūtāṅgada of Subhaṭa	N.S. Press, Bombay 1935.
Nāgānanda of Śrī Harṣa	Ed. by Dr. M.A. Karandikar and Mrs. S. Karandikar, Bombay.
Nāṭakalakṣaṇaratnakośa of Sāgaranandin	Oxford University Press, London, 1937.
Nāṭyadarpaṇa of Rāmacandra and Guṇacandra, II Edition	G.O.S. Baroda, 1959.

Nāṭyaśāstra	Kāvyamālā, N.S. Press Bombay 1943. (II Edition)
-do-	K.S.S
Nāṭyaśāstra with Abhinavabhāratī	G.O.S. Baroda, Vol. I (2nd Ed.) and Vols. II, III and IV.
Nāṭyaśāstra	Ed. by J. Grosset, Paris 1898.
-do-	Vol. II Ed. by M. Ghosh, Asiatic Society Calcutta, 1956.
Nāṭyasarvasvadīpikā (MS.)	B.O.R.I. No. 41 1916-18.
Nāradīyā Śikṣā with the commentaries Vivaraṇa and Prakāśa	Śrīmanmahārāja Saṁskṛta Mahāpāṭhaśālā Patrikā, Mysore March-June 1943.
Pratāparudrīya of Vidyānātha with Ratnāpaṇa	Ed. by Chandra Shekhar Shastri, Madras, 1914.
Prabodhacandrodaya of Kṛṣṇamiśrayati with Candrikā and Prakāśa	N.S. Press, Bombay, 1935.
Priyadarśikā of Śrī Harṣa	Ed. by Prof. N.G. Suru, Poona, 1928.
Bālarāmāyaṇa of Rājaśekhara	Banaras Edition, 1869.
Bṛhaddeśī of Mataṅga	Ed. by K. Sāmbaśiva Śāstrī T.S.S., 1928.
Baudhāyana Dharmasūtra	K.S.S., No. 104.
Bhagavadajjukīyam of Bodhāyana Kavi	Ed. by P. Anujan Achan, Ṭrichur, 1925.
Bharatakośa	by M. Ramakrishna Kavi, The T. T. Devasthanam Press, Tirupati, 1951.
Bharatabhāṣya of Nānyadeva (MS.)	B.O.R.I. No. 111, 1869-70
Bharatārṇava of Nandikeśvara	Ed. by K. Vāsudeva Śāstri, Sarasvati Mahal Library, Tanjore, 1957.
Bhāvaprakāśana of Śāradātanaya	G.O.S., Baroda, 1930.
Bhāsanāṭakacakra	Ed. by Prof. C. R. Devadhar, Poona Oriental Series No. 54.

Mattavilāsaprahasana of Mahendravikramavarman — Ed. by T. Ganapati. Sastri, Government Press, Trivandrum 1917.

Manusmṛti, (8th Ed) — N.S. Press, Bombay, 1929.

Mahābhārata — Chitrashala Press, Poona.

Mānasollāsa, Vol. I & II & III. — G.O.S. Baroda.

Mālavikāgnimitra of Kālidāsa — Ed. by Prin. R. D. Karmarkar, 1937.

Meghadūta of Kālidāsa — Ed. by V.G. Paranjape, Poona, 1941.

Mudrārākṣasa of Viśākhadatta with the commentary of Dhuṇḍirāja — Ed. by M. R. Kale, Bombay, 1900.

Mṛcchakaṭika of Śūdraka with the commentary of Pṛthvīdhara, (4th Ed.) — Ed. by K. P. Parab, Bombay, 1916.

Yājñavalkyasmṛti (4th Ed.) — N.S. Press, Bombay 1936.

Raghuvaṁśa of Kālidāsa — N.S. Press, Bombay 1925.

Ratnāvalī of Śrī Harṣa — N.S. Press, Bombay 1918.

Rāmāyaṇa, — N.S. Press, Bombay 1930.

Laṭakamelaka of Śaṅkhadhara — Kāvyamālā No. 28, N. S. Press, Bombay 1923.

Vāyupurāṇa — Veṅkaṭeśvara Press, Bombay.

Rasārṇavasudhākara of Śrī Śiṅgabhūpāla — T.S.S. 1916.

Viṣṇusmṛti — Smṛti-sandarbha, Prathama Bhāga, Calcutta 1952.

Veṇīsaṁhāra of Bhaṭṭanārāyaṇa — Ed. by Dr. G. K. Bhat & Prof. R. N. Gaidhani, Continental Prakashan, Poona 1957.

Vikramorvaśīya of Kālidāsa with the commentary of Raṅganātha — N.S. Press, Bombay, 1925.

Vikramorvaśīya — Ed. by Prof. H. D. Velankar, Sahitya Akademi, New Delhi, 1961.

Viṣṇudharmottarapurāṇa (3rd Khaṇḍa) — Ed. by Dr. Priyabala Shah, Oriental Institute, Baroda 1958

Vyākaraṇamahābhāṣya (with the Marathi Translation by Mahāmahopādhyāya Vasudevashastri Abhyankar) — Deccan Education Society, Poona.

Śārṅgadharapaddhati — Ed. by Peter Peterson, Bombay Sanskrit Series, No. 37 1888.

Śilparatna of Śrīkumāra — T.S.S. 1929.

Śṛṅgāraprakāśa of Bhoja Vol I Parts I & II — Ed. by Dr. V. Raghavan, Karnatak Publishing House, Bombay, 1940.

Śṛṅgārahāṭa (Caturbhāṇī) — Ed. by Dr. Motichandra and Dr. V. S. Agrawal, Hindi Granth Ratnakar Private Ltd. Bombay 1960.

Saṁgītamakaranda of Nārada — G.O.S. No. 16, 1920.

Saṁgīta-ratnākara of Śārṅgadeva with the commentary of Kallinātha, — Anandashram Edition, Poona.

Saṁgīta-ratnākara with the commentaries of Kallinātha and Śiṅgabhupāla, Vols. I-IV. — Adyar Library, Adyar, Madras.

Saṁgītasamayasāra of Pārśvadeva — Ed. by T. Gaṇapati Sāstrī Trivandrum, 1925. (T.S.S.)

Saṁgītasārāmṛta of Tulajā — The Music Academy, Madras 1942.

Samarāṅgaṇasūtradhāra of Bhoja, Vol. I & II, — G.O.S. No. XXXII

Sāhityadarpaṇa of Viśvanātha, (Ed. II) — Ed by P.V. Kane, Bombay 1923.

Subhadrādhanañjaya of Kulaśekhara — T.S.S., Ed. by T. Gaṇapati Sāstrī, 1912.

Svapnavāsavadatta of Bhāsa — Ed. by M. R. Kale, Bombay 1929.

Harivaṁśa — Chitrashala Press, Poona.

Articles in the Journals etc. and Journals consulted.

Acharya, P.K. — 'The Playhouse of the Hindu Period', Dr. S. Krishnaswami Aiyangar Com. Vol.

Appanna, T. — 'The Origin of Drama', Raja Sir A. Chettiar Com. Vol.

Athavale, R.B. — 'The Problem of Nāndī and Pūrvaraṅga, paper in A.I.O.C. 1953.

Athavale, R.B. — 'Ancient Sanskrit Drama and Music', Paper in A.I.O.C. 1961.

Barua, Hem — 'The Theatre in Assam', Illustrated Weekly Feb. 5, 1961.

Bloch, T. — 'Caves and Inscriptions in Rāmgarh hills', Archaeological Survey of India Annual report, 1903-4. (pp. 123-131.)

Bhaṭṭa, L.S. — 'The Mode of Singing Sāma Gāna', Poona Orientalist, Vol. IV No. 1 and 2.

Barua, B. K. — 'A Short Note on Śrī-Hastamuktāvali', J.A.R.S. 1941.

Balbir, G.K. — 'The Conception of Conventions of Speech in Sanskrit Dramaturgists' A.I.O.C. Vol. 1946.

Bhat, G.K — 'Bhāsa's Stage', J.O.I. Baroda Vol. II, Parts I-IV.

Bhandarkar, P.R. — 'Kuḍimiyāmalai Inscription on Music', Epigraphia Indica, Vol. XII.

Coomaraswamy, A.K. — 'Hindu Theatre', I.H.Q. Vol. IX 1933.

-do- — 'The Parts of Vīṇā', Journal of American Oriental Society 1931.

Chakravarti, Chintaharan — 'A Note on the Bharata-vākya' I.H.Q. Vol. V 1929.

Chakravarti, C. — 'A Further Note on Bharata-vākya', I.H.Q. Vol. VII.

Datta, Kali Kumar — 'Prologues and Epilogues in Sanskrit Drama', Our Heritage, Vol. V, 1957.

De, S.K. — 'The Curtain in Ancient Indian Theatre', Bhāratīya Vidyā Vol. IX, 1948.

-do- — 'The Śānta-rasa in the Nāṭyaśāstra' & the Dasarūpaka', Siddhabhāratī Part I, 1950.

Dave, Urmila — 'Nāndī in Theory', I.H.Q. Vol. XVII, 1941.

Desai, Chaitanya — 'Nṛtyanāṭya Va Geyanāṭya', Chanda, Māgha-Phālguna 1880.

Devasthali, G.V. — 'Viṣkambhaka and Praveśaka of Bhāsa', Journal of the University of Bombay, Sep. 1950.

Diwekar, H.R. — 'Mattavāraṇī', A.I.O.C. 1959 Vol. II Part I.

Divekar, H.R. — 'Timing of Dramatic Representations in India', J.R.A.S. G.B. & I. 1928.

Fabri, Charles — 'Five Thousand Years of Indian Theatre', Western Railway Annual 1955-56.

Gargi, Balwant — 'Dance and Music in Drama,' The Illustrated Weekly of India, Feb. 7, 1960.

Ghosh, M. — 'The Ādibharata and the Nāṭyasarvasvadīpikā, A.B.O.R.I. Vol. XV.

-do- — 'Bharata-vākya', I.H.Q. VI-1930.

-do- — 'The Nāṭyaśāstra and Bharatamuni', I.H.Q. Vol. VIII.

-do- — Prākṛta Verses in the Bharata-Nāṭyśāstra' I.H.Q. Vol. VIII, Supplement.

-do- — 'A So-called Convention of the Hindu Drama' I.H.Q. IX.

-do- — 'The Hindu Theatre', I.H.Q. IX.

Gode, P.K. — 'The Bharata and Ādibharata Problem and the MS. of Ādibharata in the Government Oriental Library, Mysore, A.B.O.R.I. XIII.

Gonda Von J. 'Zur Frage Nach Dem Ursprung Und Wesen Des Indischen Dramas' Acta Orientalia, Vol. XIX, 1943.

Hazra, R.C. 'The Vidūṣaka in Sanskrit Drama—His Origin', Journal of the Asiatic Society Vol. XIX No. 1, 1953.

Jaitly, R.S. 'Rasānātharvaṇādapi', Paper in A.I.O.C. 1959,

Joshi, Nirmala 'Some aspects of Kathak Dancing', J.M.M.A. Vol. XXV 1959.

Kapadia, H.R 'The Jaina Data about Musical Instruments', J.O.I. Baroda Vol. II, III & IV.

Karmarkar, R.D. 'The First Greek Conqueror of India', A.B.O.R.I. Vol. XXXI 1951.

-do- 'Dramatic Terms—Janāntikam and Apavāritam', 'Praveśaka and Viṣkambhaka' A.B.O.R.I. Vol. XXXV.

Levi, Sylvain 'On Some Terms employed in the Inscriptions of the Kshatrapas', I.A. Vol. 33.

Luders, H. 'Indian Caves as Pleasure Resorts', I.A. Vol. XXXIV.

Mujumdar, G.N. 'Kālidāsa and Music', A.B.O.R.I. Vol. VII.

Mankad D.R. 'Two notes on the Origin of Sanskrit drama', Acharya Dhruva Smaraka Granth.

-do- 'Bharatavākya and Bhagavadajjukam', I.H.Q. VII.

Mitra, Kali Prasada 'Dramaturgy in the Mahāpurāṇa of Puṣpadanta', I.H.Q. Sep. 1950.

Marshall, John Archaeological Report, 1911-12.

Mookerjee, M. 'The Jatras in Bengal' Calcutta Review, July 1922.

Nagendra 'Rasa Śabda kā Arthavikāsa' (Hindi) Hindī Anuśilana, Dhīrendravarmā Viśeṣāṅka.

Nayar, S.K. 'Kūṭiyāṭṭam', Annals O.R.I. Centenary Number.

Parikh, J.T. 'The Orthodox Tradition about the Origin of Sanskrit Drama', J.O.I Baroda, Vol. I No. 4.

Pisharoti, K.R. 'The Ancient Indian Theatre', Rajah Sir Annamalai Chettiar Commemoration Volume, 1941.

Pisharoti, K.R. 'The Time of staging a Sanskrit Drama', I.H.Q. June 1950.

Przyluski, J. 'The Shadow Theatre in Greater India and in Greece', Journal of the Greater India Society, Vol. VIII, No. 2

Raghavan, M.D. 'Traditions and Chronicles of the Dance in Ceylon (Separated from Spolia Zeylanica, Vol. 28, Part II)

Raghavan, V. 'The Vṛttis', J.O.R. Madras, Vol. VI & VII.

-do- 'A Note on the name Daśarūpaka', J.O.R. Madras, Vol. VII.

-do- 'An Outline Literary History of Indian Music', J.M.M.A. Vol. XXIII, XXIV.

-do- 'Why is the Mridanga So-called ?' J.M.M.A., Vol. XXIV & XXVI.

-do- 'The Social Play in Sanskrit' Indian Institute of Culture, Bangalore 1952.

-do- 'Nāṭyadharmī and Lokadharmī' J.O.R. Madras Vol. VII & VIII.

-do- 'Yakshagana', Triveni, Vol. VII No. 2.

-do- 'Bhāgavata Mela Nāṭaka' The Journal of the Indian Society of Oriental Art, Calcutta June-Dec. 1937.

Raja, Kunjunni, 'Kūṭiyāṭṭam', Samskrita Ranga Annual 1960.

Rao, S. Ramchandra 'Tragedies in Sanskrit', A.I.O.C. Vol. 1935.

Ramanathan, S. 'Gramas and Musical Intervals', J.M. M.A. Vol. XXXI 1960.

Ramachandran, K.V. 'Dance Traditions of South India', Triveni, Madras Vol. VII No. 4 & 6.

Ritha Devi 'The Manipuri Tradition of India', The Illustrated Weekly of India, Nov. 20, 1960.

Ruben, Walter Über Die Ursprunge Des Indischen Dramas', Tūrk Tarih Kurumu, Belleten, Ankara, 1940.

-do- Über Die Literatur', Der Vorarischen Stämme Indiens' Akademie-Verlag, Berlin, 1952.

Shastri, Nilakantha 'The Origin of the Sāma-veda', J.O. R.M. Vol. IX.

Sankaran, C.R. & Deva, B. Chaitanya 'Studies in Indian Musical Scales', Taraporewala Memorial Volume, 1957.

Saxena, M.N. 'Bharatokta Śrutyantara', Nādarūpa (Hindi) Jan 1961, College of Music and Fine Arts, Banaras Hindu University.

Sen, R.K. 'Suśruta, Caraka and Bharata', I.H.Q. March 1954.

Sharma, H.L. The Critical and Comparative Study of Indian Aesthetics', Journal of the Ganganatha Zha Research Institute, May-August 1958.

Sivaprasad 'A Note on the Popular Element in the Classical Sanskrit Drama, A.I.O.C. 1922.

Vaidya, P.L. 'On the use of Prakrit dialects in Sanskrit Dramas', A.B.O.R.I. Vol. XXXIII.

Wijesekera, O.H. de A. 'Buddhist Evidence for the Early. Existance of Drama' I.H.Q. Vol. XVII.

Wadeyar, S.S. Yakshagana and Tala-maddale', Bihar Theatre No. 10, Feb. 1958.

Varma, K.M. 'Hasta-prachāras Three or Five' O.H R.J. Vol. V.

Wells, H.W. 'Eastern Drama and the Western Stage', The Illustrated Weekly of India, Feb. 11, 1962.

Zha, Vibhutinath 'Bharata-vākya', I.H.Q. Vol VI

Journals

The Illustrated Weekly of India, March 6, 1960.

Mārga — Bharatanāṭyam

-do- Kathakali.

-do- Kathak.

Souvenir Kala Vikash Kendra, Cuttack 1958.

ADDITIONAL BIBLIOGRAPHY FOR KŪṬIYĀṬṬAM

Books

(1) A Temple Theatre of Kerala—Its History and Description, by Clifford Jones; A Ph.D. Dissertation, University of Pennsylvania, U.S.A., 1967.

(2) Āścaryacūḍāmaṇi (Malayalam)—compiled and edited by K.P. Narayana Pisharoti; Kerala Sangeet Natak Akademi, Trichur, 1967.

(3) Asokavanika Anga (Malayalam)—An Attaprakaram for the act in the Aścaryacūḍāmaṇi; Kerala University. Trivendrum.

(4) Koothampalangalil (Malayalam)— A study by K.P. Narayana Pisharoti; published by the author, Trichur, 1981.

(5) Kūttampalam and Kūṭiyāṭṭam—by Goverdhan Panchal; Sangeet Natak Akademi, New Delhi, 1984.

(6) Mantrankam (Malayalam)—by P.K. Narayanan Nambiar; Kerala Sahitya Akademi, Trichur, 1930.

(7) Natyakalpadrumam (Malayalam)—by Mani Madhava Chakyar; Kerala Kalamandalam, 1975.

(8) Purusharthakkoothu (Malayalam)—by V.R. Krishna Chandran; Kerala Sahitya Akademi, Trichur, 1978.

(9) Rājasūyam Prabandham (with an old Malayalam commentary)—published by Dr. K. Raghavan Pillai; Kerala University Malayalam Series No. 100.

(10) Sree Krishnacharitam Nangyarammakkoothu (Malayalam) —by P.K. Narayanan Nambiar; Kerala Kalamandalam, 1984.

(11) The Wondrous Crest Jewel (in performance)—Edited by Clifford R. Jones; Oxford University Press, Delhi, 1984.

Articles in the Journals etc.

(1) "A Pattern of Survival: Literary and Epigraphical References to the Chākyārs—Custodians of the Sanskrit Drama in the Temples of Kerala"—by Dr. Clifford R. Jones, U.S.A.

(2) "Bharata's Stage in Action"—by Goverdhan Panchal; Sangeet Natak No. 34, New Delhi, 1974.

(3) "Curtain in Classical Drama"—by Goverdhan Panchal; Sangeet Natak No. 25, New Delhi, 1972.

(4) "Eloquent Eyes—Netra-Abhinaya in Koodiyattam"—by L.S. Rajagopalan; Journal of the Music Academy, Madras, Vol. XLV, 1974.

(5) "Inside a Temple Theatre"—by J.C. Mathur; Sangeet Natak No. 26, New Delhi, 1972.

(6) "Is Kudiyattam a Museum Piece?"—Christopher Byrski; Sangeet Natak, No. 5, New Delhi.

(7) "Kūṭiyāṭṭam"—by K.B. Bharata Iyer; The Times of India Annual, Bombay, 1962.

(8) "Kūṭiyāṭṭam"—by Dr. V. Raghavan; Sanskrit Ranga Annual No. V, Madras, 1971.

(9) "Kūṭiyāṭṭam and its Links with Classical Sanskrit Theatre"—by Goverdhan Panchal; Reprinted from Journal of the Oriental Institute, Vol. XXVI, No. 3, Baroda, March, 1977.

(10) "Kūttampalam and its Links with Bharata's Stage"—by Goverdhan Panchal; Journal of the National Centre for the Performing Arts, Vol. VI No. 1, Bombay, March, 1977.

(11) "Kūttampalam—Sanskrit Stage of Kerala"—by Goverdhan Panchal; Sangeet Natak No. 8, New Delhi, 1968.

(12) "Kūttampalam"—by Goverdhan Panchal; Keralotsav Souvenir, Shreyas Foundation, Ahmedabad, 1976.

(13) "Music in Kootiyattam"—by L.S. Rajagopalan; Sangeet Natak No. 10, New Delhi, 1968.

(14) "Notes on the Restoration of a Temple Theatre for Sanskrit Drama"—by Clifford R. Jones; Quarterly Journal of the National Centre for the Performing Arts, Bombay, March 1975.

(15) "Source Material for the Construction of the Nāṭyamaṇḍapa in the Śilparatna and the Tantrasamuccaya—Śilpabhāgam"—by Dr. Clifford R. Jones; U.S.A.

SUBJECT INDEX

ILLUSTRATIONS

Plate I

Single hand-gestures

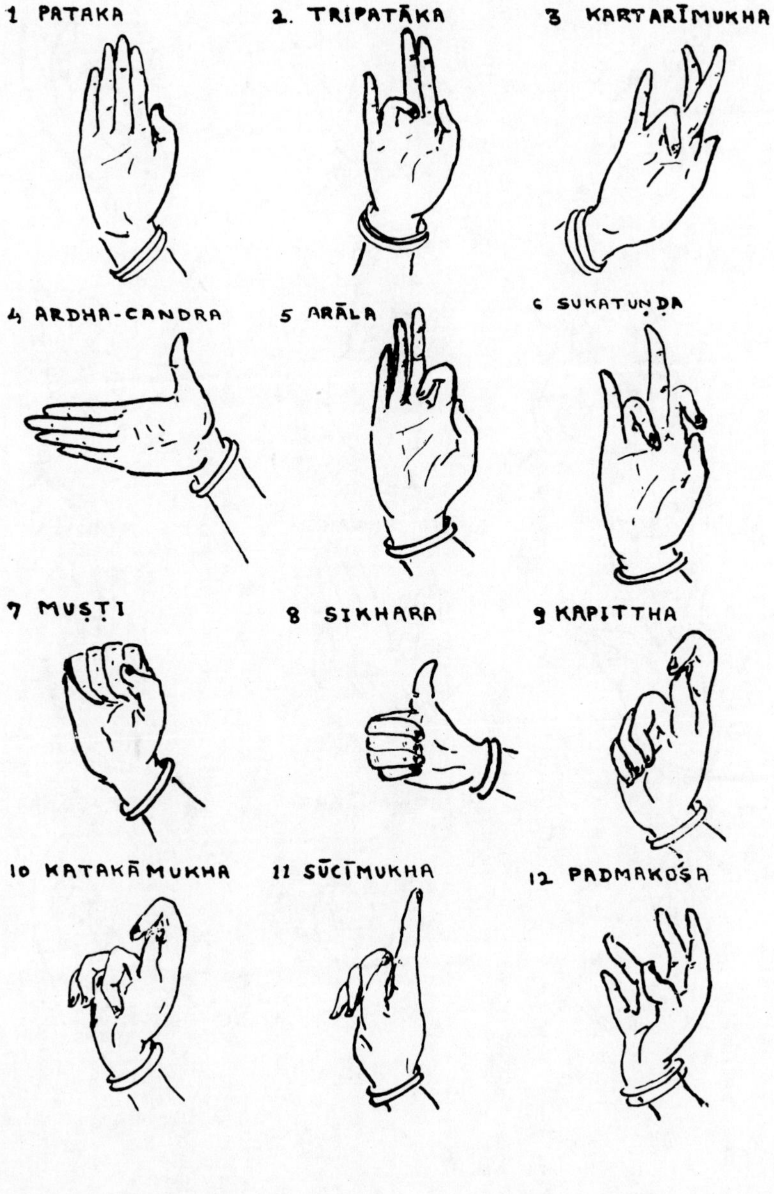

Plate II

Single hand gestures

13 SARPASĪRṢA

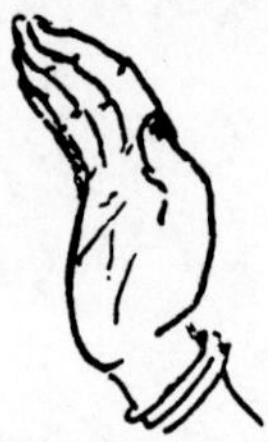

14 MṚGASĪRṢA

15 KAṄGULA

16 ALAPALLAVA

17 CATURA

18 BHRAMARA

19 HAṀSĀSYA

20 HAṀSAPAKṢA

21 SANDAṀŚA

22 MUKULA

23 ŪRNANĀBHA

24 TĀMRACŪDA

Plate III

Double hand-gestures

1 AÑJALI

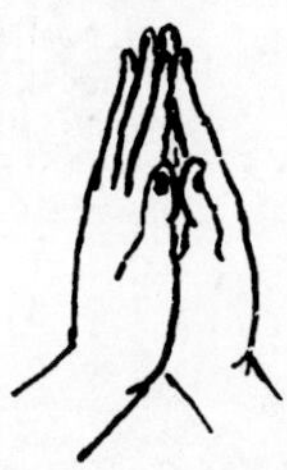

2 KAPOTA

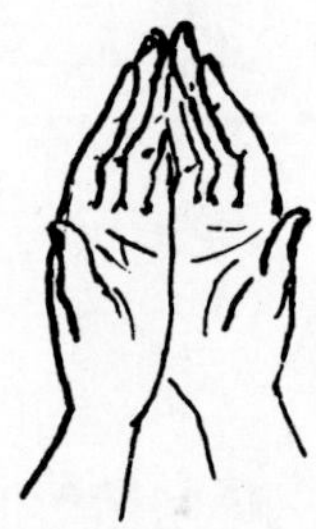

3 KARKAṬA

4 SVASTIKA

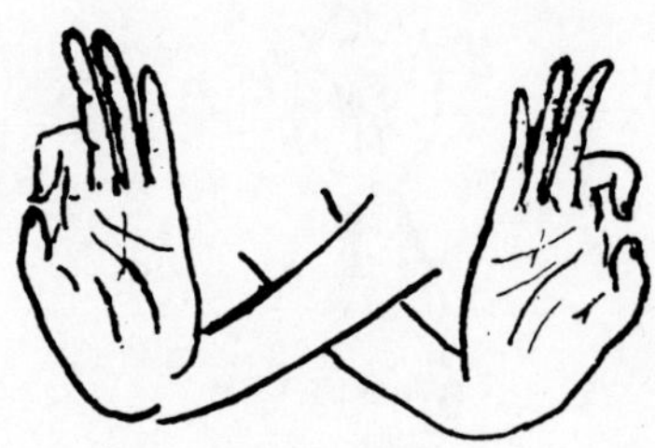

5 KAṬAKĀVARDHAMĀNAKA

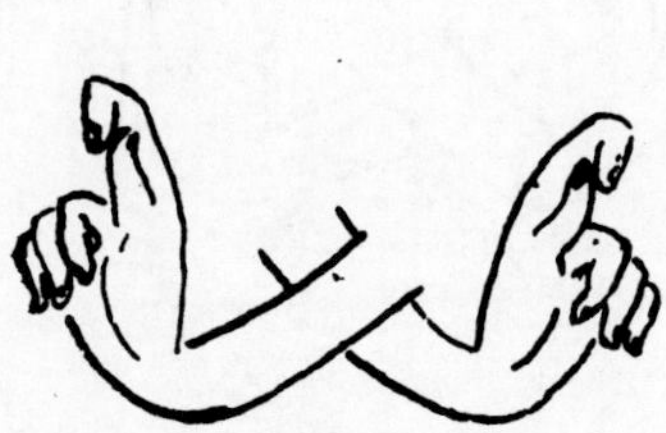

6 UTSAṄGA

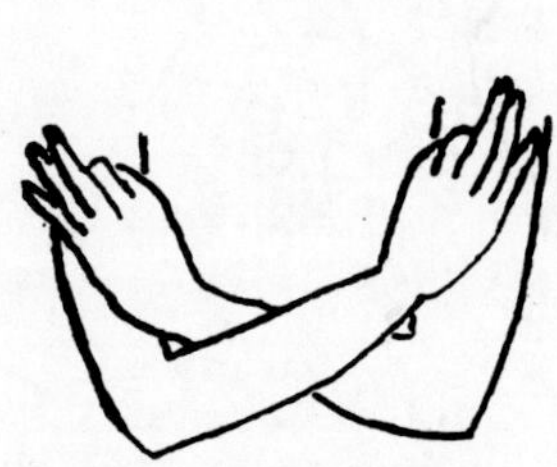

Plate IV

Double hand-gestures

7 NIṢADHA

8 DOLA

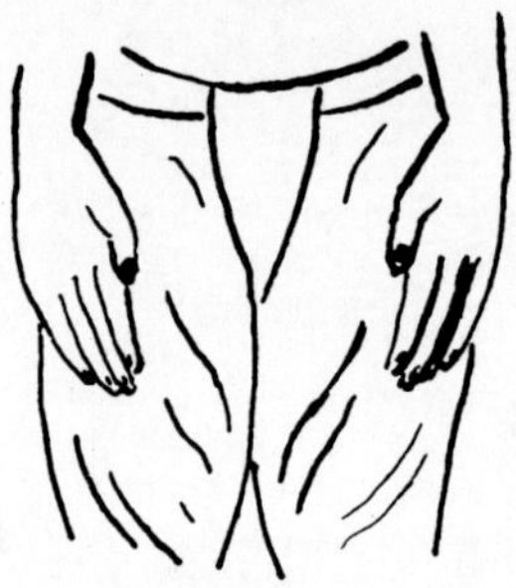

9 PUṢPAPUṬA

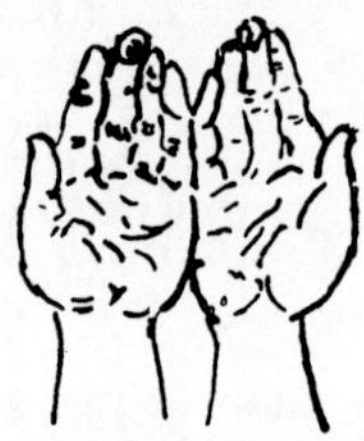

10 MAKARA

11 GAJADANTA

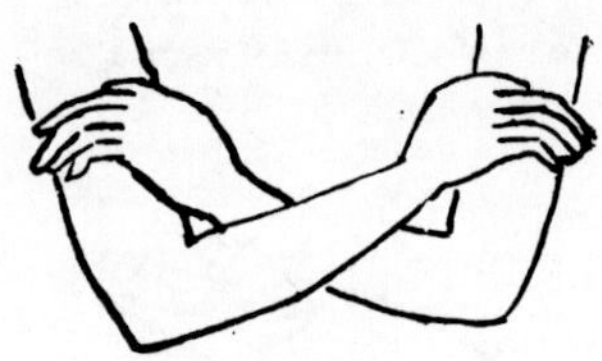

12 AVAHITTHA

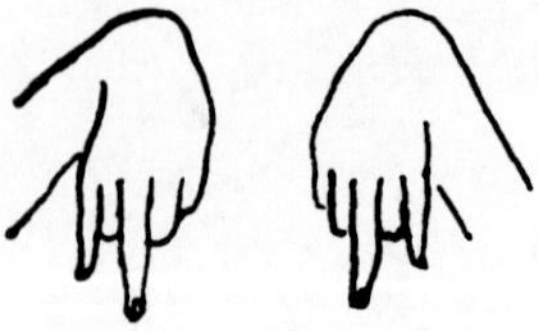

13 VARDHAMĀNA

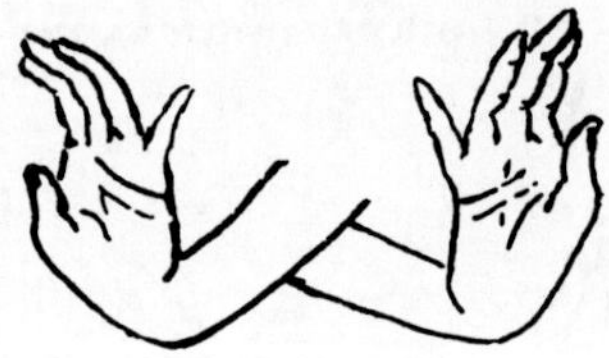

Plate V

Some Musical Instruments Found in Ancient Indian Sculpture and Painting –

VIṆĀS –

(Bharhut) Vipañcī Vīṇā

(Bharhut) Citrā

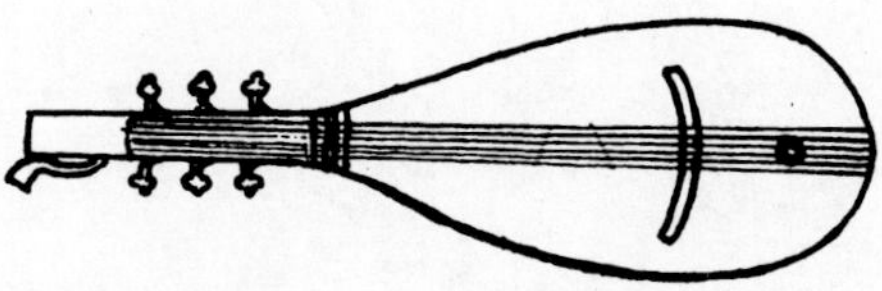

(Amaravati, Pawaya, etc.) Kacchapī(?)

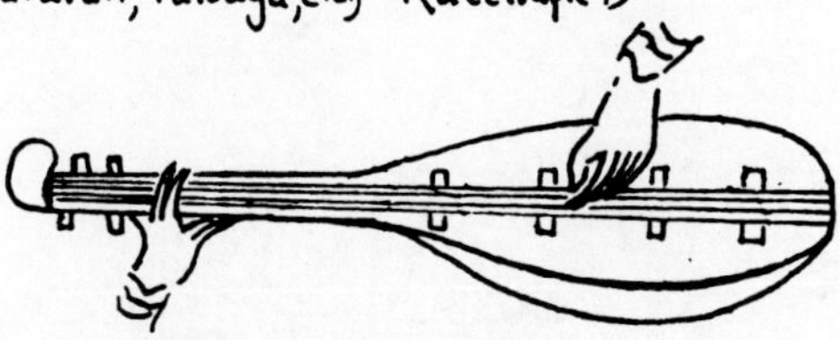

(Pattadkal)

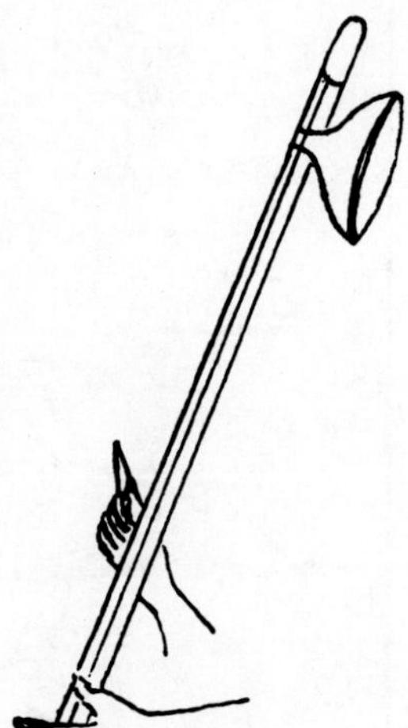

(Ajanta)

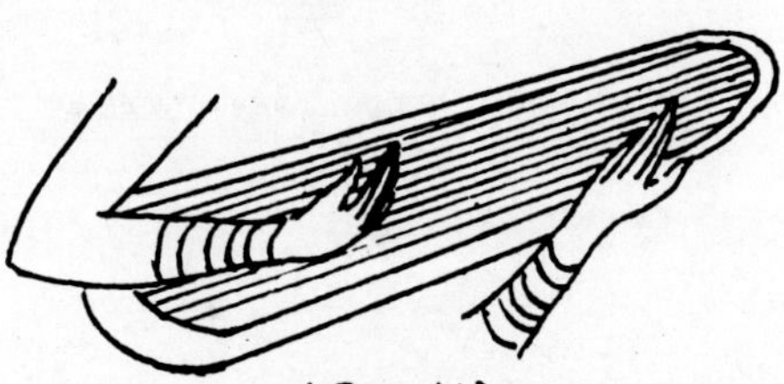

(Sanchi)

Plate VI

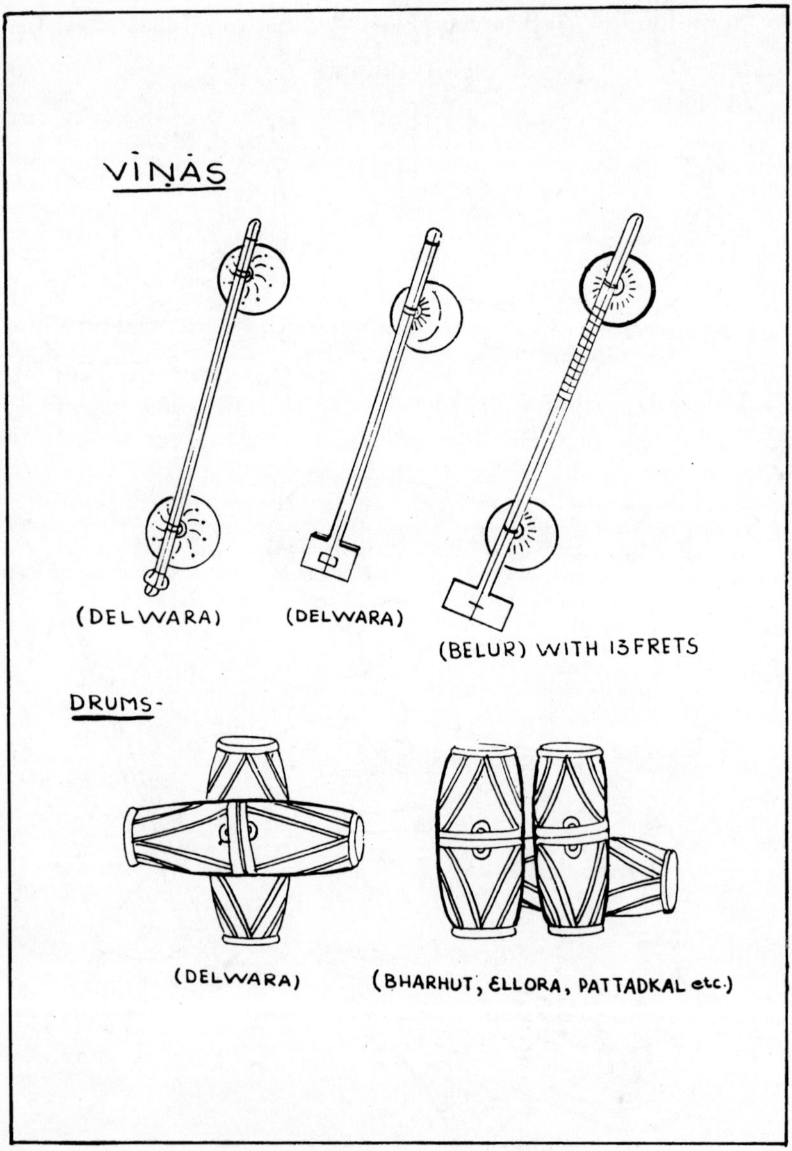
VINAS
(DELWARA)
(DELWARA)
(BELUR) WITH 13 FRETS
DRUMS-
(DELWARA)
(BHARHUT, ELLORA, PATTADKAL etc.)

Plate VII

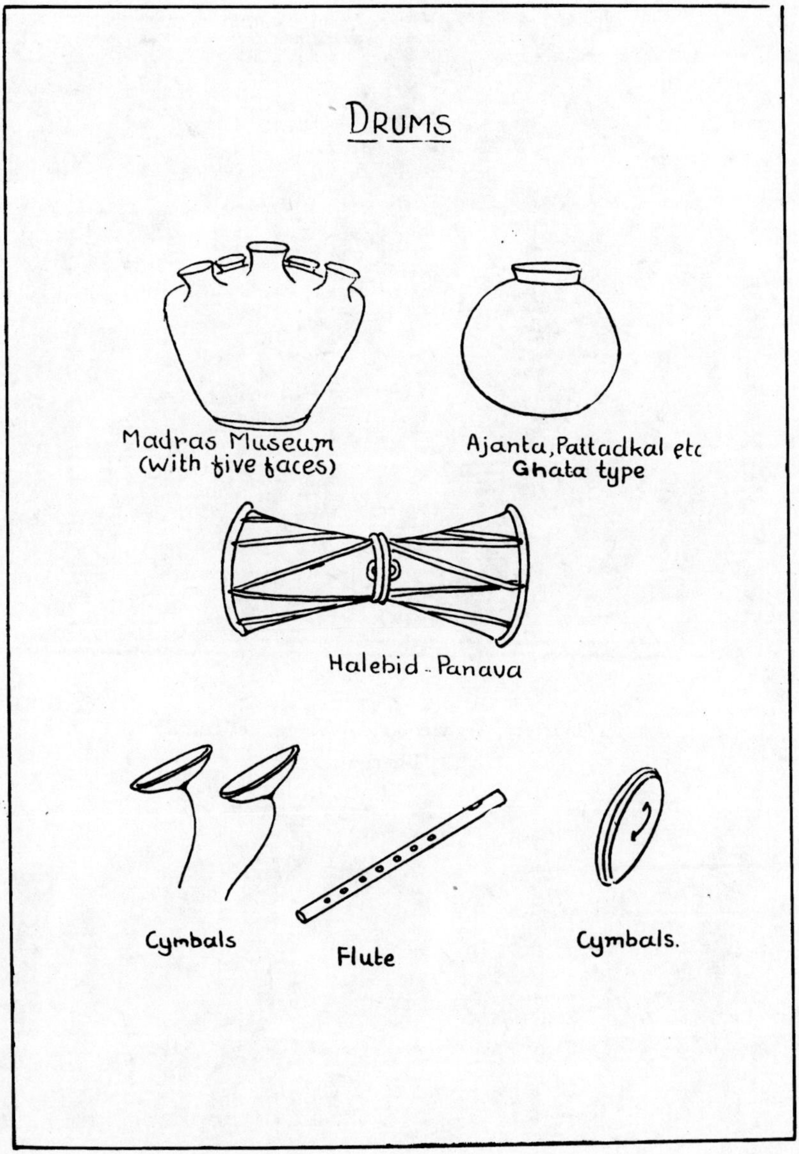
DRUMS
Madras Museum
(with five faces)
Ajanta, Pattadkal etc
Ghata type
Halebid - Panava
Cymbals
Flute
Cymbals.

Plate VIII
Some Dance Panels in Indian Sculpture
Bharhut

(Courtesy, Archaeological Survey of India)

Bharhut

(Courtesy, Archaeological Survey of India)

Plate IX
Some Dance Panels in Indian Sculpture

Khajuraho

Delwara

Nagarjunkonda

Plate X

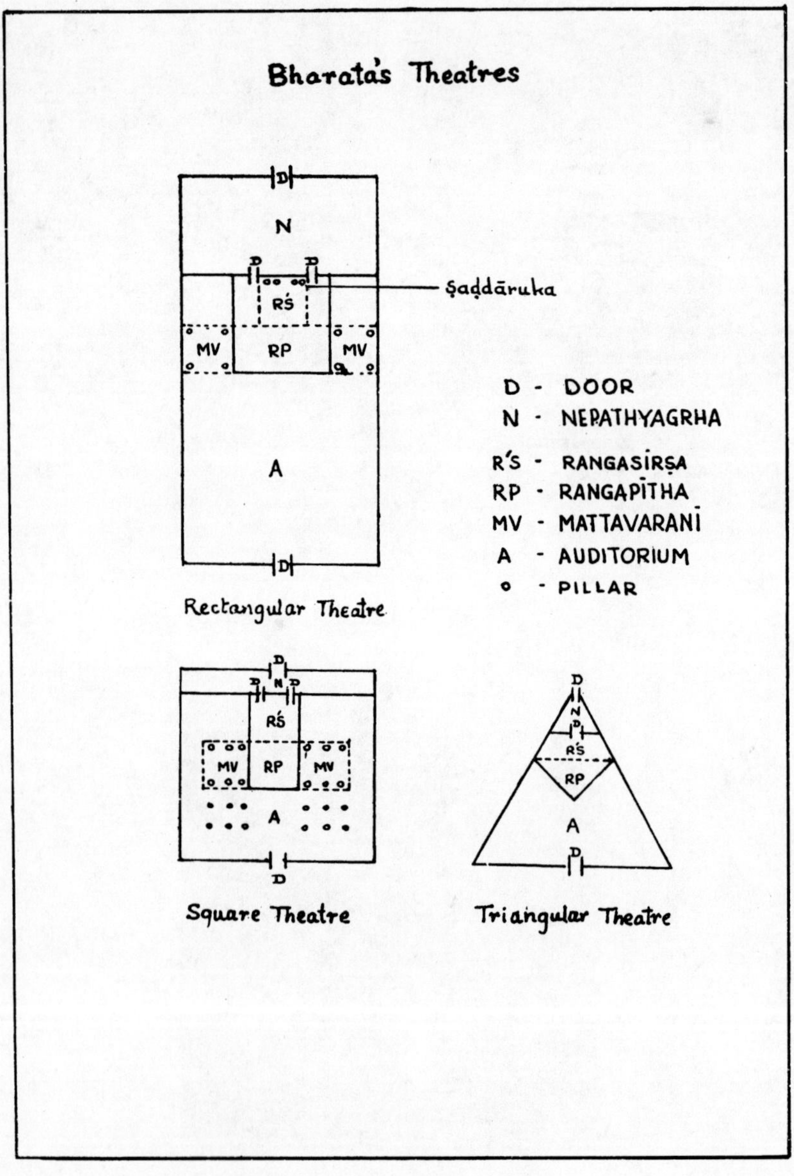
Bharata's Theatres
D
N
D D
Ṣaḍḍāruka
R'S
MV RP MV
A
D
Rectangular Theatre
D - DOOR
N - NEPATHYAGRHA
R'S - RANGASIRṢA
RP - RANGAPĪTHA
MV - MATTAVARANĪ
A - AUDITORIUM
o - PILLAR
D
D N D
R'S
MV RP MV
A
D
Square Theatre
D
N
D
R'S
RP
A
D
Triangular Theatre

Plate XI

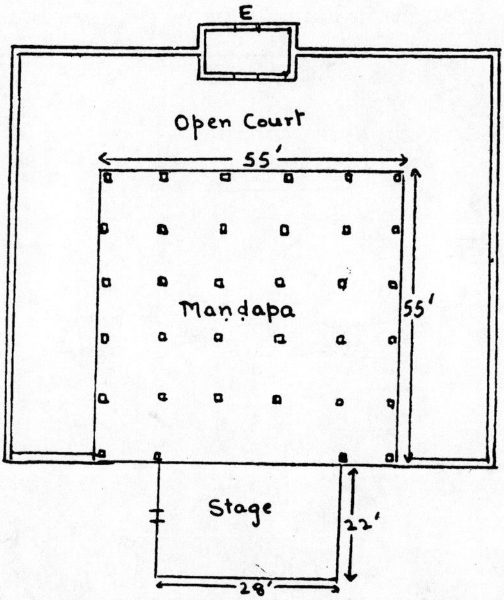

Prekṣāgṛha unearthed at Nagarjunkonda

▫ : Pillar

E : Entrance

Shakespearean Stage

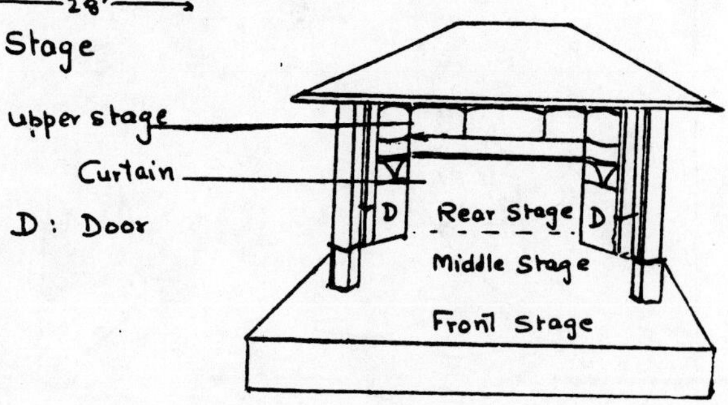

Chinese Stage

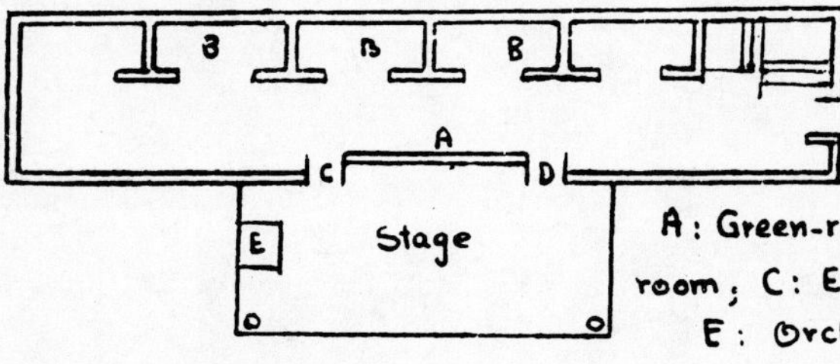

A : Green-room ; B : Dressing room ; C : Entrance D . Exit E : Orchestra place

Plate XII

Mudrās in Kūṭiyāṭṭam

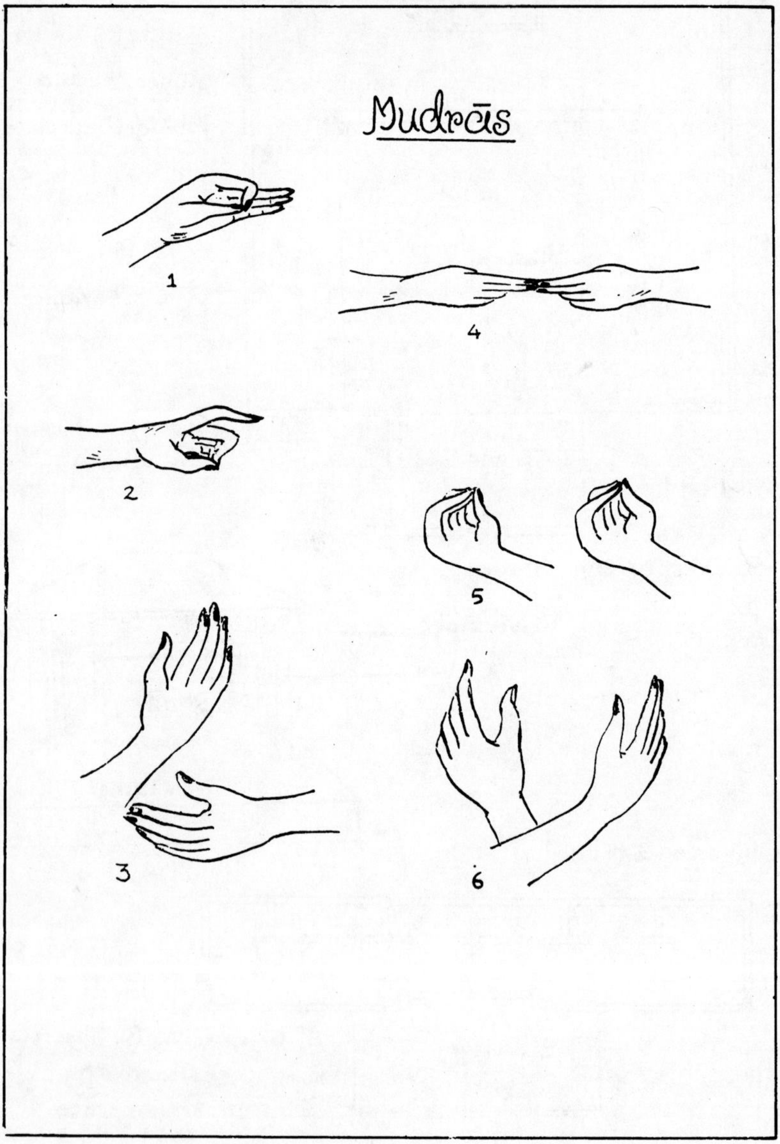

Plate XIII

Mudrās in Kūṭiyāṭṭam

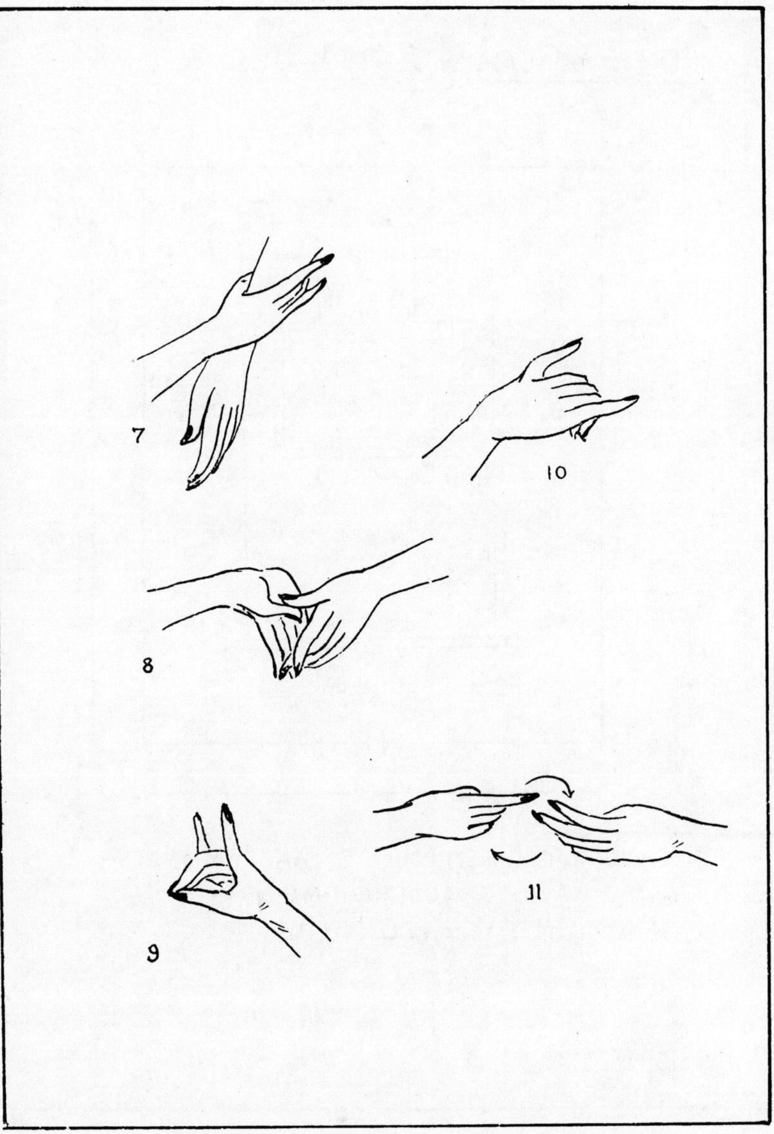

Plate XIV

KUTTAMPALAM TRICHUR

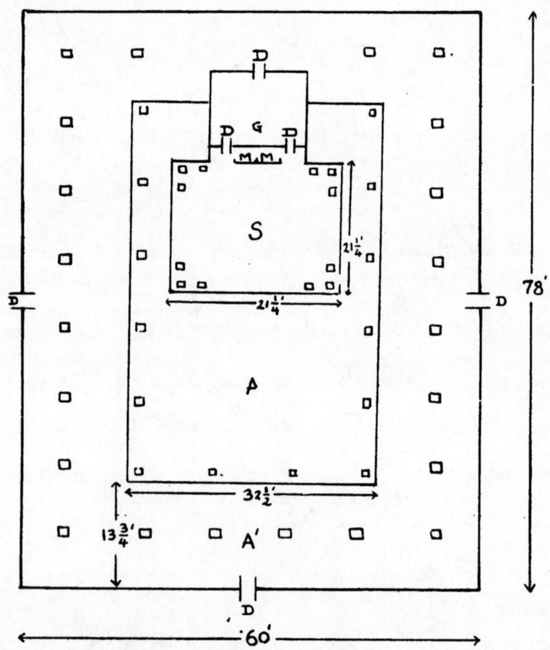

D: DOOR; G GREEN ROOM; S-STAGE; M-PLACE-FOR MILAVU; A-AUDITORIUM; (*Raised*)
A'-AUDITORIUM (*LOWER*) ▫-PILLAR

Plate XV

Kūttampalams

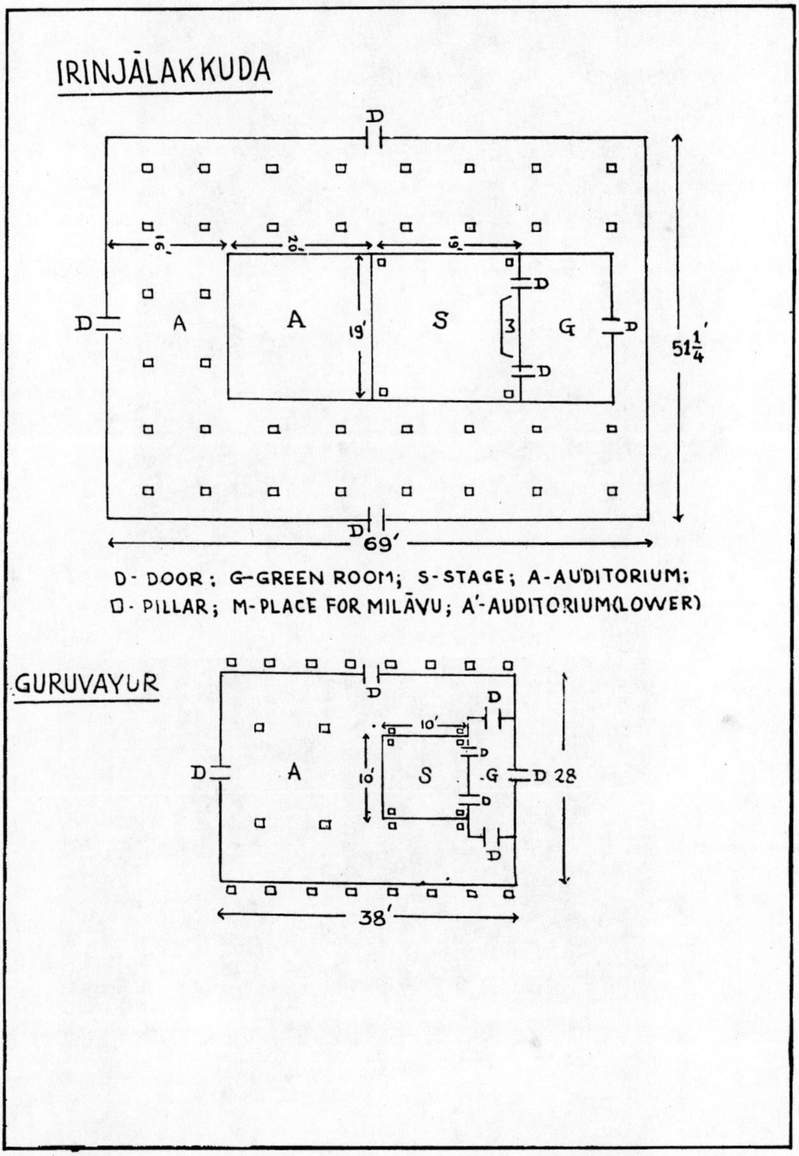

Plate XVI
Kūṭiyāṭṭam Photos

1

3

Plate XVII
Kūṭiyāṭṭam

Plate XVIII
Kūtiyāṭṭam

4 

 5

Plate XIX
Kūṭiyāṭṭam

Plate XX
Kūtiyāṭṭam

7

10

Plate XXI
Kūtiyāṭṭam

Plate XXII
Kutiyaṭṭam

Plate XXIII
Kūṭiyāṭṭam

11

12

Plate XXIV
Kūṭiyāṭṭam

13 

 14

Plate XXV
Kūṭiyāṭṭam

15

16

Plate XXVI
Kūṭiyāṭṭam

Plate XXVII
Kūṭiyaṭṭam

Plate XXVIII

Kūṭiyāṭṭam

Plate XXIX

Bhita Medallion

PLATE I

(Courtesy, Archaeological Survey of India)

Plate XXX

Plate 2

A Kūṣāṇa Sculpture, National Museum, New Delhi
(Courtesy, National Museum, New Delhi)